Intelligence in general, and peacekeeping intelligence in particular, have long been highly sensitive subjects at the UN. Because intelligence is vital for the successful implementation of risky peacekeeping operations, the topic will continue to be important, if controversial, at the UN. This useful volume should help generate a more sophisticated debate thereon in the future.

David M. Malone, President
International Peace Academy

As several of the contributions in this book make clear, in peacekeeping operations the threat is often much more diffuse and harder to identify than in conventional military operations. The enemy is less clearly defined and regular military forces can be largely absent. Instead, paramilitaries, volunteers, self-declared police forces or criminal gangs often dominate the situation on the ground. Clearly, intelligence is a much-needed asset in such an environment, as this book rightly emphasises. Where there is an intelligence failure, in the end there will be nearly always the human victims, on the side of peacekeepers, or more often, on the side of the civilian population.

Danielle Cailloux, Chief, Victims and Witnesses Section
International Criminal Tribunal for the former Yugoslavia

Peacekeeping Intelligence
Emerging Concepts for the Future

Foreword by
Dame Pauline Neville-Jones

Editors
Ben de Jong   Wies Platje
Robert David Steele

OSS International Press
Oakton, Virginia

This book and others in the series are available at quantity discounts for group or class distribution. Please communicate with the publisher.

OSS International Press is the book-publishing arm of Open Source Solutions Inc., publisher of *Proceedings of the Global Information Forum* (annual), *OSS Notices* (occasional series), and the ten-book series *ON INTELLIGENCE*. Visit www.oss.net.

Published by OSS International Press (OSS)   April 2003
Post Office Box 369
Oakton, Virginia 22124 USA
(703) 242-1700 Facsimile (703) 242-1711
Email oss@oss.net, Web: www.oss.net

Printed and bound in the United States of America

9 8 7 6 5 4 3 2

LIBRARY OF CONGRESS CATALOGING-IN-PUBLICATION DATA

Platje, Wies, Ben de Jong, and Robert David Steele (editors)
    Peacekeeping Intelligence: Emerging Concepts for the Future/edited by Ben de
Jong, Wies Platje, and Robert David Steele
    p.   cm.
Includes bibliographical references and index.
ISBN 0-9715661-2-7 (alk. paper)
1. Intelligence service. 2. Military intelligence. 3. Law enforcement intelligence. 4.
    Internet. 5. Organizational change. 6. Strategic planning. 7. Leadership. 8.
    Information Technology. 9. Knowledge, theory of. 10. Power (Social sciences).
    11. Information science—social aspects. 12. National security—management of.
    13. Political planning.
I.   Title.
JK468.I6S74 2003
327.1273—dc21   00-029284

Foreword

Dame Pauline Neville-Jones

Since the end of the Cold War, peacekeeping has assumed a renewed saliency and importance. For many years in the second half of the twentieth century, up to the 1990s, peacekeeping had become largely synonymous with the preservation of stalemated post conflict situations, where men in blue berets patrolled temporary boundary lines between unreconciled communities pending the permanent political settlement of the dispute in question. There was little military activity and little challenge to the peacekeeper's authority.

The conflicts in the former Yugoslavia saw the attempt made, on a scale not seen for a very long time, to engage in preventative peacekeeping, the aim being to forestall the outbreak of full-scale warfare. UNPROFOR was a brave attempt but at best only very partly successful in its mission. Important experience was however gained, not least in developing more effective, if still imperfect, techniques for commanding disparate multinational forces in potentially or actually unstable situations. Since Bosnia, peacekeeping under the UN aegis has become yet more ambitious in its aims and, even if still too dependent on the skills of a few nations and the quality of individual commanders, has become increasingly able to cope with difficult, and largely unfamiliar, situations on the ground.

Well-led peace keeping forces have shown themselves to be capable of considerable robustness and resilience and, even in turbulent and challenging situations, of being able to assert their authority with minimal use of force. It is mark of how far modern peacekeeping has come that employing multinational peacekeeping forces to provide the initial framework for the restoration of law and order in post conflict nation building has become the norm.

Current preoccupation with the danger to international stability posed by weak and failing states seems likely to guarantee an indefinite future to international peacekeeping as a military and paramilitary activity. Major combat interventions under Chapter VII of the UN Charter seem likely to be reserved for rogue states offering challenges with strategic implications - and not necessarily all of those. Below the strategic level, however, it seems all too probable that interventions of a peace keeping variety, with the assent of at least some of the parties to a given conflict and with the aim either of preventing further deterioration in the situation, or of restoring law and order after fighting, or both, will increasingly be needed. If peacekeeping is to be a regular multinational activity, and is to be successful in its own terms, it cannot be done on a hand to mouth, make-it-up-as-you-go-along-basis. There have to be some generally accepted basic principles to which all forces involved in an operation sign up. The starting point has to be minimising the risk to the forces involved while maximising their effectiveness. A learning process regarding the collection, dissemination and use of intelligence needs to be part of increased resilience.

The acceptable level of risk is a crucial issue, and is not just a matter for the military. Civilian public opinion tends to have strong views. A level of risk which is perceived as acceptable in cases where defence of the homeland is involved, will not necessarily be acceptable in the context of providing security to societies other than one's own. In the colonial era, the role of the military as an aid to the civil power was well-practised and understood. In the political climate of the post colonial world, such a role for the military has been largely eschewed and some of the arts associated with it, forgotten (not least the important one of creating a viable relationship between the civil authority and military command, which itself can be a big determinant of the level of risk inherent in an operation). As a general proposition however, it is fair to say that peacekeeping operations will only be politically sustainable if the levels of risk involved for the peacekeepers are not disproportionately high in relation to the goals of their mission. This in turn must mean that the risks are sufficiently under the control of the peacekeepers that they can actively mitigate and manage them - implying a level of superiority in capability and a capacity rapidly to escalate such that they can meet any challenges that may emerge during the course of the mission. Thus, in the modern political context, low intensity warfare does not permit of primitive battlefield control.

Good intelligence is always important to soldiers and can be crucial. Its generation and use is - or should be - a two way process between the unit in the field and command headquarters. If some units, in effect, opt out, the overall quality of intelligence will be the poorer. The multinationality of a force does not lessen the value and importance of good intelligence, though, for reasons I will discuss later, the two way process may not work as well as in a wholly national context and, as a result, intelligence may be less available to forces on the ground and less well used by them than in a national context. In principle, precisely because international peacekeepers cannot necessarily rely on as good an information flow as would be forthcoming in a national command structure and because they are likely to be up against irregular forces with a vastly superior knowledge of the local terrain, they need to compensate for shortcomings in intelligence collection, assessment and distribution, by being active themselves in the generation of their own local, tactical, information base. The bottom up part of the process can assume unusual importance.

Even in so called Chapter VI situations, where the peacekeepers are doing their job with the assent of the host government, it would be unwise to assume that information supplied by the local authorities or their forces will be either sufficient or reliable. If the soldiers in the field cannot test, against their own observation, what they are told by the local authorities and other third parties, they will be risking operational blindness. There is also the danger of a false sense of security if they are unable to test information obtained from covert sources against what they themselves have observed. 'Intelligence' can be wrong, and can certainly be out of date.

How serious a handicap lack of locally generated tactical information is however, will depend on the peacekeepers' level of capability vis-a-vis hostile forces and how they choose to accomplish their mission. In any multinational peacekeeping operation, there is likely to be more than one style of peacekeeping in evidence. An emphasis in the field on heavy armour and force protection, resulting in less flexible patrolling and less contact with the local population, will be likely both to generate less useful tactical intelligence and to rely on it less. A more extended concept of peacekeeping, in which troops get out and about, patrolling with the aim of making local contact, will generate more and need more. The combination that is least likely to work, and most likely to put peacekeeping troops at risk, is one where their capability is barely, if at all, superior to that of hostile forces, their information poor and their exposure to third party activity high.

iii

In such a situation, information isolation can be very dangerous. Locally generated intelligence will be very important, but almost certainly not enough. Strategic intelligence, and top down information generally, which extends the range of the individual unit's information base, increasing its ability to predict correctly the movement of hostile forces and to interpret accurately the longer range significance of activity in the immediate locality, will all be vital assets in threatening environments.

Except, therefore, in the most formulaic of peacekeeping missions, in situations where the embers of conflict have long since died and only political animosity still stands in the way of settlement (readers can think of instances), it is hard to envisage the possibility of capable and effective peacekeeping without the availability of good quality, timely, intelligence. At the same time, since most peacekeeping forces, and certainly peacekeeping forces of any size involving a mission of any complexity, are almost certainly going to involve troops of more than one nationality, the requirement for providing and using that intelligence poses a challenge not encountered in one nation forces.

Intelligence and trust are intimately linked. And trust is a quality frequently lacking between the component elements of a multinational peacekeeping force. Many factors can be involved, ranging from radically different military traditions, differing levels of capability, language difficulties, sheer lack of familiarity with each other, different, and possibly divergent, interpretations of the mission, and a tortuous, indirect and inefficient command structure, open to challenge, arising from all of these considerations. In the case of UN mandated forces, in those instances such as UNPROFOR in Bosnia, where the ground troop command structure led back to New York, lack of intelligence capability and a unambiguous and fulltime command at the top greatly magnified the consequences of the structural weaknesses of the forces further down the line. In the Bosnian case also, the extreme heterogeneity of the composition of the force was itself a seriously aggravating factor. The zones designated to the different national battalions often became virtually isolated fiefdoms where the forces did their own thing which, all too often, was not very much. As a result, only parts of UNPROFOR really functioned. Some commonsense has to be exercised about the likely effectiveness of a force that is composed of a multiplicity of units that have never before operated, or even exercised, together.

PEACEKEEPING INTELLIGENCE: Emerging Concepts for the Future
Foreword—Dame Pauline Neville-Jones

A weak, loose, command structure is extremely inimical to the willingness of those governments possessing intelligence capabilities to make the product freely available. They see the risk of compromise of the information, or the sources of information, through careless handling or deliberate misuse, as being too great. On the other hand, they will not want their own, or closely allied, force components to be deprived of intelligence which will increase their levels of security or improve their operational effectiveness, or both. The effect of these conflicting imperatives is to bring into existence a force in which the various nationalities are operating against the background of differing levels of intelligence and consequently, of potentially seriously differing assessments of the strategic and tactical situations in which their forces finds themselves. Such a situation inevitably reinforces existing divisions in command and communication and can itself be a source of mistrust. This in turn can have very damaging consequences in situations where the peacekeeping forces, or parts of them, come under threat.

Are there mitigations which can be put in place to alleviate this situation? The answer is some, over time. It is not the case, in my view, that intelligence is so uniquely a one nation activity that it cannot be shared with any other. Were this the case, the British-American intelligence community, which includes the shared generation and use of intelligence, would never have come into existence. That relationship also shows, however the importance of some of the conditions precedent, shared priorities; shared outlook; close structural co-operation between the intelligence agencies of the two governments; willingness and ability in operational situations of their respective armed forces to form a single command structure, all of which go up to maximising the utility of covert source information. Such a situation did not, of course come into being fully fledged. It sprang out of particular circumstances in the mid twentieth century and has developed over time. It has reached the point that, having survived many vicissitudes, it has itself become a binding element in the bilateral relationship (though it would be an illusion to think that it would survive a strategic breach generated by other factors).

This example may be special, but not so special, I think, that elements of its composition cannot be transposed into the world of multinational operations. The crucial factor is not so much a single loyalty - these are, after all, two sovereign nations owing different loyalties - as a common understanding of the shared benefits as well as penalties involved in breaches of trust. If such understanding cannot, over time, be developed in the multinational context, then it is not only international peacekeeping that is likely to remain disproportionately hazardous to the peacekeepers, it is the whole idea of 'coalitions of the willing' that will be stillborn. The more ambitious the multinational operation and/or hostile the environment in which it takes place, the more the forces involved will need to be able to rely on effective intelligence co-operation.

In the so-called war against terror, the level of active international co-operation among civilian authorities and intelligence agencies has been stepped up considerably, including between governments not traditionally thought of as natural partners in such matters. Such co-operation no doubt increases the risk of compromise of sources, but has to be accepted in the interests of effective action. Risk to sources has been reassessed in relation to the rising risk to civilian populations. As they say, needs must. There could well be lessons here for intelligence co-operation in the military sphere also.

Increasing the ability to use intelligence for operational purposes in a multinational force cannot be divorced from strengthening the lines of command within such forces. Genuine unity of command, in practice as well as in theory, is a prerequisite for effective co-operation in the dissemination and use of operational intelligence. This in turn implies that a relationship of confidence and trust exists up and down the line within which procedures for the handling and use of intelligence can be agreed and strictly adhered to. The conditions for this were lacking in UNPROFOR in Bosnia. A NATO led and commanded operation on behalf of the United Nations, on the other hand, has the capacity to rectify many of the observable shortcomings in more ad hoc command structures and to devise secure ways of transmitting and using operational intelligence. While it is inherently likely that the most sensitive intelligence will continue to be withheld from multinational peacekeeping command structures - thus ultimately limiting what can be achieved by such forces - there is much that can be achieved to ensure that the sort of operational errors of the early peacekeeping operations in the Balkans are not perpetuated. That there is increased operational resilience in challenging conditions is already clear. How far the improvements have gone will in due course repay study. The conduct of the current operation in Afghanistan will be an instructive test case.

Table of Contents

PEACEKEEPING INTELLIGENCE: Emerging Concepts for the Future
Table of Contents

Preface

'Peacekeeping and Intelligence: Lessons for the Future?' On 15 and 16 November 2002, this subject brought together international historians, journalists, intelligence experts and military personnel in The Hague at a conference organised by the Netherlands Intelligence Studies Association (NISA) and the Netherlands Defence College (IDL).

Until recently 'Peacekeeping and Intelligence' was a hardly touched upon issue in military and political studies and deliberations. However, the dramatic events in the former Yugoslavia during the last decade of the previous century, clearly indicate that the planning and execution of international peacekeeping operations can only be carried out successfully when supported by adequate and timely intelligence.

The conference coincided with an inquiry by the Netherlands parliament into the dramatic events in Srebenica in the summer of 1995, when a UNPROFOR battalion belonging to the Royal Netherlands Army failed to prevent the massacre of five thousand Bosnian Moslem men. Dr. Cees Wiebes, who was a member of the team of the Netherlands Institute for War Documentation which investigated the massacre, concludes in his *Intelligence and the war in Bosnia 1992-1995: The role of the intelligence and security services* (LIT Verlag: Berlin/London 2003), that the lack of knowledge about Serb plans to overthrow the UN enclave contributed to the failure of this peacekeeping mission. Apart from the fact that this UN mission, for various reasons, was 'destined' to be unsuccessful, Srebenica was also an intelligence failure.

With this book, NISA wishes to contribute to a better understanding of the necessity of timely and adequate intelligence support for political and military decision makers during international peacekeeping operations.

The editors express their gratitude towards the speakers at the conference in The Hague. Without the high quality of their presentations and their willingness to participate in the project, the publication of this book would not have been possible. Originally based on the papers presented at the conference, the addition of six seminal past publications (and two extracts) by prominent authors has added extra value to this volume. We are grateful to the publishers for their permission to reprint.

Finally, as the editors completed their work, it was realised that three forms of reference material would be helpful to UN leaders and others engaged in the vital task of devising concepts and doctrine for peacekeeping intelligence. Therefore we added extracts from the Brahimi Report, as this mature vision could become the primary guide for broad UN reform. We agreed that a more concise version of the book, organised by level of war and by intelligence function, would be helpful even through it would repeat some points. Also we added reference pages pointing to mostly free online references, among which the North Atlantic Treaty Organisation documents on Open Source Intelligence (OSINT) have special relevance to any UN intelligence endeavour.

As the book goes to press, Canada has agreed to host the second annual peacekeeping intelligence conference—details are at the back of the book. It is our hope that this book will be the beginning of a new era in which UN peacekeeping missions have added strength from strategic intelligence (the right mandate and the right force structure), operational intelligence (complex situational awareness spanning civil as well as military dimensions) and tactical intelligence (avoiding surprise, substituting intelligence for violence).

The Netherlands Intelligence Studies Association and the Netherlands Defence College (sponsors of the conference), and OSS (sponsor of the book), dedicate this reference work to all UN peacekeepers: not only military men and women sent abroad to restore peace and stability and to protect the lives of people in a hostile environment, but also the increasing numbers of law enforcement, relief, and other civilian personnel who help the UN address complex emergencies.

Ben de Jong Wies Platje
Robert David Steele
Editors

Part I combines six senior perspectives based on deep experience in the multinational peacekeeping environment. As a group, the author-practitioners call for the professionalisation of peacekeeping intelligence, to include the establishment of a standing United Nations peacekeeping intelligence organisation able to do complex worst-case estimates essential to ensuring the correct mandate is devised at the strategic level; and the establishment of full and diverse multi-disciplinary intelligence collection, processing, and analysis capabilities at the tactical level of operations.

Chapter 1. Strategic Intelligence and the United Nations. Intelligence and the United Nations is not only a complex but also a controversial subject. Terminology problems blur the discussion. What is considered to be 'information collecting' by some, is considered 'intelligence gathering' by others. Again, what is labeled 'strategic intelligence' by some, is labeled 'espionage' by others. The traditional attitude within the UN system is that intelligence gathering is contrary to the open nature of the UN system and is therefore absolutely forbidden. During peacekeeping operations intelligence provided by the permanent members of the UN Security Council reflects the different policies of the respective governments. FRANK VAN KAPPEN

Chapter 2. Intelligence in Peacekeeping Operations: Lessons for the Future. The chapter examines the role of intelligence in UN peacekeeping operations. What lessons can be learned from the past for future peacekeeping operations? Among others, the subjects covered in this chapter are: the Brahimi recommendations, the United Nations as a source and as a recipient of intelligence and the role of intelligence role in the planning and execution of operations. The author comes to the conclusion that the military information structure should be tailored to worst-case scenarios, take into account the mission and include counterintelligence. Sufficient military information should be made available by the use of Humint teams, headquarters and field specialists, special equipment, aerial photography and aerial reconnaissance. Access to satellite imagery and national databases of troop-contributing countries are also needed, as well as a geographical-cell capability. The author emphasizes the need for information security and underlines the necessity of the implementation of the Brahimi recommendations and the establishment of an analysis and early warning secretariat at United Nations headquarters. PATRICK C. CAMMAERT

Chapter 3. Peacekeeping and Intelligence: An Experience in Bosnia-Herzegovina. The chapter is to a large extent based on the author's experience as commander of SFOR's Multinational Division South-West in Bosnia-Herzegovina where the area of operations of the division covers about 40 percent of the land mass of the country. An important part in the intelligence process is played by National Intelligence Cells (NICs) which are directed through national channels. Some NICs have more personnel than the contribution of their countries to SFOR and national characteristics determine to a large extent the ways the cells operate. With the arrival of Lord Ashdown as High

1

Representative in Bosnia-Herzegovina, the exchange of information between SFOR and the Office of the High Representative has considerably improved. TONY VAN DIEPENBRUGGE

Chapter 4. Peacekeeping and Intelligence: Experiences from United Nations Protection Force 1995. All personnel assigned to a peacekeeping mission must have basic understanding of the population, culture and political situation in the area of operations. Past UN operations tell us that commanders and soldiers often lack information about the situation they are facing. This lack of knowledge may cause unnecessary complications and possibly loss of life. To understand a conflict like the one in the Balkans, you have to learn the history, religion, culture and way of thinking of the countries concerned. One of the lessons learned is that what is irrelevant in Stockholm or The Hague may be very relevant in Pale. In a peacekeeping mission military tasks are generally carried out by small units. One can find a lot of information/intelligence on the battalion level but it is often fragmented and difficult to interpret for the battalion commander. Most UN missions are executed in battalion structures and it is therefore necessary for battalion commanders to have access to operational and strategic information. JAN-INGE SVENSSON

Chapter 5. Bridging the Gap: Intelligence and Peace Support Operations. The author argues that by bridging the gap between theory and practice in intelligence work, intelligence for command functions can improve considerably in quality. The chapter focuses on operational and tactical level intelligence as these levels mainly provide intelligence support to operations. Intelligence work mostly tends to be pragmatic and requires field experience. It is multidisciplinary and does not belong to one particular field of the social sciences. Both the intelligence community and academia can benefit from exchanging views and practices. The main area of common interest is in analysing collected data in a well-established methodological way. As more and more technological analytical tools are developed, these could be applied to the planning of intelligence operations as well as to analysis. PASI VÄLIMÄKI

Chapter 6. Intelligence and Peace Support Operations: Some Practical Concepts. Peace support operations (PSOs) require a dedicated and specific intelligence support. During PSOs, intelligence organisations will operate in a 'global information environment' rather than a traditional 'military information environment'. Knowledge of the intentions of parties will be crucial. Relying exclusively on high-tech sensors will only offer a partial and therefore incorrect picture of the situation. A comprehensive picture can only be obtained by fully engaging the human factor in all steps of the intelligence cycle, focused on studying and understanding the attitudes and aspirations of the parties. Force protection is the limiting factor for the implementation of the mandate during PSOs. The importance of force protection implies that at all times special attention should be paid to counterintelligence. RENAUD THEUNENS

2

Strategic Intelligence and the United Nations

Frank van Kappen

When asked to contribute to a book on Peacekeeping and Intelligence, I felt initially rather uneasy and I still do. The reason is that during my tenure as the Military Adviser to the Secretary General of the United Nations, I have struggled with this subject more than once and I have not always come out of the battle unharmed, to say the least. The subject matter is not only complex, but also controversial. I realise that I never managed to get on top of this subject. The danger therefore exists that at the end of this chapter I will leave you with more questions than answers. The confusion starts with the fact that within the Secretariat of the UN in New York, there are many widely different views on the subject. In addition, terminology problems blur the discussion. What is considered collecting information by some is considered intelligence gathering by others, what is labelled 'strategic intelligence' by some is labelled 'espionage' by others. In addition, not everybody understands the difference between strategic and tactical intelligence and those who understand the difference can not agree on where the dividing line between the two should be drawn. A confusing debate that leads nowhere and has all the characteristics of a turf fight.

The traditional attitude within the UN system is that intelligence gathering is contrary to the open nature of the UN system and is therefore absolutely forbidden. This point of view is most strongly voiced by the humanitarian components of the UN system like UNHCR, UNDP, UNICEF etc. The reason is that the humanitarian community is worried that the safety of their personnel is endangered if it is associated with intelligence gathering. Another reason is that the humanitarian agencies are not accountable to the Security Council for their operations.

3

For the Secretariat in New York the situation is of course different. Within the Secretariat, the Department of Peacekeeping Operations (DPKO) and the Department of Political Affairs (DPA) are directly involved in the preparation and execution of peace support operations (PSOs) and are accountable to the Security Council for these operations.

Traditionally the UN Secretariat was opposed to intelligence gathering in support of PSOs: 'it was just not done'. In addition, it was not considered necessary for traditional peacekeeping where consent of all the parties involved was a leading principle. When I started at the UN in July 1995 this was still the majority view. But some within the Secretariat had come to the conclusion that the nature of conflict had changed. The UN was now asked to intervene in civil wars and failed states. The UN now had to deal, not only with governments and their soldiers, but also with multiple factions and their motley bunch of fighters. Governments are susceptible to international pressure, factions are not. Soldiers follow orders, fighters often do not. The risk on the strategic and tactical level of these so-called 'second generation PSOs' is therefore considerable.

Gradually more and more people within DPKO and DPA came to the conclusion that it *might* be necessary to take this into account. Good intelligence might after all be a critical factor to improve the success rate of PSOs executed under the auspices of the UN. I formulate this a bit awkward and hesitant, because that is the way it was. Many within the Secretariat came only with great reluctance to this conclusion and even now there are those who do not agree. When I joined the UN in 1995, this last group was still considerable in size and they considered the shift in thinking about the need for intelligence as something negative and even despicable. They blamed this shift in thinking on the increased influence of the military staff within DPKO. DPKO, and in particular the military staff, had continuously pointed out that the lessons learnt during the operations in Somalia, Rwanda and Bosnia should not be ignored and that it was dangerous and unprofessional to engage in any second generation PSO without having access to solid intelligence. At this point I have to resist the temptation to continue on the subject of so called 'Second Generation PSOs', but it would lead us too far astray. Suffice it to say that it is not only the increased risk, but also the fact that the root causes of civil wars and failed states are complex and require a multidisciplinary approach. It involves activities like restarting the economy, rebuilding the justice system and all those other institutions and structures that are crucial to ensure a sustainable

4

peace. The military operation alone will not create a sustainable peace, it only provides the security umbrella underneath which the real peace process has to take place.

The real peace process is complex and requires a wide variety of civilian actors. To be successful these operations need a comprehensive strategy. Strategic intelligence is absolutely necessary, not only to assess the political and military risks of an intervention, but also to produce a workable and comprehensive plan. I am personally convinced that the lack of strategic intelligence has been an important factor in the failure of a number of UN operations. Fact is that the UN has no intelligence capability of its own and is totally dependent on the member states for intelligence support. For strategic intelligence the UN is mainly dependent on the permanent members of the Security Council. Fact is, what has been provided to the UN in the recent past has not always been 'politically neutral', to say the least. Personally I have a strong suspicion that the permanent members of the Security Council find it rather convenient that the UN depends on them for strategic intelligence. At least they do not consider this to be a problem and there is certainly no urge to change the situation. However in the mid-1990s, after lengthy deliberations, some kind of solution was found to accommodate the wish from DPKO to have access to intelligence to support the planning and the execution of peace support operations. The solution that was implemented reflects not only the internal strive within DPKO, but also the attitude of the permanent members of the Security Council concerning this subject.

Within the Situation Centre at the UNHQ in New York, a separate section was formed. Intelligence experts from the five permanent members of the Security Council man this section. These experts have access through their national channels to the intelligence agencies of their respective nations. Requests for intelligence information from the various departments within the Secretariat can be put forward through this section to the intelligence agencies of the permanent members.

Although occasionally this section has provided some useful intelligence, there are obviously some problems attached to the arrangement. It is for example not clear *who* is in charge of this section, *how* it is managed and *who* is responsible for *what*. During my time at the UN, the arrangement constantly created tension and friction within the Secretariat. In addition, many officials inside the

Secretariat looked at the product of this section with great distrust and not without reason.

On more than one occasion I had the strong suspicion that the information provided by the individuals in this section was intended to steer DPKO into a certain direction or worse, to manipulate DPKO. During the humanitarian crisis in the Great Lakes region in 1997 the intelligence provided through this section about the number, the fate and the condition of the refugees was rather confusing. The reason was that the intelligence provided reflected the difference of opinion between the permanent five about the desirability of a humanitarian intervention. If the nation providing the intelligence was in favour of an intervention, the intelligence provided indicated that the number of refugees was enormous, their suffering unbearable and disaster was imminent. If the nation was *not* in favour of an intervention, the intelligence provided indicated that the number of refugees was not *that* high and their condition reasonable. The number of refugees and their condition became a hot political issue, the whole affair was rather shameful. I am also personally convinced that in some cases crucial information was not provided to the UN, because it was considered to be politically inconvenient at the time. Let me give you an example. I think it is a well-known fact nowadays, that the US was actively involved in the training of the Croatian Army for the Krajina offensive. This was done through a Washington based 'private military contractor'. DPKO was never officially informed about these activities. DPKO was also not warned that an attack by the Croatian Army was imminent. An attack that led to some gruesome killings amongst the civilian population in the Krajina and some dead and wounded UN soldiers. Now don't get me wrong. This example happens to mention the involvement of the US, but I could give you many more similar examples concerning the involvement of other permanent and non-permanent members of the Security Council. I am also not attempting to take the moral high ground by moaning and groaning about the fact that the world is not a fair place. I know by now that the world of international politics is far removed from 'fairy tale la-la-land where we all float around on pink clouds hugging each other.' Sometimes 'things happen,' but it can be extremely frustrating if you are caught in between.

Another problem is that sometimes the intelligence was only provided face to face, verbally and with the caveat that the information could only be shared with a limited number of officials mentioned by name and with nobody else.

On more than one occasion I was not allowed to share the information with the desk-officer who was responsible for the operation within my staff or with the civilian political desk officer in DPKO responsible for the political aspects of the mission. It was sometimes extremely difficult to work effectively under these circumstances and to maintain the necessary team spirit. Let me give you an example. During the United Nations Transitional Administration for Eastern Slavonia, Baranja and Western Sirmium (UNTAES), Belgium provided the force commander and also the framework for the military staff. Because Belgium is a NATO nation, NATO was requested to provide UNTAES with intelligence. NATO agreed on the condition that the intelligence section of UNTAES was to be manned *exclusively* by officers from NATO countries. Because Belgium was the only NATO country participating in this operation, this condition implied that the intelligence section could only be manned by Belgian personnel. This situation created anger and frustration amongst the major troop contributors to UNTAES Russia, Pakistan, Ukraine and Jordan. The fact that the Belgian force commander could not share intelligence, provided by NATO, with his Russian deputy and the officers on his staff from non-NATO countries, created not only tension and frustration within the UNTAES staff, but also within DPKO in New York.

A number of officials within DPKO and also a number of permanent representatives from the troop contributing nations felt the situation to be unacceptable and humiliating. This situation was certainly not conducive to create a climate of trust and cooperation; it caused me a lot of headaches at the time. Again, don't get me wrong. I understand the reluctance of the nations to share intelligence with DPKO. Often intelligence is not shared with the UN Secretariat because the nation that owns the information is afraid its intelligence sources may be compromised, or else certain technical capabilities may be revealed. The Secretariat is as watertight as a sieve, it is nearly impossible to keep anything under wraps. An intelligence official from one of the member states once apologised to me with the words: 'I am sorry. I realise this caveat creates a difficult situation for you personally, but I have no choice. You know how it is in this place. If you even think about something in this building, it is known in 189 capitals the next day.'

Another complicating factor is that many troop contributing nations increase their intelligence efforts in the area of operations where their own troops are deployed. Understandable from their point of view, but it complicates the overall picture considerably. Examples are the activities of the British SAS in Bosnia when UNPROFOR was deployed and the activities of US Special Forces and Delta Force in Somalia when UNOSOM was deployed. Needless to say that these Special Forces operate under national control and the UN is most of the time officially not informed about their presence and their mission. I have to resist the temptation to continue on this subject, doing so, however, might be counterproductive. Suffice it to say that this practice can lead to some awkward and even dangerous situations that get people killed. Still, although DPKO is not officially informed about these intelligence activities, there are often UN officials who know. They know because intelligence operatives from a variety of member states inform them. Not about their own intelligence activities, but about the intelligence activities conducted by *'the others'* The motivation is in these cases not always obvious. It is done for a wide variety of reasons but in general, let's say, 'because it suits their own purpose.' What is obvious, is that also *other* nations than the 'usual suspects' are involved in covert operations in UN mission areas. You really have to be extremely cautious when you are caught in this dangerous game. It does not take much to make a wrong assessment and the next thing you know is that things go terribly wrong and people get killed.

An example of the latter is what happened in Rwanda. The Force Commander of the UN-force in Rwanda, General Romeo Dallaire, had intelligence from various sources that a terrible massacre of the Tutsi minority in Rwanda was imminent. The information he had received was quite detailed. He even knew the location of the secret arms caches of those who had planned the massacre. He informed UNHQ in New York and asked permission to take preventive action. New York considered General Dallaire's warning another unconfirmed rumour, or even another attempt to manipulate the UN. New York denied permission to take preventive action. The massacre that followed in Rwanda was of biblical proportions. This incident took place before I joined the UN, but I spoke many times with General DelAire about his Rwanda experience. He is still haunted by this disaster. It illustrates the distrust within the Secretariat about intelligence and the fear to be manipulated. In this case however, the intelligence was correct. In this chapter I have hinted several times at the existence of a wide variety of informal structures intertwined with the formal structure of the Secretariat. Unofficial information networks form a substantial part of these informal structures and they are often used to pass intelligence. However, it is extremely difficult to verify the information obtained via these

8

informal networks. It is therefore dangerous to base important decisions on this information. Sometimes it is possible to verify specific information by comparing the results obtained from several separate informal networks. However this is not easy. You never know if the information from these separate networks eventually originates from the same source.

Another method is to use the humanitarian organisations within the UN system to verify certain intelligence received from member states. Organisations like UNDP, UNHCR and others are present all over the world. The UN system has therefore potentially an inherent and considerable capability to collect information and therefore intelligence. What is needed to develop this potential is a system to tap the necessary information from these organisations and to subsequently process it in a professional way. The problem is, as I stated earlier, that the humanitarian side of the house has understandably no intention whatsoever to co-operate. I must admit that despite all this, I have occasionally used my personal network within the humanitarian part of the UN system to get crucial information to protect my soldiers. I am sure others within UNHQ in New York have done the same for a wide variety of reasons. I am also sure this practice will continue. These activities are not structured and are strictly based on personal networks. At least at this time they are.

At the end of my chapter I would like to stress the fact that my account is a *personal* one and therefore far from neutral. It is probably also not very balanced, it can't be. I was part of what happened at the time and my perception may differ from the truth. However, the editors asked me to provide a personal account, that was my mandate and that is what I stuck to.

Last but not least: from what I have said here, you may get the impression that the UN is an ineffective and cumbersome organisation. To a certain extent that is true but I would like to remind you that despite all the drawbacks the UN has saved millions of lives and, apart from some well-known disasters, has also achieved some striking successes. We should keep in mind that the UN has few resources of its own. We, the nations, provide it with the necessary resources. The United Nations is what we, the nations, want it to be.

10

Intelligence in Peacekeeping Operations: Lessons for the Future

Patrick C. Cammaert

> *'We are fully aware of your long-standing limitations in gathering information. The limitations are inherent in the very nature of the United Nations and therefore of any operation conducted by it.'*
>
> UN Secretary-General U Thant to the Commander of the UN Operation in the Congo (UNOC), Lt-Gen. Kebbede Guebre, in a coded cable on 24 September 1962.

In the last forty years we have seen a quantum leap in technology, weaponry, military capability, war fighting ability and tempo of operations, but in the field of UN Peacekeeping operations little has changed! Our greatest capability remains the 'Mark I eyeball'. Too often a UN mission is judged as a success or failure based on peacekeeper casualties rather than innocent lives saved. In today's changing environment, pro-active operations and force security become paramount for successful peacekeeping – in a chapter VI (peace support) or chapter VII (peace enforcement) operation. These are dependent on accurate intelligence. In peacekeeping as in all military operations, the basis of all successful operations is:

- Accurate, timely intelligence
- How the commander utilises this, his most precious asset, in the application of his forces to achieve his mission objectives.

Aim

The aim of this chapter is to examine the role of intelligence in UN peacekeeping operations (PK)—specifically, what lessons we can learn for application in future PK operations. Subjects covered are:

- Introduction
- Role of intelligence in peace support operations
- Terminology
- UN peacekeeping and intelligence
- Brahimi recommendations
- The UN as a source of intelligence
- The UN as a recipient of intelligence
- The role of intelligence in the planning and execution of peacekeeping operations
- Elements of the intelligence process in UN peacekeeping operations
- Some intelligence lessons learned in UN peacekeeping operations
- General intelligence lessons learned
- Conclusions
- Recommendations

Introduction

> *'What is called ''foreknowledge'' cannot be elicited from spirits, nor from gods, nor by analogy with past events, nor from calculations. It must be obtained from men who know the enemy situation.'*
>
> Sun Tzu

Ethnic, religious and political Inter-state and Intra-state conflicts continue to destabilise regions and lead to the formation of belligerent groups of whom it is becoming less and less clear whether they are freedom fighters, national military forces, guerrillas or terrorists. As the Brahimi report recommendations and recent initiatives have demonstrated, the UN Secretariat and Security Council are becoming more aware of the need for early warning and preventative interventions in the form of peacekeeping operations. Despite the digitalisation of the battlefield with remote sensors, on-line satellite imagery and digital data burst transmissions, in a post-September 11 world the role of intelligence, and specifically human intelligence (Humint), has become more and more crucial.

The Role of Intelligence in Peace Support Operations

Peacekeeping operations normally refer to peace support operations (PSO)—which may be conducted in relatively stable environments where belligerent parties have demonstrated a capability to abide by cease-firing agreements, or in highly unstable environments where conflict has developed or is ongoing. The efficient gathering and processing of information, and the dissemination of military information, is critical to the success of peacekeeping missions and the safety of mission personnel. This is especially relevant in UN peacekeeping operations where location and capability of belligerents are often known through 'observations' and 'overt intelligence'. But the crucial information of 'personalities', 'motives' and 'intent' can only be obtained through traditional Humint means. (NATO definition: 'a category of intelligence derived from information collected and provided by human sources'.) Commanders at all levels require accurate military information support in order to effectively execute their tasks. Poor intelligence means you often do not have the right forces with the right equipment at the right place and time. This is often reflected in the number of casualties – either peacekeeper lives as we have seen in Rwanda and Somalia, or the lives of the innocents that the mission was initiated to protect – the genocide in Rwanda and massacres at Srebrenica serve to illustrate this. In PSOs, military requirements for accurate and timely information are the same as elsewhere in the spectrum of conflict and in the continuum of operations. Military information gathering within a PSO relies heavily on observation of events through military observers and force elements—including mobile units, observation posts, airborne reconnaissance and a broad spectrum of surveillance devices. High-tech intelligence collection methods such as imagery intelligence (Imint) or signals intelligence (Sigint) are for the most part timely and accurate. While the sources and associated products attract considerable attention, largely due to the technologies involved, they cannot provide complete knowledge of the environment, local attitudes, emotions, opinions, identities and importance of key players and their role in the situation. Humint, on the other hand, gathered by well-trained troops in an area of operations, from interacting with the complete range of local human sources, provides this nature of critical information from which a complete picture can be developed. It is the major contributor to understanding the population, its culture and needs and how these relate to the operational environment.

In the Balkans, both French and British officers emphasized the value of Human intelligence and the fact it was particularly lacking. However BRITFOR obtained 98% of their information from Humint sources, primarily from their own soldiers on patrol. British intelligence officers stated the tactical picture had to be built up by piecing together Humint and by interpreting the totally biased Serbian/Croat/Muslim radio.

Initial Impressions Report French and British
Operations Other Than War (OOTW)
Former Republic of Yugoslavia

PSOs differ from conventional military operations in the sense that the collection of information and processing it into analysed material may be politically restricted. Furthermore, information acquired must be guarded from all belligerent parties to a dispute, to ensure that the impartiality of the mission is not compromised and the consent of the parties in the conflict is maintained and fostered. So it is imperative that a secure channel is established for transmission of sensitive information to DPKO level and that a mechanism is in place for that information to be received, analysed, briefed to the right level on a 'need to know' basis and kept confidential.

Terminology

By design and definition, the UN is a highly transparent organisation. Due to political sensitivities, for many years 'intelligence' within the UN was not considered an acceptable term, activity or process. However, this view has to some extent changed in recent years. The UN now realises that basic 'overt intelligence' must be provided in order to ensure force protection and enhance the capability of the force to achieve its mandate. However, in the interest of projecting a non-threatening presence, the term military information (MI) is used instead of 'military intelligence'. Despite the UN terminology, the basic intelligence processes are still present in all PSOs, as they cannot operate without an organised system to collect, analyse, interpret, predict and disseminate the sum of knowledge and understanding of the environment in which military activities are conducted. Not only does this include knowledge pertaining to the activities, capabilities and intentions of belligerent parties, but also to 'neutral sympathisers' of the belligerents and the physical environment where a military force is expected to achieve its mission. This is generally accepted practice, but the level of success is often linked to the level of confidential information that is obtained in this process. The most controversial issue remains the methodology used to get the confidential information needed, and the question is if force protection gives us enough leeway to actively collect critical information in a mission situation.

UN Peacekeeping and Intelligence

It has been said that the UN is a sieve for information – but this is not a flaw – it is a design feature to enable people and countries, some of which may be in conflict with each other, to work together and to be part of an organisation that has international organisational objectives. However, this makes it difficult for national intelligence agencies to work closely with the UN Secretariat. If the rationale for intelligence gathering at UNHQ level is to inform political decision-makers, then the logical place for it to interact with the UN is where it currently does, via the member states representatives in the legislative bodies, particularly the Security Council. Peacekeeping operations should 'a priori' be non-political. However, it is in the missions themselves where the knowledge and intelligence needed lie. Transmitting this sometimes confidential intelligence through the political filters to the right level is one of the greatest challenges we face.

Brahimi Recommendations

Change in the UN system is crucial in order to address deficiencies in the peacekeeping process. Important Brahimi report recommendations in this respect include:

- United Nations military units must be capable of defending themselves, other mission components and the mission's mandate. Rules of engagement should be sufficiently robust and not force United Nations contingents to cede the initiative to their attackers.

- The Secretariat must not apply best-case planning assumptions to situations where the local actors historically have exhibited worst-case behaviour. It means that mandates should specify an operation's authority to use force.
- United Nations forces for complex operations should be afforded the field intelligence and other capabilities needed to mount an effective defence against violent challengers.
- A new information-gathering and analysis entity should be created to support the informational and analytical needs of the Secretary-General and the members of the Executive Committee on Peace and Security (ECPS).
- The proposed ECPS Information and Strategic Analysis Secretariat

> *The 'EISAS' secretariat has since been referred to as a 'system wide information and analysis' effort. It is the closest the Secretariat has come to establishing an official intelligence capacity, however its implementation is fraught with potential obstacles. However, this is a specialist subject for discussion on its own.*

- (EISAS) would create and maintain integrated databases on peace and security issues, distribute that knowledge efficiently within the United Nations system, generate policy analyses, formulate long-term strategies for ECPS and bring budding crises to the attention of the ECPS leadership.

- Rapid deployment standards and 'on-call' expertise
  The first six to twelve weeks following a cease-fire or peace accord are often the most critical ones both for establishing a stable peace and the credibility of a new operation. Opportunities lost during that period are hard to regain. The Brahimi report recommends that:

  > 'A revolving "on-call list" of about 100 experienced, well-qualified military officers, carefully vetted and accepted by DPKO, be created within UNSAS. Teams drawn from this list and available for duty on seven days' notice would translate broad, strategic-level mission concepts developed at Headquarters into concrete operational and tactical plans in advance of the deployment of troop contingents, and would augment a core element from DPKO to serve as part of a mission start-up team'.

It would be crucial to include qualified intelligence officers in this process, particularly those who have proven track records of capability and excellence during peacekeeping deployments.

- Adapting peace operations to the information age
  Another Brahimi recommendation is that modern, well-utilised information technology (IT) is a key enabler of many of the objectives, but gaps in strategy, policy and practice impede its effective use. In particular, UN headquarters lacks a sufficiently strong responsibility centre for user-level IT strategy and policy in peace operations. A senior official with such responsibility in the peace and security arena should be appointed and located within EISAS, with counterparts in the offices of the Special Representative of the Secretary-general (SRSG) in every United Nations peace operation. Headquarters and the field missions alike also need a substantive, global, Peace Operations Extranet (POE), through which missions would have access to, among other things, EISAS databases and analyses and lessons learned.

Many of these recommendations cover the field of intelligence. The effective use of intelligence often depends on a Secure Communication Channel. One of the critical failures of the UN system is that there is no really secure confidential channel for sensitive intelligence to be sent from the field to DPKO. Information must pass through many channels to get to the level where it can be used to brief at Security Council level, making it potential public knowledge. Looking at the broader picture, there are two parts to the UN's relationship with intelligence:
- The UN as a source of intelligence
- The UN as a recipient of intelligence.

The United Nations as a Source of Intelligence

There are elements of intelligence gathering for which United Nations peacekeeping missions are uniquely suited. An easy example is the United Nations Mission to Ethiopia and Eritrea (UNMEE) with its Temporary Security Zone (TSZ). Whilst interested national governments inevitably have sources of information in both capitals, only the UN has observers spread across the TSZ. They are able to offer independent assessments of troop movements and other

17

relevant changes on the ground, for example changes in local administration, local command structures and attitudes of ground level commanders. This information gathering forms part of the dual role of UNMOs on a peacekeeping mission that is to prove confidence to the parties by acting as an independent observer. But it also provides independent and objective advice to the international community on the behaviour of the two parties who have sought the intervention. The UN can then confirm to each party what the other is doing in terms of adhering to the peace process. The UN also provides member states (who have invested in the peace and who make the political decisions about mandates etc.) with an objective assessment of whether the parties are in fact abiding by their commitments.

Similarly, the nature of UN staff engagement with local authorities means that it can and does receive a breadth of impressions and information that would not easily be acquired by national agents. The catch is how this information is passed on (think Rwanda again, or East Timor). There is undoubtedly a systemic problem with passing critical information to the Security Council from the field, in part because of lingering Cold War fears and in part because what the UN Secretariat knows is potentially public knowledge. Therefore it can embarrass its employers, member states, whose decisions to act or not on any given crisis will not simply depend on right or wrong, but also on national interests.

The Brahimi reports recommend telling the Council what it *needs to know,* not what it *wants to hear.* This is a solid and worthwhile position, but Secretariat officials (including even secretaries-general) have been severely punished for doing this in the past (e.g. Hammarskjöld on Congo when the USSR refused to speak to him, U Thant on Vietnam when the US refused to acknowledge him and set out to discredit him and even in the post-Cold War era: Boutros-Ghali on Bosnia and Rwanda. The problem remains..!

The United Nations as a Recipient of Intelligence

The United Nations is a deliberately transparent organisation, although it has been described as so transparent it is opaque, with no instrument to filter through the volumes of incoming data. However, accurate intelligence would clearly be of use to it, in determining how to respond to events on the ground in peacekeeping. The difficulty lies in finding a route to transmit classified

18

intelligence material to those within the UN who need to know and ensuring the ongoing confidentiality of that information in the process.

The route cannot always be via the senior staff on a mission. Senior mission appointments are always political. This is inevitable and will not change. Without questioning the integrity of top mission appointments, it is a fact that the direct transfer of information during missions can be dictated by and influenced by the politics and national affiliations of the top-level political appointments of those missions.

The proper mechanism is through the Security Council and its related Military Staff Committee, which is set up by the UN Charter. It is questionable whether a new methodology for rendering the Military Staff Committee more effective has emerged after the end of the Cold War (the effectiveness of the committee was severely restricted by Cold War antagonisms). It should, however, be made more operationally effective. There have been various proposals from academics and others to this effect, but this is on a different note.

The Role of Intelligence in the Planning and Executing of Peacekeeping Operations

When looking at the role of intelligence in PK operations, there are two basic phases in the process, namely the Planning Phase and the Execution Phase:

a.   Planning phase
       This is the military strategic level where PK operations are initiated by
       the Secretariat and planned by DPKO. A wide spectrum of information
       is needed here and there is a large degree of dependency on open
       sources of information, fact-finding missions and intelligence from the
       national intelligence agencies of troop contributing nations. Experience
       has shown that PK missions are often destined to succeed or fail based
       on the scope and accuracy of the intelligence available for planning at
       this level.

b.   Execution phase
       PK missions normally follow the sequence of:

i.   deploy an advance party to conduct limited reconnaissance and liaison with the emphasis on evaluating the situation on the ground

ii.   meet the belligerents, initiate the logistics of deployment

iii.   re-evaluate force security aspects. Determine exact deployment areas, Area of Responsibility (AOR), phase of deployment and expansion

iv.   execute deployment, expand mission in pursuit of the mission objectives (e.g. TSZ, buffer-zone, demilitarisation, demobilisation)

In all of these phases we have learned that Intelligence Preparation of the Battlefield (IPB) is critical.

A force commander needs planning information on roads, terrain negotiability, infrastructure, hazards such as minefields and of course tactical positions and strengths of the belligerents. As the mission unfolds and force elements and military observers are deployed on the front line amongst the belligerent forces, force security and force protection becomes a critical issue. To be effective you must know the threat.

Tactical positions of belligerent forces, personalities of commanders and occurrences in the mission area which may impact on the tactical situation become critical as the mission moves towards some form of separation of forces, creating of a buffer, security or demilitarised zone, removal of heavy weapons to barracks or cantonments and some form of demilitarisation through demobilisation.

With all of these processes, force protection is a critical issue. To be effective, peacekeepers in conflict zones must proactively acquire and painstakingly analyse information about conditions within the mission area. This is especially true if the mission is conducted in a hazardous and unpredictable environment and the lives of peacekeepers are threatened. Accurate intelligence on the location, deployments and intentions of belligerents provides more force protection than having (greatly outnumbered) armed troops on the ground. It is here where the type, nature and structure of intelligence assets available to the force commander become critical.

Elements of the Intelligence Process in United Nations Peacekeeping Operations

The intelligence structure and functioning for a PKO is planned at DPKO level. As a force commander you must use what you get. Often the basic structure and elements are there but are far from ideal. Some of my experiences in this regard are as follows:

a. Organic intelligence ability and structure of deployed contingents
    It is my experience that certain contingents which have a Humint collection orientation and their own organic intelligence structure and capabilities are several times more effective in controlling their AOR than other contingents with only an equivalent combat capability. I found to my dismay in my peacekeeping experience that there are some contingents to which in practice the word 'intelligence' is a foreign and theoretical concept. Ideally, a force commander should have some good qualified and experienced intelligence officers with each contingent to direct the process of information collection and the intelligence cycle for those contingents' AORs down to ground level.

b. Dedicated Humint field collection capability
    There is much controversy over the concept of having dedicated groups of Humint teams in PKOs. In reality, the entire military component should be Humint information gatherers, although ideally every contingent should have a few specialist Humint collection teams which should be planned as part of a force structure. The least we should have is a good Humint orientation and training programme in the pre-deployment phase for contingents.

c. Strong intelligence analysis section at headquarters level
    I have found that one or two really sharp officers are of more value to me as a force commander than having a intelligence section of fifteen people who are engaged in a 'process'. That process tells me history, not implications, predictions and expected belligerent Courses of Action (CAOs) which I need to know. This brings me back to the point of selection and training as well as the concept of having a stand-by list of experienced officers to deploy into critical posts on missions. We urgently need a military intelligence training wing at one of the

21

international peacekeeping training institutions to address the issue of doctrine, training, selection and standards related to military personnel in peacekeeping operations.

d.   Intelligence photo interpreter capability at force headquarters
During the start-up of UNMEE, I had a dedicated aerial photo reconnaissance unit with a P-166 aircraft and a large team of technicians, photographers and support personnel, but no photo interpreter. They could take aerial photos for me but that was it. This was a critical resource for me in the investigations to determine the TSZ boundaries and subsequent changes which we made to accommodate more accurate facts on the ground. Fortunately I found one of the UNMOs, a young South African captain by the name of Peter Roos to be a specialist military intelligence photo interpreter. I brought him to headquarters and he did great work in assisting me with the analysis required to get an accurate picture of the TSZ during the sensitive process of getting a separation of the forces on the ground. However, there was no photo interpretation equipment available. Captain Roos offered to go and borrow some specialist equipment from his Defence Force. I thought this was a great idea but then we spent months trying to get the UN civilian administration to reimburse him for the excess baggage costs of getting the twenty kilograms of equipment there and back.

e.   Terrain analysis/Military geography team
The most beneficial aspect of the available Geographic Information Systems (GIS) technology is the ability to integrate information from various sources on top of digital maps of the theatre of peacekeeping operations. To be of effective value to a force commander, they need to deploy at the earliest possible moment and assist in Intelligence Preparation of the Battlefield (IPB). This should include terrain negotiability analysis, route maps, effect of weather on terrain, land-mine data, AOR maps and other GIS and mapping products utilising available databases, digital imagery, satellite support and Landsat imagery. However, I have found that like many other emerging technologies where capabilities and processes are not fully understood by all, there is a distinct lack of user functionality built into the GIS projects. During UNMEE we were using maps based on a 1937 survey

22

updated in 1974. I needed maps with accurate roads annotated using Global Positioning System (GPS) route tracking data but lack of a $5 download cable to get the info from the GPS to a computer delayed this project for more than eight months.

f.   Force security threat
Here I include the concept of information security and particularly in the information technology (IT) field. The UN is potentially the best and most accurate source of information and intelligence for belligerent parties. We are vulnerable in our communications and data security, from Humint to the IT field and plain old-fashioned document security.
In DPKO missions we have embraced the wonders of the computer age with LANs, WANs, servers, share drives and firewalls. The only thing we have not done is addressed the human factor. We have people on missions with little or no previous exposure to computers. I have found sensitive information being placed in low security locations and open share drives, through negligence and lack of security awareness.
During UNMEE, two years after mission start-up we received state-of-the-art firewall hardware to prevent hackers getting into our systems; essential, but not my ideal time scale.

It is important to remember that a belligerent group will often only allow you as much access to tactical information (through observations and liaison) as their confidence in the UN mission's ability to safeguard that information allows. This often translates directly into freedom of movement and level of co-operation on the ground, which is the primary data collection process in pursuit of the mission's mandate and objectives. It is therefore critical to have counterintelligence and security specialists as part of a force structure to address Humint and IT vulnerabilities through monitoring, investigations, threat assessments and security awareness training.

Some critical counterintelligence aspects that should be considered include:

- pre-deployment analysis of intelligence collection capability of the opposing groups in a mission theatre

- qualified force counterintelligence officer at headquarters
- computer network information security specialist
- availability of IT hardware such as firewalls at mission start-up
- field investigation/interviewing teams.

g.   Skills and Capabilities

The old adage of 'a few good men' (or women), is always relevant in any field, but particularly so in the military information field. It is almost 'mission critical' to have a core group of competent, experienced and capable military information officers. TCCs more often than not fail to provide the right profile of military information personnel, often it is not even a military information specialist who ends up in the military information section. One solution already mentioned is the establishment of a specialised UN military information centre or training wing at one or more of the established international peacekeeping training centres. Here the doctrine of 'intelligence in peacekeeping operations' can be developed, military information courses presented and standards of training and competencies determined, evaluated and implemented with teams assisting national training similar to the UNMO training concept.

Some Intelligence Lessons learned from United Nations Peacekeeping Operations

Rwanda

With the UNAMIR mission in Rwanda, accurate information was available on the planned Hutu COA (genocide of the Tutsis). However, this 'intelligence product' was based not on an extensive military information system of collection, analysis, corroboration and a Military Intelligence Preparation of the Battlefield (MIPB), but largely on the information of 'Jean Pierre', a single highly-placed militia leader informant.

The MIPB process was lacking and politically restricted, not resulting in a proper flow of information which would lead to detailed analysis of the situation, development of belligerent COAs and possible 'triggers'.

24

The impression created was that 'bang', out of the blue, DPKO headquarters received a horrific tale of planned genocide based largely on the information from one person. The often-quoted reaction in that fateful coded cable was really to be expected:

> Subject: Contacts with Informant
>
> We have carefully reviewed the situation in the light of your MIR-79. We cannot agree to the operation contemplated in paragraph 7 of your cable, as it clearly goes beyond the mandate entrusted to UNAMIR under resolution 872 (1993).

More than half a million people died in the Rwandan genocide. Perhaps hundreds of thousands of lives could have been spared through decisive peacekeeping intervention. This was dependent on immediate and decisive Security Council member state support, however it was not forthcoming. The question needs to be asked: 'If the information on planned genocide had been seen to be coming from a broad-based, multi-source MIPB process using established Humint resources over a period of time, would the Security Council and member states have reacted differently and could the world have been spared more than half a million deaths?'

Intelligence must be the product of the analyses of multiple sources of information over a period of time, there must be a system and commanders at all levels must have confidence in that system through consistency. With Rwanda, if there had been better intelligence and more confidence in that intelligence at United Nations headquarters level, they might conceivably have changed the mandate of UNAMIR to allow pre-emptive operations. This might have either stabilised the situation or bought enough time for reinforcements to be brought in which could possibly have made a difference.

<u>United Nations Protection Force (UNPROFOR) – Bosnia</u>
Ethnic cleansing was not a new concept to the Balkans. It was practised during the occupation of the Balkans by the Ottoman Turks and during the Second World War. One of the most valuable lessons from history is that history repeats itself. The break-up of the Former Republic of Yugoslavia led to renewed conflict and a cycle of violence. Lessons learnt by UNPROFOR in Bosnia should not have been new lessons. Some of these are as follows:

a.   Population really is key terrain!
     When separating the Bosnian Croats and Bosnian Muslims in Central
     Bosnia, local issues could often be resolved with prior knowledge of
     historical perspectives and emotive locations such as former battle
     sites, burial sites, religious sites, homes of local leaders, key locations
     for economic and other reasons and the list goes on. When trying to
     split formally linked communities, everyone has their own idea of who
     owns what.

b.   Military Geography
     The lines of communication overlaid with data provided by terrain and
     weather analyses and engineer intelligence, provided the convoy
     commander with invaluable information. It allowed for those normally
     unforeseen difficulties and prompted the forward basing of engineer
     plant equipment on one main supply route.

c.   Personalities
     This really does become a 10th order of battle factor and not just a
     miscellaneous element of the IPB. When faced with a military
     commander on one side who was a former JNA commander
     (disciplined, trained, etc.) and a local thug turned military commander
     on the other, this information becomes invaluable.

d.   Courses of Action
     These really do multiply with Serbs, Croats, Bosnians, Bosnian Serbs,
     Bosnian Croats, Mujahideen and even United Nations allies with their
     own third-party interests. They all have potentially conflicting
     hostilities.

d.   Language
     When faced with the problem of linguistic skills and having only
     limited resources within the Force, the obvious answer is to use locally
     employed interpreters (it was useful to use Army linguists to monitor
     what they were actually saying). However, as the aid convoys crossed
     ethnic and military boundaries, these interpreters became an issue and
     were sometimes detained. The challenge with using local interpreters is

that they are vulnerable to blackmail and coercion. They could be working for up to three different sides besides the UN.

General Intelligence Lessons learned

Debriefing
Valuable information can be gained from debriefing anyone who is available and willing. These casual sources provide mostly low-level information gathered recently in the region. This can be particularly useful when building up the database of personalities to be used for future dealings and negotiations.

Situation Awareness and Information reporting
Even the 'mail run' might pass that faction reinforcement convoy travelling otherwise unseen. Everyone must know the importance of reporting and how to do it. Memory joggers and acronyms should be taught at every level:
* OVERWHELM. Ordnance, vehicle type, electronics, recognition features, when, how many, equipment seen, location, morale.
* WHAT. Wheels, hull, armament, turret
* BBWT. Barrel, Baffle, Wheels, Trail.

Culture
An understanding of cross-cultural issues is essential, not just of the local population but also of your allies. For example, to a Bulgarian a nod of the head means 'no' and a shake 'yes'. Why is the Battle of Kosovo Polje so emotive? After all they lost, did they not? A basic knowledge of the language, if only to say 'hello' or 'thank you' or sometimes more importantly 'stop' or 'halt' is also very useful and conveys a message.

Mission Start-up
The beginning of a mission is often the most volatile and vulnerable, the MIPB system must operate from day 1.

MIPB
We have learnt that the ability to act faster than a belligerent is of paramount importance. Actions are based on contingency plans for possible COAs, which are dependent on accurate MIPB.

Intelligence awareness to lowest level
The best form of force protection is treat awareness.

- Every uniform member must be attuned to his role as 'eyes and ears' information gatherers.
- The MIPB concept and process should be understood and implemented at platoon commander level. It is not the exclusive domain and responsibility of the military information section at headquarters level!

A picture tells a thousand words
If there are cheap digital cameras and video recorders down to section level, with the ability to send a digital image by radio transmission or any other means to headquarters, the commander is already ten steps further ahead in the game than he would otherwise be.

Information resources
There are ways and means of enhancing open sources information collation and analysis efforts in missions. Commercially available IT and data mining products are highly sophisticated nowadays. The internet contains a vast amount of useful information which, if found, verified and assembled into a useful product, can be a valuable asset. Subscription-based products, such as FBIS and BBC Monitoring can also provide a useful flow of raw 'near intelligence' material. Of course, that raw data then has to be analysed and this requires resources, skill and effort.

Exploit expertise and experience
A commander is often only as good as his staff. Successful commanders identify and surround themselves with experience and expertise, officers who can translate vision and commanders' intent into effective military information collection plans, own force battle plans and courses of action.

Conclusions

After examination of the role of intelligence and specifically lessons learned from the deficiencies and successes of Intelligence in Peacekeeping Operations, the following conclusions are reached:

a.   Strategic/UN headquarters level

    i.   Plan military information structure to cater for worst case, not best case, tailor to mission, include counterintelligence.

    ii.   Plan for sufficient military information assets, Humint teams, headquarters & field specialists, special equipment, aerial photography capability, aerial reconnaissance, access to satellite imagery, access to national databases of troop-contributing countries, geographical-cell capability.

    iii.   Early deployment of military geographical cell.

    iv.   Greater use of commercial technology, GPS, digital cameras, satellite imagery, commercial data encryption software.

    v.   Do not let political sensitivities compromise Force Security by restricting the military information mandate to collect information.

    vi.   Implement Brahimi report recommendations of military information early warning and analysis capability at United Nations DPKO level.

    vii.   Secure channel for sensitive intelligence to United Nations DPKO.

    viii.   Military information mandate to recruit informers and collect confidential information relating to force security.

b.   Operational (mission) and tactical level

    i.   Staffing of critical posts, do not let rank inhibit function. Use your best resources.

    ii.   Utilise all assets and personnel for information gathering.

    iii.   Tap national intelligence capability of Troop Contributing Countries (TCCs) in mission.

    iv.   Aggressive MIPB, use all resources, manage the info flow process, continuously evaluate status of Periodic Intelligence Reports (PIRs), profile the personalities, monitor the bigger picture, know the history of the conflict, monitor the media and political scene, analyse motives.

    v.   Importance of digital imagery and real-time information.

    vi.   Reliability and consistency of the intelligence system and product.

    vii.   Information security.

viii. Attitude of commanders to military information, and specifically how the force commander utilises his intelligence assets and capability, is critical.

Recommendations

Although the conclusions reached for the future have addressed the aim of this chapter, I would like to stress the following recommendations:

- Implementation of Brahimi recommendations on establishment of a 'analysis and early warning secretariat' at United Nations headquarters level is crucial.
- The issue of training needs to be addressed with the creation of a military information training centre at one of the peacekeeping institutions which could have the dual role of developing doctrine and integrating emerging technologies with the military information function and setting standards for training.
- In mission planning we must plan for success, using worst history behaviour models of the actors in a conflict, not the best case. Ensure that sufficient military information capacity is provided for the structure, assets and quality of personnel.
- Use of emerging technologies from GIS to digital cameras can provide a significant near real-time and mission-wide information network. Information is power and digital images tell a thousand words.
- Secure channels should be created to ensure capability for flow of highly confidential sensitive information from mission military component to United Nations DPKO level without loss of confidentiality or 'filtering' to cater for political sensitivities.
- In complex contingencies, especially where peacekeeping operations have a force security threat or face a mission situation that could deteriorate into required intervention (peace enforcement), military information assets need to have the mandate and capability to acquire relevant confidential-level information (read: use of informants).

There will always be too many Peacekeeping challenges and too few resources. Let us not forget the hurt of the past where we could not do enough but learn from it so that we can have the power to do more in the future.

Peacekeeping and Intelligence: An Experience in Bosnia-Herzegovina

Tony van Diepenbrugge

It was a great experience to be a year in command of the Multinational Division South-West (MND (SW)) as part of the Stabilisation Force (SFOR) in Bosnia and Herzegovina. In this chapter I want to share my experiences in the field of peacekeeping and intelligence. I will first devote a few words to the area of responsibility and the mission of the division before I cover the topics related to peacekeeping and intelligence. I will look at 'situational awareness', whereby it is of utmost importance to be able to be proactive and to act when necessary. I will further examine the intelligence organisation and assets that are vital to getting the information we need in order to create the desired situational awareness. Finally I will cover some recent developments and conclude with the lessons that we learned from our experiences. Based on these lessons we can make improvements for the future.

Multinational Division South-West

I shall briefly describe SFOR for purposes of this discussion. From the top-down, the SFOR operation in Bosnia-Herzegovina is controlled by AFSOUTH in Naples and HQ SFOR in Sarajevo. MND (SW) is one of the composite units of SFOR. It is connected to the north and east by Croatia, to the east by Multinational Division North, and to the south is Multinational Division South-East.

MND (SW)—with a strength of approximately 4,250 military—consists of three battle groups and several assets at divisional level. The battle groups have a number of teams or companies varying from two to five that, with the exception of one company in reserve, have their own area of responsibility.

31

MND (SW) AOR

MND (SW) is a truly multinational division: the main troop contributing nations are Canada, the Netherlands and the United Kingdom. Representatives from Australia, the Czech Republic, Bulgaria, New Zealand, Rumania and the Slovak Republic also participate in MND (SW). The divisional area of operations is the largest in SFOR, encompassing about 41% of the land mass of Bosnia-Herzegovina; it is, however, more sparsely populated than other areas. The British battle group operates entirely in the Republica Srpska, the Netherlands battle group in most of Canton 6, and the Canadian battle group in all of Canton 1 and Canton 10. In mid-August the Netherlands battle group took over responsibility of the southern part of Canton 10 from the Canadians. The main bases are: the Divisional HQ and the Division Support Group, located in the Banja Luka Metal Factory (BLMF); the Canadian battle group with its headquarters in Zgon and companies in Bihac, Drvar and Glamoc and its air assets in Velika Kladusa. The Netherlands battle groups have their headquarters and one all-arms combat team located in Bugojno, and a second team in Novi

Travnik. The British battle group has its headquarters and two companies in different locations in Mgornic Grad, an artillery battery in Sipovo and an armoured reconnaissance squadron and a company in the Banja Luka Metal Factory. All three battle groups have several platoon bases spread over their area of operations. And finally the divisional medical facilities, an integrated unit with personnel from the three major troop contributing nations, are located at Sipovo.

Mission

The operations of the division in theatre are based on the following mission: 'MND (SW) is to eliminate any threat to the safety and security of Bosnia and Herzegovina in order to implement the General Framework for Peace'. Much of the military work necessary to allow the implementation of the civil aspects of the General Framework for Peace has been accomplished. However, the mission will not be finished until this important civil part is completed. It is therefore important to maintain a safe and secure environment in order to allow the international community to attain its strategic objectives, as described in the multi-year road map. We will act pre-emptively, or respond quickly to any activity that threatens public security. However, it is also our intention to encourage the local authorities to take responsibility for local security. Therefore, whenever possible, taking into account their limited resources, we try to let the local authorities take charge. Some good examples are crowd and riot control and the handling of unexploded ordnance.

Situational Awareness - Areas of interest

The operation in Bosnia-Herzegovina, as all operations, should be intelligence-driven. Situational awareness is of the utmost importance. It is essential that we are aware of what is going on around us in order to be able to take precautionary measures and ultimately react if necessary. Our primary mission is to control the armed forces in Bosnia-Herzegovina. But the threat, or our interest as it were, is not only military. In fact in the current situation we evaluate the military threat as low. Our focus was to prevent reserve units from quick mobilisation and to improve safety; one of our priorities was the separation of units and equipment as well as weapons and ammunition. We deployed to Bosnia just a few days after September 11, 2001, thus it is not difficult to imagine that terrorism also had our special attention. Another focus

33

was on civil developments. Ultimately a situation has to be created wherein the presence of international organisations is no longer needed. Civil developments have a great influence on a safe and secure environment. So we are very much interested in refugees and displaced persons; politics; economic development; social, cultural and religious development, and last but not least, crime and corruption.

The Intelligence Organisation

The intelligence organisation is organised along the same lines as the SFOR hierarchy. All levels have their own dedicated assets to gather and analyse information. Next to the NATO line there is a national line. The National Intelligence Cells (NICs), co-located with HQ SFOR in Sarajevo, have a special position. They are commanded in the national line. Their proximity to the operational commander differs from nation to nation.

National Assets

The National Intelligence Cells, located at HQ SFOR in Camp Butmir in Sarajevo, have direct access to national resources. They have a special position, as they are directed through national channels. All major troop-contributing nations are represented, and often put a lot effort into the operation, ranging from 5 to 50 persons per NIC. Some countries have even more personnel in their NICs, which are strictly speaking not part of SFOR, than in their contingents in SFOR. There are mutual interests between the two. NICs need information from SFOR assets to construct their picture. SFOR needs information from national channels to procure information that SFOR is otherwise unable to gather on its own. Exchange of information within the intelligence world is not simple. There exists the principle of reciprocity, nothing is for free; exchange of information is always on a give and take basis. In this field personal relations are important and often yield much better results than formal requests. Another issue is the protection of sources. A lot of information is NATO-classified and a complicating factor is the involvement of non-NATO countries in the operations.

SFOR Assets

The Allied Military Intelligence Battalion operates at SFOR level. This unit is specialised in human intelligence. Its personnel operate in all three MND AORs and are even physically located within the MND HQs. This would not be the standard concept of operations in a high-intensity conflict, where the different levels focus on different areas. Different units operating in one area create a need for close coordination and, when necessary, 'deconfliction' (i.e. de-escalation of conflict). Another unit at SFOR level is the Military Support Unit (MSU), Italian Carabinieri, whose primary task is crowd and riot control. When not employed in that manner they reinforce the patrol schemes within the MNDs, which brings them into frequent contact with the SFOR AOR. In the course of their duty, they gather a lot of useful information.

Divisional Assets

The division itself has several intelligence gathering assets. In the first place, of course, there are the sub-units of battle groups and teams with their organic personnel. The essence of what are called 'Normal Framework Operations' is all about 'constructing the picture' and getting a feeling for what is going on. It is important to note that, especially in peacekeeping operations like those in Bosnia, every single man and woman is a collector. The daily patrols, the helicopter pilot flying back to his detachment or the commander visiting one of his units, they observe what is going on and sometimes this can be valuable information. The division also has specialised intelligence elements. In the field of human intelligence the MND has personnel to handle locals that come to SFOR with information. The MND also has enhanced reconnaissance capability to actively observe if necessary, and limited electronic warfare capabilities to monitor the communications of the armed forces in Bosnia-Herzegovina. A frequently underestimated, but very important, source of information is our liaison officers. Through their almost daily contact on various levels with the armed forces, canton governments, international organisations and several non-governmental organisations, we can achieve a good and balanced picture of what is going on in local society.

The Concept of Intelligence Operations

Nations differ in their concept of intelligence operations. In a country like the Netherlands, where the concept is based on high-intensity conflict, the battalion is the lowest level with its own intelligence cell. In peace support operations like Bosnia, where a team has its own area of responsibility, the team also gets its own intelligence cell (TIC). People do their utmost, but the lack of experience is significant. British units, for example, are more accustomed to having team intelligence cells. In some cases, positions in the intelligence cells are filled for a year or even longer to ensure the continuity of 'corporate knowledge'. Another necessity for continuity is a good and easily accessible database. It would be even better if these systems could communicate with each other. There are also a few shortcomings in analysis capacity. This is not only applicable to the division level, but also to SFOR and the National Intelligence Cells. Firstly, there is a lack of sufficient numbers of experienced analysts. What we see is that the few qualified people are used preferably in the home countries. Secondly, there is very limited availability of systems like link-analysis for automatic data analysis.

Other Assets

I shall devote a few words here to the special assets available to the division. Radio Oksigen is a low cost, high impact tool for information operations. It is a very popular radio-station run by locals supervised by a UK manager. The target audience is the youth, ages 16 to 25. It covers items like: safety, co-operation, elections, etc. We can see that it has a very positive influence by the large number of people that react by telephone or mail. At the moment of my departure from Bosnia-Herzegovina the establishment and possible funding of SFOR radio-stations was under discussion.

Civil Military Cooperation (CIMIC) is another activity that provides useful information. In the early phases it concentrates on humanitarian aid and later shifts its attention to nation building. CIMIC plays a major role in improving relations with the local population. The 'hearts and minds campaign' results in regular contacts. That again leads to information and, in this sense, improves the safety of our forces. A British warrant officer, for example, was coach of a Bosnian youth football team. As part of the education he warned the children of the dangers of mines and ammunition. A member of his team told him that he regularly played in a cave that contained a lot of ammunition. Since extracting weapons and ammunition is one of the main efforts of SFOR, this proved to very useful information and resulted in the extraction of more than nine tons of mine-and-mortar grenades. The boy was rewarded with a football.

Downsizing SFOR

The situation in Bosnia and Herzegovina changes over time and influences the concept of operations of SFOR and, of course, the way SFOR collects and handles information. Both the military and other organisations show symptoms of Bosnia fatigue. This leads to downsizing of SFOR, from 60,000 troops to 18,000 in 2001, further to 12,000 by the end of 2002. But not only is SFOR downsizing, also the International Police Task Force (IPTF), which consisted of 1800 policemen on the ground, changed into the European Union Police Mission (EUPM), comprising 450 policemen in the higher management levels. UNHCR plans to leave by the end of 2003, the last year that property can be claimed under the Property Implementation Law. The OSCE and even the Office of the High Representative (OHR) are planning to leave in a few years. The size of the force and the changing concept of operations have influence on the intelligence process. Initially military units can cover their whole area of responsibility with their own means. They have enough troops, intelligence assets and liaison personnel available to field outposts (company, platoon and troop level) where necessary. The downsizing of the force has brought us to a point where further reductions render it impossible to cover the whole area with our own means. This makes it necessary to work together with other organisations that are in fact facing the same problems. The challenge is to enhance situational awareness by synchronising the efforts of the international community, local authorities and (major) NGOs.

'Complementary footprints' is a way by which SFOR and other organisations have to work together. Every organisation previously had representatives in the same place, for example, in a cantonal capital. That is not possible anymore. Therefore we have to develop a system together with other organisations like OHR, EUPM, OSCE, etc. to divide the locations and develop a system to exchange information in a coordinated way. This coordination, chaired by OHR-representatives, has to be organised on several levels. Fixed meetings and fixed agendas are a tool for getting a real grip on problems which have to be tackled together. The necessary actions can then be divided between the organisations. At the end of my command this system was implemented and the start was very promising. One might wonder why we did not develop this earlier, as it seems to be very beneficial. Initially, all organisations have the tendency to guard their own ground, to be self-supporting. Sometimes it takes some pressure, for example lack of resources, to work together. In the end it proves beneficial and leads to an integrated exchange of information.

New High Representative

Recently Lord Ashdown was appointed High Representative of the OHR. His main concern is the lack of the rule of law and therefore his top priority is fighting crime and corruption. Lord Ashdown strives for good relations between OHR and SFOR, and the cooperation between SFOR and OHR has clearly improved since his arrival. One of the improvements is the exchange of information, which has recently been organised in a more structural way. This touches upon an important point, namely, that SFOR has to stay within its mandate. Military assets can be used for a lot of purposes, but can and should they assist the state border service, should military units look for drug trafficking or for white slave trade? Different countries have different opinions on this matter. But in principle normal military units are not well equipped and trained for this kind of 'police' work. The military is also not the best means of fighting large-scale corruption. To tackle this enormous problem whereby offenders make widely use of the 'electronic highway', we have to bring in IT and banking specialists, but information that is gathered in the normal line of duty should not get lost. Cooperation between SFOR and OHR is therefore valuable.

Lessons

In conclusion, I will summarise the lessons we can learn form our experience in Bosnia-Herzegovina. Situational awareness, which is vital to a military operation, can be improved in several ways. First of all the slogan for the intelligence organisation should be: 'Organise and train as you fight'. This means that if you work with intelligence cells at team level during operations, this should also be the way units are organised and trained in their homeland. Another important factor is continuity. Some vital posts in the intelligence organisation have to be staffed by personnel that stay longer in theatre than the regular six months. This ensures that new units are well informed and prevents important information from getting lost. Furthermore, analysis capacity has to be enhanced. The shortage of trained personnel and capable systems decreases the value of intelligence. Information from a source is not always properly analysed and copied in reports. Moreover, the exchange of information can be improved by enhancing the interoperability of the different intelligence systems. Intelligence procedures have to be adapted when circumstances change. Fewer forces lead to a different concept of operations. The necessity to adjust collection, analysis, and exchange of information, for example, by using the principle of complementary footprints, is clear. Another issue we have to tackle is avoiding tensions between intelligence assets of different national origin in the divisional area of operations. In peace operations like SFOR it is a fact of life that several of these assets operate in the divisional area. Good co-ordination helps to avoid negative experiences or accidents. And finally: the mandate is the touchstone, a card that otherwise will be played by the senior national representatives.

Conclusion

One year in command of the Multi National Division (South-West) was a unique, once in a lifetime experience. It is very inspiring to work together with soldiers from so many nations in a truly multi-national military organisation. I have now shared my experiences in the field of peacekeeping and intelligence. Of course we can and must draw lessons and try to make improvements where possible. But I cannot overemphasize the respect I have for all the soldiers and civilians of the division and SFOR, who did and still do a great job for a better future in Bosnia-Herzegovina.

Peacekeeping and Intelligence Experiences from United Nations Protection Force 1995

Jan-Inge Svensson

The opinion of the world is that the United Nation operation in former Yugoslavia, particularly in Bosnia-Herzegovina and Croatia in the 1990s, failed. This is difficult for me to accept after spending a year of my life there and saying farewell to fallen UN soldiers. It is true that the UN did not stop the war, because the mandate told us to support humanitarian work and protect the so-called safe areas. We failed to protect the safe areas and UN-intelligence made an incorrect analysis concerning the fall of Srebrenica and Žepa. In my opinion we did a good job covering the conflict in Croatia and we also made a very reliable assessment before the fall of Krajina. Long term assessments by UNPF G-2 (United Nations Peace Forces HQ Intelligence Branch) sent to New York were appreciated and laid the foundation for political decisions.

In traditional peacekeeping operations there is no enemy. Instead you have warring factions towards which you have to remain impartial. In the UN, 'intelligence' is a non-word often replaced by 'military information'. 'We are UN – we have no secrets'. In this ideal world, the UN have access to open sources which they get from the warring factions, third parties and their own forces. Among military personnel, concerned with intelligence information, attitudes differ significantly. Some fully adhere to the UN culture and insist that 'information service' is something distinctly different from the 'intelligence service'. Others consider that the two terms are just alternative names for the same thing. After one year as head of G-2, I adhere to the latter interpretation.

When I arrived in the mission area however, I was still influenced by the Swedish view that it was impossible to release intelligence to the UN. On my

41

leave to Sweden, I reported to Swedish Headquarters that we had to look with different eyes on disseminating information to the UN. As a result from experiences made by the troops in the area, Swedish Headquarters realised that the mission in former Yugoslavia was fundamentally different from other UN missions in which Sweden had participated.

I was an experienced intelligence officer and knew that national interest was the guideline for collecting and sharing information. I also had good knowledge of the ways of the real 'intelligence world' with its own rules. The policy in UNMIO (United Nations Military Information Office) was familiar to me and I was convinced that the policy should be my guideline as head of the Military Information branch. However my first day experiences told me that I was wrong. The G-2 in UNPF HQ in Zagreb used methods similar to those of an ordinary military HQ and it was easy for me to adapt the rules in use.

All personnel assigned to a peacekeeping mission must have basic understanding of the population, culture and political situation in the area of operations. Experience from UN operations tells us that commanders and soldiers often lack necessary information about the situation that they are facing. The lack of knowledge concerns political, social and religious conditions in the mission area and may cause confrontation and critical situations, and – in extreme situations – loss of life, as was indeed the case in former Yugoslavia.

In a peacekeeping mission military tasks are generally carried out by small units. One can find a lot of information/intelligence on the battalion level but it is fragmented and difficult to interpret for the battalion commander. Most of the UN missions are executed in battalion structures and it is therefore necessary that battalion commanders also have access to operational and strategic information in order to interpret their own information and the pattern around them. In my experience, this information does not get to the battalion level and the battalion commander does not always know the political play behind the mission.

In a traditional UN operation it is crucial that the troops act impartially and enjoy the confidence and respect of the warring factions, who have to know that any information collected will not be used by the other side. Confidence between troop contributing nations is also necessary. Some countries have well-developed intelligence resources, outside UN control, to support their own troops. Some of this information is not available to other participants. The troop contributing states sometimes have their own interests that may be contrary to the mandate. This may cause the country to refuse to deliver information to the mission. Political reality teaches us that we cannot avoid that some participating nations have an agenda of their own. My experience from UNPF HQ is that there was a flow of information beyond my control. As an intelligence officer coming from a non-aligned country, I had some problems getting all the necessary information, as supporting countries did not release intelligence to G-2 but to their own officers who were assigned to the branch. Some of my senior NATO officers had access to the FC (Force Commander), DFC (Deputy Force Commander) and COS (Chief of Staff) and carried out briefings on a weekly basis. I have no knowledge of what was said during these briefings. I suspect that the commanders got more than one assessment and that the assessments sometimes contradicted each other.

During the air strikes in Bosnia-Herzegovina in September 1995, it was impossible for me and my staff to make an overall assessment. Our own information was insufficient and we were not granted access to information collected by NATO technical devices, Special Forces and other NATO intelligence sources. Most of G-2 was excluded from 'the inner circle' and all information and damage assessment went from NATO to the FC. The UN chain of command did not function. I understand that the decisions were made on the political level, but my opinion is that all these exemptions on the chain of command have to be settled before a mission is launched. However I have to admit that my co-operation with NATO intelligence officers was excellent, though on an informal level.

In a UN or multinational, mission it is necessary that there is a free flow of information relevant to the mission for all participants. The only restriction should be measures taken to protect the sources. It is, however, also important that the UN do not leak information. During the air campaign in Bosnia-Herzegovina, in the autumn of 1995, both Admiral Smith (CINCSOUTH) and General Janvier (Force Commander UNPF [United Nations Peace Forces]) confided that there was a serious problem with leakage of secret operational information in both headquarters. In that perspective it is fundamental to preserve operational security, since lives depend on it. But steps taken should not be allowed to hamper the activity in the multinational headquarters, as it

43

did. There is hardly a resource as invisible to the warring factions as a national collecting/processing unit from a troop contributing nation itself. The UN has to rely largely on the resources available from some of the member states. As to an organisation's need of credibility and impartiality, the UN mission has to deal with the exchanged information in a proper way.

One UN principle is that all information and its storage has to be public, open and transparent. This principle restrains some national intelligence agencies from providing information to the UN and those principles need to be changed. Otherwise it is impossible for MIOs (Military Information Officer) (G-2) to provide the commanders with relevant intelligence as a basis for the decisions they have to make.

Intelligence is traditionally very sensitive by nature, and countries are reluctant to grant unauthorised personnel full access to it. One way to solve this problem is to have all troop contributing nations deploy a National Intelligence Cell in the mission area, and to let the NICs cooperate and share information and assessments amongst each other and provide the UN HQ G-2 with indispensable information.

The troop contributing countries also have to reach agreements about how and to whom the information should be disseminated. Intelligence officers assigned to a UN or multinational HQ have to reach agreements with agencies of the intelligence providing nations in order to get access to information pertinent to the mission. Another problem is to get information from the troops. Sometimes there are blank spots on the map due to the fact that, due to their own agenda, a certain battalion from a certain nation does not wish to send the information to a higher level. It is therefore important to have both human and technical sensors all over the area. A UN operation does not have its own reconnaissance units. Therefore one must use all conceivable sources. During my time in former Yugoslavia, our collecting plan consisted of all UN agencies and NGOs that were willing to provide information. We reimbursed them by providing reliable risk assessments. The most useful organisation was the UNMO (United Nations Military observers). They were a sort of reconnaissance unit, which we could steer for various intelligence requirements. However in order to achieve that we had to co-operate with the commanding officer of UNMO. The UNMO commander was not in the same chain of command as the G-2 staff, so we had to rely on his good will. UNMO also operated under a different mandate than

44

the battalions. In my opinion, UNMO has to be directly subordinated to the chain of command.

In HQ G-2 we received reports from different levels in the organisation. Daily information summaries were sent from commands, sectors and battalions. The reports from the battalions were very detailed and their assessments reflected fragments of the overall conflict. Our analysts were literally swamped with details. The reports from sectors and commands were sometimes contradicting. The reporting system confused the intelligence officers on the mission level and also caused the staff to work with too many details. The reason for 'not following the chain of command' in the reporting system, I believe, is the fact that the higher echelon did not rely on the assessments from the commands and sectors because of involvement of troop contributing nations and possible political pressure on the commanders and staff members. The lesson learned is to let the information flow up and down the chain of command.

The mission in former Yugoslavia was very 'NATO' and the G2 staff was, to a large extent, manned by officers from NATO countries and they had information superiority over non-NATO officers. As a Swedish officer, and coming from a non-aligned country, I had no access to intelligence coming from NATO by natural means. By building up confidence and credibility, I succeeded in getting information that was necessary for me in order to evaluate the analyses of my staff and to give me an understanding of the situation. In a conflict infected by different conceptions of the solution and of how to attain it, it was an advantage for me to view it all with impartial eyes. My striving to be impartial caused a lot of clashes with my peers. However in the long run, the G-2 earned a good reputation among the commanders and at the UN in New York, thanks to the high quality of the analyses provided by it.

My experience, when I arrived to Zagreb, was that MIO worked too much with day-to-day problems and too little with assessment. I immediately transformed the table of organisation and methods. The organisation concerned enabled me to assign officers coming from different countries, with different culture and knowledge, to an appropriate desk. In that way we could capitalise on their special competence. Some troop contributing nations appointed officers without intelligence training and some of them had insufficient knowledge of the conflict.

45

I have already mentioned that we failed to predict the fall of Srebrenica. We had a good view of the warring factions in and around the area. What we did not know were their intentions. We had vague information concerning troops deployed in the BSA (Bosnian-Serb Army) area and their movements. The reason was that the warring factions did not respect the UN freedom of movement and we did not have full access to the area. Most of the current information we got from UN troops by 'combat contact', but by then it was too late and the fall of the city was a fait accompli. The incentive to the offensive still rests hidden in the minds of the Bosnian-Serb leaders. One plausible explanation could be that the offensive was Bosnian-Serb retaliation for the air strikes, another that they wanted to prevent the Bosnian coalition forces from launching assaults into Bosnian-Serb territory. Now and again we reported that the Bosnian-Serb troops had the capacity to conquer the enclaves at any time, but that they would not do it because of the likely political consequences.

To understand a conflict like the one in the Balkans you have to learn the history, religion, cultures and ways of thinking in the countries concerned. The lesson learned is that what is irrelevant in Stockholm and The Hague may very well be relevant in Pale. In a future UN mission, co-operation between military analysts and political analysts has to be closer. We experienced that during the last month of the war and the weekly discussions with the SRSG (Special Representative of the Secretary General) political unit resulted in upgraded and more reliable assessments. It is also necessary that the UN change its attitudes towards military intelligence and that the troop contributing nations provide the Force Commander and the commanders in the field with intelligence.

Bridging the Gap:
Intelligence and
Peace Support Operations

Pasi Välimäki

This chapter does not represent the official views or opinions of the Finnish Defence Forces, but only of the author.

To gain strategic advantage in order to avoid war and bloodshed, nations require accurate information and insight. The same applies to crisis management and peace support. As Robert D. Kaplan points out, 'an irony of the post-World War II generation (and of the media, which reflects its values) is that it proclaims an era of human rights while abusing the profession [intelligence community] that historically provides advance warning of gross human rights violations'.[1] In the last decade, nations have been increasingly engaged in crisis management and prevention. To this end, the significance of intelligence[2] has increased.

In this chapter I will try to show that by bridging the gap between theory and practise in intelligence work, better support will be provided to command functions. I shall not attempt to give complete answers, but rather to raise questions and present ideas. This chapter is based on a presentation given at the IDL/NISA conference in The Hague in November 2002. It focuses on operational and tactical level intelligence, since these levels are the chief providers of intelligence support to operations.

Most of the theoretical work on intelligence has been conducted by intelligence practitioners, who are either academics involved with strategic intelligence, or

47

military functionaries involved with military intelligence. In consequence, the approach to studies in intelligence has been more pragmatic than theoretical. There is also a rather traditional gap between practitioners and scholars. Practitioners view theory as too academic, full of abstract diagrams and incomprehensible jargon. Scholars claim that practitioners make conclusions too hastily, are uncritical, and make too simplistic generalisations.

Let us begin with two sceptical anecdotes to which those who have worked as intelligence officers in peace support operations (PSO) can probably relate. Firstly, from Murphy's law of combat, that 'professionals are predictable, the amateurs are dangerous'. Secondly, from Clausewitz, that 'many intelligence reports in war are contradictory; even more are false, and most are uncertain ... in short, most intelligence is false'.[3] Both anecdotes make a valid point. In traditional ground warfare, the theoretical framework of command, control, communications, computers and intelligence (C4I) is based on written manuals and doctrines, which are derived from studies of past wars. In PSO, actions are planned and executed according to different rules: the scope, aims, capabilities, constraints and limitations are all just 'different' from traditional warfare. To meet requirements set by the changing operational environment intelligence practitioners need to adjust their practices.

Operational Environment – setting the requirements

One could argue that most PSO's in the last decade dealt in fact with conflicts where coercive diplomacy or strategic coercion had been used.[4] The rationale behind coercive diplomacy[5] is to 'resolve without violence, or with only minimal violence, those conflicts that are too severe to be settled by ordinary diplomacy and that in earlier times would have been settled by war'.[6] In peace support the conflict has already taken place and its nature is something less than war. Factions and actors can, but may not necessarily be organised in a military fashion. It is unlikely that actions, battles and skirmishes are executed according to written manuals or doctrines. In PSO's there does not exist as such a baseline for which operational and tactical level intelligence officers are trained. There is no clear structure, no clearly defined tasks and operational plans, no basic rules (ten tanks to a company), and no clearly defined weapons capabilities to assess capabilities and intentions. However, the decision-makers will continue to assess whether strategic coercion[7] can be used. This requires the assessment of different variables and factors that are politically,

48

demographically, and economically related, as well as context dependent. Military capabilities and intentions exist, but are not the only key factors. Detailed and precise information is imperative to decision-making.

Furthermore, the potential use of military power sets even more detailed requirements on timely information, which needs to be developed into intelligence. Precision guided munitions, air power, and the use of Special Forces require more detailed and precise information, not only to eliminate specific targets but also to minimise collateral damage and protect troops.

The complex operational environment is unpredictable and asymmetric. It is unlikely that crises and confrontations will ensue according to the traditional rules of combat. There will likely be an absence of moral restrictions normally associated with armed conflicts, supported by the use of new technologies. The use of new technologies by new radical actors creates asymmetric situations that cannot be handled in traditional ways. It is very difficult to get an early warning on forthcoming incidents. The intelligence community is expected to define 'basic noise ratio'[8] and to find the essential signals rising from the noise, and the normal situation in the operational environment. In PSO's the indicators can be difficult to identify and follow as they can change according to ethnic background, geographical location, and the economic and political situation. The time pressure and time-span in which decision-makers have to operate is to some extent different from that of traditional warfare. Operational tempo in peace support is less intensive, since most of the time nothing seems to be happening. Activity can flare up for several hours from a car collision, flag waving, or a drive-by-shooting.

In this operational environment the strategic-operational-tactical levels are becoming obsolete as far as information is concerned. The explosion of a shell causing a mass of casualties can have significant impact in a very short time.[9] Simple linear cause-and-effect assessments are not enough to explain and predict the PSO environment. More in-depth holistic assessments and information are required. The fact is that crisis management, with or without coercive diplomacy, requires intelligence support at all command levels. A solid theoretical baseline and methodology could help intelligence officers to cope with this complex environment.

Theoretical aspects

The task of a scientific theory is to abstract, to generalise and to connect.[10] By abstracting a group of incidents, people and objects, such as weapons that are not identical, are put together. For this, one needs well-defined concepts and criteria by which to sort and combine. To generalise one needs to examine what else these things that have been identified by the same concept have in common, not as matter of logic but as a matter of fact. Connecting then requires making links and sequences to incidents and people. Theories have room for anomalies, like hand-grenade attacks in new places. Theory requires clear conditions and concepts under which it applies. Explanatory power, however, does not equal predictive power. Good theories provide relevant and useful conceptual frameworks, which help to understand the general requirements of actions, and the general logic associated with its effective employment. Such theoretical-conceptual knowledge is critical not only for policymaking, but also for command and control. In any case practitioners consciously or subconsciously make use of some kind of theory or conceptual framework.[11]

The real challenge is the ability to combine different scientific fields, taking into account the factual limitations and conditions under which they apply. We should look at international relations theories on how nations and coalitions interact and, furthermore, how the operational environment on a higher level works. We should also examine the use of military power in crisis management. This is social science in a broad sense – intelligence is 'socially constructed' and the qualitative and quantitative methodology of social science can be used to enhance analysis work.

The main use of theoretical or generic knowledge[12] is to compile information about uses and limitations of intelligence in crisis response, derived from the study of past experience. This knowledge can also be useful for perspective in new situations. Generic knowledge should be created to benefit both the intelligence practitioners and the actors. The aim is to make conscious choices in creating theoretical and conceptual frameworks for decision-makers to rely upon.

In the last 5-7 years it has become popular to use Boyd's OODA-loop[13] as a theoretical baseline for C3I concepts ranging from NetCentricWarfare to Combat Net Radio systems. OODA-loop does not help to explain nor understand Intelligence – Command and Control (C2) interaction. I maintain that Lawson's C3I process model does. I will not further define how the model works, but one can observe from Figure 1 that it addresses the intelligence and C2 cycles. Also single source and all-source links to C2 functions are described. This model is worth examining.

In the applied model, single source analysis provides near real-time input to the C2 process to create situational awareness. This can be quite dangerous unless the personnel are very experienced and have good access to the 'larger picture', as data has to be analysed and interpreted before it is forwarded. Furthermore, we should note that all source analysis provides direct input in the decision phase. The model lacks a feedback link from the C2 process and the highly underestimated feedback link within the intelligence process, which would verify how the analysis coincided with reality, and the reasons for success and failure.

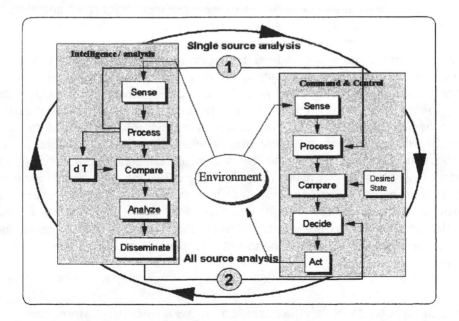

Figure 1 Adaptation of Lawson's C3I Process Model.[14]

Lawson's model has been used in practise in the Finnish battalion in KFOR. It has proven to support not only the battalion but also the brigade in their C4I efforts. The original idea was to provide the command functions at all levels with timely and reliable intelligence support, create common intelligence situational awareness through a virtual IntelNet, and to support on-scene commanders with an intelligence liaison officer to provide all-source and single source information. IntelNet ensured that once a report was released it appeared as new information on intelligence and operations workstations and message terminals. All intelligence players received messages simultaneously and the command functions were supported in near real-time single source and all-source analysis.

Planning and guidance[15]

Planning the intelligence support begins with a focused Intelligence Preparation of the Environment (IPE). The traditional Intelligence Preparation of the Battlefield (IPB) has to be adjusted to meet the local PSO requirements and situation. Once again new variables and factors need to be addressed which are very much like the variables and factors in coercive strategies/diplomacy.[16] Lawson's model does not address the operational planning process nor the direction and guidance of intelligence. However, this aspect is well addressed in most manuals describing staff procedures and C2 functions. Basically, the experience from past operations becomes practice and model in field manuals. Planning of the use of intelligence assets to retrieve information and to meet prioritised intelligence requirements should result in a comprehensive collection plan that forms the basis for all collection and intelligence operations. However, in many operations the collection plan has become so general in nature that it can be used from mission to company levels. To provide accurate direction and guidance for intelligence collection the collection plan has to be adjusted to meet the local PSO requirements and situation. It is also vital to develop this in conjunction with subordinates.

Collection[17]

Humint appears to be a rather inexpensive way to collect information, but demands special skill from the operators. For basic data collection it is very cost-effective to have patrols collecting general information on infrastructure, demographics, and politics. But to gain access to the vital information—

information that the other side does not want you to have—demands specialist skills, time and patience. It requires trained teams working in-theatre for extensive periods of time. Sometimes information is gained through ad hoc contacts, sometimes through contact handling. Recent findings place Humint as a top priority in modern PSO's. It is not covert cloak-and-dagger spy work but a carefully planned and executed collection that is sensitive in nature. Most collection means are sensitive in nature. Sigint, Comint, Elint, and EW support, have proven to be very effective in cueing other assets and providing early warning/force protection. Intercepting conversations and networks has provided valuable substantive information on what is going on, as well as on target organisation structures, morale and leadership. Humint is probably the fastest developing area. UAVs have provided a relatively cost-effective and timely means to deliver imagery on high value targets. Humint as well as other single sources require connection to the larger picture and all-source intelligence products to give high quality analysis and assessments. Osint's role is rather obvious. Today the internet provides a platform for extensive search for information. Approximately 80% of all information can be derived from open sources. However, it is rather difficult to derive intentions from Osint sources. Counter-Intelligence directly supports force protection actions. However, in PSO most intelligence activities aim at supporting force protection. The counterintelligence specialists have a different approach from Humint and other means of collection. They tend to look inside, conducting concrete threat analysis on possible actions against one's own troops, whereas the other collection means look outside. One frequently used means of collection is the unofficial channel of liaison to other than military players. NGO's, international organisations and other players can provide worthwhile information in a discreet, mutual manner. A lot of background information can be obtained through civil-military cooperation that can be further developed into intelligence. It is vital to neither use these contacts as a primary means for collecting intelligence, nor to compromise the source and recipient.

Findings and common sense suggest that intelligence system capabilities should be tailored in accordance with realistic information requirements placed by commanders and the operations branch. This is not always the case, as very often the intelligence branch defines the requirements. This further complicates creating an intelligence concept of operation and organisation. Furthermore it is necessary to create a C4I structure that properly supports the intelligence system. The tendency toward more and more detailed real-time information places extreme demands not only on the collection system but also on the C4 system. Real-time data is basically required only in functions where the actions that take place are very high-speed air and naval operations. Looking at Predator imagery at 3-5 different level command centres is interesting, but is it really what should be done? Even though it seems old-fashioned and against the principles on how to use national assets, it is vital to have centralised management and co-ordination within each single source and within theatre intelligence resources. There is a requirement to create an in-theatre intelligence centre in order to have a network that can exchange information and coordinate efforts.

The most difficult challenge collection faces is meeting the time-lines set for the prioritised intelligence requirements. It is a fact that the operational tempo and timeframe in which information can be gathered, considering the activity level of the targets, does not meet the requirements set for the collection system. The expectations from the command functions are unrealistic when they expect fast results. The single source has positive and negative aspects. It can be used to identify and report indicators from the normal noise. This information can be reported in nearly real time. One undesired aspect is that it provides keys to micro management, passing the chain of command. All source analysis requires a large mass of detailed information that can be obtained only by a comprehensive collection system. This information can be obtained and processed into a proper product only through time and solid field experience. This requires not only good basic training but also in-theatre training in specialist skills. Through specialist training (search, Humint, helo, etc.) the motivation and focus of reconnaissance elements can be maintained in long deployments. However, basic reconnaissance skills and information on the area of operation need to be developed before deployment.

Assessment and production[18]

Especially in the production of analysis and assessments, solid theoretical-conceptual frameworks can be useful. Conceptual frameworks can help the analyst in establishing a solid analytic process through a well-defined method. In some situations, the worst-case[19] approach is justified, but it very often results in overreaction and loss of confidence, and not always in playing it safe. Threats and possible actions should always be analysed through capabilities and intentions, considering what is possible and what is likely. Common sense and field experience are necessary to create solid and reliable intelligence products. Products should embody probability estimates like 'likely', 'possible', 'probable' as well as substantive information and assessment on future development.[20] End products can be categorised as what Sherman Kent terms 'current-reportorial' intelligence, describing what has happened recently and what is happening now. The term 'basic-descriptive' centres on relatively fixed facts on situations, places or events. 'Speculative-evaluative' reports deal more with the future assessments. All these products can be found in today's PSO's.

As mentioned above, the expectations of fast results are unrealistic. It is necessary to emphasise that proper analysis requires time to compare and confirm information before it can be called intelligence. Sometimes this takes more time than writing the end product, but it is vital that this phase of the intelligence process or cycle is not skipped over. Often the consumers are prisoners of their own preconceptions and resistant to any explanation other than their own. Ultimately the intelligence product can be considered successful only if the consumer has read and understood it. It is then their task to decide whether or not to take notice. But until the moment of decision it remains the responsibility of the intelligence providers to offer decision-makers products that meet their requirements, which include a proper written format, level of analysis, specific details, maps etc. Our normative perceptions colour our empirical perceptions. Our own belief system does not help in understanding the actions of an agent with a different belief system (Western versus Eastern).[21]

The creation of a thoroughly analysed intelligence product is very demanding. There is a great challenge to meet on methodology in analysis. All data gathered for analysis focuses either on the target's intentions, or on its capabilities. Traditionally intelligence analysis concentrates on assessing capabilities and actions from a cause-and-effect perspective, which is a very Machiavellian approach. According to Hollis and Smith, Machiavelli argued that 'history is a sequence of cause and effect; theory does not create practice but is created by practice; politics is not a function of ethics, but rather, that ethics is a function of politics, and morality is a product of power'.[22] One possible approach is to apply a positivist approach in analysing events through methods of natural science. However, explaining events and incidents solely by empirical evidence has its limitations. The analyst is only really doing his job when an understanding of motives and intentions is exhibited. Do the actors apply a rational actor model, sound logic, or basic instincts? Are their actions the result of pragmatic thinking, hate-related or normal practise in conducting business affairs? Another frequent fault is to analyse an actor's behaviour within the framework of our own (belief system). On the other hand, reason and common sense in considering context and way of life can produce good results, but that requires field experience and extremely capable personalities.

Another approach could be described as hermeneutic which aims at understanding the intentions and motives behind the actions and use of capabilities. This approach is not very typical for the military, even though we do try to understand why people act as they do in order to be able to predict their actions next time. The central hermeneutic theme is to understand actions from within and not to reflect our own perceptions or guess. Most analysts consider that understanding intentions is the most important and at the same time the most difficult thing to do.[23] In PSO, environmental rules are different from causal laws, which is why it is so difficult to establish rules under which actions take place. These rules are constructed and applied at an individual level and they change constantly.

Hollis and Smith note that Weberian explanatory understanding is a matter of assigning the action to the right 'complex of meanings'.[24] Approaching this through history, one looks for the particular motive that moved a particular actor toward a particular incident. Methodologically this approach could be developed to help intelligence practitioners. In any case a holistic approach is required to give information meaning and the right context. Intelligence analysis in PSO, in cases where demographics, cultural factors, non-security issues and even economics are not taken into account, reverts to the linear cause-effect analysis of warfare in the desert. Academic generalisations cannot be the end products, as there is a requirement to produce pragmatic and self-explanatory reports that address both capabilities and intentions. To do this year after year and analyst after analyst, a proper well-established method would be worthwhile.

Most of the intelligence products can be classified as current-reportorial products that are produced periodically, e.g. daily intelligence reports and intelligence summaries. However, these products appear to be more like a unit's daily situation reports, stating basic facts with very little interpretation. How do these reports help decision-makers? Do these reports mainly serve the intelligence community? An important question to ask is what the ratio is between end user products (outside) and intelligence-only products (inside). A division of labour can be carried out not only in collection, but also in creating and maintaining basic intelligence products. Demographics and infrastructure data could be delegated to the civil-military co-operation branch, since their conception and analysis could be very useful.

In PSO's, statistical trends are shown afterwards. It is much more difficult to use these statistics for predicting the future than for explaining the past. Very often single events and incidents can be identified later on as focal points, yet they remain anomalies, never occurring again. For example, KFOR intelligence had identified that at a specific place along a main supply route, there was a potential threat of drive-by-shooting. The troops were alerted frequently as some indicators were identified. But alerts that result in no action tend to decrease trust and confidence on intelligence, and readiness for action consequently decreases. One afternoon a drive-by-shooting did take place, resulting in a larger incident causing riot and havoc. Intelligence had given early warning, and the threat had been identified. However it was impossible to make an educated guess on timing. Another point that makes quantitative interpretation very demanding is that the number of incidents is rather small. This adds to the difficulties in creating a mechanism for indications, and warning indicators need to be defined as something that has been confirmed to be (1) necessary for the actors (2) unambiguous (except for purpose), and (3) capable of being monitored by the intelligence collection system.[25]

Since operations deal with the issue of information, management becomes important. Intelligence products are effective only if distributed timely to end-users. Today most products in PSO's are still delivered in hardcopy or on CD-ROM. As the collection system has been well established and operating, the amount of data, information and developed intelligence is growing fast. It is a prerequisite to create databases for the collected data. It is quite surprising that only very few collection systems have updated information systems supporting PSO intelligence requirements. Information security and assurance are key 'show-stoppers' in securing information distribution to all the necessary bodies. The fact is, and will be, that some are more privileged than others. It is essential that not all information is shared, but that all relevant information is shared. This has improved in the last 5-7 years, but often only because the people on the ground have personally decided to forward information.

In the end it is very often the case that decision-makers and even senior intelligence officers are unwilling to draw unpleasant conclusions from intelligence they have received. Quite often decision-makers and analysts had all the necessary information at their disposal.

Conclusions

Intelligence work is foremost very pragmatic and requires field experience. On an academic level, it is multidisciplinary and cannot be categorized into one specific field of social or political science. However, I believe that both the intelligence community and academics could benefit from exchanging views and practices. The main area of common interest is in analysing collected data in a well-established methodological way. Furthermore, as more and more technological analytical tools are developed, these could also be applied in the planning and analysis of intelligence.

In the military, theories are very often derived from past wars and conflicts as they are studied. Senior officers and scholars then develop doctrines and field manuals from these experiences and new systems capabilities. This practise could also be applied in academia in the developing of research methods and testing of theories.

The aim of this chapter has been to show how a good theoretical baseline can support intelligence work in peace support operations. In many ways this has been the case, especially in the last 5-7 years as armed forces have gained experience from operations like those in Haiti, Bosnia and Kosovo. Lessons have been learned from these operations. What still remains to be done is applying the 'mental tools' of academia to the military. All of these may not be able to be applied, but I maintain that there are still some new ones yet to be discovered.

Endnotes

[1] Robert Kaplan, *Warrior Politics: Why Leadership Demands a Pagan Ethos.* (New York: Vintage Books 2003) p.43.

[2] Pasi Välimäki, *Intelligence in Peace Support Operations,* (Helsinki: National Defence College Helsinki 2000) pp.44-45: 'Intelligence is an uninterrupted process that lends support to the command and control process, its end product being "acquired, compared, combined, analysed, evaluated and interpreted information".'

[3] Carl von Clausewitz, *On War*, M. Howard and P. Paret (editors), (Princeton: Princeton University Press 1976) p.117.

[4] Lawrence Freedman (editor), *Strategic Coercion, Concepts and Cases* (Oxford: Oxford University Press 1998) pp.1-15. For more on coercive diplomacy and compellence see Thomas Schelling, *Arms and Influence* (New Haven: Yale University Press 1966) and Alexander George and William Simons; *The Limits of Coercive Diplomacy* (Boulder, Colo: Westview Press, 1994).

[5] Alexander George and William Simons, *Limits of Coercive Diplomacy*, p.2: 'The general intent of coercive diplomacy is to back a demand by an adversary with the threat of punishment for non-compliance that will be credible and potent enough to persuade him that it is in his interest to comply with the demand'. According to Lawrence Freedman this definition is too narrow.

[6] Charles W. Kegley Jr., and Eugene R. Wittkopf, *World Politics: Trend and Transformation* (New York: St Martin's Press 1999) p.443.

[7] For a definition of strategic coercion see Freedman, *Strategic Coercion, Concepts and Cases* p. 15: 'The deliberate and purposive use of overt threats to influence another's strategic choices'.

[8] Michael Handel, *War, Strategy and Intelligence* (London: Frank Cass 1989) p.237.

[9] For example, the Sarajevo Market Place II incident, followed by Operation Deliberate Force in August 1995. For more information see Välimäki, *Intelligence in Peace Support Operations*, p.108.

[10] Martin Hollis and Steve Smith, *Explaining and Understanding International Relations* (Oxford: Clarendon Press 1990) pp.61-67.

[11] George and Simons, *Limits of Coercive Diplomacy*, pp.3-4.

[12] Ibid, pp.20-21.

[13] Editors' Note: Orient-Observe-Decide-Act (OODA). For a biography on Colonel John Boyd, see Robert Coram, *BOYD: the Fighter Pilot Who Changed the Art of War* (Boston, MA: Little Brown and Company, 2002).

[14] George Orr, *Combat Operations C3I: Fundamentals and Interactions.* (Maxwell: Maxwell Air Force Base 1983) pp.2-3. On applying Lawson in PSO see Välimäki, *Intelligence in Peace Support Operations*, pp.44-49.

[15] For additional information on findings see Välimäki, *Intelligence in Peace Support Operations*, pp.107-116.

[16] George and Simons, *Limits of Coercive Diplomacy*, pp.16-20.

[17] For more on collection means see, Välimäki, *Intelligence in Peace Support Operations*, pp.55-88, 135-148.

[18] For more information see, Välimäki, *Intelligence in Peace Support Operations*, pp.51-55, 127-135.

[19] Handel, *War, Strategy and Intelligence*, pp.247-248.

[20] Michael Herman, *Intelligence Power in Peace and War* (Cambridge: Cambridge University Press 1996) pp.100-144.

[21] Herman, *Intelligence Power in Peace and War*, pp.84, 239; Handel, *War, Strategy and Intelligence*, pp.249-251.

[22] Hollis and Smith, *Explaining and Understanding International Relations*, pp.22, 43. Hollis and Smith refer to E.H. Carr, *The Twenty Years' Crisis 1919-1939*. Reissued with a new introduction and additional material by Michael Cox. (London/Basingstoke: Palgrave Macmillan 2001) pp.63-64.

[23] Handel, *War, Strategy and Intelligence*, pp. 239-241.

[24] Hollis and Smith, *Explaining and Understanding International Relations*, pp. 78-80; Handel, *War, Strategy and Intelligence*, p.250.

[25] Handel, *War, Strategy and Intelligence*, pp.246-247.

Intelligence and Peace Support Operations: Some Practical Concepts

Renaud Theunens

The opinions expressed in this chapter are purely personal and do not represent the views of the Belgian Ministry of Defence or the United Nations.

Introduction

The past decade was marked by a remarkable increase in the number of peace support operations. The lessons learned from the UNAMIR, UNOSOM and UNPROFOR operations[1] have shown that peace support operations require a dedicated intelligence support and should, preferably, have an integral intelligence capability. Therefore it soon became popular to describe peace support operations as 'intelligence-driven operations', notwithstanding that it has proven to be anything but easy to put this slogan into practice.

The inflation in the number of peace support operations, together with drastic changes on the geo-political level have provoked a radical transformation of the environment wherein intelligence and security services are expected to accomplish their mission. Whilst large parts of Western European militaries, when not involved in operations, function according to the somewhat routine '9 to 5' schedule, intelligence and security services see themselves facing a very different situation, where there is no distinction anymore between operations and 'non-operations', or to it put more bluntly, between peacetime and wartime. In fact, intelligence and security services are, in essence, confronted with something tantamount to permanent war occurring all over the world. In order to be able to face this challenge with some degree of success, it is of paramount importance that the structures of intelligence and security services are modular and flexible, and last but not least, that these services can rely on the required amount of manpower with the right qualifications.

More than ever, intelligence services are expected to be permanently vigilant and fulfil the role of alarm bells. These expectations can only be met if the 'Indication and Warning' process is performed in a professional way. This includes, among other things, the monitoring of not just conventional political and military indicators, but also less common parameters like cultural, sociological and other tailor-made indicators that have to be regularly reviewed, reassessed and updated.

Another interesting aspect is that almost simultaneously, the influence of the international media has expanded beyond all expectations. International and national media now have to be considered as key factors in the political decision-making process. They are not just opinion shapers anymore, but have developed into policy drivers.[2]

The Changing Face of the Threat: the Need for 'Other' Intelligence

In peace support operations, the threat is much more diffuse and harder to identify than in conventional military operations. The enemy is less readily defined and regular (military) forces often only play a secondary role. Paramilitaries, volunteers, self-declared police forces, freedom fighters, or even criminal networks and the gangs they control, dominate the situation on the ground. These groups are fully integrated in and assimilated with the local population and often maintain close relations with the local power centres. Due to the nature of the conflict, the local power centres amalgamate military, economical and political power. The objectives of the local parties are often determined by hard to quantify and qualify political and socio-cultural factors, which may appear irrational in our 'Westernised' judgement. The peace support mission is confronted with a 'Catch-22' situation: in order to implement its mandate, the mission will have to co-operate with these local power centres, which, at the same time, represent the biggest threat to the realisation of the mandate. This imposes particular constraints on the intelligence structure.

Instead of focussing on purely military information and intelligence, peace support operations require a much broader span of information: political, economical, geographic, ethnic, linguistic, social, sociological, cultural, religious, demographic, biographic, ecological intelligence, etc. In addition, the fact that the potential area of responsibility has become much larger has an immediate impact on the size of the area of intelligence interest.[3]

In concrete terms, this means that the intelligence organisation and its personnel during a peace support operation do not operate in a 'military information environment', but in a 'global information environment'. It is obvious that this new situation imposes particular demands, not the least on the collectors and the analysts, and on their intellectual flexibility. They have to be able to handle a much larger amount of information, dealing with a much wider range of issues, in much less time. Most importantly, much more than was the case during conventional military operations, analysts will have to be able to get out of the paradigm; 'get out of the box!' and think in a more unconventional way. This situation imposes a new and maybe unorthodox approach to recruitment and training of analysts. There may be a need for the temporary hiring of people (academics, NGO workers) with particular backgrounds or relevant experience, not available in the military. Some of the work may have to be outsourced to specialised research institutes or think tanks, etc. Analysis techniques have to be reviewed too. Link analysis, supported by specialised software has become a very important technique, although over-reliance on electronic tools (that should in fact only assist the analyst) could lead to erroneous conclusions.

Needless to say that this multi-layer intelligence picture should be available before the political decision to send troops, or participate otherwise in the peace support operation, is taken. Once this decision is taken, intelligence personnel should be among the first to be deployed to the mission area, before the other troops arrive.

The mission of the peace support operation is determined by its mandate. In reality, however, force protection tends to be the limiting (and therefore determining) factor for the implementation of the mandate and therefore the objectives of the peacekeeping operation. Force protection is not only a concern in the mission area, but also elsewhere; not the least on the territory of the troop contributing nations or other parts of the world where these nations have particular interest, as there can be a risk of retaliation. Force protection implies that there is at all times particular attention for counter intelligence (subversion, espionage and terrorism). Notwithstanding that most Security and Counterintelligence professionals will argue that the distinction between their discipline and intelligence needs to be maintained, based on the importance of force protection during peace support operations, the maximum integration of both disciplines should be pursued.

Force protection is also an appropriate area to illustrate the influence of the media. The 'zero casualty'- doctrine that marked some Western powers during the 1990s and the concern of our political leaders to safeguard above all a good public image, have put the media in a privileged position. Media play an ambiguous role during peace support operations. On one hand they can be a particularly valuable and essential source of information (as a component of Osint), but on the other hand, their influence and 'subjectivity' can be counterproductive. Media can create myths or legends that can make the working conditions for the peace support mission and for an intelligence organisation quite difficult. The conflict in the Balkans and the way it was covered by most international media are a good example of this situation.[4]

Media can even become competitors to intelligence organisations. International media can produce 'breaking news' from anywhere on the globe, at an unbeatable speed. Still, the political and military decision makers will expect from their intelligence services that they will be able to investigate these media reports and answer all their questions provoked by the media reporting and all this under tight time constraints.

It was mentioned earlier that the intelligence organisation and its personnel during a peace support operation do not operate in a 'military information environment', but in a 'global information environment'. Related to this, it is argued by some, that the purpose of intelligence has changed too. The Defence Committee of the UK House of Commons concluded after the NATO Kosovo bombing campaign in Spring 1999 that it is an error to believe that intelligence is intended to predict the future and the reactions of the opponent with the highest probability. The real aim of intelligence is to identify and analyse all possible options and reactions of the opponent, even if they seem irrational, to avoid surprise and allow the planners and decision-makers to best prepare for all contingencies and avoid strategic surprise. At the same time, the decision-makers have to define their intelligence needs more precisely and also critically evaluate the intelligence that is produced.[5]

Impact of Peace Support Operations on the Intelligence Organisation

Particularly during UN-led peace support operations, neutrality and transparency will be two crucial aspects. The mandate can only be implemented if the peacekeeping mission has the lasting trust and confidence of all the parties involved. Therefore, the term intelligence is often replaced with 'military information'.[6]

If the gathering of information is perceived to be too aggressive, it will be considered 'espionage' and will most likely affect the trust of the parties in the neutrality of the force and as such weaken or even undermine the whole operation. This problem can also arise within the peacekeeping force itself[7], particularly if troop contributing nations disagree about the solution to the conflict, because they have particular relations with one of the parties, have conflicting interests, or for other reasons. This was particularly obvious during the UNPROFOR peacekeeping operation in the former Yugoslavia (1992-1995).

Because the threat in peacekeeping operations is more diffuse and harder to identify, the traditional differentiation between tactical, operational and strategic intelligence - which usually reflects directly on the structure and procedures of intelligence organisations - proves to be counterproductive. Tactical developments can have or develop strategic implications and vice versa. The intelligence structure needs to be flexible enough to allow the permanent exchange, integration and synthesis of these three disciplines. The backlash of this situation is that there is a distinct risk of 'micro-management', when leaders at the strategic level (mis)use their direct access to real-time tactical information to attempt to influence tactical developments.

The knowledge of the parties' intentions will be crucial and actually be more important than their measurable military capabilities.[8] WHAT do the parties want to achieve, and WHY? These intentions are much wider than just political or military objectives and as mentioned earlier, may seem sometimes irrational. Relying exclusively on sensors and detectors (Istar)[9] will only provide a partial and therefore most likely incorrect picture of the parties' intentions. It is vital to

UNDERSTAND, to grasp the parties. This cannot be done by computers, but only by fully engaging the human factor in all steps of the intelligence cycle, focused on studying and understanding the attitudes and aspirations of the parties.

It is commonly accepted that Humint and Osint are the dominating disciplines in Peacekeeping operations. Still, Sigint (Comint) and Imint will be important disciplines too (e.g. Imint to monitor buffer zones or demilitarised zones; observation satellites are crucial for Indication and Warning). The use of certain intelligence disciplines can be prohibited by the Rules of Engagement (e.g. field Comint). Osint consists not only of the systematic monitoring and exploitation of local and international media and other news sources, but also of the setting up of databases with the names of academics, journalists, NGO workers and others who have relevant knowledge of the area of intelligence interest and can be called upon when needed.

Humint is subject to a number of caveats. Because of the nature of the operation, all military personnel should be considered potential collectors. Logistical and humanitarian convoys cross the whole mission area and can provide very valuable information on the situation there. The same is valid for engineers, medical personnel, and Civil-Military Co-operation (CIMIC) and Information Operations teams. Liaison officers are in privileged position to collect information from the local authorities. All these people need to be made aware of their role as collectors and to receive basic training to carry out this task. But it has to be clear that the use of this wide range of mostly inexperienced collectors -who have to be systematically debriefed- includes a number of risks like 'information overflow' and even misinformation. Additionally, many are wary of anything they think might undermine perceptions of their objectivity and intelligence collection is often accused of tainting the likes of CIMIC personnel.

When it comes to local contacts and sources, one should always consider why they want to help the peace support operation (often against their own people). It is quite obvious that their motives are often less noble than we expect them to be. This brings us to the importance of the screening of sources and keeping contact and source records, and, last but not least, source protection. The constant rotation of military personnel, every four or six months, represents an additional handicap in an area where confidence and confidentiality are key.

66

The military peace support force does not operate alone.[10] Most often, civilian organisations (like for example UN Civil Affairs, the EU, OSCE, NGO's), with different corporate cultures, and their own approach to intelligence and security are present in the region too.[11] All these organisations collect information. Civilian organisations will need to have access to military intelligence and vice versa. This means that procedures need to be agreed upon to permit a smooth sharing of relevant intelligence, before the start of the operation. The most ideal solution, but most likely wishful thinking, is the creation of a fusion centre, where representatives of the various organisations come together and share and exchange intelligence in an organised way.

In case the military peacekeeping mission is based on ad hoc coalitions (Combined Joint Task Forces), procedures for the sharing of information and intelligence will also be required within the mission, not only to enhance the capabilities of the whole force and ensure force protection, but, also, and not least, to avoid distrust and friction within the force. The UNTAES and SFOR operations provide a good picture of the complexity of intelligence fusion and releasability.[12]

Some Practical Concepts

- The *Military Intelligence Liaison Officer* concept has existed for a long time in the United Kingdom. The aim is to have a group of trained intelligence officers available with a broad background who could be quickly deployed to any potential mission area, to assist in the planning and preparation of any potential peacekeeping operation (prior to the deployment). They can also be assigned as temporary reinforcement in case particular intelligence requirements have arisen.

- *National Intelligence Cells* are actually a very common concept in contemporary peace support operations. One could wonder though whether the NIC concept has always been applied like it should be. Should a NIC be limited to a liaison element or should it act like a mini-CJ2? Taking into account the lack of qualified personnel intelligence services are confronted with, it seems to be logical to limit the role of a NIC to that of a liaison element. It should be underlined that liaison implies the exchange of information and/or intelligence in two directions.

67

- *JASIC*: Joint All Source Intelligence Cell: During peacekeeping operations, nations can decide to deploy collection assets a battalion or a battle group (BG) normally does not have in its inventory. Examples of this are battlefield surveillance radars, specialised reconnaissance, Field Humint teams, Comint teams. In addition, the BG may have its own CIMIC and Information Operations teams, and a PIO cell under its control. This means that there is a whole range of new intelligence collection assets available to the BG commander. The regular S2 cell will most likely be overwhelmed and unable to adequately use all these assets. The idea of the JASIC would then be to create a kind of intelligence centre with a modular composition, where all the information collected by the aforementioned assets can be collated, analysed and further disseminated. The modular configuration of a JASIC consists of a command element, a CCIRM (Collection Co-ordination and Intelligence Requirement Manager) and an analysis element.

Endnotes

[1] *Activiteitenverslag, Vast Comité van Toezicht op de Inlichtingendiensten, Conclusies en aanbevelingen,* (Brussel:1996) pp 139-140, at http://www.comiteri.be/rapports/rapport%2096nl.pdf (accessed on 12 November 2002); *Report of the Secretary-General pursuant to General Assembly resolution 53/35 'The fall of Srebrenica',* UN Doc A/54/549, 15 December 1999, at http://www.uni-frankfurt.de/fb01/INPE/srebrenica.pdf (accessed on 12 November 2002); *Report of the Somalia Commission of Inquiry, Volume 3, The military Planning System, Military Intelligence,* July 1997, at http://www.dnd.ca/somalia/vol3/v3c25ce.htm (accessed on 12 November 2002).

[2] Bruce Hoffman, *Inside Terrorism* (London: Victor Gollancz 1998) p. 152.

[3] Andrei Raevsky, *Managing Arms in Peace Processes: Aspects of Psychological Operations and Intelligence* (Geneva: UNIDIR 1996).

[4] See CNN-effect and the IRMA (Instant Response to Media Attention)-effect. The latter acronym was introduced by a senior UNPROFOR officer in Sarajevo when a troop contributing nation decided to send a transport plane to evacuate a Bosnian girl called Irma.

[5] *Lessons of Kosovo, Volume I, Reports and Proceedings of the Committee, Defence Committee, Fourteenth Report* (London: House of Commons 23 Oct 2000).

[6] Daniel Villeneuve 'Intelligence and the United Nations, Lessons from Bosnia - A Canadian Experience', *Military Intelligence Professional Bulletin* (Oct-Dec 1996).

[7] Andrei Raevsky, *Managing Arms in Peace Process.*

[7] Andrei Raevsky, *Managing Arms in Peace Process.*

[8] David A. Charters, *'Virtual War? Virtual intelligence?': Alternative Visions of Future War and Intelligence* (Lecture at CASIS Conference Ottawa: September 2000).

[9] ISTAR: Intelligence, Surveillance, Target Acquisition and Reconnaissance

[10] Compare the UNPROFOR and UNTAES operations and SFOR, KFOR. Whilst a UN civilian (SRSG or Transitional Administrator) was the overall chief in the UNPROFOR and UNTAES operations, there is no subordination relation between SFOR and the High Representative, nor between KFOR and the SRSG UNMIK.

[11] Pär Erikson 'Civil-Military Co-ordination in Peace Support Operations – An Impossible Necessity', in Woodstock and David (eds.) *Analysis of Civil Military Interaction* (Cornwallis Park: The Canadian Peacekeeping Press 1999) pp. 17-35.

[12] Particularly during the UNTAES operation, Russian officers serving in the force headquarters were convinced that colleagues from NATO countries were collecting information on them. This led on some occasions to tensions within the HQ.

Part II presents three diverse perspectives on what lessons can be learned from academic study of historical situations. Most noteworthy is the common view that peacekeeping operations simply cannot do without effective intelligence, despite the historical antagonism within United Nations circles toward 'intelligence', as it is perceived to be associated with espionage. Historical experience clearly does provide a basis for devising intelligence concepts and doctrine that can be shared in a multinational environment. However, the hostility of some nations toward the idea of peacekeeping; and the tendency of nations to regard intelligence support to peacekeeping as a national activity with only national beneficiaries, remains as great an obstacle to strategic and tactical peacekeeping success, as does the current cultural negativism of the United Nations toward intelligence. Peacekeeping, and especially peacekeeping in conditions that are neither war nor peace, but rather a complex mix of warlords, criminal gangs, natural disasters, and leaderless mobs, clearly demands multinational intelligence capabilities of the highest order, and presents a challenge to the intelligence profession that is as great, if not greater, than any conflict between clearly-defined states.

Chapter 7. From Ireland to Bosnia: Intelligence Support for UK Low Intensity Operations. The UK experiences with intelligence support to low intensity operations in Ireland and in Bosnia contain some remarkable similarities. Common themes are identified and then employed to suggest that the boundaries between intelligence support for different types of low intensity operations are less significant than is commonly believed. First, intelligence addresses the problem of surprise that can undermine political resolve to pursue operations, either within states or within coalitions. Second, intelligence helps to employ resources efficiently in operations where forces are often improbably over-stretched. Meanwhile, the UK journey from Ireland and Bosnia also allows us to observe a rare example of institutionalised learning. The long period of UK intelligence operations in Ireland has allowed time to conduct detailed operational analysis and review. Does this offer transferable lessons and experience, or should each fresh situation be considered anew? Finally, some attention is given to the vexed issue of 'intelligence sharing' in Bosnia. Resistance to the pooling of intelligence partly reflects the sensitivities of secrets, but it also appears to be connected to the wider issue of 'red carding', which made all UN and NATO forces effectively national forces. RICHARD J. ALDRICH

Chapter 8. Intelligence, Peacekeeping and Peacemaking in the Middle East. The Middle East has been the scene of numerous peacekeeping and peacemaking efforts over the past five decades. The success of UN peacekeeping forces in this region is often inherently dependent on information for their roles in monitoring compliance of treaties and agreements. This chapter examines the contradiction between UN and national use of intelligence in peacekeeping and peacemaking efforts in the Middle

East. UN forces in the Middle East reject intelligence collection since it could damage their impartial standing in the Arab-Israeli conflict, while national governments use their intelligence services as tools of covert diplomacy. Intelligence services have turned into an indispensable tool of peace or at the very least a stabilising factor in a region plagued by decades of conflict. SHLOMO SHPIRO

Chapter 9. The Second Iraq Intervention, 2002-2003. The United Nations and the United States present immediate problems in a paper designed to investigate intelligence and peacekeeping in the context of a future conflict against Iraq. To many in the United Nations the thought of intelligence is anathema while peacekeeping is an activity which is not only unpopular in the United States but one at which that state does not excel. It is clear that if there is to be military activity aimed against Iraq, it will be in the form which suits the United States best: military intervention. The author makes the point that when peacekeeping eventually comes, as part of post-conflict resolution and nation building, the peacemaking and peacekeeping phase will in all probability be more complex than the military intervention. RICHARD CONNAUGHTON

From Ireland to Bosnia: Intelligence Support for UK Low Intensity Operations

Richard J. Aldrich

Introduction

Why compare the UK experience with intelligence support to low intensity operations in Ireland and in Bosnia? While both deployments involved divided states and multiple factions, and although both deployments encountered 'mission creep', significant differences obtain. Ireland was primarily an internal security problem and was dominated by a mixture of aid to the civil power and counter-terrorist activities, while Bosnia was, at first glance, an international situation that involved peacekeeping, humanitarian assistance, policing and monitoring. Although both deployments involved diverse activities, the emphasis was quite different. Moreover, in Ireland activities were unilateral and under national command, in Bosnia they formed part of international and latterly, multinational operations.[1]

Notwithstanding this, two arguments are advanced here to suggest that there is value in connecting and comparing UK intelligence experiences in these two environments. Firstly, we must consider the boundaries between different sorts of low intensity operations. Much abstracted writing suggests that many post-cold war tasks are not only 'new' but also specific in their nature. A literature now exists on humanitarian operations and peace operations that is very different to the counter-insurgency literature of the 1970s and 1980s. In particular, there now exists a significant body of writing on the discrete issue of intelligence support for peacekeeping.[2] By contrast, Thomas Mockaitis recently argued that most low intensity operations enjoy a generic quality that crosses boundaries between specific tasks. Old operations of counter-insurgency were often complemented by humanitarian assistance, while recent

73

peace operations, typically in Somalia, look like counter-insurgency. He asks, are peace enforcement and peacemaking just 'new names for old games'? More specifically, Mockaitis has argued that peace enforcement, like counterinsurgency or even conventional war are ultimately all military operations. Like all military operations, they require two things to succeed: the resources to accomplish the mission and the political will to see the mission through to a successful conclusion.

Mockaitis's arguments have a bearing on intelligence support to low intensity operations. Indeed, the impact of intelligence reinforces the argument about the generic quality of low intensity operations. All low intensity operations have substantial generic psychological dimensions and constitute a test of political will. Unpleasant surprises quickly erode national political will or coalition solidarity that are vital to sustaining both peacekeeping and counterinsurgency. (The events in Somalia in 1993 are but one illustration of this.) Good intelligence can offer a cushion against the unexpected. Intelligence also allows the efficient deployment of resources. David Kahn has recently argued that the most promising avenue towards a substantive theoretical definition of intelligence lies in the realm of economic theories that conceive of intelligence as the kind of information that permits the most efficient action.[3] Again this has importance for peacekeeping and counterinsurgency operations, where resources and personnel are often notoriously thin. This was never more so than in Bosnia where small numbers of peacekeepers were scattered across a vast and difficult terrain. Arguably, while intelligence is important for all kinds of military operations, it is of additional importance for low intensity operations because of these general characteristics.[4]

The second reason for comparing Ireland and Bosnia is to trace the impact of policy learning. UK intelligence had operated in Ireland for decades but found itself in the unfamiliar territory of Yugoslavia at very short notice. Under the pressure of these adversities, UK intelligence repeatedly drew on its experience in Ireland to inform its activities in Bosnia, simply because this was what it knew best. Practitioners themselves made the comparison at the time and continued to make the comparison in the context of other operations such as Kosovo and Macedonia. When UK troops arrived in Kosovo one of the first thing that Richard Holbrooke reportedly asked them was 'What would you do if you were in Northern Ireland?' This was a question to which the UK contingent had plenty of ready answers, although they were not all appropriate to the local situation. Such longitudinal comparisons are methodologically more problematic, but they are also potentially more interesting.[5]

This chapter suggests that the UK deployment in Ireland, a uniquely intelligence-led area of activity, has been critically important in terms of shaping how UK intelligence thinks about all low intensity operations. This importance is partly explained by the simple fact that UK forces have been there so long. Over a period of three and a half decades of continuous operations they achieved what they had not achieved elsewhere, a learning curve that involved not only individual experience but also institutionalised learning, constructed upon detailed operational analysis. Moreover, the sophistication required of UK forces by the 1980s was considerable, given that the opposition also 'learned lessons' and had raised the level of its 'game'. As a result, the British Army had developed a depth of expertise in the running of both technical and human intelligence operations. This is in marked contrast to almost every other low intensity operations that Britain has been involved in since 1945, where lessons were often learned and then lost.[6]

One obvious obstacle to meaningful comparison is the issue of unilateralism versus multilateralism, a difference that has already been alluded to. In Bosnia, the UK was working in the context of UNPROFOR, IFOR and eventually SFOR which created unique problems that arose out of international liaison and intelligence sharing amongst troop contributing nations. Moreover, the UN itself proved to be 'allergic' to intelligence, presenting further problems. But as this chapter seeks to suggest, activities in Ireland required more international co-operation than has previously been appreciated. Meanwhile, security constraints in Bosnia meant that, for some states, the flow of intelligence was primarily national. Indeed, for the UK, intelligence sharing mostly consisted of traditional bilateral Anglo-American exchange. Meanwhile, in Ireland and Bosnia the scale of UK deployment was quite similar. In Ireland, the British Army despatched 3,000 troops in August of 1969, rising to 32,000 at the height of the troubles in 1972. Since then the British Army have deployed between 11,000 to 26,000 troops in Ireland at any given moment. In 2002 there were 16,000 troops in Ireland. Similarly, the British Army had 16,000 troops in Yugoslavia in 1990s. In 2002 it had 2,000 troops in Bosnia, 3,200 in Kosovo and some 200 in Macedonia. Significantly, in both Ireland and Bosnia, UK forces were often spread thin.

Did these 'Irish lessons' result in an overall improvement in the intelligence aspects of UK low intensity operations doctrine? Or have they resulted in a situation in which UK forces enjoy overweening arrogance, while at the same time preparing for the last war, rather than the next. It is easier to reflect on the past than to correctly anticipate the future, or as Michael Howard once put it, historical analogies are a lazy substitute for hard analytical thought.[7] Does comparison of everything with Ireland, as some serving officers are inclined to do, lead to misplaced confidence? Certainly in UK military academies one does not have to search for long to find an officer who will argue that having 'defeated' the Irish paramilitaries through an intelligence-led campaign, dealing with the aftermath of conflicts in the Gulf, Bosnia and Afghanistan was fairly straightforward.

In this chapter, comparisons are pursued at three levels. First, the macro level considering intelligence support to political, strategic and diplomatic developments. Second, at the mid-level, reviewing the place of intelligence in operational and logistical concerns. Finally some attention is given to the micro level where intelligence interfaces with tactical or training issues, together with matters of administering humanitarian assistance on the ground.

At the Top, Intelligence at the Macro Level

Political intelligence provides the most obvious area of commonality. In both Ireland and Bosnia complex and highly factionalised situations needed strong intelligence to support negotiations directly. Intelligence was employed to identify opportunities and appropriate time phases for negotiation to be brought forward. Intelligence also supported operations designed to bring hostilities temporarily to a low enough level and to keep them at a low enough level for negotiations to succeed, or to thwart the efforts of elements who were working in an instrumental way to disrupt negotiations. In both cases, intelligence agencies not only supported negotiation but negotiated, through the provision of the additional service of 'para-diplomacy', allowing contact to be kept open with parties who would rather not be seen talking to each other openly. This is a time-honoured tradition, exemplified by the use of Britain's SIS to talk to Germany during the Second World War and the American use of the CIA to talk to Communist China during major international conferences in the 1950s when Washington did not recognise the People's Republic and did not maintain diplomatic relations. Similarly, for years the UK government kept open lines of political communication to the IRA, sometime through SIS officers operating out of Dublin. The existence of these conversations at the height of communal tensions in Ireland would have caused a public outcry. Nevertheless, the continued dialogue was essential to the long-term building of mutual confidence between opponents. Intelligence cannot solve deep-seated political problems of divided communities, but it can build institutional trust between negotiating parties.[8]

Intelligence has a strong role to play in supporting policy-makers attempting to negotiate solutions to bitterly divided communities. In both Ireland and Bosnia, policy makers often entered negotiations at short notice and with only limited knowledge of the local situation. Additionally, when a large number of diverse organisations are engaged in a broad political, economic, informational, and military effort to bring peace and stability to specified peoples the need for sophisticated intelligence fusion is very apparent. Here, it has been argued, timely intelligence can play an 'educational' role in emphasising the extent to which the conflicts were not only political but also multinational, multi-organisational, multi-dimensional, and multi-cultural. Good intelligence is needed to support working effectively in a complex environment and to encourage 'mind-set adjustments that will allow leaders to be comfortable with political ambiguity and at ease as part of a synergistic process.'[9]

The relationship of intelligence and senior political or administrative figures engaged in negotiation is not always a comfortable one. While many came to appreciate the importance of detailed briefings and timely political intelligence in the context of both Ireland and Bosnia, in both cases it was sometimes difficult to extract high-level approval for necessary operations or for clear guidance that allowed agencies to work with confidence. Intelligence gathering in such highly charged situations involves the continual taking of calculated risks, something which rarefied policy animals were sometimes unable to appreciate. Aggressive intelligence gathering, where it occurred, in both Ireland and Bosnia, tended to originate at the mid-level from those managers who appreciated its value, rather than from the highest level where caution often prevailed.

Intelligence gathering was complicated by continual shifting of objectives. In modern parlance this has become known as 'mission creep', but it was also observable in Ireland in the 1970s as the UK military presence expanded and

77

became more permanent. UNPROFOR's mission in Bosnia was blurred from the start and while it emphasised providing humanitarian aid together with protection and security, it permitted a degree of peacemaking where this was required to fulfil the mission. The perception of the outside world was that the other functions were being performed, including covert assistance to favoured factions. Different missions required different sorts of intelligence and were hard to mix. Matters were especially complex when a shift occurred from intelligence gathering to covert action. Efforts to influence the situation on the ground almost always involved co-operation with factions. As the UK discovered in Ireland and as the US discovered in Bosnia, intelligence played a large part in subterranean support for favoured factions. Both found returning to the previous state of impartiality is nigh impossible.

Intelligence support in the initial stages of most low intensity operations tends to follow a familiar pattern. Policy-makers inhabit an optimistic world and prefer to anticipate activities which are short-lived and low-cost. Contrary to initial expectations, the operations in Ireland and Bosnia were neither. This presumption tends to lead to poor intelligence investment at the outset precisely when a strong information flow would be most valuable. Intelligence operations, especially human agent operations, are intrinsically long-term and do not respond well to the stop-go atmosphere of crisis and response. But this is no excuse for minimising intelligence support and this mistake was made by the UK in 1969 when Whitehall believed that 3.000 troops would go to Ireland on a temporary basis. Thereafter, the UK forces stayed for a period of more than three decades in which a third of a million soldiers have done duty in the province. Similarly in Yugoslavia, UK forces stayed in Bosnia for longer than expected and the Kosovo deployment was bigger than originally anticipated. Intelligence operations in the wake of these deployments have had to run hard to catch up.

General Sir Roderick Cordy-Simpson, who was variously General Sir Michael Rose's Director of Operation and Chief of Staff in Bosnia, expressed himself on the problem of intelligence prior to arrival in Bosnia very frankly. He asserted that in the run-up to deployment they were 'totally unprepared', in a way that the UK should not have been, for what happened in the Balkans. Neither decision-makers, nor local commanders understood the nature of the conflict at the outset. At the beginning the main source of 'information' was emotive television pictures from CNN and ITN which prompted knee-jerk reactions and public calls for intervention. He remembers one of the briefing packs that were sent by the Foreign Office during his first weeks in Bosnia:

> I can remember it quite clearly what flora and fauna I would find, that lead-free petrol would be difficult to find (there was not a single petrol station that had not been blown up by the time we got there), what type of money would be used, not that there was a bank because they had all been raided by then. To be honest, we were living in the Dark Ages. We had militarily no intelligence virtually, and certainly at the strategic level I do not think the nation had much true understanding of the nature of the conflict. I do not know at what stage we should have begun to understand it, probably in the early stages of the Croatian/Serb war that started at Vukovar or subsequently, I do not know, but we did not understand the conflict when we deployed.[10]

This lack of understanding about the complexities fed into decision making at all levels. One of the results was a desire to over-simplify the situation and employ a reductionist labelling of factions as 'good guys and bad guys'. No-one appreciated that on the ground, elements of two factions could be allies at one point in the sector, but fighting each other ten miles down the road, largely as a result of particular combinations of personalities or family relations. Absence of intelligence contributed to a situation in which the UK did not enjoy a clear consensus about why it joined UNPROFOR or an idea of what would amount to success and thereafter what would comprise a well crafted exit strategy.

For military planners at the strategic level, intelligence has always been vital to try and extend the efficacy of thinly stretched forces attempting to cover too much ground. Indeed, one of the most important ways in which intelligence and the doctrine of low intensity operations connect is efficient use of resources. This applies to military operations of all kind, but *especially* to low intensity conflict where the ratio of security forces to problem can be very low. In Ireland the UK forces often found that 16.000 troops were kept at full stretch by only 300 active terrorists. UK operations in Northern Ireland absorbed between 20% to 33% of all UK infantry battalions at any one time between 1969 and 1993. Ireland and Bosnia together in the early 1990s pushed the British Army to the limit and growing numbers of reservists had to be called in to fill the gap.

The problem of efficiency continues to be central at a time when the British Army has had to accept that it is unlikely ever to meet its current recruiting targets.[11]

Intelligence quickly identified aspects of the situation in Ireland and Bosnia that were linked to other areas of security. Most importantly, the factions proved to have substantial links to organised crime. In Ireland extortion, bank-robbing and petrol smuggling was widespread. Factions in Yugoslavia in particular were almost without exception linked to organised crime including prostitution and narcotics. In Bosnia it was important to know whether the local commander that one was dealing with had a background as a sober Army officer or local Mafioso. Ireland and subsequently Yugoslavia, re-affirmed the intense and unseen linkage between the growing importance of 'global issues' such as organised crime, drugs and illegal trafficking in light weapons on the one hand, and local or regional conflicts on the other.[12]

Links to organised crime and light weapons trafficking underline the fact that most low intensity operations have complex international dimensions. Moreover the control of light weapons flows seems increasingly important in conflict termination.[13] Similar situations obtained in Ireland and Bosnia with a view to arms supplies. Vast resources were deployed to enforce efforts to prevent shipments of weapons, while the factions resorted to ingenuity to evade them. In both cases, arms trafficking gave local conflicts an international dimension. In Eire and the UK governments co-operated to cut off seaborne weapons shipments to the factions in Ireland. Concerted intelligence work uncovered a Libyan effort to provide aid to the IRA in the amount of 9 million pounds sterling in the 1980s. They shipped 130 tons of weapons to the IRA between 1985 and 1987. UK intelligence also supported the UN arms embargo in Yugoslavia. This proved to be more complex because so many states, even those who were troop contributing nations, who were legally committed to enforcing the embargo, had their favourites amongst the factions and were simultaneously turning a blind eye to the import of small arms or even helping to circumvent the ban.

Ireland and Bosnia were therefore both local conflicts with a strong global dimension. In the early years of the Ireland conflict UK intelligence was dubious about the commitment of its American partners to preventing weapons and money from reaching Republican factions, but as co-operation improved the FBI carried out some spectacularly successful arrests against Republicans seeking to buy anti-aircraft missiles in the US. The IRAs decision to attack British Army bases in Europe in the 1970s ensured that intelligence co-operation on this matter became NATO-wide. Over time substantial programmes were built up with both the German security service BfV and the Dutch security service BVD who ran agents against terrorist cells on the Continent. Similarly, representatives of the factions in Bosnia were active on a global scale.

Ireland and Bosnia both resulted in strains on the Anglo-American intelligence relationship. In Bosnia, strategic intelligence exchange proved to be a major problem as the political objectives of the two allies diverged. The United States was clearly offering arms and assistance to the Bosnian Muslims and to the Croatians on a large scale, often via third parties or via private military companies. Germany also clearly favoured the Croatians and supplied them, reviving old historic links to that part of Yugoslavia. The UK did not agree with these illegal transfers. In 2002, the International Criminal Tribunal on the former Yugoslavia (ICTY) was investigating the United States for its assistance to military operations conducted by Croatia against rebel Serbian forces.

Admiral Davor Domazet, chief of Croatia's military intelligence during the country's four-year war against secessionist Serbian guerrillas, was recently questioned in Zagreb by two investigators from the ICTY and a representative of the prosecutor's office at The Hague. The investigators asked about the US role in aiding Croatian forces in the 1993 Medak Pocket operation and the 1995 lightning offensive known as Operation Storm. It appears the real purpose of the questioning was to investigate the role of US intelligence officials in these operations, according to off the record comments by officials. The tribunal investigators were interested in Croatia's use of unmanned drones during Operation Storm, which were especially effective in enabling Croatian military forces to locate positions of rebel Serbs on the ground. The Hague investigators also asked about Zagreb's signals intelligence, high-powered satellite dishes used for electronic surveillance that the Croatians reportedly received from the US National Security Agency. It was reported that, during and after Operation Storm, the CIA operated unmanned drones from a military base near Zadar on the Adriatic coast. It has also been reported that the United States provided encryption gear to each of Croatia's regular army brigades and that Washington shared extensive electronic surveillance data with Zagreb.[14]

81

Where policy diverged, intelligence flow between allies slowed down. At the strategic level, UK intelligence knew about, but preferred to ignore, the flow of illegal arms to Bosnian Muslims. Cameron Spence, a member of the Special Air Service (SAS) recalls the dismay of his superiors when his unit discovered the extent and nature of arms transfers by their US allies. SAS units on the ground in Yugoslavia contacted SAS in Germany who were located near the US airfields where supplies were being shipped from. They noticed the distinctive dress of those loading the crates into C-130s, 'guys with shades and earpieces wearing T-shirts'.[15] In practice, the US seems to have been only part of a wider programme which involved Germany, Turkey, Saudi Arabia, Iran and Pakistan in the airlifting of supplies to both the Bosnian Muslims and the Croatians.[16] Most memoirs of American officials from this period refer to the US official proposal for 'Lift and Strike', lifting the embargo on arms to the Bosnian Muslims and striking the Bosnian Serbs with airpower, pressed for by US Secretary of State Warren Christopher in 1993. But they do not refer to the covert implementation of this policy after it was rejected by European states that same year.[17]

Differences of policy between Britain and the United States had a significant impact upon the texture of the Anglo-American intelligence alliance.[18] Reports have circulated regarding the possible American interception of UK communications in Bosnia, typically those of SAS units providing ground observation. This is not unlikely for three reasons. First, the sheer antiquity some of the UK communications equipment would have made this straightforward. Second, the status of British troops as 'UN Forces' would have put them into a grey category regarding US-UK Sigint agreements forbidding the interception of each others traffic. Third, so many factions had such good Sigint facilities that traffic intercepted by one element was often re-intercepted by others as it was communicated. It is widely thought that signals intelligence gathered by the Croats or the Bosnian Muslims may have been intercepted by Bosnian Serbs. As one observer recalls 'the Serbs were bugging the buggers'. For a while London-Washington tensions were obvious, with a growing reluctance to share information that bore directly on current political issues.[19]

Disputes over intelligence exchange in Bosnia were not dissimilar to Ireland. Restrictions were lateral in terms of service or nation and also horizontal. In Ireland, the intelligence services developed good technical and human intelligence sources, but were reluctant to share this material widely,

82

suspecting, quite rightly that there might well be penetration of government offices by the paramilitaries. In Yugoslavia too, although the UK was deriving good intelligence from both technical and human sources, distribution was highly restricted. The UK sat on some of its own Humint and had its own Sigint distribution system. General Sir Michael Rose was given a unit that resembled the Second World War Special Communications Units for Ultra that were attached to theatre commanders. In other words, a four-man team from the Royal Signals deployed with very secure communications equipment to provide Rose with high-grade intelligence which was absolutely not for circulation at an operational level.[20]

That Rose's office in the Residency at Sarajevo was being kept under technical surveillance by both the Americans and the Bosnian Muslims has been asserted by one of his staff, Milos Stankovic. Moreover, the general problems of omnipresent surveillance have been alluded to by Rose. He recalls that sensitive discussions about, for example, attempts to snatch war criminals had to be conducted in a special room that had been comprehensively de-bugged. Stankovic was suspicious of some of the high-grade communications equipment given to Rose by US technicians whom he dubbed 'The Hidden Ones'. He complains of 'their forest of antennae and funny boxes ... busy hoovering up every bleep and fart, every single electronic emission to come out of the Residency'. But as he himself concedes, security with the UNHQ was so weak that Rose and his successor, General Rupert Smith, had long become accustomed to working in an office which they assumed to be transparent.[21]

Remarkably, and despite these annoyances, strategic Anglo-American intelligence exchange remained good. In Bosnia, the post-cold war intelligence alliance was complex, with elements of mutual surveillance, but also with genuine and substantial exchange that was vital to the fortunes of UNPROFOR. While there were disagreements over factions, more important were issues of intelligence distribution. High-grade Sigint and imagery from the United States and the UK could not be passed to other allies and could not be passed beyond Michael Rose's immediate circle. His Director of Operations, General Sir Roderick Cordy-Simpson, testified to the critical importance of the high-quality intelligence he received from the Americans. Recalling his experience in Bosnia, he argued that any type of difficult operation simply cannot, presently, be undertaken without the United States' support, if for no other reason than their immense fighting power. He then added:

83

They have also got something which is irreplaceable and that is their intelligence capabilities. When I was in Bosnia there were 35 different nations providing intelligence to us. I would have to say that I do not know the exact figure, but I would have thought that somewhere around 70 per cent of the intelligence came from two nations, ourselves and the Americans. The rest of the nations, frankly, put very little into the pool. They took quite a lot out but they put very little in to what we were getting. If we had not had the Americans with their amazing capabilities, I think I for one would simply not have survived. When I consider some of the things that we were able to find out because the Americans had the capability which no-one else had, we would have been in dead trouble in any operation without them. ... I would re-emphasise time and time again that the intelligence which the Americans brought with all their capabilities was something that I know that as a commander on the ground I simply would not have survived without. UK plc gave me a great deal but there were masses of things I could not even have got from them.[22]

US Sigint capabilities in Yugoslavia were very good, as were the Sigint capabilities of the various factions, but UK capabilities remain obscure.[23]

Conversely, as UNPROFOR was replaced by IFOR, the United States came to admire and value sophisticated European Humint capabilities. The contrasting approaches were not hard to see. American forces, being somewhat risk averse, were required by their senior commanders to go on Humint missions in full battle dress in convoys of no less than four vehicles, a procedure which did not contribute much to clandestinity. Meanwhile, as American after-action reviews have observed: 'The United Kingdom had a great deal of background in these types of operations based on its experiences in northern Ireland and, was able to effectively apply this experience in Bosnia.' This was especially noticeable in the context of the G-2 element of Ace Rapid Reaction Corps, a UK-led operation, which made substantial contributions to IFOR intelligence activities.[24]

In the Bosnian case, much has been made of the problems of lateral flow, ally to ally, and these were certainly severe. But in both Ireland and Bosnia the issue of intelligence flow up and down the chain of command was no less crucial.

Hierarchical military instincts combined with 'need to know' provision kept a lot of good information at the top. But the nature of the operation muddled any clear division among the strategic, theatre, and tactical levels. At the tactical level, the deployed functional units contributed to the reconnaissance and surveillance plans, to the intelligence reporting process, and to the synthesis of information that painted the picture for the commanders. But in Bosnia, tactical commanders at the brigade, battalion and company levels needed access to political intelligence and so-called 'strategic intelligence'[25]

As Cees Wiebes has pointed out, one of the disconcerting aspects of low intensity operations is that tactical events often have strategic consequences. Traditional military thinking tells us that three tanks moving down a road is a tactical issue. But in the context of ethnic cleansing, it may be the preface an event of world-wide significance. In other words, a disturbing blurring of levels of analysis characterises intelligence for low intensity operations. Moreover the 'CNN effect' ensures that small events, seemingly selected at random and not necessarily representative of the whole situation, often have a large impact on public perceptions. The same has arguably been true of Ireland. The real problem is how to move intelligence quickly and securely from a strategic level to those who needed it at a lower echelon, or vice versa.[26]

Operations Intelligence at the Mid-level

At the operational level, existing UK military intelligence doctrine was found to be inappropriate when troops arrived in Northern Ireland and later in Bosnia. Extensive intelligence experience, albeit passed on by personal experience rather than formalised training, in counter-insurgency intelligence operations in Kenya, Malaya, Aden, Hong Kong, Cyprus, and many other colonial outposts, was carried over directly into the first phase of activity in Ireland. But unsurprisingly, the UK forces discovered they could not apply brusque colonial approaches and methods due to the status of Northern Ireland as part of the United Kingdom.

Specifically, the media were vigilant in Ireland, constituting a kind of informal oversight and providing continuous commentary on modes of behaviour. Accordingly, the UK had to abandon traditional techniques like 'interrogation in-depth' because they soon aroused accusations of 'torture', which were subsequently investigated by a special commission headed by Sir Edmund

Compton. Widely publicised were methods of sleep deprivation and sensory deprivation, including the use of hoods. Another technique widely used, but less publicised, was simply to take a Republican suspect and drive him into a Unionist area, acquaint the locals with the identity of the person in the car and threaten to leave him alone for half an hour. There were also instances of suspects being taken up in helicopters and confronted with the possibility of an 'accidental fall'. In short, physical brutalisation was rare in Ireland, but psychological torture was widespread. The uproar over using 'interrogation in-depth' on prisoners caught UK military authorities off-guard since these techniques had been taught at the Joint Services Intelligence School for some time. Substantial efforts were taken to bring practices into line with public expectations and thereafter, European legislation pushed the process of regulation further.

Bosnia represented a further step in the direction of caution and correctness. The level of media coverage in Yugoslavia was again high and intelligence gathering activity was required to not only be benign but to be visibly benign, indeed there was rarely any reference to intelligence at all. 'Information' was gathered as a result of patrolling and interrogation was almost unheard of. This was replaced by widespread interviewing of the local population who proved to have, by word of mouth, remarkably good information about the local factions, often as a result of family connections.

In both Ireland and Bosnia, UK forces had to acclimatise to environments in which operations had not only to be successful in difficult circumstances, but also in which any use of force had to be publicly justifiable in some detail. Real precision was required if any military action was taken and in both cases the need to demonstrate imminent threat was paramount. Here, experience in Ireland seemed to prove valuable. UK forces were much better at assessing tactical intelligence about imminent threats and were, at an individual level, better at deciding whether the circumstances warranted the return of fire. This experience allowed UK forces to defend themselves more confidently and led to the local nickname for 'Britbat' becoming 'Shootbat', a tag that not all commanders welcomed, but which added to their deterrent status.

In Ireland the actions of its personnel were individually accountable under the provisions of UK law. Thus if a soldier exceeded his authority he might well be charged and tried in a criminal court. (The Army objected to civil prosecution

86

of military personnel and eventually the Government accepted that soldiers would only appear in military courts.) Accordingly, UK forces issued 'Yellow Cards' to each soldier to outline what could be done. For legal reasons these rules of engagement were set below what the law allowed. This covered routine situations, however, in practice the majority of armed confrontations between paramilitaries and the Army occurred during intelligence-led operations and involved special forces. For almost a decade, the SAS were involved in maintaining covert observation over reported terrorist weapons dumps and, once weapons were recovered from the dumps, the soldiers were permitted to fire, and often did so. However, this led to a public outcry about 'ambush' and this was exacerbated when mistakes were made when innocent civilians approached the dumps.[27]

By the 1980s, the Army in Ireland found that it was under pressure to attack terrorists only when they were actually on the way to an active operation. This required a high level of sophistication in which the IRAs Active Service Units were penetrated with human agents. Alternatively, the weapons in weapons dumps were bugged with electronic equipment. This remarkable process, known as 'jarking' a weapon, allowed the army to listen in to terrorists on their way to attack a target. The epitome of this activity was the thwarted attack by the IRA on a police station at Loughall in 1987. Nine IRA men died in a hail of gunfire as they approached the target. However, the complexity of such operations was underlined by the fact that one of the nine men killed was an Army informer. Nor was this the only operation in which an informer was eliminated by the security forces. Crucially, the sophistication of intelligence operations was being driven not by military requirements, but by the need to be publicly perceived as using force in a constrained and legitimate manner.[28]

Accordingly, UK forces were ready for the surreal situation in Bosnia where forces could only fire on those who were actively attacking them, but not, for example, when those forces were fleeing after having conducted an attack. While wishing to be seen as having robust response capabilities, the UNPROFOR rules of engagement were not robust. Air strikes were under a bizarre 'dual key' arrangement in which required approval from both the UN and NATO. The local joke was along the lines of 'if you make a wrong move, I will speak to my colonel who will ask the general to ask our national defence minister to ask the prime minister to ask the rest of the UN to order me to open fire, so be warned.' Separating civilians from military in targeting for air

87

attacks created an insatiable demand for the most detailed intelligence, often provided by Unmanned Aerial Vehicles or 'drones'. But in both Bosnia, and later in Kosovo, there was a grim acceptance that, even with the unprecedented levels of intelligence provided by these new sources, avoiding all civilian casualties would mean complete halt to air operations.[29]

Issues of legitimacy and the complexities of public relations were areas in which the UK had learned painful lessons in Ireland. In both Ireland and Yugoslavia, intelligence was able to support three primary goals for UK information operations: First, winning public confidence (or at least reducing hostility to UK military presence) through a 'winning the hearts and minds' or at least, 'winning passive acceptance' campaign; second, countering misinformation spread by the paramilitaries and by spontaneously generated damaging rumours, and third, spreading misinformation to damage or unbalance the paramilitaries. In peacekeeping, responses to direct and indirect threats must be as much political/psychological as military. Intelligence is a vital component of 'soft' political, economic, psychological, and moral power, supported by information operations, careful intelligence work, and surgical precision at the more direct military or police level.[30]

Intelligence speaks very directly to issues of public perceptions and the legitimacy of force. In 2002, the UK released a dossier of intelligence material which attempted to demonstrate that Iraq was in breach of UN requirements to disarm and dispose of a range of weapons. The disclosure of this dossier, effectively a sanitised Joint Intelligence Committee report, was hailed as 'unprecedented'. In fact this was merely an incremental development of a trend which had been emerging for more than twenty years and had its origins in Ireland. Here a unit known as Information Policy was set up by intelligence officers to influence public opinion. Periodically, sensitive intelligence material was shown to journalists on an unacknowledged basis, where the Army felt that its case for action had been strong, or where it felt that public criticism of an operation was unjust. This process was continued in the context of Bosnia, and later was clearly illustrated during the air war against Serbia. The UK encountered great pressure to release intelligence, particularly imagery, to inform public opinion. A major debate developed in which these public pressures to release intelligence to show that targeting was discriminating and effective was set against the need to maintain operational security. The growing relationship between the secret world of intelligence and the very public world of media relations was one of the major lessons of the former Yugoslavia. After conducting a retrospective review of all its intelligence activities in Yugoslavia over a decade, the UK government has announced: 'We are now looking to streamline procedures for the sanitation, declassification and release of intelligence into the public domain.'[31] At the operational level, the SAS played an important and sometimes controversial role in both Ireland and Yugoslavia. The SAS were a vital resource for operational commanders on the ground. SAS personnel began operating in Ireland selectively as individuals in 1971 and then later as acknowledged SAS units in 1976. In Ireland they were employed in intelligence gathering, reconnaissance and surveillance. But as Ireland became an intelligence-led war the demand for SAS type operations became so great that the SAS spent much time training regular UK military units in covert observation techniques. They were also involved in ambushes and retaliatory raids. A parallel process took place in which Army technicians were trained widely by members of MI5 and GCHQ in technical aspects of surveillance. This high-level training activity, which greatly expanded the covert capabilities of the British Army as a whole, was an unseen but important change, taking place over a period of several decades.[32]

In Bosnia, General Sir Michael Rose, the commander of UNPROFOR was keen to have SAS at his disposal, in part because of his own period spent with the regiment in Aden in the 1960s. In Bosnia much of their work involved reconnaissance for the purpose of directing airdrops and air strikes. On 6 April 1994, SAS units penetrated Serb lines and directed air strikes against Serb positions around the town of Gorazde. One of a team of seven was killed withdrawing from these operations. On 30 August 1995 a similar SAS operation took place to direct air strikes around Sarajevo. As early as 1994 the SAS were being employed to find alleged war criminals. On 10 July 1997 a Bosnian Serb wanted for war crime charges was killed and another man arrested by a 10-man SAS squad. The operation, codename Tango, aimed at the detention of Simo Drljaca and Milan Kovacevic by an SAS team in the area of Prijedor, north-west Bosnia. The men were identified and tailed covertly before being challenged. Drljaca offered resistance and was fatally wounded in the exchange of fire.[33]

Despite the fact that UNPROFOR was an international operation, while Ireland was an internal problem, issues of intelligence sharing at the mid-level were remarkably similar. In Ireland, British Army intelligence was theoretically operating 'in assistance of civil authorities'. This meant sharing intelligence with the Special Branch & MI5 and SIS, which it did not enjoy. Periodic tangles occurred between the various intelligence services and as early as 1979 Maurice Oldfield was despatched to Ireland as an Intelligence Co-ordinator to try and unravel the confusion. But it was only in 1989 that the emergence of an effective machine, known as Tasking and Control Groups, began to integrate Army and police operations, preventing collisions on the ground or competition for agents.[34] For years, different elements of UK intelligence in Northern Ireland behaved not unlike the National Intelligence Cells (NICs) in UNPROFOR, sharing intelligence slowly, reluctantly and often on a horse-trading basis. In both Ireland and Bosnia, mechanisms were slowly evolved for the sharing of some intelligence but this was never complete. In Bosnia, one of the main contributors to the sense of frustration in the theatre was the sheer number of intelligence entities, denoted by the presence of the ubiquitous portakabin. Typically, in Sarajevo, there were perhaps a dozen NICs primarily dedicated to providing intelligence that was releasable only to their own national elements. At the level of the NIC, human intelligence often generated by local forces was the stock-in-trade, while NATO-releasable Sigint was too diluted to be of great value. Imagery was plentiful owing to the growing number of platforms from which this was collected, including some unconventional ones such as gun cameras. In Bosnia, material that was circulated widely at the UN or even NATO level was regarded a being effectively public domain.[35]

Intelligence support to factions is perhaps one of the most secretive, but intriguing aspect of both Ireland and Bosnia. Over the last ten years it has become increasingly clear that links between the British Army's Force Research Unit and the intelligence arm of some of the more violent protestant paramilitaries were strong. Discussions have focused upon the role of Brian Nelson, a former soldier planted on the paramilitaries who rose to be intelligence co-ordinator for the UDA and became a conduit for passing Army Intelligence on supposed IRA members to the UDA, who then took action. This extraordinary state of affairs became very public when the UDA was accused of eliminating the 'wrong men', and in order to substantiate their claims that they had attacked the 'right men', duplicated and pasted Army intelligence documents on the walls of Belfast. (The extent to which even terrorist organisations were having to release targeting intelligence to the public, albeit in an ersatz manner, to legitimate their activities was a startling aspect of this

90

episode.)[36] In Bosnia too, there were links to the intelligence components of the factions, some of which have yet to be discussed. American intelligence officials in Sarajevo hardly bothered to disguise their close relations with the BiH Intelligence Chief in Sarajevo.[37]

In a more mundane sense, in both Ireland and Bosnia, intelligence became an integrated part of preparation and training. In the early years, intelligence training for service in Ireland was either non-existent at worst or haphazard at best. The first deployments were intended as a short-term emergency measure and it was only in 1973 that institutionalised learning began to materialise. Eventually, the UK developed a procedure by which each battalion on orders to go to Ireland would send an advanced intelligence party some weeks before the main body arrived, to familiarise themselves with the situation on the ground as well as to extract knowledge from the unit scheduled to rotate out. This was important because in some areas the Royal Ulster Constabulary's intelligence-gathering capabilities were weak when the British Army intervened in 1969. The Army had to start building its own intelligence system from scratch which meant pouring in a large amount of effort. It was a long time before the UK received the full return on their investment in intelligence-gathering activities.

Intelligence was fed into purpose-built training areas for Ireland such as the NITAT (Northern Ireland Training Team) facility at Sennelager in Germany. The success of this influenced the decision to provide specialised training for operations in Bosnia using a similar UNTAT (United Nations Training Assistance Teams) facility at Westdown Camp on Salisbury Plain for operations in Bosnia. But such activities take time to develop and short-notice deployments to Kosovo, East Timor and Sierra Leone prevented the development of full training packages and were characterised by the familiar pattern of 'learning on the job' and limited prior intelligence. Good information and training about local situations, customs and dispositions is essential when dealing with factions whose armed elements are sometimes dressed in plain clothes, making them indistinguishable from the local population. Poor briefing or inadequate training can lead to grave mistakes, loss of life and associated public humiliation.

Intelligence on the Ground, the Micro Level

In both Ireland and Bosnia, units on the ground appreciated the importance of a holistic approach to intelligence. Intelligence was vital to support even the smallest units and every patrol devoted time and attention to intelligence gathering. Patrols were often high-profile affairs whose main function initially was to reassure public and to assert authority. In both environments, patrols required intelligence support from covert observation points to reinforce their security. Substantial numbers of covert observation posts had to be established in order to reduce the number of patrol incidents. In Ireland, soldiers, often trained by the members of the SAS, would lie in cover with binoculars, high-powered telescopes, and night vision devices for days or weeks on end in order to observe specific individuals or areas. Such covert observation posts could link with patrols in order to dominate an area. But the work exposed them to attack if their location was uncovered by passing civilians. Patrolling in Bosnia, and indeed later in Kosovo, presented some of the dilemmas experienced in Ireland. Random patrolling produced little result and potentially exposed patrols to unnecessary danger, because it was difficult to provide appropriate support. By contrast, predictable and repetitive patrolling made it easier for attackers to conduct ambushes. A varied pattern that was nevertheless co-ordinated allowed proper coverage of an area, and enabled commanders to have patrols reinforce one another if necessary.

In both Ireland and Bosnia, tactical intelligence gathering was lent an additional importance because the flow of intelligence from the higher echelons to those on the ground was weak. Intelligence at ground level flowed up, but not down. The 'poor bloody infantry' gathered a great deal of useful material but were not well informed by higher echelons. Partly because of anxieties about communication security, dedicated intelligence units tried to keep information to themselves, or at least at a high level. Reviewing the Bosnian experience, the UK authorities have concluded: 'Commanders in theatre are already supplied with good intelligence from the UK, but we are also looking at how best to provide real-time information to the commanders and forces on the ground about the disposition of their opponents, including intelligence material obtained by Intelligence, Surveillance and Reconnaissance assets.' In other words, the issue is how to employ new technologies to extent the benefits of high grade intelligence to those at the forward edge in a manner that is secure and timely.[38] At the battalion level the numbers devoted to full-time intelligence

92

have been increasing. In Ireland the standard compliment of the battalion intelligence section, 5 or 6 people, went up to 30 or 40 people. Most remained in plain clothes throughout the units tour of duty. In Bosnia the picture was the same, except that matters were complicated by the UN abhorrence of 'intelligence,' Instead Bosnia saw the setting up of 'milinfo' sections. Eventually the UN became a little more relaxed about 'intelligence' if it was gathered to enhance the mission directly.

Although both Ireland and Bosnia are often represented as intelligence efforts dominated by individuals with binoculars and a notebook, technical intelligence played a vital role even at a low level. In Ireland, fixed wing aircraft and helicopters undertook vast amount of surveillance activity. The role of helicopters in particular as surveillance platforms has been underplayed. Helicopters not only carried cameras with very large aperture lenses with high magnification, but also TV cameras. Arguably these platforms providing television footage in real time (and known in local parlance as 'Heli-tellies') were the direct predecessors of the drones that send live video feed back from the mountainous areas of Yugoslavia.[39]

At all levels, one of the toughest lessons that UK forces had to learn in both Ireland and Bosnia was that of COMSEC. Rigorous communications security is essential, even against non-state enemies. So often the armies of states presume that non-state or faction-based opponents will not resort to anything as sophisticated as signals monitoring. IRA security and intelligence gathering was good. British Army clear voice communications were being monitored by the IRA in the early 1970s and later the British discovered that the IRA had 'bugged' telephones in British military headquarters. All the factions in Bosnia gave a high priority to technical intelligence gathering.[40] In Bosnia, British Army COMSEC problems were multiplied by poor equipment. Conventional military radios were unsuitable for urban operations. The British military fulfilled some of their equipment needs with commercial off-the-shelf technology including mobile phones, a bad habit. The poor intelligence flow to the lower echelons was partly the product of the disastrous failure of the UK to provide its forces with a modern radio system, a requirement that had dragged on unfulfilled for years. The 1970s Clansman radio system used by the infantry was an antiquarian relic and very insecure, but its long overdue replacement had not arrived. There are few more glaring examples of front line units poorly served by defence bureaucrats and procurement bunglers. Outdated communications systems also meant that signals staff were badly over-stretched.

When UK forces first arrived in Bosnia, COMSEC was a disaster at every level. General Sir Roderick Cordy-Simpson recalls: 'When I was first out there in Bosnia, I have never known a nightmare like it was in 1992. It was quicker for me to drive the 12 miles to Phillip Morrillon's separate headquarters than it would be to chance getting through to a telephone, which I would guarantee was being listened to by all three sides. So it was much quicker to drive and talk to him face to face.'[41] Almost ten years later the UK was still being forced to resort to stopgap measures. In October 1999, the UK began to install a commercial protected communications system in Pristine, which overcame some of the reliability and security shortcomings of the Clansman system. It was announced in February 2000 that a contract had been let to provide wide area communications in the UK sector in Kosovo, as well as in the UK sector in Bosnia, providing modern and reliable communications. One of the repeated lessons of the UK experience is the high cost of treating 'COMSEC' as a poor relation, but there is no sign of this changing.[42]

Conclusion: Learning Lessons?

The literature of 'lessons learned' fills every staff college library to over-flowing. Indeed the US Army has its own specialised outfit with the pedagogical title 'Centre for Army Lessons Learned'. Unsurprisingly, there is a great deal of literature on Army experiences in Ireland, and increasingly on Bosnia. But there is not much on lessons transferred. Moreover, there is little literature on the problems of transferability of lessons between different types of low intensity operations. This is a significant question for specialists on intelligence and for observers of wider military issues. If there is a generic kind of 'low intensity operations intelligence' then this process should be beneficial and relatively unproblematic. But if different types of low intensity operation have their own distinct qualities, then forces are confronted with business of learning the parameters of each situation anew.

This chapter seeks to suggest that there is a generic low intensity operations intelligence. Its doctrine is yet to explored and defined. Yet its salient points are already observable and indeed to some extent obvious. Typically, local geographical knowledge and linguistic skills are going to be critical in all such operations in the future. When separating the Bosnian Croats and Bosnian Muslims in Central Bosnia, local issues could often be resolved with prior knowledge of historical perspectives and emotive locations such as graveyards and former battle sites. The same is true in Ireland Personalities are a critical aspect of the intelligence picture for every commander and the challenge is acquiring this sort of local knowledge at an improbable speed. In Ireland the UK forces had the luxury of more than 30 years to learn their craft. Having been in Yugoslavia for more than ten years, UK forces are learning a local trade there too. But few low intensity operations have this sort of duration, how are the emergency deployments to be accommodated?

A comparison of Ireland and Bosnia also has interesting insights for academic observers of intelligence, in the area of alliance and liaison. At first glance Bosnia seems quite different from Ireland in this regard. But on closer inspection, Bosnia was often like Ireland, with national intelligence operations running in parallel, characterised at best by controlled bilateral sharing. Accordingly, experiences in Ireland, a unilateral environment, will continue to inform UK intelligence operations even in the context of multinational or international operations, because of the dependence upon national intelligence systems and the absence of anything that might be called 'UN intelligence'.

Indeed, perhaps the divide here is not between national operations and multilateral/international operations, but instead between the two worlds of the academic and the practitioner.[43] The academic literature on intelligence and peacekeeping support has continually bemoaned the mismatch between the multinational or international character of the forces provided by UN or NATO and the fissiparous nature of intelligence provided through national 'stovepipes'. There have been repeated calls for an expansion of UN intelligence and for states to become accustomed to pooling sensitive intelligence while developing more confidence in the UN's ability to handle this material efficiently and discreetly.[44] But a close reading of the practitioner literature reveals that intelligence was not particularly out of step with the real nature of operations in Bosnia, or elsewhere in the former Yugoslavia. Intelligence flows often followed the composition of the forces, which were themselves often operating as *de facto* national units with hidden national vetoes. General Wesley Clark captured this succinctly in his perceptive memoir when he talked about the increasingly open 'dirty secret' of NATO operations. He asserts: 'NATO commands were like puppets, with two or six or sometimes

95

dozens of strings being pulled from behind the scenes by the nations themselves, regardless of the formalistic commitment of forces. Commanders were subject to constant scrutiny and potential veto by contributing nations.' He continues: 'This was practice that had originating with UN forces in Bosnia called "red carding" where nations temporary withdrew their forces and refused to participate in operations ordered by higher commanders. All UN and NATO forces were in practice national forces.' If troop contributing nations continue to regard their forces as their 'own' and feel at liberty to backslide on decisions taken centrally when they feel so inclined, as some have done in Yugoslavia, we have a situation of parallel national operations rather than international or multilateral operations. In such a situation, one can hardly hope for anything other than parallel national intelligence support.[45]

Endnotes

---

[1] I am indebted to Alice Hills, Vanessa Pupavac and others for comments and suggestions on earlier drafts of this paper.

[2] For literature that discusses a specific peacekeeping intelligence see: Hugh Smith, 'Intelligence and UN Peacekeeping', *Survival* 3 (1994) pp.174-94; A.W. Dorn and David J.H. Bell, 'Intelligence and Peacekeeping: The UN Operation in the Congo, 1960-64', *International Peacekeeping* 1 (1995) pp.11-33; David Ramsbotham, 'Analysis and Assessment for Peacekeeping Operations', *Intelligence and National Security* 4 (1995) pp.162-174; Paul Johnston, 'No Cloak and Dagger Required: Intelligence Support to UN Peacekeeping', *Intelligence and National Security* 4 (1997) pp.102-112; Thomas Quiggin, 'Response to 'No Cloak and Dagger Required: Intelligence Support to UN Peacekeeping Missions', *Intelligence and National Security* 4 (1998) pp.203-207; A.Walter Dorn, 'The Cloak and the Blue Beret: Limitations on Intelligence in UN Peacekeeping', *International Journal of Intelligence and Counterintelligence* 4 (1999) pp. 414-447.

[3] David Kahn, 'A Historical Theory of Intelligence', *Intelligence and National Security*, 3 (2001) pp.79-93.

[4] Thomas R. Mockaitis, 'From Counterinsurgency to Peace Enforcement: New Names for Old games?', *Small Wars and Insurgencies* 2 (1999) pp.41-57.

[5] Todd Landman, *Issues and methods in comparative politics* (London: Routledge 2000) pp.23-77.

[6] On UK intelligence and earlier low intensity operations see: K. Jeffery, 'Intelligence & Counter-Insurgency Operations', *Intelligence & National Security* 1 (1987) pp.118-

150; Richard Popplewell, 'Lacking Intelligence: Some Reflections on Recent Approaches to British Counter–Insurgency, 1900–1960' *Intelligence & National Security* 2 (1995) pp.336-346.

[7] Michael Howard, *The Lessons of History* (Yale University Press: Yale 1992).

[8] As early as 1972, SIS officer Frank Steele, together with officials from the Northern Ireland Office, met with Gerry Adams to attempt to negotiate a cease-fire, PREM 15/1009, Public Record Office. His successor was Michael Oatley, see Peter Taylor, *Brits: The War Against the IRA* (London: Bloomsbury 2001) pp.67-70.

[9] Max G. Manwaring, 'Peace and Stability Lessons From Bosnia', *Parameters: Journal of the US Army War College* 4 (1998) pp.28-38.

[10] UK House of Commons, *Select Committee On Defence*, Examination of Witnesses (Questions 220 - 242), Wednesday 3 February 1999, evidence from Lt General Sir Roderick Cordy-Simpson KBE CB, Director of Operations.

[11] The British Army has been between 8,000 and 12,000 short of its recruiting targets for several years, Tania Branigan, 'Sisters in Arms', *Guardian* 12 February 2001.

[12] The SIS global issues section was set up in the 1990s, Mark Urban, *UK Eyes Alpha inside British intelligence* (London: Faber and Faber, 1996) p.229.

[13] J. Spear, 'The Disarmament and Demobilisation of warring Factions in the Aftermath of Civil Wars', *Civil Wars* 2 (1999) pp.1-22.

[14] Jeffrey T. Kuhner, 'Tribunal Probes U.S. Aid To Croatia', *The Washington Times*, 6 December 2002.

[15] Cameron Spence, *All Necessary Measures* (London: Michael Joseph 1998) pp.102-104.

[16] J. Spence; 'Ex-ISI Chief Reveals Secret Missile Shipments to Bosnia defying UN Embargo', Special SAT Report *South Asia Tribune*, Issue No 22, December 23-29, 2002. I am indebted to Mazhar Aziz for bringing the latter to my attention.

[17] For example General Wesley K. Clark, *Waging Modern War* (NY: Public Affairs Press 2001) pp.97-98. Richard Holbrooke asserts that the United States 'played no role' in the covert assistance but could not object to it at a time when the survival of the Sarajevo government 'hung by a thread', R. Holbrooke, *To End a War* (NY: The Modern Library 1998) p.51.

[18] Richard C. Holbrooke identifies the Summer of 1994 as the low point in Anglo-American relations, Holbrooke, *To End a War*, p.333.

[19] Milos Stankovich, *Trusted Mole: A Soldier's Journey into Bosnia's Heat of Darkness* (London: Harper Collins 2000) pp.250-252

[20] Urban, *UK Eyes Alpha*, pp.210-219.

[21] Stankovich, *Trusted Mole*, pp.252-253. See also Sami Fournier, Tasos Kokkinides, Daniel Plesch, and Richard Thomas, 'Implementing Dayton: Arms Control and Intelligence in Former Yugoslavia', *BASIC PAPERS: Occasional papers on International Security Policy*, (March 1996) No.15.

[22] UK House of Commons, *Select Committee On Defence*, Examination of Witnesses (Questions 220 - 242), Wednesday 3 February 1999, evidence from Lt General Sir Roderick Cordy-Simpson KBE CB, Director of Operations. In the same session Professor Thornberry remarked: 'On the intelligence side also, it has to be said that certainly again in South West Africa in Namibia without American backing at that level, working in the joint commission on the intelligence side in South Western Africa, we would have been in very, very serious trouble.'

[23] Cees Wiebes, *Intelligence and the War in Bosnia: 1992-1995*. (Berlin and London: Lit Verlag) pp.219-310, passim.

[24] Larry K. Wentz, (ed.) *Lessons from Bosnia: The IFOR Experience*, National Defense University: Viena, VA 1997) Chapter IV: 'Intelligence Operations'; see also C. Agee, 'Joint STARS in Bosnia: Too Much Data, Too Little Intel?', *Military Intelligence*, 4 (1996) pp.6-10, 40-41; and L.T.C. Perkins, 'Humint/CI', Office of DCSI at http://call.army.mil/products/spc prod/humint/humint.htm (accessed in January 2003).

[25] Wentz, (ed.) *Lessons from Bosnia*.

[26] UK House of Commons, Select Committee on Defence, Examination of Witnesses (Questions 880 - 902), Wednesday 17 May 2000, evidence from Sir John Goulden and Vice-Admiral Paul Haddacks.

[27] General Sir Peter de la Billiere, *Looking for Trouble: SAS to Gulf Command* (London: HarperCollins 1994) p.315.

[28] Mark Urban, *Big Boys Rules, the secret struggle against the IRA* (London: Faber 1992) pp.224-237. Also private information.

[29] Clark, *Waging Modern War*, pp.299-300.

[30] R.R. Smith, 'Psychological Operations in the Return to Normality in Bosnia-Herzegovina', *British Army Review* (1996) pp.114, 13-18; T.D. LaBahn, 'Information Operations in Bosnia', *FA Journal* 6 (2001) pp.32-37; Thomas K. Adams, 'Psychological Operations in Bosnia', *Military Review* 6 (1999) pp.29-37; S. Collins, 'Army PSYOP in Bosnia: Capabilities and Constraints', *Parameters* 2 (1999) pp.57-73.

[31] MoD Report, 'Kosovo: Lessons from Crisis' (London: HMSO, June 2001) para 6.33.

[32] Tony Geraghty, *The Irish War: The Hidden Conflict between the IRA and British Intelligence* (Baltimore, MD: Johns Hopkins 2000) pp.154-173.

[33] Tim Butcher, 'SAS kills Serb war crime suspect and grabs another', *Daily Telegraph*, 11 July 1997.

[34] Martin Dillon, *The Dirty War: Covert Strategies and Tactics Used in Political Conflicts* (London: Routledge, 1990) p.425.

[35] G.K. Gramer, Jr., 'Operation Joint Endeavor: Combined-Joint Intelligence in Peace Enforcement Operations', *Military Intelligence*, 4 (1996) pp.11-14.

[36] More on this complex case continues to spill into the public domain, see Ed Moloney, 'Panorama missed the real story of collusion in Ulster', *Daily Telegraph*, 25 June 2002.

[37] Stankovich, *Trusted Mole*, p.251.

[38] MoD Report, 'Kosovo: Lessons from Crisis', paras 6.33, 8.26.

[39] L. Shiner, 'The Air Force's latest remotely operated reconnaissance marvel gets its first real-world test in the skies over Bosnia', *Air And Space Smithsonian* (2001) 16, 1: 48-57.

[40] Wiebes, *Intelligence and the War in Bosnia*.

[41] UK House of Commons, Select Committee On Defence, Examination of Witnesses (Questions 220 - 242), Wednesday 3 February 1999, evidence from Lt General Sir Roderick Cordy-Simpson KBE CB, Director of Operations.

[42] MoD Report, 'Kosovo: Lessons from Crisis' paras 6.33, 8.26.

[43] Christopher Hill and Pamela Beshoff (eds.), *Two Worlds of International Relations: Academics, Practitioners and the Trade in Ideas* (London: Routledge, 1994).

[44] Smith, 'Intelligence and UN Peacekeeping', p.184

[45] Clark, *Waging Modern War*, pp.404-405.

Intelligence, Peacekeeping and Peacemaking in the Middle East

Shlomo Shpiro

The Middle East has been the scene of extensive international peacekeeping and peacemaking efforts for the past five decades. In 1948, the newly created United Nations organisation dispatched its first-ever peacekeeping mission to the Middle East. From the early 1950s and even today, the Middle East has constantly been a key focal point of UN peacekeeping operations, with three different peacekeeping missions operating simultaneously throughout the region. The intricacies of the Arab-Israeli conflict meant that there was an invariable need for impartial observers to monitor cease-fire lines and border transgressions as well as to physically separate between the warring sides. Through its peacekeeping operations in the Middle East, the UN gained respect and trust on both sides of this difficult and bitter conflict.

A discussion of intelligence and peacekeeping in the context of the Middle East is one of a clear contradiction. On the one hand, United Nations peacekeeping forces reject the notion of gathering intelligence, though their very duties are often inherently dependent on collecting information. On the other hand, intelligence services of countries outside the region, commonly associated with military force and conflict, fulfil important functions in regional peacemaking. This chapter focuses on the role of intelligence in peacekeeping and peacemaking efforts in the Middle East, in the years 1948 to 2002. It begins by examining the intelligence aspects of UN peacekeeping forces and UN policy towards intelligence in peacekeeping missions in the Middle East. It then examines the role of national intelligence services in regional peacemaking efforts. The chapter concludes with an analysis of the interaction between intelligence and peacemaking in its Middle Eastern context.

UN Peacekeeping and Intelligence

United Nations peacekeeping efforts in the Middle East have traditionally been aimed at freezing the situation and preventing escalation. However, those efforts have rarely been successful in significantly moderating the overall level of both inter-state and intrastate conflict in the region. UN peacekeeping in the Middle East could be divided into three separate types of activities: observer missions, buffer zones and treaty verification missions.[1] Observer missions are inherently operations aimed at the collection of information. The very essence of observers is, indeed, their ability to identify and collect information on relevant issues. Treaty verification is also dependant on timely information being collected, information that would indicate compliance or transgressions. Although information, or in other words, intelligence, was crucial for the success of many peacekeeping efforts in the Middle East, there is traditionally great reservation among UN forces in this region when discussing the issue of intelligence. Most UN officials would strongly deny that UN peacekeeping operations in the Middle East are engaged or even interested in intelligence. The very term 'intelligence' seemed to carry a negative connotation when applied to UN peacekeeping in this region.

The reason for this rejection of intelligence is connected to the perceived image and activities of intelligence, which are liable to create suspicion and damage goodwill and mutual trust. The UN rejection of intelligence as a legitimate activity in peacekeeping is not limited to the Middle East. The *Peacekeepers Handbook* notes that '... any form of covert intelligence... can damage relations and diminish the trust and confidence that the disputants would wish to have in the (peacekeeping) Force's impartiality.'[2] By engaging in, or even being suspected of, covert intelligence-gathering activities, UN forces could be perceived as assisting one side or the other in the conflict, thus losing their impartial and neutral status. This status of impartiality is an important guarantee not only for political success but also for the physical security of UN troops in the region. With over 250 UN peacekeepers killed in the Middle East, more than in any other region of the world, the first priority for UN commanders in the field is force protection.[3] In such a heavily armed conflict, peacekeeping can only work by consent, and UN forces are dependent on political and public goodwill for their success. Such goodwill could easily be damaged if UN troops are perceived to be engaged in 'spying'.

UN forces stationed throughout the Middle East took great care not to engage in covert intelligence gathering actions or any actions that could be associated with espionage. The debate over peacekeeping and intelligence reached its peak in late 2000, following the kidnapping of three Israeli soldiers by Hizbollah militants while patrolling the Israeli side of the Lebanese-Israeli border. United Nations officers of UNIFIL stationed on a hilltop overlooking the kidnapping site observed, photographed and even filmed part of this event. Information on this observation was, however, withheld from Israel for almost 18 months, despite desperate Israeli efforts to discover the fate of the missing soldiers. Even after the existence of the films was made public, UN officials refused to provide Israel with copies or even allow Israeli officials to view the film, arguing that Israel could conceivably gain intelligence advantage from the film material. Israeli officials were finally allowed to watch the films at UN Headquarters in New York only after some parts were cut out, possibly to prevent recognition of individuals or vehicles. United Nations peacekeeping has a long tradition in the Middle East. It is so ingrained into the fabric of the conflict that even when UN missions become obsolete or lose their effective peacekeeping value, they still remain in place due the fact that no country party to the conflict wishes to be seen as the one rejecting UN efforts in making peace. Thus the mandate of the three main UN missions in the Middle East, UNTSO, UNDOF and UNIFIL, is annually ratified almost automatically by the General Assembly, with little real debate over the political value of their operations. The United Nations Truce Supervision Organisation (UNTSO) was established in June 1948 to assist the work of the UN Mediator in Palestine, Count Folke Bernadotte. However, Jewish extremists assassinated Count Bernadotte shortly afterwards and UNTSO was tasked with supervising the truce between Israel and Jordan and the border dividing Jerusalem. Until 1967, UNTSO observers manned observation posts, conducted patrols along the Israeli-Jordanian border and reported border violations to the UN Secretary-General. For information on treaty transgressions, the observers relied on visual sightings and on close liaison with the Israeli and Jordanian armies. The June 1967 war removed the border from Jerusalem and the 1994 Israeli-Jordanian comprehensive Peace Treaty replaced the old truce agreement, making UNTSO's mission redundant. But the UNTSO operation, now 55 years old, continues to this day. Although it does not fulfil today any practical peacekeeping functions directly relevant to its mandate, some UNTSO personnel have been attached to UNIFIL and UNDOF.[4] Practically though not officially, the 150 observers of UNTSO now form a nucleus for UN peacekeeping training and are often used for missions in other parts of the region and throughout the world.[5]

Some early successes of UN peacekeeping in the Middle East depended on the effective collection of information. For example, the UN mission headed by Ambassador Pier Spinelli, which operated in 1949-1950, was able to use clear evidence collected through monitoring activities that contradicted official propaganda and prevented the escalation of conflict between Israel and Jordan.[6] On another occasion, an aeroplane carrying the Jordanian King was almost shot down by Israeli forces due to a failure to notify the flight plan. The UN mission was able to indicate the error and prevent fresh hostilities. Ambassador Spinelli was later appointed Head of UNYOM, the United Nations force in the Yemen.[7]

The United Nations Disengagement Observation Force (UNDOF) was dispatched to the Golan Heights in June 1974 and is operating there to this day. It is tasked with supervising the cease-fire agreement between Israel and Syria, maintained since the end of the October 1973 war. UNDOF's task is to collect information on Israeli and Syrian force size and dispositions in the Golan Heights area and in adjacent Syrian territory. For this purpose, UNDOF personnel conduct vehicle and foot observation patrols within clearly defined routes in an area extending 25 km on each side of the border, often known as the 'Area of Limitations'. UNDOF officers compile lists of specific types of armaments, including tanks, artillery and armoured personnel carriers and of observed troop movements. These lists form the base for analysis to ensure that both sides do not keep more forces in the Golan than was agreed upon in 1974.

Information collected by UNDOF observations is processed by Military Information Officers (MIOs), a UN euphemism for intelligence officers, who form part of UNDOF's headquarters staff.[8] UNDOF is perhaps unique in UN peacekeeping operations in that its observation work was directly complemented by US intelligence collection. For many years, U-2 aircraft flew weekly reconnaissance missions over the Golan, providing aerial photography evidence on the size of forces maintained by Israel and Syria.[9] The U-2 photos were provided to both sides, further strengthening UNDOF's function of preventing a military surprise attack. UNDOF is generally considered to be very successful at its tasks and the Israeli-Syrian border has been virtually quiet for almost three decades. UNDOF officials argue that their information-gathering operations are not intelligence work but rather open observation,

104

since their visits are announced and their routes well known. But regardless of semantics or terminology, UNDOF is dependant on the collection, analysis and dissemination of information, albeit from open observation, and does so in a way that gained the confidence of both the Israeli and Syrian sides.

The United Nations Interim Force in Lebanon (UNIFIL), stationed in southern Lebanon since 1978, faced completely different tasks and attitudes towards intelligence. UNIFIL has been dispatched to confirm the withdrawal of Israeli forces that invaded Lebanese territory following terror attacks against Israel and to assist the Lebanese Government in restoring peace and security. However, in the stark realities of war torn Lebanon, UNIFIL quickly became a target in itself. In the 1980s, UNIFIL troops operated in some of the most dangerous areas in the world, locations saturated with armed militias, terrorists and constant military operations. Only lightly armed and virtually unable to prevent violence, UNIFIL quickly deteriorated into a force mainly concerned with guarding its own security. UNIFIL personnel could sometimes not even leave their own strongholds without the agreement of some local militia chief or leader, and their movements were also often obstructed by the Israeli or Lebanese military. UNIFIL often failed to prevent terror attacks from being launched through its territory and across the border into Israel. For operational information, UNIFIL depended on the goodwill of the countries in the region, and that goodwill was often very sorely lacking. Since each individual UNIFIL battalion supervised a separate and in some cases partially disconnected section of the border area, little information could be collected by its personnel outside their immediate area of operations. The movement of UNIFIL personnel was often severely restricted and its officers could only collect information they personally saw or heard. On many occasions, UNIFIL positions came under attack from groups unknown to UNIFIL commanders. This lack of an overall intelligence picture severely hampered UNIFIL's operations for many years. In addition to that, the frequent turnover of staff officers in its units, due to the harsh conditions of service in Lebanon, limited UNIFIL's ability to gather effective local knowledge.

The UN experience of peacekeeping in the Middle East has been a mixture of success and stagnation. UNTSO and UNIFIL fulfilled few of the hopes entrusted in them, partially due to the peculiar circumstances of the conflict. UNDOF serves an important function as an impartial collector of military intelligence, or as its officers would argue, of 'peace-related information', used to ensure both Israel and Syria that 'the other side' does not plan any military surprises in the Golan region.[10]

External Intelligence Services and Regional Peacemaking

While the UN openly shuns intelligence in peacekeeping, national intelligence services of are increasingly playing the part of peacemakers in the Middle East. The strategic importance of the Middle East has made it an important arena for intelligence operations since the 19th Century. Competition between the European powers, and later between the US and Soviet Union during the Cold War, over influence in this region meant that decision makers required accurate and timely information on the Middle East. Throughout the 20th Century, this region became a high-priority focal point for the intelligence services of many countries. While intelligence collection was the primary task for those services, some western intelligence services developed a long history of serving as channels for covert diplomacy in the Middle East, trying to bridge between enemies while providing contacts insulated from adverse publicity and media attention. These services have also made significant contributions to peacekeeping and peacemaking efforts in the region.

In November 1936, King Abdullah of Jordan, great-grandfather of the current King Abdullah, secretly met with Moshe Sharet, later to become Israel's Prime-Minister, to discuss security cooperation. 'My situation is always difficult, and you Jews must remember this,' said the King, referring to the grave personal risk undertaken by moderate Arab leaders who choose to have contacts with Israel.[11] Fifteen years later, King Abdullah was assassinated in East Jerusalem by extremists who rejected his contacts with Israeli leaders. The need for secrecy became a paramount element in future contacts between Israel and Arab leaders, many of whom were to pay with their lives for their wish for peace.

The need for covert channels of communications became apparent as Israeli Prime Minister David Ben-Gurion organised Israel's intelligence community in the early 1950s. Israeli Mossad was established not only to collect information on Israel's enemies but also to serve as a secret channel of relations with countries that had no diplomatic relations with Israel. The Mossad was often called Israel's 'second foreign ministry' and its heads were responsible for initiating contacts with moderate Islamic countries including Turkey, Sudan and Iran. These relations culminated in the formation of a secret intelligence alliance, known as Trident, which brought together the four countries into close security co-operation.[12] Unlike conventional foreign ministries, intelligence services could ensure total secrecy for high-level meetings and political negotiations, decreasing the risk of adverse media publicity as well as ensuring the personal safety of the participants. Information collected by the Mossad often served to enhance covert relations with Arab leaders. One such opportunity came in July 1958, when Mossad agents received information on an Egyptian plot to assassinate the Jordanian King Hussein. The information was passed to King Hussein via the British government and the Jordanian security service was able to thwart the planned coup.[13] This was the beginning of over thirty years of close but secret relations between the Mossad and the Jordanian monarch. Hussein met the heads of the Mossad and developed with them security co-operation against the PLO, which by the mid 1960s was becoming a serious threat to the stability of Jordan. The relationship between King Hussain and the heads of the Mossad became a focal point for Jordanian-Israeli relations until both countries signed a comprehensive peace treaty in 1994.

The strategic surprise of the October 1973 war and the high cost of the war made Israeli leaders reconsider the role and structure of their intelligence community. In September 1977, the Mossad played a key role in paving the way for Egyptian President Anwar Sadat's historic visit to Jerusalem. Israeli Prime Minister Menahem Begin signalled to Egypt his willingness for territorial concessions in return for peace through a plethora of secret channels including the US, Rumania, India, Iran and Morocco. President Sadat, being aware of the personal and political risk involved in negotiations with Israel, was reluctant to rely on mediators and sought direct contacts with senior Israeli officials. The Mossad smuggled Israeli Foreign Minister Moshe Dayan to a secret meeting in Morocco with Egyptian Deputy Prime Minister Hassan Tohami. With the help of western intelligence services, the Mossad has closely monitored Egypt's policy change towards peace. The Dayan-Tohami meetings opened the way for Sadat's landmark visit to Israel two months later, leading the way to the Israeli-Egyptian Camp David peace accords.[14]

Throughout the late 1970s and the 1980s, the Mossad and Israeli Military Intelligence (AMAN) played an increasing part in the relations between Israel

107

and the Christian population in Lebanon. Following Israel's 1982 invasion of southern Lebanon, the Mossad established a station in Beirut and played a key role in Israel's attempts to achieve a peace agreement with Lebanon.[15] Although such an agreement was drafted, the assassination of Lebanese President Bashir Jumayel had put an end to hopes of peace in Israel's northern border. Israeli military presence in southern Lebanon continued until summer 2000.

The 1993 Oslo Accords profoundly changed the political map in the Middle East. In 1994, the Palestinian Authority received control of large urban areas in the West Bank and the Gaza Strip. Many Western intelligence services began assisting the Palestinians in establishing their security apparatus, made up of eight different services. The CIA led the way by establishing special training programs for Palestinian security officers. It also provided the nascent Palestinian intelligence services with sophisticated espionage equipment for monitoring communications and observation. The principal policy element guiding western intelligence support to the Palestinian Authority was that only an effective Palestinian effort could eliminate the threat of terrorism, a threat that could derail the entire peace process. By providing training, equipment and funds, the CIA and its European counterparts hoped to create an effective Palestinian force that would fight terrorism.[16] However, the CIA ignored the fact that many of the officers of the newly created Palestinian security services were former terrorists from PLO camps in Tunisia and Yemen. Many of those had no intention to combat terrorism and used the skills and equipment gained from western services to mount attacks against Israeli targets.

Israeli-Palestinian security co-operation, one of the key elements of the Oslo Accords, continued until late 1996. This co-operation was effective in neutralising many terror threats in the region. However, violent clashes between Israeli and Palestinian forces, which erupted in September 1996, signalled the end of this short era of close co-operation. As increasing terror attacks engulfed the region with blood, Israeli and Palestinian security officials became more dependent on the intercession of foreign intelligence officers in trying to break the political deadlock. The CIA station in Tel-Aviv became the focus of US peacemaking efforts in the region as CIA officials attempted to broker co-operation and encourage the Palestinian Authority to combat terrorism within its territory. The rapid deterioration in Israeli-Palestinian relations, which followed the October 2000 outbreak of the 'Intifada', made any official

108

contacts between the two sides almost impossible. Attempts by numerous international actors, including the US administration, the European Union and European governments to broker an agreement that would end the violence failed repeatedly. The intensity of terrorism and violence in the region, which in the years 2000-2003 cost the lives of over 2000 Palestinians and Israelis, made any attempt at open diplomatic mediation efforts futile because of strong public rejection both in Israel and in the Palestinian Authority to any form of direct negotiations.

In the absence of direct talks between the two sides and the failure of international mediation efforts, the intelligence services of third countries became the only effective channel of contacts between Israel and the Palestinian Authority. By March 2002, the level of terror attacks in Israel has reached its peak, with suicide bombings at urban centres being carried out on a daily basis. Following the assassination of Israeli Tourism Minister Rehavam Zeevi by terrorists, the Israeli army launched operation 'Defensive Shield', a wide sweep throughout the Palestinian areas and the arrest of hundreds of militants. Israeli troops laid siege to Yassir Arafat's Headquarters at the 'Mukataa' in Ramallah, where Zeevi's killers were hiding. The Israeli army also surrounded the Church of the Nativity in Bethlehem, one of Christianity's holiest shrines, where over 200 militants took refuge as Israeli tanks stormed the town.

The situation at Arafat's Headquarters and the Church of the Nativity created a crisis of international proportions. A military attack into the Mukataa would have signaled the end of the Palestinian Authority as a viable political entity, while any damage to the Church of the Nativity could have aroused grave misgivings throughout the Christian world. Mediation attempts by the Vatican and by prominent world leaders for solving the stalemate failed, as Israel was determined that Zeevi's killers could not be allowed to go unpunished. The task of negotiating this delicate issue was submitted to the CIA and to intelligence officials representing the European Union, who still enjoyed the trust of both sides.

In order to break the deadlock between the two sides, western intelligence services formulated creative solutions designed to address the core problem issues without resorting to wide political concessions from any side. The resulting agreement over Arafat's Headquarters, hammered out over weeks of

109

tense negotiations, called for the imprisonment of Zeevi's assassins, who were convicted by a hastily convened Palestinian court martial, in a special jail in Jericho guarded by British and US officers. This unique solution enabled Israel to believe that the assassins would be punished while not forcing the Palestinians to hand over prisoners to the Israeli justice system. CIA agents transferred the convicted terrorists to Jericho, where they remain in prison, and Israeli troops left Arafat's headquarters.[17] As of early 2003, the six Palestinians are still imprisoned in Jericho, guarded by British prison officers.

The siege of the Church of the Nativity, which lasted almost a month, was ended by a solution that called for the exile of 13 men suspected by Israel of being responsible for numerous terror attacks.[18] A British military aircraft took the thirteen men to Cyprus, and they were later dispatched to different European countries that agreed to offer them temporary residence. The success of western intelligence officials at Arafat's Headquarters and in Bethlehem hinged on their ability to propose constructive, though unconventional, solutions that aimed to defuse the immediate cause of the problem. By disconnecting the immediate problem of terrorism from its overall political context, the mediating intelligence officers could defuse potential flashpoints and provide both sides with face-saving solutions. The Mukataa and Bethlehem sieges demonstrated the usefulness of intelligence mediation in solving sensitive and potentially explosive local security problems that could have severe regional repercussions.

The intelligence services of Egypt and Jordan also joined peacemaking efforts to calm the situation in the Palestinian areas. In summer 2002, Egyptian President Hosni Mubarak dispatched his head of intelligence, General Omar Suleiman, on several mediation missions to Israel. The Egyptian plan, known as the 'Pilot Plan', called for Israeli military restrictions to be lifted in specific areas in Gaza, which would then be policed by Palestinian forces.[19] Once the Palestinian Authority could prove its ability to dam terrorism in those areas, Israeli restrictions could safely be lifted over wider areas. The Egyptian intelligence services enjoy significant influence in the Gaza Strip and General Suleiman, perceived by many as President Mubarak's designated successor, exerted effective pressure on the Palestinian leadership in Gaza to moderate, if not eliminate, suicide terror attacks. The efforts of Egyptian intelligence were complemented by assistance from their Jordanian counterparts, who traditionally enjoyed considerable influence in the West Bank. An unofficial division of labour evolved, whereby the Egyptian intelligence services negotiate in Gaza and the Jordanians in the West Bank.[20] These contacts proved useful for maintaining the dynamics of at least a minimal core of Israeli-Palestinian intelligence dialogue.

Conclusions – Intelligence and Middle East Regional Stability

Intelligence activities have played an important role in numerous peacekeeping and peacemaking efforts in the Middle East over the past five decades. Many of the UN operations in this region depended on collecting and disseminating information of a military nature, intelligence in all but name. National intelligence services acted as covert go-betweens and mediators, undertaking secret and often highly sensitive diplomacy missions aimed at peace and stability.

Within the context of UN peacekeeping operations in the region, the role of intelligence was best demonstrated in the UNDOF experience. Effective UNDOF monitoring has significantly contributed to the Golan border being the quietest border in the Middle East for many years. Through reliable UNDOF information collection, complemented by US intelligence activities, both sides in the Golan border could be sure that the other was not planning a surprise attack, similar to that of October 1973. UNTSO and UNIFIL operations also benefited, albeit on a smaller scale, from information collecting activities. While it could be argued that none of the three UN missions achieved its designated tasks of peace, they have contributed at different times to regional stability.

The role of intelligence in regional peacemaking efforts took an expanded turn after the outbreak of large-scale violence in October 2000. In the absence of domestic legitimacy for direct Israeli-Palestinian negotiations, the covert contacts brokered by western intelligence services between Israeli and Palestinian security officials were aimed at four issues: exploring the possibilities for a wide political deal between Israel and the Palestinian Authority; finding solutions for immediate local security problems and crises; examining potential areas for security co-operation; and forming a wider understanding of the views and needs of the other side. The real importance of the intelligence contacts, however, lay in keeping open one last channel of

111

communication between Israel and the Palestinian Authority, one which functioned even under the enormous strain of daily terror attacks and Israeli military activities. The intensity of the conflict and the geographically interwoven landscape meant that a total breakdown of contacts could quickly escalate into a deeper crisis, possibly prompting a total Israeli take-over of the West Bank and the dissolution of the Palestinian authority as a functioning political entity. As long as some form of contact still existed, immediate flashpoints could be addressed, decreasing the risk of a general escalation.

In a Middle East torn by terrorism and political violence, intelligence services currently perform the role of peacemakers since they are the only actors that still enjoy the confidence of both sides of the bitter Palestinian-Israeli conflict. Although these services pay a price for their peacemaking involvement, mainly through their public exposure and decreased ability to covertly collect information, they fulfil an essential function for enhancing stability in the Middle East. While the activities of UN peacekeeping missions in the region are increasingly marginalised, covert peacemaking efforts conducted through intelligence services have turned into an effective tool of foreign policy for enhancing regional stability. As such, intelligence activities will continue to play a key role in regional peacemaking in the Middle East in the years to come.

Endnotes

---

[1] For the development of UN peacekeeping policy see Marrack Goulding, 'The Evolution of United Nations Peacekeeping', *International Affairs* 3 (1993).
[2] *Peacekeepers Handbook*, (New York: International Peace Academy, Pergamon 1984) p.39.
[3] In the years 1948-1990, UNTSO had 28 fatalities, UNDOF 24 and UNIFIL 170. See *The Blue Helmets* (New York: United Nations Department of Public Information 1990) pp.419-427. UNIFIL fatalities since 1990 have been estimated to be about 40-50.
[4] *Watching from the Heights*, Report by New Zealand naval officer and UNTSO observer Lt. Commander Pete Waa, October 2002, http://www.navy.mil.nz (accessed in January 2003).

[5] Author's interviews with UNRWA officials in Vienna.

[6] *Peacekeepers handbook*, p.337.

[7] *Canada and Peacekeeping Operations – Yemen UNYOM: Report No. 13*, (Canadian Forces Headquarters: Directory of History December 1966) p.26.

[8] *Watching from the Heights.*

[9] *Near East Report*, (Washington DC: AIPAC 7 February 2000).

[10] For UN assessment on how peacekeeping in the region could be improved see *Improving the Capacity of the United Nations for Peacekeeping*, (Report of the Secretary-General, UN Document A/48/403 14th March 1994).

[11] See Y. Melman and D. Raviv, *A Hostile Partnership: The Secret Relations Between Israel and Jordan* (Meitam: Tel-Aviv 1987) pp.28-37.

[12] See Shlomo Shpiro, *European-Mediterranean Intelligence Cooperation: A Hidden Element in Regional Security* (RIEAS: Athens 1995).

[13] Melman and Raviv, *A Hostile Partnership*, p.49.

[14] See Y. Bar-Siman-Tov, *Israel and the Peace Process 1977-1982*, (New York: SUNY Press 1994).

[15] See Z. Schiff and E. Yaari, *Traitorous War*, (Tel-Aviv: Schoken 1984).

[16] See Shlomo Shpiro, 'Stabilität im Nahen Osten? Der Beitrag der Geheimdienste zur Konfliktpraevention', *Internationale Politik*, 12 (2002) pp.39-44.

[17] See A. Hess, 'At the End of Intensive Negotiations, Six Palestinians Leave for Jericho Prison', *Haaretz*, 2 May 2002.

[18] See A. Ziegelman, 'Negotiation Team Comprised of IDF, Shabak and CIA Officials', *Haaretz*, 22 April 2002.

[19] For General Suleiman's missions see D. Bahor, 'Omar Suleiman Will Come Again to Israel', *Yediot Aharonot*, 16 July 2002, also 'Egyptian Spy Chief on Mid-East Mission', *BBC World News*, 7 July 2002.

[20] For Jordanian intelligence and Palestinian terrorism see Z. Barel, 'Hamas Activity Has Not Been Blocked', *Haaretz*, 1 September 1999.

113

114

The Second Iraq Intervention 2002-2003

Richard Connaughton

A Rationale for War

Military Intervention lies two clicks beyond peacekeeping in a spectrum of military activity wherein the intensity of operations ebbs and flows along the length of the spectrum. If there is to be armed conflict in Iraq in which the United States performs the task of the framework state, then it will begin by resembling a full-blown UN Chapter VII enforcement operation and only after a period of time might we see peacekeeping emerge as part of the post-conflict arrangements. The nature of the intelligence task also changes to reflect the decline in intensity of the original military operation. We have seen for example in peacekeeping operations in Kosovo, Sierra Leone and Afghanistan how military intelligence has become involved in countering organised crime.

If we wish to examine how the United States functions in the collective security environment then that environment is increasingly likely to be one of military intervention rather than what is properly understood as 'peacekeeping'[1] duties. The American military are not natural peacekeepers: the use of lethal force only in self-defence runs contrary to the nation's culture. And this is a nation whose leaders have a perception of peacekeeping as an activity unworthy of the world's sole superpower. This is not a new concept since in the early years the armed forces of the Permanent Five Members of the Security Council were not engaged on UN Peacekeeping operations.

Cartoon by Plantu
Le Monde, 1991

The study of what might be the lead-up to a 'coalition of the willing's' military operations against Iraq is complicated by a tension which exists between a war on terrorism, specifically the al-Qa'eda faction and its global franchises, and Iraq. The catalyst was the shock arising from the 11 September 2001 attack on New York and Washington but examined objectively, there is an undeniable credibility gap between the grotesque activities of knife-wielding al-Qa'eda hijackers and Iraq and her weapons of mass destruction (WMD).

We have a curate's egg of an intelligence picture, good in parts, but where it is not good is in making the essential linkage between the doctrinally opposed al-Qa'eda faction and Iraq. We heard Secretary of State Powell's testimony before the Senate how 'we saw the telephone exchange light up in Baghdad'. This is emblematic of the use of intelligence for political or diplomatic negotiations prior to military action. Moreover it was a ploy in depth. The CIA released satellite photographs of the al-Salim palace in Baghdad and the Department of Defense showed videos from Southern Watch aircraft of mobile surface-to-air missiles, all designed to put pressure on Saddam Hussein.

Equally, enormous pressure had been placed upon the CIA and MI6 to identify an association between al-Qa'eda and Iraq. Dissatisfied with the CIA's performance, Secretary of Defense Rumsfeld has established a competing unit within the Pentagon, attracting the accusation that he was 'trying to politicise intelligence information to suit his hardline agenda'.

The original October 2001 report which linked Mohammed Atta, the hijack leader, to a meeting with an Iraqi intelligence officer in Prague was of profound importance in justifying the taking of military action against Iraq. But no such meeting took place; a fact confirmed by President Vaclav Havel of the Czech Republic. There have been subsequent reports of clandestine meetings in Baghdad but no evidence has been forthcoming, allegedly in order to protect sources. Despite the allocation of resources specifically designed to find the evidence, Secretary of Defense Rumsfeld has said that it does not matter that there is no evidence to link Saddam Hussein to the hijackers. That much is evident from an October 2002 poll which revealed that 63 per cent of Americans believed Saddam Hussein to have been implicated in the attacks upon New York and Washington.

There is a momentum at large which will not be still until New York's agony is reprised in Baghdad. The risk-taking and decision-making processes should involve careful consideration whether the consequences of the removal or attempted removal of Saddam Hussein do not outweigh the significant, negative points which accrue from the taking of military action. We have here a *where you stand is where you sit* scenario with the American Way and Manifest Destiny on the one hand and the majority voice of world opinion on the other. The reason Prime Minister Blair's position in support of the USA is ambiguous is because he is pursuing the foreign policy of a foreign power whose interests and national psychology are at odds with the British Way. What many observers outside the USA see, rightly or wrongly, is the gathering of forces to exact revenge, to take up unfinished business and to deal finally with an individual who had the effrontery to challenge the might of the superpower. Part of the American rationale for confronting Saddam Hussein is as a deterrent, *pour encourager les autres*. There is the prospect that pursuing this course of action might precipitate the very response which America's moves against Iraq are designed to prevent.

If we go back 40 years to the 1962 Cuban Missile crisis and President J.F. Kennedy's Democrat Administration, it is possible to observe similar responses to that threat to America's security and national sovereignty. America's reaction to the developing Soviet threat on her doorstep is redolent of the culture and traditions which are peculiarly American. Among the observations to be drawn from that experience is the one that military intervention need not develop into a shooting war but more importantly, there are two particular

117

indicators which relate to international law and the use of force which reveal that American thinking has not changed in 40 years. What Dean Acheson said at the time could equally have been said today by hardliners in the Bush Administration. 'The power, position and prestige of the United States has been challenged by another state, and law simply does not deal with such questions of ultimate power, power that comes close to the source of sovereignty.' The message was, and still remains, initiatives which challenge American power will be dealt with.

Despite the enormity of the risk at the time, America's friends had confidence in the Kennedy Administration and evidence of the threat posed by Soviet intermediate ballistic missiles was proven through photographic images from reconnaissance flights. This intelligence succeeded in buttressing the resolve of allies as surely as it showed Moscow that they had been caught red-handed. No pun intended. Again, this evidence proved irrefutable and was a sound basis for taking a strong diplomatic position which insisted the Soviets withdraw or face the military consequences. The lesson relevant to us to emerge from the Cuban missile crisis was the importance of revealing to a potential 'coalition of the willing' the existence of a threat through incontrovertible evidence and intelligence. The use of intelligence in this case to justify the military threat of action succeeded, which was not the case when the same formula was employed by Prime Minister Blair in September 2002.

The British have a different culture, tradition and geography from the Americans (and the Continental Europeans) and therefore it is unsurprising that the latter's case for invading Iraq would not be embraced automatically by the public of the former. Facing up to this political challenge, Prime Minister Blair reassured the unconvinced British public that he had evidence of the threat Saddam Hussein posed to global security. It is a sign of the times that the common people do want to be convinced that a leader's decision to go to war is justified and it seems that the day has almost passed when a leader can take his country to war without the express authority of Parliament. Some time would elapse before Mr Blair released his Dossier of evidence.

The Dossier, dismissed by Mr Putin as 'propaganda' did not live up to its promise of pinpointing the 'unique' threat, that is capabilities and intentions, posed by Saddam Hussein. The fact that it was only released by a government adept at news management three hours before it was presented in parliament

118

suggests that the Blair government had little confidence in something intended to reveal a *casus belli* for an attack on Iraq. Politically it was an error of judgement because the Dossier assembled by the UK's Joint Intelligence Committee (JIC) did not come close to identifying a real and immediate threat to justify the use of force against Iraq. More persuasive evidence may be available but fear of prejudicing sources could mean that it is being held back for a future occasion.

The Dossier provided details of plans to conceal WMD and of the availability of medium-range missile systems on short response times. The point is made in the Dossier that the possession of WMD is central to the maintenance and preservation of Saddam Hussein's power base. Space is also given to allegations of grotesquely inhumane treatment of his own people.

There are 3 facts which arise from the analyses of Mr Blair's data, none of which reveals Iraq to be a current threat to other sovereign states:

1. A man whose assassination has been publicly encouraged in Washington will, if forced into a corner, use WMD. George Tenet, head of the CIA, reported to Congress that military action could provoke Saddam Hussein into unleashing a chemical or biological attack on the USA but short of such provocation, no attack seemed imminent.

2. Under a different mindset, the use of WMD could be deterred as it was in 1991. There is no evidence to show that there has been any intention to use force against other states since 1991. Militarily, containment appears to be working.

3. Thompson says of his second principle: 'there is a very strong temptation in dealing both with terrorism and with guerrilla actions for government forces to act outside the law'.[2] This observation is equally as true of peacekeeping as it is of intervention, which will invariably have been necessitated due to a breach of international law. For the interventionist forces to break that same law leaves them open to the charge of *tu quoque* and the forfeit of any right to lay claim to the moral high ground.

119

Prime Minister Blair has declared that the UK will act within the law in her confrontation with Iraq. But, in the final analysis, the authority to embark upon armed conflict is essentially within the collective gift of the Permanent Five members of the Security Council whose initial conduct is not one of Wilsonian *noblesse* but mirrors precisely their own national interest. President Bush has declared his intention of taking the UN Security Council route but, had this debate not coincided with the mid-term Congressional elections and a poll revealing 63 per cent of Americans wishing to take the UN route, then his response might arguably have been different. The United States is committed to regime change and this presumably means that if Russia and France obstruct America's wishes in the Security Council she will demonstrate her sovereignty, act unilaterally and operate outside the law. Mr Bush's understanding of regime change has subsequently been modified so that Iraqi compliance can also be understood to mean that the regime has changed.

The United States' unilateral adoption of the 'Bush Doctrine' of pre-emptive self-defence bends the meaning of UN Article 51, self-defence, to a point that it breaks. International law is *international* and it is undesirable for example that such a device is available to be used by such states as Iraq to justify an attack on Israel or India and Pakistan upon each other. The White House appears to have no respect for that international law which threatens her national sovereignty. In an example of which the colloquialism is 'lawfare' Washington has refused to allow her servicemen to face prosecution at the International Court of Justice. If the United States succeeds in picking and choosing those parts of international law which she finds convenient, the law will be held in contempt and terrorism and lawlessness will be used elsewhere as means of achieving national aims. A display of contempt for international law can only work to the advantage of the anonymous forces ranged against the USA. Nothing can be more guaranteed to swell the ranks of Muslim extremism than international law being set aside to effect a predetermined intention to attack Iraq. This legal preamble leads into the key intelligence point that an attack upon Iraq will severely inhibit access to essential intelligence from moderate Muslim sources which is vital if threats posed by Muslim extremists are to be countered.

Congress has given President Bush a national authority to 'use the armed forces of the United States as he determines necessary and appropriate…against the threat posed by Iraq'. The wide margin of approval was due to the capitulation

120

of Democrats fearful for their re-election prospects at the mid-term at a time when the American public showed themselves to be pro-war. Meanwhile, efforts to draft a suitable UN resolution ran into difficulty. The euphemism for the use of enforcement measures, 'all necessary means', was conceded by USA/UK in favour of the threat of 'serious consequences' if Iraq failed to comply with the new resolution. These subtle changes in phraseology are important. The responsibility for ensuring that Iraq complied with the letter of Resolution 1441 rested with the Chairman of the United Nations Monitoring, Verification and Inspection Commission (UNMOVIC), Hans Blix. UNMOVIC's predecessor, the United Nations Special Commission (UNSCOM) was withdrawn from Iraq in 1998. A high proportion of CIA operatives formed part of the inspection team. Since the UN has no intelligence means, it has been customary, even for the EU, for monitoring teams to include intelligence personnel with access to national intelligence means. It would be difficult for the ostensibly neutral Mr Blix to locate and destroy Saddam Hussein's WMD without the active support of the CIA. In his seminal work on the intelligence situation in Bosnia with particular reference to Srebrenica, Cees Wiebes draws attention to the poverty of intelligence available to UNPROFOR. This is not a factor which will arise in a confrontation with Iraq which is perceived to be a vital US interest.

Russia and France persisted in objecting to the USA/UK draft and methodology, thus threatening the ability of the USA to use the winter 2002/spring 2003 window of opportunity before the summer heat conspired to make the wearing of nuclear, biological and chemical (NBC) protective dress impossible. Iraq has until 8 December to provide the Security Council with a full, accurate and complete declaration of its holdings of WMD, something which Saddam Hussein has insisted he does not have. The plan was to resume inspections within 45 days of the resolution being agreed and for Hans Blix to have an optimistically short period of 2 months in which to submit his report. That would take the submission of the Blix report to the Security Council to February 2003, too late to launch what most military observers believe will be a protracted, difficult operation. Conspiracy theorists envisage Saddam Hussein scrupulously avoiding giving any pretext to Hans Blix to blow the whistle to set in train a suspected *démarche* towards a Rambouillet-style *dénouement*.

It will be recalled that at Rambouillet, Serbia was presented with ultimata and conditions which no elected representative of a sovereign state could accept.

121

As Henry Kissinger conceded, 'the Rambouillet text…was a provocation, an excuse to start bombing'. The question is, are there not triggers within the Iraq weapons inspection programme so designed to justify armed conflict? The answer is clouded in uncertainty not least because it has proved impossible to discover what comprises a breach of the resolution.

It was no mean diplomatic achievement for the UN to pass Resolution 1441 unanimously. A combination of reasons would suggest that it is possible the Powellites will have their way over Rumsfeld's hawks. For example, Saddam Hussein's hunger for power is equally as strong as Milosevic's. If forfeiting WMD means that he can remain in power, it seems that this is something he would be prepared to do. There will be humiliation and he will become more vulnerable to a palace coup but compliance with the UN weapons inspectors is the best of what for him are two bad choices. In the United States, senior politicians and generals remain casualty averse, so much so that the non-conflict scenario may appear positively attractive. The benefits to the west in taking the non-conflict route are substantial. Not only will Iraq's WMD stocks be neutralised but steps can be taken to draw the sting of international terrorists insofar as sanctions against Iraq can be brought to a conclusion and US forces can be withdrawn from Saudi Arabia.

The central problem is what happens hereon in Iraq is subject to the whims of American domestic policy. President Bush used the events of 11 September and confrontation with Iraq as rally events to secure political advantage in the mid-term elections and strengthened his position in Congress. His political strategists will now be concentrating upon the re-election of the President in 2004 and what happens now in Iraq will have that requirement to the forefront of Republican planners' minds.

As we will show, the armed conflict option is so fraught with danger as to beg the question whether the United States can persist in attacks, which will involve damage to civilian property and the deaths of non-combatants, long enough to win. Before that however there will remain one significant hurdle to be overcome.

Despite Saddam Hussein's denials, he obviously does have stocks of chemical and biological weapons. Moreover, western intelligence sources know the locations of some but not all the weaponry. The first pressure on the trigger will

122

be Saddam Hussein's acknowledgement that he has WMD. The second pressure on that trigger will arise if there is any mismatch found in the locations of stocks as declared by Saddam Hussein compared to that which is already known by the intelligence services. This could be one of a number of events deemed to be non-compliance for which the UN Security Council would be reconvened. This is where the hurdle lies, for the USA and UK will argue that a new resolution is not required to authorise an attack on Iraq whereas France, Russia and China are likely to insist that is not the case. Resolution 1441 is not an 'all necessary means' resolution and therefore, arguably, France, Russia and China are correct. If the USA moves against Iraq without proper UN authority, this will represent a clear breach of international law. The use of Kuwait as the launch pad for the major thrust into Iraq is conditional upon such an attack being authorised by the UN.

Concurrently with moves to link action against Iraq to some form of UN fig leaf came a revelation which dissolved the logic of Washington's stern position against Iraq. The CIA has known for the best part of two years that North Korea, which like Iraq and Iran is an 'axis of evil' state, had reneged on a 1994 agreement with the USA and had developed its own nuclear weapons programme. Intelligence reported that North Korea had at least one, possibly two nuclear weapons. Iraq has none. The intelligence report revealing North Korea's nuclear weapons program was submitted to Pyongyang on 3 October 2002 and confirmed as correct by the North Koreans the next day. Washington suppressed this information for a fortnight until after Congress had been persuaded to give the President the authority to attack Iraq.

The focus upon Iraq has become a dangerous distraction from the main issue. The rapid succession of terrorist attacks against western targets from al-Qa'eda worldwide is evidence that it is not rogue states at play here but a co-operative of often middle-class, stateless terrorists stirred by grudges and causes. It may be that a global view taken from within the Beltway can argue that the Iraq and North Korean situations are different. But for many who see the world from a different perspective, the Washington position appears as a double standard founded upon a dangerous policy that could be argued as being anti-Muslim, pro-oil and dedicated to the support of Israel. A US Gallup poll taken in April 2002 showed that Republicans favoured Israel over the Palestinians by 67 per cent to 8 per cent and Democrats by a margin of 45 per cent to 21 per cent. It seems that unless a more equitable solution is formulated to deal with problems

123

posed by hostile sovereign states, Washington and her coalition partners will continue to stoke the fires of assured, terrorist-inspired, long-term retribution.
The outcome of an attack upon Iraq could fall a number of ways. It could be a case of capitulation but many observers have a sense of foreboding that urban conflict will involve substantial combat and non-combatant casualties. The Iraqis are a proud people who have endured 12 years of deprivation through UN sanctions and who are unlikely to regard an assault by the sponsor of arch-enemy Israel in terms other than hostile.   Saddam Hussein is not a beloved leader and his overthrow would be well nigh universally welcomed. What this putative operation must not do is immortalise Saddam Hussein as a new Saladin or Che Guevara. The balance of analysis is that operations against Iraq would be a war of choice not of necessity. There are other, more urgent priorities.

A strategy aimed at confronting the threat posed by stateless terrorism must contain measures which deny the terrorist his oxygen, to deprive him of his causes, thus isolating those who indulge in political violence from the moderate mainstream. Sequentially, a move against Iraq should not precede addressing the political solution to the causes of the Israel-Palestine crisis within a regional strategy. It may be that the Arabs' sense of humiliation for the way in which they see their brother Palestinians being treated has not registered in a Washington subject to the tyranny of the ballot box. Nevertheless, it is essential to bring moderate Arab opinion on-side and this will not be achieved by attacking Iraq, which a majority in the west and Middle East do not see as being the first priority. General Anthony Zinni, formerly the US envoy to the Middle East, expressed his view that the USA should only focus upon the five most important threats to her national interest. He rated Iraq as the seventh greatest threat to US interests. As King Abdullah of Jordan said: 'in the light of the failure to move the Israeli-Palestinian process forward, military action against Iraq would really open a Pandora's Box'. Whereas there is powerful intelligence to point to al-Qa'eda as a significant present threat to international peace and security, there is no corresponding intelligence to indicate Iraq is an immediate threat. The Bali attack should have been taken as an opportunity for reappraisal. The requirement is not therefore an ill-conceived military intervention followed by post-conflict peacekeeping but a strategy to deal with the causes which drive terrorists to adopt political violence as a means to an end.

Concurrently, the preparations for armed conflict have begun. There have been US/UK attacks on Iraqi air defence facilities and the movement of American ground forces into the region continues. As many as 60,000 American troops may already be in theatre and the call-up of reservists continues. The parading of the hardware of *capability* is being matched by presence to emphasise an *intention* aimed either at persuading the Iraqis to comply with the inspections or, if that fails, for the launching of an invasion. The movement of British ground formations has not yet begun and may not do so unless Mr Blair is either convinced he has the legal authority or is prepared to fudge the issue. As the USA demonstrated in Afghanistan, other than Special Forces she is content to operate with the support of a political coalition. Technologically, Europe's armed forces have fallen so far behind the American standard as to be not interoperable. That observation includes the UK which plans to make available an armoured division to support four American divisions. Three months will be required from embarkation to readiness. The USA criticised British formations in Kosovo, and Exercise Saif Sareea held in Oman in November 2001 highlighted problems with British equipment. The USA could therefore go ahead without British ground support. There must be an element of surprise somewhere within the Pentagon's plans.

Next Moves

If there should be a hidden agenda set upon invading Iraq come what may, then the importance of the consideration of the next moves up to and including the exit strategy becomes self-evident. The debate has been focused upon the justification or otherwise of an attack on Iraq, the supposition being that once the green light has been given, the result will be a foregone conclusion. That is far from certain. It has been a revelation to hear so many pressing for war yet not having the first idea of what is involved. The weakening of Saddam Hussein's military position since 1991 leaves him in no position to attempt manoeuvre warfare. If he is to have any prospect of minimizing the USA's qualitative superiority in men and machines he will have to select Iraq's urban areas as his battlefield. Asymmetric conflict sees the weaker party drawing upon psychological factors to outwit the stronger. The full range of asymmetric possibilities and responses available to a targeted state and its sympathisers has so far not been revealed to its fullest extent. If Iraq controlled the terrorist groups, it would be possible in due course to come to a state-to-state agreement to cease whatever form hostilities had taken. But since the initiative would be in

125

the hands of dispersed, non-state actors it is a very difficult proposition to bring the perceived attacks on homeland USA and her interests worldwide to a conclusion. There is not a central authority with which to negotiate. The expansion of terrorist cells worldwide must be nipped in the bud.

The negative factors to be weighed against marginal benefits can be usefully examined under the controlling criteria for military intervention, low risk, low cost, short duration. The *risks* involved in invading Iraq are high, not low. The level of attacks on the USA and the west and their interests will intensify. That much was predictable before the attack in Bali, another intelligence failure. If Iraq is 'liberated' there is a strong possibility she will break up in the same way as Yugoslavia. Iran will allow exiled Iraqi Shi'ites of the Badr Brigade to return to Iraq to help achieve the overthrow of Saddam Hussein. Shia's, with or without the assistance of the Iran-based Supreme Council for the Islamic Revolution in Iraq, might attack the minority Sunni's. It is possible that the Kurds in the north could seize the opportunity to join with their kin in Iran and Turkey to declare a new state of Kurdistan, anathema and unacceptable to Turkey. Measures have been proposed to prevent the implosion of Iraq. Democracy is viewed as a positive measure on the alleged grounds that democracies do not go to war, but the liberal western model of democracy is not appropriate for a state which, like Afghanistan, has one tribe predominantly more numerous than any other. However, Bahrain held the region's first fully democratic election in October 2002, but with an Islamist majority. A solution to circumvent the division that exists among Iraqi opposition parties is to appoint a US General as proconsul to rule Iraq after liberation. This initiative would be misunderstood as a form of imperialism. General Douglas MacArthur's mission in Japan had little by way of similarity but the idea of a US proconsul is probably an example of psychological operations, – an attempt to increase pressure on the Iraqi opposition to launch a palace coup, the implication being, 'you sort out the problem or we shall run the country'.

However, when in 1945 a casualty-averse General MacArthur, the future proconsul for Japan, returned to liberate Manila, 100,000 non-combatant Manileños died in the ruins of their city – up to 40,000 dying due to firepower being used in preference to infantry to clear streets and buildings.

No American General will relish fighting through Baghdad or other *Saddamgrads* where water and power may be cut off to force capitulation.

Presentationally this will be no Grozny because it will be subject to full international media scrutiny. Public opinion brought the Vietnam war to an end, and the public's casualty-aversion played a central role in 1991 in the decision that coalition forces would not follow-on into Baghdad. The west's public were equally as averse to needless Iraqi casualties as they were to their own. The combined effects of the destruction of private property and the killing of non-combatants are certain to erode any domestic or international support for continuing a war against Iraq. No matter how good the quality of intelligence it will never overcome the ultimate erosion of public will.

A US military urban exercise conducted at Fort Polk in October 2002 ended with over half the attackers killed or wounded. 'In a real assault', said the commentary, 'such losses would most likely have caused the US forces to pull back'.[3] If American forces do have to invest and attack Iraqi cities, they will enter an area of military operations which they cannot win. The defended cities scenario is more probable than possible. Militarily it makes no sense to embark upon a conflict in which such a scenario is likely to manifest itself. The nature of conflict has changed. The power to weight relationship between states and non-state actors has also changed to the benefit of the latter. It is far better for a superpower to swallow pride, allow diplomacy to run its course rather than enter into a regional conflict it cannot win, with all the profound global implications.

It has been a risk to withdraw Special Forces from Afghanistan to open the second front in Iraq. The risk is that the limited achievement in Afghanistan will be forfeited as a finite capability is hurried into another campaign, the start of which is by any standard premature.

The financial *cost* of invading Iraq will be high. The shock effect upon a weak international economy will be profound. Initially, oil could reach $50 a barrel. Washington has had to authorise the biggest increase in defence spending in two decades to fund the war. In the UK, taxes are already going to have to rise to plug a £7bn budgetary deficit. Armed conflict would adversely affect the British government's ability to deliver on improvements to health and education. An operation in Iraq of a duration of a year or more will cost London up to £5 billion or 7.5 billion dollars or Euros. Other, incalculable costs will include unintentional regime change, damaged regional relationships and a cost in lives of combatants and non-combatants. The cost of a post-conflict military

127

security commission of an estimated 75,000 personnel is influenced by duration and the level of passivity encountered among the Iraqis. Peacekeeping will only arise if there is peace to be kept. If there is a significant force protection requirement, the strength of the military security commission will need to rise to 150,000 and beyond for the duration of the insurgency. There has to be a pre-established plan to deal with such a contingency.

Short duration is of course associated with risk and cost but some would argue that in a war of obligation as opposed to a war of choice it should not be a substantive consideration. The occupation of Iraq would not be of short duration. The argument here however is that an invasion of Iraq is a war of choice in so far as there is no immediate obligation. The coalition needs a clear idea of what for them constitutes success, the end game and, most important, what the exit strategy will be. It is bad enough to enter a conflict that cannot be won but to have no face-saving exit strategy is inexcusable. We now face what seems to be the possibility of what will be one of those reviled wars, similar to Vietnam.   When we look back in retrospect, as we surely will, we will reflect upon the ignorance of identifiable politicians who set the whole business in motion.

Six Weeks in Politics

This final section was written six weeks after the Conference on Peacekeeping and Intelligence, to review what was said at the time, to contemplate what has happened to date and provide a prognosis for the future. During those six weeks which takes us to the end of December 2002, there has been evidence of al-Qa'eda's presence throughout Europe but more seriously in Mombassa where an Israeli-owned hotel facility was attacked and Israelis and Kenyans killed. What has not changed is the prevailing sense of inevitability that the United States wants its war and will not be deterred. The intelligence situation has been re-assessed because it seems not to be as good as believed and not as good as it should have been. Mention was made how it was in the United States' interest to help Mr Hans Blix locate the WMD which Saddam Hussein on 7 December 2002 denied having. Yet we have seen Mr Blix accusing the USA and the UK of denying him the essential intelligence required to prove Saddam Hussein to be in material breach of UN Security Council Resolution 1441.

The indicators that US Intelligence may be limited include the emphasis placed on encouraging Iraqi scientists to come forward to describe their work and the locations of WMD. The excuse that intelligence is not being released to the UN for fear of revealing capabilities and resources is untenable. With free-range UN inspection teams loose in Iraq, it is difficult to envisage how surreptitious advice given to Mr Hans Blix to check out a factory at 'X' or a specific grid reference in the desert could prejudice sources. It may be that potential targets are on a reserved list to be included as targets in the first phases of a future bombing campaign. It is however Mr Blix's evidence which should legitimise such a bombing campaign through a declaration that a material breach of UN Security Council Resolution 1441 had occurred. It is a fundamental American interest that Hans Blix should detect Saddam's 'smoking gun'. Moreover it seems preferable for sites to have the benefit of ground inspection to avoid a repetition of acts similar to bombing the Sudanese pharmacy. Perhaps there is no sensitivity to such a consideration.

The stirring of a modest UK ground intervention to an uncertain trumpet was evident at year's end but too late for a mechanised formation to be involved in a Spring 2003 offensive. The importance of the British contribution as the lesser partner in what appears to be a two-state coalition is politically symbolic, not militarily. Conventional British mechanised ground participation at formation level would have to be held over until autumn. This delay may prove unacceptable to the United States who will not want their deployed force kicking its heels throughout an entire Kuwaiti summer. Unlike the British, the Americans have a plethora of high-tech night-fighting devices which would permit them to engage the Iraqis in the relative cool of the night. What the British have to avoid is responsibility for, or a major role in, the messy, dangerous and protracted post-conflict 'peacekeeping' mission, even though it is a mission to which they are better suited than most.

The unanswered question is, will the United States, whose public require their government to take the UN route, argue that UN Security Council Resolution 1441 provides all the authority that is required, or concede that a second 'all necessary means' resolution is unavoidable? Washington would not take this latter step unless absolutely certain there was no prospect of an embarrassing veto from either France or Russia. The veto is not the only bear trap along the UN path within the Security Council. The other potential problem is Syria. Syria is the only Arab state occupying one of the rotational seats inside the

129

Security Council. Although she does not have the veto, it would not augur well for a policy aimed at keeping Arab states on-side if, at the time of the consideration of the second UN resolution, Syria voted against the invasion of Iraq and that Arab opinion were to be ignored by America.

The advantage to the USA of being seen to take the UN route is that it is likely to minimise the extent of furious retribution which will follow an invasion of Iraq. We have seen among the hawks a growing exasperation at being led down the UN path. The mission of the apparent warmongers in the Administration is understandably unclear but that is what worries the public. Are the public seeing intense sabre-rattling intended to put pressure on Saddam Hussein to comply with the wishes of the UN or is this a group of people who do want war at any cost? The problem with sabre-rattling is what happens when there is no reaction? Can the superpower back down? The answer is probably 'no'. The fact remains that it is in America's interest to resolve the Iraq problem short of war not only due to predictable repercussions but also to avoid a breach with mainstream Arab states which could take years to repair.

The problem the hawks have with the UN and its Security Council is precisely that enunciated by Dean Acheson in 1962 and it concerns national sovereignty and the superpower's determination that its sovereignty will not be shackled by international law. It is anathema to the right wing that the President, the Commander-in-Chief, should have his power limited by lesser states within the Security Council. The states most likely to veto an 'all necessary means' resolution are France, with whom the USA does not enjoy the most consistently cordial relations and Russia, soundly beaten in the Cold War. There is a growing international realisation of how essential is this second resolution if Arab leaders are to have any prospect of carrying their people with them. But planners have to have their eyes on the end game and the UN has proved adept at pulling hot potatoes out of the fire. Overall therefore, Washington's policy towards the UN needs to be carefully thought through.

If the USA were to invade Iraq under the aegis of Resolution 1441, there would be a theoretical point of separation both politically and militarily with her principal ally. Prime Minister Blair has said he is committed to operating within international law but he has also said that he would not allow a veto to stop military action. If a veto should arise during this pursuit of the UN option, ignoring it would require the passing of an illegal order to the national military

130

commander. A significant element of his own party and an increasing number within the opposition parties will seek to hold him to his earlier commitment. There is no precedent in modern British history of British armed forces being engaged in armed conflict contrary to the will of the people. The discovery of Saddam Hussein's smoking gun is as important to Mr Bush as it is to Mr Blair but an individual is not a state and it remains difficult to see how a war against another sovereign state with all the attendant death and destruction and collateral risks can be justified to achieve the removal of one despot.

The growing realisation that the UN Security Council will provide too high a hurdle for some to negotiate may have prompted NATO's Secretary General to declare that it was a 'moral obligation' for his organisation to become involved in Iraq. The reality is that NATO's Article V is founded upon Article 51 of the UN Charter, Self-Defence. The offer to involve NATO in Iraq could be said to be a ploy to open up an option to move the decision making away from a reluctant premier international organisation to one that is assumed to be more compliant, pro-American. The truth is that if the Security Council route will not legitimise an attack on Iraq, neither can NATO. If Washington does see it as being politically important for British forces to make what Blair described as the 'blood sacrifice', it creates enormous uncertainty when planning a five division military operation to find at the last critical moment that national politics have intervened to prevent the only other western national division in the coalition from taking part.

The Pentagon has a number of contingency plans and it is apparent that there has been debate as to the relative merits of the heavy or light options although neither is mutually exclusive. Integrating a foreign component into the manoeuvre phase is likely to be counterproductive, particularly for a high-tech military force sensitive to the risks of blue on blue incidents. British light forces however could have utility operating within boundaries in an amphibious or urban environment.

It is not possible to report that the aforementioned credibility gap has closed. The contrary is true. Israel is pressing the USA to tackle Iran after Iraq yet Korea is a more potent threat than either of the other two 'axis of evil' states. White House spokesman Ari Fleischer has sought to explain why Iraq is to face armed conflict and why Korea is to face diplomacy. 'The situation in Iraq involves somebody who has used force in the past to attack and invade his

131

neighbours. That is not the case of North Korea in the last 50 years', said Fleischer. Iraq attacked Iran and Kuwait with the encouragement of the USA. The US Ambassador in Baghdad reportedly told Saddam Hussein that the USA had 'no opinion on Arab-Arab conflicts, like your border disagreement with Kuwait'. She is on record as having admitted to the *New York Times*: 'Obviously, I didn't think and nobody else did, that the Iraqis were going to take *all* of Kuwait'.

Militarily, there is a difference in scale between Iraq moving across an undefended line in the sand compared to what North Korea would have to do in attacking the Republic of Korea's sophisticated defence line south of the UN Demilitarized Zone (DMZ), a line buttressed by the presence of 37,000 American troops. It is understandable therefore why North Korea has not contemplated an attack across the DMZ but that is not to say that over the past 50 years she has not been involved in numerous attacks on South Korea. Among these, in 1983, North Korean assassins assassinated members of South Korea's Cabinet during an international conference in Rangoon. In 1987, a South Korean airliner was destroyed. In September 1996, there was a North Korean submarine infiltration into South Korean waters in which 24 North Koreans died. In June 1999, a North Korean navy ship was sunk in a naval battle.

On 9 December 2002, a Spanish naval boarding party stopped and checked a North Korean freighter, the *So San,* and discovered on board 15 Scud missiles, 15 conventional warheads and 85 tons of chemicals. The weapons were bound for Yemen, ostensibly a friend of the USA and an ally in the war against terrorism. The combative Donald Rumsfeld described North Korea as the single largest proliferator of missile technology. After taking responsibility for the missiles from Spain, the USA released the consignment back to Yemen. 'There is no provision under international law prohibiting Yemen from accepting delivery of missiles from North Korea', declared Ari Fleischer. The following day, North Korea announced the re-commissioning of the key Yongbyon nuclear power plant to compensate for America's suspension of fuel oil shipments. It is said that history repeats itself.

There is an argument that an attack on Iraq is justified because Saddam Hussein has weapons of mass destruction and might make them available to the enemies of America. But why should that be the case? The Oklahoma bombing and the anthrax attack in America were launched domestically by American nationals and the manufacture of ricin in London which was prominent in the international press was achieved through the processing of beans readily available in the market.

The message to emerge from the 14-19 December 2002 London meeting of 315 delegates from 50 Iraqi factions and ethnic opposition groups was not propitious. Many of those present had been among those encouraged by President Bush senior to rise up in 1991 only to find America spectating on the sidelines as the Kurdish and Shi'ite uprisings were met with force. The obsessive desire for power within the region will provide the Americans with another opportunity but among the heated arguments and bickering there seems little prospect of a democratic government emerging from what was on view in London. There is a growing argument that it may be preferable to keep Saddam Hussein and his power structure in being rather than forcibly remove this Tito of Iraq and face the consequences of regional instability and disorder. This is not a precise comparison but near enough. What is of concern in the proposal to attack Iraq is the obvious conclusion that no one has the first idea how, once set in motion, the business will come to an end. What can be predicted is that relative to the neutralisation of Saddam Hussein, the management of the post-conflict period will be more difficult. To restate the three principles of military intervention, low risk, low cost and short duration, for the United States and the United Kingdom, the risk analysis indicates the risk far exceeds any possible benefit. The cost remains as stated. It is the third factor which has come under the closest scrutiny in the past few weeks.

The American proconsul idea is a non-starter, as is the hope of installing a preferred candidate from among those who gathered in London in December 2002. The individual will be seen as a puppet through whom a neo-colonialist America will exert her national interest to achieve strategic and economic goals. The belief that there is an oil-based rationale for conflict with Iraq has developed since early November 2002. Iraq's oil reserves are four times greater than the USA's. The difficulty in establishing a credible and competent government works directly against the 'short duration' philosophy. However, it must be a fundamental priority to remove interventionist armed forces from Iraq at the earliest opportunity, particularly if there have been significant non-combatant deaths and damage to private property. Their continuing presence in Iraq will merely serve to sustain terrorist attacks upon their homeland, their interests and their people. If this foolhardy intervention proceeds, this may be one post-conflict resolution period in which the UN is reluctant to become involved, particularly if international law had been set aside. The end game is under such a fog as to challenge the wisdom of setting out along a path which requires those who destroy a regime to recreate a suitable alternative. The dutiful British have created for themselves a foreign policy disaster; treated with contempt by Israel and despair by former friends in the Middle East. In fairness to Prime Minister Blair he does recognise the connection between global terrorism and the Palestinian crisis and showed commendable initiative in convening an international conference in London to resume the quest for a political settlement.

Prime Minister Ariel Sharon used a murderous Palestinian bomb attack against Israel to deny Yasser Arafat and his delegation permission to travel to London. International observers looking to Washington to make a suitable representation asking Sharon to rescind his decision were fascinated by the silence. Why was this? A State Department official said: 'If there is to be a political solution for the Arab/Israeli problem, it will be under American chairmanship'. The problem is deeper than that and entwined in American domestic politics. In April 2002, George W. Bush intervened diplomatically in the then deteriorating Israeli-Palestinian conflict. He told Sharon, Prime Minister of an apparent client state, to withdraw from West Bank towns and settlements. Sharon's refusal humiliated the President and his Secretary of State.

The proportion of the Jewish vote in the United States represents 2.2 per cent of the electorate but that proportion is concentrated in a number of key marginal constituencies. Sharon will be aware what happened in 1992 when Bush senior involved his party in Jewish politics. It was Secretary of State James Baker's testy ultimatum to Israel that, if Washington was paying it expected compliance. That action was seen as a contributory factor towards President George H.W. Bush losing the 1992 election. The son needs no reminding how close was his victory in 2000. At a time when the international community is looking to the superpower to show responsibility, inspired leadership and political courage, they have been given George W. Bush.

Finally, there is a clearer picture of the elements which form the rationale for what former Secretary of State Madeleine Albright described as President Bush's 'irrational exuberance' for wanting to attack Iraq. These are:

134

- The message of the Superpower to lesser states, that challenges to her power and authority will not be tolerated.

- A need for revenge which will be satisfied with the removal of Saddam Hussein.

- The re-election of the President in 2004.

- A shared interest with Israel to destroy Iraq's power base of which WMD are one component.

- The control of Iraq's oil reserves.

Endnotes

---

[1] Under UN Chapter VI peacekeeping duties, the blue berets operate *impartially*, with the *consent* of the contesting parties and use lethal force only in self-defence.
[2] Sir Robert Thompson. *Defeating Communist Insurgency* (London: Chatto & Windus 1967) p. 52.
[3] *USA Today*, 31 October 2002.

Part III presents four practitioner views on changes that must be adopted if peacekeeping intelligence is to become codified and effective. The first author-practitioner points out that the United States of America must, in essence, change its ways and become more effective at being responsive to and sharing intelligence with non-governmental organizations, the most important of which is the United Nations. The second, with deep experience in managing the Joint Intelligence Committee in the United Kingdom, recommends the development of international doctrine and especially of multiple levels of collaborative intelligence enterprises. The third focuses on modeling and simulation as a means of both estimating future challenges, and training peacekeepers. Lastly, the keynote speaker-practitioner from the conference presents specific suggestions on 'seven standards for seven tribes', in what may be the beginning of a unifying doctrine that establishes both unity and continuity of intelligence operations across national, military, law enforcement, business, academic, NGO-media, and religious-clan-citizen lines of authority and capability.

Chapter 10. International Peacekeeping Operations: The intelligence Challenge for America in the 21st Century. Over the past decade, the US intelligence community's performance during a number of high-profile international peacekeeping assignments has improved dramatically, such as in Haiti, Bosnia and Kosovo in the 1990s. The best measure of this success is the lack of casualties from hostile fire among the US peacekeeping troops who participated in these operations. But conversations with a number of American intelligence officers reveal that there is a great deal of room for improvement, both in terms of how the US intelligence community supports American peacekeeping troops, and perhaps more importantly, how the U.S. co-operates and shares intelligence with its international partners in current and future peacekeeping operations around the globe. Of particular concern is the rising volume of complaints received from America's European allies about the inability or unwillingness of the US to share intelligence, or work co-operatively in the intelligence field during peacekeeping operations. Further, the US has not resolved the larger and more difficult question of how to provide intelligence support to the United Nations, as has been recently demonstrated during UN weapons inspections in Iraq. MATTHEW M. AID

Chapter 11. Intelligence Doctrine for International Peace Support. International peace support operations rely on national intelligence collection under national control, with some pooling of the results. In particular they need international *assessment* of these results, as a preliminary and distinctive input to policy planning and decision-taking. No effective machinery for assessment of this kind – preferably combining an international drafting staff with provision for national inputs, discussion and agreement – at present exists at the top inter-governmental level, for example for the Security Council and NATO Council. The procedures of the British Joint Intelligence

137

Committee (JIC) and the American National Intelligence Estimate should be adopted for international use to fill the gap. At lower, theatre levels of command the British precedent of 'local' JICs could be added similarly to the conventional military intelligence structures, to encourage national inputs and discussion at these levels and to meet the need for broad, mixed political and military ('pol-mil') assessment. An international doctrine of intelligence in peace support is needed to promote these and other desiderata. MICHAEL HERMAN

Chapter 12. Modeling and Simulating Transitions from Authoritarian Rule: New Analytic Techniques for Peacekeepers. Traditional intelligence architectures offer unique and often intractable challenges to peacekeepers. These issues are unlikely to resolve themselves soon, indicating a need for innovative approaches to meeting the peacekeeper's requirements for predictive analysis. One common situation confronting peacekeepers that requires this type of predictive analysis is the transition from authoritarian rule. Recent mathematical research into iterative function systems suggests that complex phenomena, such as transitions from authoritarian rule, can be reasonably accurately modeled. These models, in turn, can form the basis for a simulation of a transition from authoritarian rule. The author develops exactly such a model, based on research into Eastern European and South American transitions. Building on the model and using Hungary in 1993 as a test case, a simulation was developed and executed. The results of the simulation correlated closely with real life observations in Hungary on a wide variety of measurable indices. Afghanistan in 2002 was also examined with the identical generic model in mind. The initial results indicated that it, too, would be suitable for development as a predictive simulation. In addition to the predictive results, the Hungarian simulation confirmed earlier results from other studies regarding simulations generally as excellent tools for training not only for peacekeepers but for policymakers, aid workers and students alike. KRISTAN WHEATON

Chapter 13. Information Peacekeeping & The Future of Intelligence. The future of global intelligence is emergent today. There are five revolutionary trends that will combine to create a global information society helpful to global stability and prosperity. **First**, the traditional national intelligence tribe will be joined by six other intelligence tribes, each of which will gradually assume co-equal standing in a secure global network. **Second**, in those specific areas generic to all tribes, collaborative advances will be made, and codified in 'best practices' defined by the International Organization for Standardization (ISO). **Third**, multi-lateral information sharing rather than unilateral secrecy will be the primary characteristic of intelligence. **Fourth**, intelligence will become personal, public, & political. **Fifth** and finally, intelligence will transform peacekeeping by making the case for greater investments in 'soft power' together with substantial funding for peaceful preventive measures. ROBERT DAVID STEELE

138

International Peacekeeping Operations: The Intelligence Challenge for America in the 21st Century

Matthew M. Aid

It will come as no surprise to any reader familiar with the US intelligence community to learn that the US government's perspective on providing intelligence support to international peacekeeping operations has been largely shaped by the American experience in peacekeeping over the last 20 years, particularly our involvement in Lebanon in the 1980s, followed in the 1990s by operations in Somalia, Haiti, Bosnia, Kosovo, and now in Afghanistan.

What follows is the perspective of a number of American military and civilian intelligence officers interviewed over the previous year, all of whom have participated in one or more international peacekeeping operations over the past two decades. The purpose of this chapter is to share their thoughts as to how the US intelligence community could improve its intelligence support for ongoing or future international peacekeeping operations based upon their experiences in the field. The first thought I would like to impart is that, in the opinion of these intelligence officers, despite ups and downs, including a number of dreadful miscues over the last quarter century, American intelligence support for international peacekeeping has improved dramatically in the last decade, in large part because of the harsh lessons that the US intelligence community learned a decade ago in Somalia.

With each subsequent peacekeeping operation that the US has participated in we learned something new, the lessons of which were incorporated into how the US intelligence community approached subsequent operations. We also

139

watched carefully and made note of the intelligence performance of our allies who participated in the UNPROFOR peacekeeping operations in Bosnia in the early to mid-1990s and other UN-sponsored peacekeeping operations which the US did not participate in. The net result is that within the US military today, there is a much greater understanding and appreciation for the value and importance of good intelligence support during peacekeeping operations. Almost unanimously, American military commanders that I have spoken to voiced the opinion that probably the single most important reason why virtually no American soldiers have been killed on peacekeeping duties over the past decade in Bosnia and Kosovo is largely because of intelligence.

Lessons Learned

So the question is: What practical lessons have the US military and intelligence community learned from these peacekeeping experiences that are applicable to the new global geostrategic environment in the 21st Century? These lessons can be divided into two separate but inter-related categories: (a) lessons that are applicable to the performance of peacekeeping intelligence functions within the US intelligence community; and (b) lessons relating to intelligence co-operation with foreign nations in peacekeeping operations.

Better Intelligence Preparation for the Peacekeeping Environment

The US intelligence community has learned the hard way from its involvement in previous peacekeeping operations, especially American involvement in Lebanon in the 1980s and Somalia in the 1990s, that they have to do better basic intelligence preparatory work before the first American soldiers are sent in to participate in a peacekeeping operation. It is ludicrous to believe that American peacekeepers can adequately perform their duties without fear of loss of life if we do not intimately understand the political, economic and social environment that our forces must operate in. The American journalist George Wilson, has written: 'If you don't understand the cultures you are involved in; who makes the decisions in these societies; how their infrastructure is designed; the uniqueness in their values and their taboos, you aren't going to be successful.'[1] The intelligence officers that I have spoken to strongly believe that too many American lives have been needlessly lost in past operations because our intelligence community did not adequately prepare our political leaders or

140

military forces for the mission that they were tasked with performing. In Lebanon, one author has concluded that 'The disastrous bombing of US Marines in Lebanon in October 1983 that cost almost 300 American lives, is largely attributable to a lack of understanding of the nature of the threat... US forces in Lebanon had little knowledge of how various Lebanese and Palestinian Liberation Organisation factions were likely to respond as the US escalated military actions.'[2] In Somalia, virtually all sources agree that the chief intelligence failure was the inability of senior American commanders to understand the fundamental aspects of Somali societal structure and culture, which were the driving forces behind the bloody Somali civil war and resultant famine. Few American commanders or intelligence officials in Somalia understood the dynamics of clan structure and politics in Somalia, which in retrospect we now know to have been a crucial intelligence failure.[3] The first UN commander in Somalia was particularly mindful of these aspects of Somali culture and politics, whereas his successors were not. The resulting intelligence disaster and loss of life, as popularised in the film *Black Hawk Down,* should speak for itself.[4]

Better Integration of Intelligence

Another key lesson learned is that intelligence must be completely integrated into all aspects of the planning and execution of peacekeeping operations. Although the importance and relevance of this fundamental point would appear to be self-evident, it has not always been practiced by commanders in the field in the past. Recent experience has shown that American peacekeeping commanders who ignore or give short shrift to intelligence do so at their peril. There have been instances in the past where American military commanders on peacekeeping assignments, not understanding or realizing the importance of good intelligence information for the successful performance of their mission, have relegated intelligence to a secondary priority and have not paid as much attention to the subject as they should have. For instance, the inattention to intelligence of the US Marine Corps commander in Beirut in 1983 is a stark example of what can go horribly wrong if peacekeeping commanders do not pay attention to the information that their intelligence staffs provide. At 6:22 a.m. on the morning of October 23, 1983, a Shi'ite suicide bomber detonated a massive car bomb outside the US Marine barracks in Beirut, killing 241 American servicemen. Largely forgotten by history is the fact that on the same

141

day, a second suicide bomber detonated an equally large bomb outside the barracks housing French forces in Beirut, killing 59. This disaster could probably have been avoided. On September 27, 1983, NSA sent out a warning message to the White House and the CIA stations in Beirut and Damascus, which indicated that on the basis of a September 24, 1983 intercepted telephone conversation between the Iranian ambassador in Damascus and an an official with the Iranian Foreign Ministry in Teheran, a group calling itself the Husaini Suicide Forces Movement, led by a Shi'ite terrorist supported by Iran named Abu Haidar, intended to 'undertake an extraordinary operation against the Marines' in Beirut. The warning, however, did not give a place or date for the operations, the specific identity of the target, or how the attack would be carried out. As a result, the warning message, like so many before it, was given short shrift by the Marine commanders in the field until after the attack took place.[5]

The American military's participation in the United Nations Operation in Somalia (UNOSOM) peacekeeping mission during the early 1990s was also marked by repeated intelligence miscues. For instance, US military Human Intelligence (Humint) collection assets were not among the first echelon of forces deployed to Somalia. Rather, the deployment of these units and their equipment was pushed back in order to make way for higher priority combat and combat support units.[6] Not surprisingly, the subsequent performance of US Humint in Somalia left much to be desired, in the opinion of military intelligence officers who served in Somalia.[7] Moreover, poor intelligence directly contributed to the death of 16 US Army Rangers during an operation in the Somali capital of Mogadishu on October 3, 1993.

Senior US military commanders did a much better job of integrating intelligence into planning for the 1994 intervention in Haiti, but field commanders interviewed repeatedly complained about the paucity of hard intelligence they received prior to and during the operation from both the CIA and the military intelligence organisations.[8] It was not until the US military was sent into Bosnia in late 1995 following the signing of the Dayton Peace Accords that intelligence was fully integrated into the planning and execution of a major American military peacekeeping operation. The success of the US participation in the IFOR peacekeeping operation in Bosnia since 1995 speaks volumes about the relative importance of intelligence in the conduct of international peacekeeping operations.

Tailor Intelligence Resources for the Task

The US intelligence community has also learned that insofar as intelligence collection in peacekeeping operations are concerned, they must do a better job of tailoring the intelligence collection and analytic resources committed to peacekeeping operations to be able to collect both political and military information in the country and/or region where the operation is occuring.

There have been instances in the past where American military forces have been committed to peacekeeping operations with a 'standard' intelligence package that was designed for monitoring enemy military forces on a European-style battlefield, but was incapable of performing even the most rudimentary political intelligence gathering.[9] The need for political intelligence gathering capabilities in a peacekeeping environment is absolute. The experience of the US intelligence community in Lebanon, Somalia, Haiti, Bosnia and Kosovo showed with stark clarity that the protagonists in these fractured political environments oftentimes say one thing publicly, but then do something completely contrary to their public statements. Therefore, it is the job of intelligence in a peacekeeping environment to penetrate the subterfuge of the various political actors so as to clearly understand what their true intentions are. This means that American intelligence units deployed to the field in support of American peacekeeping forces must be capable of monitoring and assessing both political and military developments with equal skill.

Better Co-ordination of Effort among Intelligence Units

US intelligence officers believe that support of peacekeeping operations can only be successful in the future through better and more consistent co-ordination of effort amongst the multitude of American military and civilian national, operational and tactical intelligence collection and analytic units participating in, or peripherally supporting these operations. For example, there have been instances in the recent past where American military intelligence personnel participating in peacekeeping operations in the Balkans were not given intelligence information collected by their civilian counterparts at the CIA or State Department diplomatic reporting, and vice-a-versa.[10]

Why Not Use the Best Intelligence Assets?

The American experience in peacekeeping operations over the past decade has demonstrated that while US forces sometimes contributed intelligence from their 'top-of-the-line' national intelligence collection assets, principally satellite imagery and Signals Intelligence, for the most part what the US intelligence community has contributed to past peacekeeping operations, especially those in Bosnia and Kosovo in the 1990s, has been generally low-level intelligence product derived from tactical intelligence assets that can hardly be described as the best product the US intelligence community had to offer at the time.[11]
The reason for failing to make available the best intelligence available to peacekeepers is simple: the security concerns on the part of senior American intelligence officials.

A Better Balance in the Mix of Intelligence Resources Committed

It is also clear that the US intelligence community must achieve a better and more appropriate balance in the mix of intelligence collection resources that it dedicates to peacekeeping operations in the future. Too often in the past, the US military has dedicated far too many technical intelligence sensor systems that had, at best, marginal utility in peacekeeping operations instead of more appropriate low-tech intelligence collection resources. The US intelligence community's dependence on technical intelligence sources at the expense of other means better suited for operations in the less-developed world has been a source of concern for many knowledgeable observers for many years. For example, the commanding general of Saudi forces during Operation Desert Storm in 1990-1991 noted that: 'I was struck by the fact that in their intelligence gathering the Americans depended overwhelmingly on technology, satellite surveillance, radio intercepts and so forth, a very little on human sources.'[12]

The problem has been that these high-tech intelligence collection sensors, more often than not, do not work in the low-tech peacekeeping environments where they have been deployed in the past. For instance, American intelligence officials confirmed that on the whole, Sigint collection systems deployed to Bosnia during the mid-1990s produced little in the way of useable intelligence.[13] Attempts by US Army Sigint personnel to secretly eavesdrop on

144

conversations being held in buildings in central Bosnia proved to be futile because the equipment was big, designed for use on the battlefield, and as such, not particularly well suited for use in an urban peacekeeping environment.[14]

Moreover, the intelligence information generated by these systems has proven to be extremely difficult to use, and posed critical problems about how to share this information with our allies, if at all. For example, an officer who served in Somalia in the 1990s has written that 'The US propensity to push the use of sophisticated technical collection equipment caused a number of problems. It made the products difficult to sanitise and distribute and delayed the arrival of more effective Human Intelligence collection assets.'[15]

Greater Emphasis on Human Intelligence

Publicly available materials and sources interviewed for this report also tend to agree that American intelligence support for future international peacekeeping operations must place greater emphasis on Human Intelligence (Humint). In virtually every instance of US forces participating in peacekeeping operations in less-developed countries during the 1980s and 1990s, such as in Lebanon, Haiti, Somalia and Bosnia, Human Intelligence has far proven by far to be the most useful intelligence resource available. It is a matter of considerable embarrassment among American intelligence officers, who have participated in international peacekeeping operations that, according to one officer, 'other countries often are more effective than the US in gathering human source intelligence.'[16] Part of the problem is that the CIA and the Pentagon have ignored Humint for the last 25 years. Intelligence officers interviewed have stated that rare indeed have been the instances where the CIA or US military have had an existing Humint network in place and operating at full capacity in the countries where US forces have been deployed on peacekeeping operations in the last twenty years. In Lebanon in 1983, for instance, American Humint resources in that country had recently been destroyed when a car bomber destroyed the US embassy in Beirut, killing all but one member of the CIA Beirut station. In Somalia the US had no Humint network in place at the time US forces were sent into the country in 1991.[17] Moreover, American military commanders had complained frequently that it has taken the CIA and US military intelligence too long to establish viable Humint networks in previous peacekeeping operations. Intelligence professionals respond that it takes a

145

relatively long period of time to establish agent networks. Ludwig Mundt, the former chief of operations of the German foreign intelligence service, the *Bundesnachrichtendienst* (BND), stated in a June 2001 speech that it can take up to five years to build an effective agent network.[18] But the intelligence officers interviewed for this paper also emphasize that the US intelligence community must do a better job of effectively using what Human Intelligence resources that are available in future peacekeeping operations, since CIA and American military Human Intelligence performance in recent international peacekeeping operations has left something to be desired in their opinion.[19] For example, in Somalia, Haiti, Bosnia and Kosovo, rather than take the time to organise and develop Human Intelligence networks, which the British experience in Northern Ireland indicates can take years if one does it right, US intelligence officers have resorted to the time-honored expedient of making large cash payments to sources in return for intelligence information.

In the short term, this yielded some intelligence, but over the long-term the reliability of what the sources were passing to their American handlers proved to be dubious, at best. In Somalia, so much false or misleading information was finding its way into American Human Intelligence reports that many commanders stopped reading them. Moreover, once the cash payments stopped, the local informants became vindictive and stopped providing intelligence.[20]

Another often-heard criticism is that American Human Intelligence collectors have all too frequently not availed themselves of the best intelligence sources available: in this case, the 'bad guys' on the other side of the firing lines. In Somalia, the UN military commander (an American general) initially made a point of meeting regularly with the most important local warlord, Mohammed Farrah Aideed. The American military commanders who followed him, however, cancelled the meetings and abandoned all contact with Aideed and his aides because of political directives received from Washington. But in the process, however, the US lost its best and most reliable source of intelligence.[21] Unable to have direct contact with the leaders of the forces hostile to the peacekeeping forces, US Human Intelligence collectors were forced to depend on much lower-level local sources who turned out, more often than not, to be unreliable and whose primary motivation was their own financial betterment. This has resulted in some painful intelligence failures, such as the inability to

146

find Aideed in Somalia, or a warning that the local populace had become hostile to the continued presence of American forces in Mogadishu.[22]

In Bosnia and Kosovo there is documentary evidence that US Army Human intelligence operatives overused their sources. Post-mortem reviews of US Army Human Intelligence performance in Bosnia in the mid-1990s found that there were too many Human intelligence collectors chasing to few sources. This often resulted in the same source being interviewed by two or three American Human intelligence operatives a week, each of whom was asking basically the same questions.[23]

Relax Political Constraints on Intelligence Collection

Then there is the problem of American peacekeepers not being aggressive enough in collecting intelligence by getting out more into the local environment. Because of political concerns about suffering casualties akin to the disasters in Beirut in 1983 and Mogadishu in 1993, American peacekeepers have become virtual prisoners in their kasernes in Bosnia, Kosovo and Macedonia. This has severely impeded productive Human intelligence collection, which can only be gathered through face-to-face contact with friends and enemies alike. It has also led to an unhealthy dependency on technical intelligence sensors for intelligence. When US Human Intelligence collectors were allowed out of their barracks, security considerations made them look conspicuous. In Bosnia, US Army regulations requiring all Army troops, including intelligence collectors, to wear full battledress uniform, carry weapons, and travel in conspicuous four-vehicle convoys was found not to be particularly conducive to eliciting information from sources in Bosnia towns and villages. Efforts to get these restrictions lifted were largely unsuccessful.[24]

Linguistic Shortages

A shortage of trained linguists has severely hampered the effectiveness of American Human Intelligence during virtually every peacekeeping operations over the last decade, and helped contribute to some of the intelligence failures of the past. The advantages of possessing good linguists is supported by this post mortem of the Somali operation:

One of the biggest successes were the contracted Somali interpreters from the United States. Although limited to English translation, they provided keen insight on Somali culture as well as language. These interpreters, many of whom were Washington, D.C. cab drivers, also interpreted body language and facial gestures - not only of Somalis to western troops, but vice versa. They were able to explain to Somalis the body language (frustration, anger, etc.) of Americans, which would otherwise have gone unappreciated. Two way understanding was important. The Somalis needed to know what we thought and felt as much as we needed to understand them.[25]

American intelligence officers who have participated in peacekeeping operations in Lebanon, Haiti, Somalia and the Balkans virtually unanimously agree that the US intelligence community as a whole must do a better job of integrating the vast amounts of intelligence information that it obtains from the wide variety of technical and human intelligence sources available, and more importantly, ensuring the timely synthesis, analysis and reporting of intelligence information collected by these various means to the peacekeeping force commanders.[26]

A More Entrepreneurial Approach to Peacekeeping Intelligence

Intelligence officers participating in supporting peacekeeping operations must become more entrepreneurial. They must be willing to throw away their doctrinal manuals and be more open to new, unorthodox ideas about how to collect intelligence in a peacekeeping environment. For example, one of the findings stemming from America's participation in peacekeeping operations in Bosnia, Kosovo and now Afghanistan is that men and women trained as professional intelligence officers now must become diplomats, police officers, construction workers, public works planners, and even foreign aid officials. One junior US Army intelligence officer in Kosovo found himself as the de facto mayor of a small town, where he found himself responsible for settling family disputes, erecting a new court system, policing traffic, and even installing a new electric grid and sewer system. Although it was not an intended result, the trust engendered from these activities led the inhabitants to begin bringing their new mayor the latest gossip and information about what was going on the surrounding region, oftentimes in the form of complaints. Still, this officer

148

quickly became one of the best Human intelligence collectors for the US military in his part of Kosovo.[27] Experience in Kosovo since 1999 has shown that Human intelligence collection in a peacekeeping environment can be expanded at virtually no cost by having the Human Intelligence collectors work more closely with their military police colleagues, who were among the few American forces permitted to roam freely through their area of operations. In addition, by merging their efforts with UN civilian police units in Kosovo (UNCIVPOL), the Human Intelligence knowledge base was expanded even further, especially when it came to hunting for known criminals who threatened the peace in the region.[28] In addition, intelligence officers supporting peacekeeping operations must be willing to explore non-traditional sources of intelligence information.

Time after time, American intelligence officers involved in peacekeeping operations over the last decade have found that oftentimes their best sources of hard information came from aid officials and relief workers employed by non-governmental organisations, such as the Peace Corps, the Organisation for Security and Co-operation in Europe (OSCE), the International Committee of the Red Cross, or CARE. These individuals generally have been present in the region far longer than the Human intelligence collectors, speak the languages of the countries involved, know and have the trust of local officials, and have a deeper perspective on the events surrounding them than the Human intelligence collectors.[29]

The problem is that the historical relationship between the US intelligence community and NGOs has been, to put it mildly, less than harmonious. NGOs have resisted co-operating in any substantive way with the US intelligence community rather than prejudice their legitimate position as humanitarian relief organisations around the world.[30] As such, these non-traditional sources of information should be treated with great care. They are not part of the US government, so no attempt should be made to co-opt them in return for temporary gains. Moreover, it should be recognised that the interests of the NGOs will not necessarily coincide with those of the intelligence collectors, so great care should be taken when examining the information provided by NGO actors.

Relax Current Security Restrictions

Existing security rules and regulations must be modified to take into account the unique aspects of providing intelligence support to peacekeeping operations. There have been too many instances in recent peacekeeping operations, such as in Bosnia during the early to mid-1990s, where national-level strategic intelligence information was deliberately not made available to American intelligence officers operating on the ground because of the fear on the part of security officials that the information could find its way into the hands of our foreign peacekeeping partners who were not cleared for access to the information.[31]

More and Better Intelligence Sharing With Our Allies

By all accounts, the CIA and US military intelligence have made dramatic strides in the last decade in trying to work more closely with their multinational partners in international peacekeeping operations. But the US intelligence officers interviewed for this chapter have made clear that the nature and extent of US intelligence co-operation and information sharing with our international partners in peacekeeping operations, which has been a longstanding problem and a source of continual tension with our peacekeeping partners, continues to be in need of massive improvement. This seemingly never ending problem is a difficult one to cure, and defies the short-term ad-hoc fixes that Washington typically prefers because they are politically expedient.[32]

There appear to be three fundamental areas which need to be addressed in a comprehensive manner before this problem begins to go away: How should the US share intelligence with its friends in a peacekeeping environment; how does the US protect its intelligence sources; and perhaps most importantly, should the US share its most sensitive intelligence information with its peacekeeping partners? Although these issues appear simple on paper, they have bedeviled politicians, military commanders and senior intelligence officials on both sides of the Atlantic for the better part of 20 years with no clear-cut resolution yet in sight. Publicly, the US intelligence community has committed itself to greater intelligence co-operation with foreign partners in multinational operations. For example, a US Joint Chiefs of Staff doctrinal document states that 'Sharing of intelligence information between coalition forces is essential to integrating all

150

resources and capabilities into a unified system that will be fulfil the prioritised intelligence needs for joint operations.'[33]

But American and foreign intelligence officers confirm that while Washington has paid lip-service to greater intelligence co-operation with multinational partners, it has consistently failed to deliver when pressed to make good on promises made. There is no question that the US must do more than pay lip service to the concept of co-operation and intelligence sharing with its coalition partners. In reality, intelligence sharing with foreign nations, even those who have been allies of the United States for decades, has oftentimes posed seemingly insurmountable problems for the US intelligence community. Senior elements within the US intelligence community have consistently viewed intelligence sharing with friends and allies in peacekeeping operations as something akin to anathema. In part this is because, as most intelligence professionals would willingly admit, the very idea of giving away one's intelligence secrets to strangers runs contrary to the some of the most basic and fundamental beliefs of virtually all intelligence officers around the world. This deeply held sentiment was confirmed a few years ago by a former senior CIA operations officer, who wrote that 'intelligence sharing is not something the comes naturally to intelligence officers.'[34] There are, of course, historical reasons for the American reluctance to share intelligence information in an international peacekeeping environment. Many past and present US intelligence officials point to an incident that occurred in early 1995, when United Nations forces abandoned a cache of sensitive American intelligence documents in Mogadishu, Somalia in their haste to withdraw from the country.[35] In some respects, the behaviour of the US intelligence community in previous peacekeeping operations has made the problem more difficult that it should be. In Somalia in 1993, delays in disseminating intelligence information was caused in part by the American propensity to label all intelligence product SECRET NORFORN, barring the sharing of the intelligence with foreign partners, regardless of their nationality. It was only thanks to the initiative of the local American military commander that some of the intelligence product was authorised for release to other coalition partners in Somalia.[36]

Intelligence information from American national sources was available, but it took in some cases days to disseminate the information to other UN units because of the need to 'sanitise' the data in order to protect sensitive sources and methods. By the time the sanitation process was completed, the time-sensitive information was practically worthless.[37]

Since Somalia, there has been, by all accounts, an order of magnitude improvement in the area of intelligence sharing with our partners, but if the complaints from allies that I have heard based on our experience in Kosovo and Macedonia have any basis in truth, which I believe that they do, we still have a long way to go. The most frequently heard complaint was that certain foreign nations were given higher quality intelligence information by the US than others. This has naturally bred considerable resentment of US intelligence sharing practices among intelligence officials from the nations that were not on Washington's 'A List.' [38]

What to do About the United Nations

Which brings us to the next sticky problem: How does the US intelligence community improve the nature and extent of its intelligence co-operation with the United Nations, which has what can only be described as a troubled history.
Given the political dynamics of the institution, the very concept of providing intelligence support to the United Nations is an extremely difficult proposition for American intelligence professionals. A former CIA intelligence officer with considerable experience in the field of providing intelligence support to the United Nations recently wrote that 'The idea of sharing intelligence between national governments and the UN has required a seismic shift in attitudes and practices on all sides.'[39] The UN has not made the process any easier for itself. UN officials have made it clear, both publicly and privately, that the idea of even admitting using intelligence information has been 'difficult and distasteful.'[40] This penchant against intelligence within the UN has frustrated that organisation's peacekeeping officials. A UN Department of Peacekeeping Operations (DPKO) post mortem study of UN peacekeeping operations in Somalia concluded 'The United Nations must continue to move beyond its earlier attitude and reluctance with respect to the propriety of 'intelligence' and its role in United Nations peace operations.'[41]

Regardless of whether it is a fair assessment or not, many American policymakers and intelligence officers, both military and civilian, frankly do not

152

trust the UN in the area of intelligence sharing and co-operation. According to a 1996 congressional report, 'Sharing information with the United Nations has been more tentative and limited due to the nature of the organisation itself (which includes countries whose interests are perceived as inimical to those of the United States) and to the lack of any effective system at the UN to control information provided by member nations.'[42]

According to one assessment, the UN's primary limitation in the field of intelligence is that it is 'a very rigid, antiquated bureaucratic operation of firmly entrenched staff, who are either unable or unwilling to change.'[43] A declassified report written by an American intelligence officer on intelligence support for international peacekeeping stated 'The UN organisation currently cannot collect or handle information efficiently or effectively.'[44] In part this conclusion stems from the fact that the UN's Office of Research and Collection of Information (ORCI), which was formed in 1988 to act as the UN's intelligence service, was forced to close its doors four years later in March 1992 for lack of sufficient resources. There are even suggestions that the unit was disbanded because it failed to effectively communicate its findings to the UN Secretariat.

Another recurring theme, again based on experience in Somalia and Bosnia, is that the UN is incapable of protecting or properly communicating classified information, or more correctly put, some member states are incapable of protecting the information within the UN context. This has created uncomfortable situations when in the early 1990s, the US denied the UN access to high-technology intelligence products during peacekeeping operations in the Sinai, Cyprus and Namibia.[45] The exception to the rule was the eight year UNSCOM weapons inspection operation in Iraq, which although not a peacekeeping operation per se, proved that under certain conditions United Nations organisations can effectively perform their functions largely to the receipt of high-level intelligence information from participating members, including the US.

How to Teach Intelligence for Peacekeeping Operations

Finally, there must be some teaching mechanism put into place whereby the lessons learned from previous peacekeeping operations are preserved and taught

153

to the next generation of American intelligence personnel participating in peacekeeping operations so that we do not repeat the same mistakes as we have in the past. Moreover, this facility should be international in scope and makeup, since American intelligence personnel must learn what it is like to work in a multinational environment. This capability sadly does not exist at the present time.

Endnotes

[1] This quote is taken from http://www.urbanoperations.com/quotes.htm (accessed in January 2003).

[2] James S. Corum, 'Air Power and Peace Enforcement,' *Airpower Journal*, 4 (1996) pp.17-18.

[3] Major Harold E. Bullock, USAF, *Peace by Committee: Command and Control Issues in Multinational Peace Enforcement Operations* (Maxwell AFB: School of Advanced Airpower Studies, June 1994).

[4] Norman L. Cooling, 'Operation Restore Hope in Somalia: A Tactical Action Turned Strategic Defeat,' *Marine Corps Gazette*, September 2001, p. 92.

[5] David Martin and John Wolcott, *Best Laid Plans: The Inside Story of America's War Against Terrorism* (NY: Harper & Row, 1988), p. 105; James Perry Stevenson, The $5 Billion Misunderstanding (Annapolis: *Naval Institute Press, 2001*) p.39n; 'New Evidence Ties Iran to Terrorism,' *Newsweek*, November 15, 1999.

[6] Bullock, *Peace by Committee*.

[7] Confidential interviews.

[8] Confidential interviews.

[9] Confidential interviews.

[10] Confidential interview.

[11] Bullock, *Peace by Committee*.

[12] HRH General Khaled bin Sultan with Patrick Seale, *Desert Warrior* (NY: HarperCollins, 1995), p. 203.

[13] Confidential interviews.

[14] Captain Robert Culp, *'TF 1-26 Intelligence AAR - Bosnia'*, undated, located at http://call.army.mil/products/trnggqtr/tq1-02/culp.htm (accessed in January 2003).

[15] Bullock, *Peace by Committee*.

[16] Helene L. Boatner, 'Sharing and Using Intelligence in International Organizations: Some Guidelines,' *National Security and the Future*, Vol. 1, No. 2, Summer (2000).

[17] Cooling, 'Operation Restore Hope in Somalia', p.92.

[18] Speech, Ludwig Mundt, International Intelligence History Study Group, Seventh Annual Meeting, June 8-10, 2001, Haus Rissen, Hamburg, Germany.

[19] Confidential interviews.

[20] Bullock, *Peace by Committee;* Cooling, 'Operation Restore Hope in Somalia' p. 92.

[21] Cooling, 'Operation Restore Hope in Somalia', p.92.

[22] Cooling, 'Operation Restore Hope in Somalia', p.92.

[23] Culp, *'TF 1-26 Intelligence AAR - Bosnia'*.

[24] CWO2 Leonard H. Holden, 'Counterintelligence: A Decade of Change,' *Military Intelligence Professional Bulletin*, 3 (1999); Culp, *'TF 1-26 Intelligence AAR – Bosnia'*.

[25] Bullock, *Peace by Committee*.

[26] Confidential interviews.

[27] Confidential interview.

[28] Major Jeff Jennings and Captain Jennifer Gaddis, USA, *'Intelligence Support to Law Enforcement in Peacekeeping Operation'*, undated, located at http://call.army.mil/products/trngqtr/tq4-02/jennings&gaddis.htm (accessed in January 2003).

[29] Bullock, USAF, *Peace by Committee: Command and Control Issues in Multinational Peace Enforcement Operations* (Maxwell AFB: School of Advanced Airpower Studies, June 1994).

[30] William E. DeMars, 'Hazardous Partnership: NGOs and United States Intelligence in Small Wars,'*International Journal of Intelligence and Counterintelligence 2* (2001) pp.193-222.

[31] Confidential interview.

[32] Confidential interviews.

[33] US Joint Chiefs of Staff, *Handbook for Joint Urban Operations*, May 17, 2000, p. III-26.

[34] Boatner, 'Sharing and Using Intelligence in International Organizations'.

[35] Confidential interviews.

[36] Bullock, *Peace by Committee*.

[37] Cooling, 'Operation Restore Hope in Somalia',p.92.

[38] Bullock, *Peace by Committee*.

[39] Boatner, 'Sharing and Using Intelligence in International Organizations'.

[40] Boatner, 'Sharing and Using Intelligence in International Organizations'.

[41] United Nations, Department of Peacekeeping Operations, *The Comprehensive Report on Lessons Learned from United Nations Operation in Somalia (UNOSOM)*, April 1992 - March 1995, undated, p.20, located at http://www.un.org/Depts/dpko/lessons/UNOSOM.pdf (accessed in January 2003).

155

[42] Commission on the Roles and Capabilities of the United States Intelligence Community, *Preparing for the 21st Century: An Appraisal of US Intelligence* (Washington, DC: Government Printing Office 1996), p.129.

[43] Commander Charles A. Williams, USN, *Intelligence Support to U.N. Peacekeeping Operations* (Washington, DC: Industrial College of the Armed Forces 1993) p.14.

[44] Williams, USN, *Intelligence Support to U.N. Peacekeeping Operations*, p.14.

[45] A.S. Henry et al., *Peacekeeping: Final Report on National Defense Headquarters Program Evaluation E2/90* (Ottawa: Program Evaluation Division 1992), p.241.

Intelligence Doctrine for International Peace Support

Michael Herman

The peace support considered here is assumed to take the form of international military operations of some kind under UN leadership or authorization, with a multinational command structure akin to that of NATO, or NATO plus other associated countries. The problem these operations pose is simple enough. They depend heavily on good intelligence, but intelligence is essentially a national activity. Intelligence for them therefore comes from a combination of national collection with international pooling of the product. Sometimes this pooling exists in formal, regular ways, as through NATO's long-standing intelligence arrangements, but this rarely applies outside NATO; and even in NATO the pooling is incomplete. The most important intelligence flows everywhere are either purely national ones to national actors, or those available internationally only on a limited 'eyes only' basis within multilateral intelligence 'clubs', principally the UK-US-Old Commonwealth one (though there may be other less well-established ones). Items from these restricted services are of course sometimes released to other nationals, but mainly on an *ad hoc* basis as part of the policy lobbying of key foreign players who would not otherwise see them. Similarly the tasking of intelligence collection in these international peace support operations remains mainly a matter for individual nations and the intelligence alliances to which they belong. All this works up to a point, especially when the Americans are the ringmasters with British assistance, as has usually been the case. Nevertheless post-mortems on peace support have regularly asked for something better. General Wesley Clark's comment on Kosovo reflects the disparaging view about alliance intelligence: 'It (NATO) had no collection and little analytic capabilities'.[1] Governments and peoples outside NATO regard intelligence with even deeper distrust; as something secret, threatening and best not discussed. The UN will only talk officially about 'information' and 'military information'. Hence the problem: can national intelligence be made more useful in these international operations? This chapter suggests contributions to an international intelligence doctrine that does not yet exist.

Intelligence Outlined

For this purpose two aspects of intelligence's definition can be sidestepped. The first is the nature of intelligence itself, and the semantic distinctions between it and the general run of other information-providers, including the other components of the American military ISR (Intelligence, Surveillance and Reconnaissance) and British ISTAR (ISR plus Target Acquisition). The same applies to the definitional differences between Sigint and ESM (electronic support measures). These all raise fascinating issues, and are important for budgeting and command-and-control purposes. But in the context of international peace support intelligence can be considered here simply as a specialist *activity* in information-gathering, processing, production and marketing, whose distinctive subject is *'them'*, and not *'us'*; or in military terms 'Red' and not 'Blue'. Peace support also involves intelligence on collaborating, neutral and environmental 'White' and 'Grey' targets, but they can be treated here as if they were all 'Red'.

The second is the relevance of the conventional 'politico-strategic', 'strategic', 'operational' and 'tactical' labels often used in explaining military intelligence. As applied in this way they denote three things: the levels of command that intelligence serves, the kinds of decisions it supports, and the levels at which intelligence is itself controlled, and the three get horribly confused. Prime Ministers at the highest politico-strategic level also take short-term as well as longer-term decisions and for them often need 'tactical' as well as 'strategic' intelligence. So-called 'strategic' intelligence assets, such as American intelligence satellites centrally controlled at the 'national' level, supply product for use at all levels in the command hierarchy; for targeting and other front-line peace support operations as often as for the top level. The resulting misunderstandings can be multiplied. So only two levels of command are considered here: the 'national capital' and 'theatre' levels, and no attempt is made to distinguish between the types of intelligence the two require.

158

Instead, for intelligence itself I differentiate between two kinds. Most intelligence is a flow of information; not 'raw data', but single-source or all-source product processed and validated in some way. The other, much less voluminous flow is of product geared to specific decision-taking issues, typically by seeing a particular situation though the target's eyes, understanding his relevant capabilities, and forecasting developments. This is the concept of the intelligence appreciation, assessment, or estimate; for convenience here I use 'assessment'. (American usage favours 'estimate', but in the UK this has some connotations of routine order-or-battle and similar publications). It is the 'Red' part of the military 'assessment of the situation'. British military doctrine describes it rather well as 'applied intelligence', or 'intelligence which is tailored to provide direct support to the decision making process'.[2]

This is familiar to military men, but hard for others to grasp, particularly for the kind of mixed political and military ('pol-mil') assessments now needed for peace support. Outside UK-US-Old Commonwealth circles, few civilians in government acknowledge the difference between an intelligence assessment, close to policy but steering clear of explicit recommendation, and the policy planning or decision-taking which draws on it. Fewer people anywhere appreciate the difference between the main intelligence flows and an assessment of them, or distinguish for example between a Situation Centre's daily brief on what is happening and the assessment of its significance. The distinction resembles that between two kinds of historians: those who tell history as narrative, and those who try to 'understand' or 'explain' it. One can argue about the nature of historical understanding and explanation, and similarly about the characteristics of an intelligence assessment; but we recognize one when we see it.

A Peace Support Doctrine

On that basis five points of international doctrine can be suggested. Thus

- Command gets its intelligence from a specialist staff, distinct from others.

- All information on 'them' flows into this staff, whether collected by special intelligence means or by others, such as normal military observation.

- Assessments produced by the staff are regular inputs to decision-taking.

- The staff tasks national intelligence collection and all other sources of information to meet its needs.

- The whole system depends on an ability to handle information confidentially, and the staff therefore incorporates intelligence's defensive security role of protecting this information from attack.

Of these the intelligence assessment is the heart of the process. Decision-taking at any level needs to be served by it. Miscellaneous information about 'Red' may do more harm than good if it does not receive proper assessment.

At theatre level this seems a statement of the obvious. The task of command there may not be straightforward; it may well be confused by the roles of the UN Secretary-General's Special Representative and other alliance representatives alongside the commander, and it always has to cope with the national 'red cards' possessed in practice by all the national military contingents. These have combined with other factors to produce intelligence shortcomings at that level that can be discussed later. But at least there normally is an international Force Commander with a recognizable intelligence structure under him, geared at least notionally to assessing, even if intelligence has to be called 'information' and the actual quality of assessment is variable. This does not apply at the top government level. Here no comparable intelligence structure exists, and the search for an intelligence doctrine for peace support needs to start there.

Top Level Assessments

Decisions are agreed at this level by governments in negotiations in national capitals, and in and around the appropriate international forums—the Security Council, the NATO Council and its subsidiaries, and perhaps its equivalents in

160

the EU and elsewhere—with the UN and NATO Secretaries-General (and sometimes the EU High Representative and others) as important operators. Negotiation and decision-taking here is a diffuse and difficult process. The more this applies, the more it would benefit from having agreed intelligence assessments on which it could be based. Inter-governmental agreement is difficult in any circumstances, but is more achievable if there is concurrence about the relevant facts and forecasts.

Here the original historical precedent can be found in intelligence support for UK-US Grand Strategy in the Second World War. The transatlantic exchanges of Sigint and other covert intelligence are well known, but less publicity has been given to the evolution of agreed inter-governmental assessments. Churchill's wartime dictum that 'Ministers should not have to argue about statistics' was applied equally to the development of the national Joint Intelligence Committee (the JIC), and after the US entry to the war to inter-governmental planning. Hence the UK-US Combined Intelligence Committee was created in 1942 as part of the machinery of the Combined Chiefs of Staff, and by the autumn of that year this intelligence committee was meeting daily.[3] There were elaborate arrangements for exchanging assessments, but one gets the impression that the British ones carried the day.

This sprang from two features of the wartime British system. The authority of JIC product came partly through reconciling different interpretations to produce agreed conclusions, and inter-service agreement of this kind came rather more easily to the British than to the American army and navy. But the British product was more than just a lowest common denominator of consensus; it had an rigour about it that was derived from its wartime drafters, the Joint Intelligence Staff (JIS), whose able and independently-minded civilians in uniform developed a corporate independence from single-service party lines. These features were carried over into the peacetime British system, and replicated in the post-war emergence of the American National Intelligence Estimates (NIEs). These reflected interdepartmental disagreements more clearly than their British equivalents, but were still single, agreed assessments and owed much in their quality to CIA's calibre and non-departmental status. In both countries the idea that assessments are products of argument and intellect, and are not tied to the court politics of power—or should not be—became part of the mental furniture, and has remained so.

161

The Second World War left one other legacy. Grand strategy was a matter for Britain and the US; there was no need to share strategic assessments with the Western European governments in exile, and good reasons for not doing so. This was entirely understandable at the time, but was a factor in formulating NATO's postwar doctrine that intelligence is essentially a national matter. The alliance has of course its intelligence structure and its formal assessments for force planning purposes, and its Intelligence Division in Brussels now has official roles of assessment, current intelligence and warning. But one gets the impression that the Division's impact is determined by its place within the International *Military* Staff, and not by any requirement to provide pol-mil assessments for use by the Secretary-General and the Divisions of Political Affairs and Defence Planning and Operations, and as a basis for collective alliance discussion in the NATO Council and its subsidiaries. It may be significant that in the current NATO Handbook references to intelligence occur on only two pages out of 536, and the NATO Intelligence Committee is not mentioned. NATO as a body still seems to feel, as in the Cold War, that intelligence is a suspect national activity, on which exchanges should remain a matter for select groups behind green baize doors, unacknowledged in the mainstream of the alliance.

The UN attitude is like NATO's, only much more so. A small assessment group (the Information and Research Cell) evolved in the 1990s within its Situation Centre, made up at one stage of British, American, French and Russian representatives with some access to national material; five officers and one NCO are said to have been working there in 1997.[4] But its role was still to write assessments for the Secretary General and UN staff, an important function indeed, but not for circulation to the Security Council members; and its members were on secondment from their nations, and not permanent international staff. In 2000 the Secretary-General established an Information and Strategic Analysis Secretariat in the Department of Political Affairs, but with assessment and policy analysis still apparently combined. Something of the same combination is suggested by the title of the EU's Policy Planning and Early Warning Unit.

Of course national assessments are circulated behind the scenes, bilaterally and multilaterally. Britain has certainly developed its service of selected JIC reports to some counries outside its main UK-US-Old Commonwealth circle, and on issues such as Saddam Hussein's acquisition of WMD the US's international use of intelligence has probably been even more extensive. It may also be assumed that key items get shown to the UN Secretary-General and other selected international officials, in the UN and elsewhere. All this is against a wider background in which international exchanges on terrorism greatly increased after September 2001, and indeed were *mandated* by Security Council Resolution 1373 at that time.

Nevertheless on assessments, where intelligence most closely bears on policy, the impression is still of irregular international exchanges, linked with specific policy issues; and perhaps also of one-way services, in which there is little reciprocal return for what the UK and US provide to those outside the UK-US-Old Commonwealth club. Certainly there are no international staffs, at the UN and elsewhere, specifically charged with putting different national assessments together and producing their own, non-national judgements, and no formal mechanism through which national leaders can discuss assessments collectively before arguing about decisions and policy.[5]

No doubt quite a lot is achieved informally, and the practical difficulties about introducing new machinery should not be underestimated. Nevertheless governments have not yet latched properly on to the advantages of making exchanged intelligence more useful through devising a routine for discussing what it means. The British JIC procedure and the device of the American National Estimate provide well-tried national mechanisms of this kind for adaptation for multilateral and international use. It is easy to despise the importance of formal machinery and routines, but they can be useful in stimulating new inter-governmental habits. Their establishment might be aided by explicit doctrine that intelligence assessment should be a preliminary to international decision-taking whenever possible.

Theater-level Assessment

The doctrinal-procedural gap just discussed does not apply at the theatre level, where intelligence staffs exist and are in a position to produce assessments. The picture given by those with experience there is of practical deficiencies: small staffs with no previous experience of working together; limitations in the amount of national intelligence supplied to international commanders; the plethora of flows on a 'national eyes only' basis, so that no one has a complete picture of who knows what;[6] and national shortcomings in intelligence training,

163

exacerbated by the problems of finding a common working language, and reflected in the quality of some of those appointed to the international staffs.[7]
I do not suggest remedies for these deficiencies here, though practical questions can be posed on one aspect. If adequate intelligence training is a serious problem, does NATO now run intelligence courses for its members and partner countries? If not, why not? And should the UN not consider the development of similar training for intelligence (or 'military information') as part of its preparation for international peace support?

Doctrinally, however, the British JIC philosophy may have something to offer to the theatre as well as the top level. The JIC is often thought of as a Whitehall system, but was in fact reproduced on a smaller scale after 1945 in regional JICs (and sometimes Local Intelligence Committees) in the British colonies and other areas where forces were deployed. Some of this machinery may still exist. Its rationale was to bring different elements together, typically the military services, police, colonial authorities and political advisers, all acting in an intelligence and not a policy mode. A version of the system was even developed to cope with terrorism in Northern Ireland.

Such a committee does not fit easily into a conventional military framework; but international peace support is not a conventional military operation, and intelligence for it diverges from a classical military pattern. As at the top level, the main theatre-level intelligence inputs are from national sources, often with national caveats on distribution. Peace support in the former Yugoslavia therefore saw the proliferation of what had already been recognized in the later stages of the Cold War: the National Intelligence Cells (NICs) established by the main intelligence nations to combine inputs to NATO with providing their own 'eyes only' services to their own national commanders and national officers in international staffs. One recollection of Bosnia is of virtually a caravanserai of NICs surrounding and outnumbering the international intelligence staff whose members they were servicing; rather as if having a NIC had become a national status symbol.[8] Some rationalization came, however, when the four Nordic NICs combined to provide a single input to KFOR. There is also anecdotal evidence of a local American suggestion at Sarajevo that all the NICs there should save time by joining with the international staff for exchanges of information and interpretations; a suggestion that in the event regrettably received no support. Nevertheless it points to the logic and potential

164

value of an in-theatre JIC to encourage pooled national inputs and international discussion.

This 'local JIC' approach, not to be confused with the American development in recent years of their rather more integrated national Joint Intelligence *Centers*, also abbreviated as JICs, might also help with the political dimension of peace support assessments. In particular the UN Special Representative could participate; perhaps he should actually run the committee, or at least be represented on it or in the drafting staff. The same might apply, *mutatis mutandis*, to the NATO Secretary General's and other political advisers. Accounts of operations in the former Yugoslavia all emphasize the importance of regular meetings of all kinds between different nations and authorities for information exchanges and problem-solving. Thus UNPF (United Nations Peace Force) Headquarters at one stage 'served as an official analytical working group that met once a week to discuss developments in the situation in Yugoslavia and the coordination of coming activities'.[9] It might be only a small step for this lesson about meetings to be applied specifically and formally to intelligence. In short, the concept of intelligence structure at theatre level could incorporate a JIC-like committee approach, under the commander's chief intelligence officer (or the UN representative), to weld together not only the variety of national inputs potentially available but also the important non-military dimension.

Cosmetics

These ideas of moving towards the regular production of international assessments seem ambitious. It is true that intelligence is becoming an increasingly international commodity, for use by communities of states against 'non-states' such as Al-Qaeda, and by 'civilized' states (however defined) against international pariahs. Yet it remains deeply wedded to its national character by its need for secrecy for source protection, the political sensitivity of covert collection, the limited worldwide understanding of the concept of objective intelligence assessment, and the general distrust of powerful intelligence as a manifestation of imperialism or authoritarianism, or both.

This is not the place to discuss how intelligence as a whole may evolve in this century.[10] However one purely semantic change can be suggested to ease the acceptance of what is advocated here. 'Assessment' instead of 'intelligence' has

165

crept in slowly over the last thirty years as a description of one of intelligence's roles. In the UK the JIS was succeeded by the JIC's *Assessments* Staff in 1968. Subsequently the Canadian Joint Intelligence Committee became the Intelligence *Assessment* Committee. More recently the intelligence-producing part of the British Defence Intelligence Staff became the Defence Intelligence *Assessment* Staff. Perhaps this move could go further. For its main function the JIC is actually a Joint *Assessment* Committee; and CIA's Directorate of Intelligence is similarly a Directorate of *Assessment* (or analysis and assessment). Changes of this kind might have little national significance. But there would be some cosmetic value if the international cooperation just advocated were labelled 'assessment' rather than 'intelligence'.

Collection and Security

This leaves the last two of the suggested five points of doctrine. These are both concerned with intelligence as a whole rather than assessment, though they still apply to it. Both need longer discussion than is possible here, but brief observations can be offered.

Intelligence is collection as well as analysis and estimating. Collection should reflect what Force Commanders need, translated into the practicalities of collection by their intelligence staffs. In peace support operations these staffs can presumably guide operational, non-intelligence units in their Force on the kinds of observation and other reporting required. But they also need to have some specialized intelligence collection geared to meeting their needs, plus an ability to state requirements authoritatively to other intelligence collectors. Meeting these requirements has always been difficult to reconcile with the NATO-derived assumption that intelligence collection is national, and unsuitable for international command. Intelligence collectors deployed in the theatres of operation have therefore tended to remain under national control, with services to local commanders and staff of other nationalities limited by whatever national 'eyes only' rules are applied to them.

In fact some 'internationalization' of these in-theatre intelligence units has occurred from time to time. Blue-helmeted tactical Sigint and photographical interpretation units developed in the UN force in the Congo in 1960 under UN control.[11] SFOR in the former Yugoslavia in the 1990s had its 'Allied Military Intelligence Battalion' as an international unit of the same kind. Some national

166

units there were put formally under international control, and there was extensive informal cooperation from others in a common cause; personal relationships and bottles of whisky sometimes circumvented the letter of the law about national 'eyes only' restrictions. In future operations it may be possible to put rather more national intelligence units formally under the international commanders of their areas. Some local imagery interpretation, for example, might lend itself quite well to this more international approach, and possibly some relatively simple Comint and Elint for immediate operational use.

Nevertheless it would be realistic to expect that most of the in-theatre intelligence collection will remain under national control. For the foreseeable future the important thing may therefore be to develop means by which a theatre commander can state his intelligence requirements to all the appropriate national authorities, with some expectation that they will be met, without seeking to control national units. To take what at present may still seem an extreme case: a joint NATO-Russian operation with a UN mandate. How under present routines would an American force commander tell his Russian partner what intelligence he seeks from Russian sources, and *vice versa* if the positions were reversed? Working out answers to such questions may be more fruitful than seeking to put all in-theatre collection under formal command.

The same applies equally at the top level. It is difficult to think of more important intelligence customers than the UN Secretary-General and, too a lesser degree, his NATO colleague. But can they and their representatives give nations their intelligence requirements and priorities? At present they probably feel it improper to seek to drive national intelligence in this way, and remain thankful for anything they get. To sum up, enabling national collection to respond to Force Commanders and other senior international requirements seems almost as important as encouraging international assessment of what is collected.

Like almost everything else in this paper this turns, however, on progress in solving the problem NATO wrestled with throughout the Cold War: how to reconcile the international dissemination of intelligence with the imperatives of national source protection. The development of techniques for the 'sanitisation' of national reports, as by the 'tear off' procedure for removing source details, is part of the answer; so too is the encouragement of realism about the degrees of source protection actually needed, and the discouragement of unnecessary 'eyes only' compartmentation. But progress in these directions depends on continued efforts, on the lines already developed in NATO and the EU, to develop minimum security standards for nations aspiring to participate in peace support.

The changes since the end of the Cold War in information security threats have made this effort all the more necessary, yet more difficult. The main threat is no longer from Russian espionage. Threats may still sometimes be of a battlefield, tactical kind, as in the examples often cited of the insecure communications of peace support contingents in the 1990s being exploited by warring parties to get tactical information about their adversaries.[12] In the main, however, the threat to sources now comes not from the intelligence collection of states and contesting protagonists, but from the media's coverage on what are regarded as transparent operations, at all levels from the top downwards. Doctrine for intelligence in peace support cannot be separated, in fact, from a complementary doctrine for the related information security and press handling.

Conclusions

Intelligence will remain mainly a national activity, and no ready-made solution is available to the problems of harnessing it properly to international peace support; but some points can be suggested. Nations should aim to make their national product available for international assessment, and assessment of this kind should be a standard ingredient of international decision-taking. Such assessments should be produced by a combination of international staff plus provision for collegial discussion by decision-taking nations, and should be pol-mil, reflecting political as well as military factors. The British and American models of the JIC and the National Intelligence Estimate provide templates for meeting these requirements at varied levels of command. The most urgent need is for some movement towards their adoption at top inter-governmental levels such as those represented in the Security Council and NATO Council, but they would also be applicable at theatre level. The complement to this use of national material for international assessment would be procedures to ensure that international officials and commanders could place intelligence requirements upon national collectors.

All this depends on changing international attitudes to intelligence's security: dispelling unnecessary mystery about it, while ensuring protection for real national secrets. For too long intelligence issues of this kind have been regarded as unsuitable for respectable international discourse. Hence the desirability of formulating international intelligence doctrine, as a means of discussing the formerly undiscussable.

Endnotes

The author is grateful to John Harrison and Stan Carlson for comments on drafts.

[1].General Wesley K. Clark, *Waging Modern War: Bosnia, Kosovo, and the Future of Combat* (Oxford: Public Affairs, 2001), p.431.

[2].Joint Doctrine and Concepts Centre, *Joint Operational Intelligence, Joint Warfare Publication 2-00* (1999), Glossary-1, expanded on p.1A-3. Note however that the descriptions of intelligence used in this paper reject the military distinction quoted on p.1A-1 of the same official publication between information ('unprocessed data of every description') and intelligence ('the product resulting from the processing of information').

[3] F.H.Hinsley with E.E.Thomas, C.F.G.Ransom, and R.C.Knight, *British Intelligence in the Second World War* Vol.2 (London: HMSO 1981), pp.42-44.

[4] Pasi Välimäki, *Intelligence in Peace Support Operations* (Helsinki: National Defence College, 2000), p.70.

[5] UNSCOM and its successor UNMOVIC developed analytic staffs for their particular targets of Iraqi WMD development. UNMOVIC is said to have taken greater care than its predecessor to employ staff as international officials free of national allegiances.

[6] As described by a speaker at the Netherlands Intelligence Studies Association (NISA) conference at which this paper was given, 'this is the fog of war in peace support; you don't know what you don't know and what others know'. An example quoted by Välimäki was when General Nambiar, the first commander of UNPROFOR, was refused NATO intelligence support because he was an Indian (note 4 above, p.111)

[7] A graphic picture of shortcomings at theatre level in the 1990s was given by a Canadian officer with experience of UNPROFOR; see Paul Johnston, 'No Cloak and Dagger Required: Intelligence Support to UN Peacemaking', *Intelligence and National Security* vol.12 no.4 (October 1997). A compatriot with similar experience took issue with the article, but mainly to argue that intelligence handling at UN Headquarters New York was even worse (Thomas Quiggin, 'Response to No Cloak and Dagger Required: Intelligence Support to UN Peacemaking', *Intelligence and National Security*, vol.13 no.4 (winter 1998)). These authors anticipated some of the conclusions of the present paper. A permanent intelligence staff in New York 'could ensure that sound

169

intelligence doctrine was institutionalized within the UN' (Johnston, p.111). 'At the operational level, leaders such as the Force Commander and Special Representative of the Secretary-General needed as much, and frequently more, political and economic intelligence as they did military' (Quiggin, p.203).

[8] Impression from speakers at the NISA conference.

[9] Välimäki, *Intelligence in Peace Support Operations,* p.137.

[10] For the author's views see '11 September: Legitimizing Intelligence?', *International Relations* vol.16 no.2 (August 2002), and chapters 1 and 13 of *Intelligence Services in the Information Age: Theory and Practice* (London: Cass, 2001).

[11] A.Walter Dorn, 'The Cloak and the Blue Beret: Limitations on Intelligence in UN Peacekeeping', *Journal of Intelligence and Counterintelligence* vol. 12 no. 4 (winter 1999-2000), pp.422-425.

[12] For example, the Croatian army in 1995 intercepted UN Military Observer reports to provide information about the Republic of Serb Krajina's forces, and used them to plan their capture of the area. (Quiggin, Response to 'No Cloak and Dagger Required', p.206).

Modelling and Simulating Transitions from Authoritarian Rule:
New Analytic Techniques for Peacekeepers

Kristan Wheaton

This chapter represents Mr. Wheaton's own work. The opinions expressed in the chapter do not represent the position of the U.S. Department of Defense, Department of State or any agency of the United States Government.

> *To capture this situation (i.e. transition from authoritarian rule), we propose the metaphor of a multi-layered chess game. In such a game, to the already great complexity of normal chess are added the almost infinite combinations and permutations resulting from each player's ability on any move to shift from one level of the board to another. Anyone who has played such a game will have experienced the frustration of not knowing until near the end who is going to win, or for what reasons, and with what piece. Victories and defeats frequently happen in ways unexpected by either player.*
>
> Guillermo O'Donnell and Phillippe Schmitter,
> *Transitions From Authoritarian Rule[1]*

Introduction

As numerous writers in this volume have noted, peacekeeping and intelligence normally mix only in difficult and uncomfortable ways. The threshold question of whether peacekeeping missions should be involved in

171

intelligence activities at all still causes considerable concern. Other, more difficult questions such as how, when and with whom these peacekeepers should share any intelligence they gather with other actors (including states) is even more difficult to answer. Even more sensitive questions of how, when and with whom states should share intelligence with peacekeepers often seem intractable. Compounding all of this, of course, is the cost of implementing traditional intelligence architecture, costs that are usually beyond the budgets of most peacekeeping missions.

Most of these concerns can be traced back to either the peacekeeper's need for neutrality in order to be effective or the need for intelligence agencies to protect sources and methods. Both requirements are legitimate and, some might say, vital to the success of the respective missions. The fact that the two goals, neutrality and secrecy, might appear to be mutually exclusive in no way undercuts the impact of both on the activities of peacekeepers and intelligence professionals or, ironically, obviates the need for some form of co-operation.

While the traditional needs of both the intelligence community and the peacekeeper might limit interaction, there appears to be room here for innovative approaches to meeting the peacekeeper's needs for timely, analysed and reasonably accurate information. I intend to discuss one such approach in this chapter. While the research I will present makes the case for this technique only in countries that are undergoing a transition from authoritarian rule, the fact that peacekeepers often find themselves in exactly these type countries makes this approach more, rather than less, relevant. This approach combines a variety of techniques, many of which the reader will no doubt be aware, in unique ways. In order to understand the unique nature of this proposal, there are several antecedent concepts that need to be explored before it can be fully evaluated.

The Number Three

Evidence of juggling can be found on Egyptian pyramids dating back nearly 2000 years before the birth of Christ. It is only in the 20th century, however, that scientists have sought to explain the complex patterns of juggling with mathematics. Using the obscure notation of site-swapping[2], mathematicians have been able to reduce the traditional, complex pattern known to jugglers as a 'three ball cascade', for example, to the number '3'. Similar notations, such as

172

'3,2,2,2', describe other, more complex patterns. Using this unique mathematical schema, scientists have even been able to derive general rules for jugglers such as, in any pattern with 3 balls, the cumulative total of the pattern must be divisible by 3 (without remainder) to succeed. If the pattern is not divisible by 3 (without remainder), one of the balls will drop. Thus the patterns '3' and '3,2,2,2' would work while the pattern '3,1' would fail. Moreover, this rule can be generalised to any pattern containing n balls.[3]

At first glance this may seem to be little more than an entertaining abstraction, of interest only, perhaps, to jugglers and the occasional Ph.D. candidate in mathematics. It also serves to demonstrate, however, that modern and unusual mathematical techniques are capable of explaining in simple terms at least some complex phenomena.

The Right Tool for the Job

Confronted with the array of data points in Figure 1, the typical social scientist would likely be intrigued by the arrangement (It represents, he would be told, an interactive social phenomenon that exists worldwide). This hypothetical scientist would immediately see the potential (if only for further study) of such an array. He would almost certainly do some sort of regression analysis on the points (after complaining about the lack of data). The heavily qualified statistical analysis might well look like the picture in Figure 2 and, if pushed hard, he might be willing to make some general comments, perhaps even a prediction or two concerning the next data point. Figure 3, representing the exact same phenomenon (albeit with data collected from a different part of the world) would likely be a bit more disturbing. While the same general phenomenon seems to be occurring, the data has now been skewed into a single quadrant. The statistical analysis of this data would certainly, our hypothetical scientist might hope, unearth some core similarities between the data sets. He would be flabbergasted, however, when forced to incorporate the data from Figure 4 into his working hypothesis. What are his realistic options? Abandoning the statistical line of inquiry does not seem justified. There are apparently some strong trends among at least some of the data and some weak correlations among the data gathered from different locations. If the phenomenon under consideration (this example represents a multi-billion dollar business) were important enough, this social scientist might put in for a grant to

173

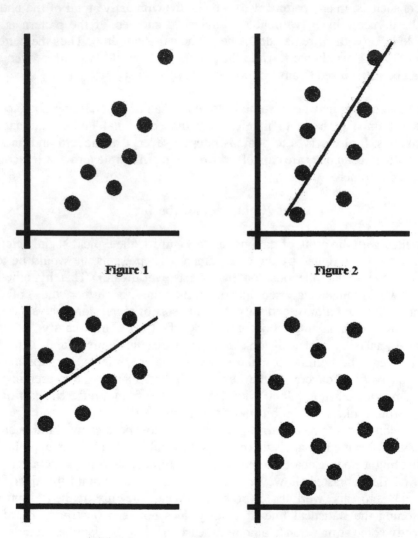

Figure 1

Figure 2

Figure 3

Figure 4

to conduct further research. Given that the diversity seems to be geographically-based, the scientist travel with adequate funding for a world wide research team. All of this is both wholly rational as an accepted process and completely and utterly useless in helping to understand this particular phenomenon. The reason is simple. The object of the study is the movement of

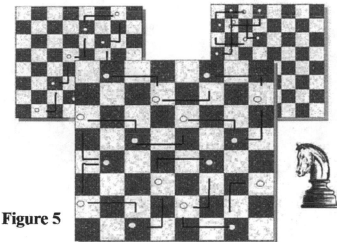

Figure 5

a knight on a chessboard (See Figure 5). Like trying to clean your ear with an ice pick, the social scientist in this example has chosen the wrong tool for the job.

This example makes two important points. First, in most people's minds there is a *presumption* that linear regression tells us something useful about a particular set of data. Clearly, there are some problems where statistical analysis, *no matter how well it is done*, does nothing to explain the actions of the object under study. In this example, this presumption of usefulness actually does far worse, it actively leads us away from a simpler, more complete explanation. Secondly, the data points in this example are relatively meaningless. That is to say, as long as the data points conform to the pattern of a knight moving across the chessboard, it matters little where those data points are on the chessboard. The phenomenon is the same regardless of the data. It can be explained completely only by focusing on the *pattern* of events and not on the data itself.

The Barnsley Fern

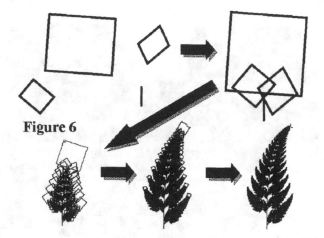

Figure 6

Figure 6 shows the growth of Michael Barnsley's computer-generated fern[4]. Beginning as a few simple objects and applying simple rules (Barnsley needed only four), the fern grows over time through what is known as an interactive function system or IFS. IFSs take the output from one cycle and make it the input for the next cycle. While such a system might not, at first glance, seem capable of achieving remarkable results, it is exactly this kind of system that is behind the recent revolution in computer graphics.

The Barnsley Fern is another stunning example of both of the previous two points: Sometimes, complex things can be represented simply and sometime pattern matters more than data. What makes this figure so extraordinary however is in the details, or rather, the lack of them. The objects used to begin the growth cycle of the fern are largely unimportant. They could be pictures, letters or entire paragraphs of words. The shapes can be altered and it might finally alter the shape of the fern but as long as the angles stay more or less the same, you wind up with a fern. In fact, absent tinkering with the four basic

176

equations that define the structure, it is extremely difficult to turn the fern into anything other than something that looks remarkably like a fern. Most of the measurable details here simply do not matter.

What, then, are the implications for peacekeepers and for intelligence? At first, these examples might seem to have little to do with the complex political systems that make up the chaos that arises from a country going through a transition from authoritarian rule. Perhaps, however, there are some useful inferences arising from this research. For example, if a complex system such as juggling can be modelled simply, perhaps there is a way to model the complexities of a transitional political system. Likewise, as with chess, perhaps such a model should focus on the patterns formed by political activity in the country and not depend so much on reams of data. Finally, maybe there is a way to ignore the expensive details that do not matter to the ultimate result and, yet, cost an enormous mount to collect and process.

These are clearly, at this point, hypotheticals. The few examples offered in no way constitute proof that such an approach would generate a useful analytic tool. Given the intelligence alternatives normally available to peacekeepers (and the costs associated with them) pursuing this alternative, however, is logical. If it is possible to compare the transition process to chess (even three-dimensional chess), if it is possible to talk about the juggling (of balls or international crises) with some degree of mathematical simplicity, then perhaps it makes sense to ask, 'How is a political system like a fern?'

Thus, iterative modelling (the type used in the construction of Barnsley's Fern and in most simulations), may be an effective way of describing the complex interactions between the various actors in a transition process. What might such a model look like? O'Donnell and Schmitter, in the quote at the beginning of this chapter, give some idea of what the process might feel like. Rustow, in his groundbreaking 1970 work, also identifies 'a two-way flow of causality, or some form of circular interaction, between politics on the one hand and economic and social conditions on the other.'[5]

I believe these intuitions are correct. I intend to make some additional assumptions and definitions, after which I will outline each phase of a model iterative process that seeks to describe transitions from authoritarian rule generally. The process itself is iterative, thus in order to understand an entire

177

transition in the light of this model it will be necessary to execute these phases a number of times. Only under these circumstances is it possible to comprehend the entire transition.

The Model

Assumptions and Definitions

First, a transition is the interval between one political system and another.[6] It has a specific beginning and ending (which will be defined and discussed later) and usually results in the replacement of those currently in power. Transitions from authoritarian rule are particularly interesting in that they provide a 'living laboratory' for a political scientist interested in studying the unrefined political process at work. The first assumption inherent in this model of transition is that the outcome is not important[7]. To study transitions from authoritarian rule based on the outcome seems to be as useful as studying football matches won by teams with the letter 'E' in their names. In order to understand the process by which these transitions take place it is just as important to study situations in which democracy does not replace the authoritarian rule as situations in which it does. A complete model of the transition from authoritarian rule must allow for any possible outcome. The second assumption is that the main goal of groups involved in the transition process is to increase their political power relative to the other groups involved in the process and to use this power to forward their agenda. Political power is further defined as the ability of one group or individual to impose its desires on other groups or individuals. While each group involved in the transition process certainly has its own agenda, it is not possible to achieve that agenda without political empowerment.

The third assumption deals with violence. The model I will develop will not account for transitions whose sole basis of legitimacy is the use of force. While these are interesting events, I believe that they are so radically different in character from internally generated transitions that they cannot be compared. In short, I am assuming that installing a prince to rule over some medieval fief is fundamentally different than the transitions of the late 20th Century.

The fourth, and final, assumption is that the transitions from authoritarian rule of the South American and Eastern European states are typical of all transitions. I will draw largely from the experiences of the South American and Eastern European states to validate many aspects of my model. Thus, I need to assume that these most recent experiences are representative of the whole.

On its face, this is my most questionable assumption. There is no obvious reason why these transitions should be any more or less typical than others. I will defend it on two grounds. The first is that these experiences run the gamut from the Velvet Revolution in Czechoslovakia to the bloody transition in Romania. This alone guarantees a wide variety of data that can be used to justify, but must also be incorporated into, any general model of transitions from authoritarian rule.

Secondly, I am not trying to say something about a specific outcome but about the process itself. For example, if I were to say, based solely on the Eastern European experience, that the Roman Catholic Church helped the transition from authoritarian rule towards democracy I would be correct (particularly in the case of Poland).[8] This would also fly in the face of previous studies concerning Latin America.[9] Since the context for my analysis is process instead of goal, I feel that I can avoid this problem altogether and legitimately make this assumption.

By way of definition, I use the terms regime, party and faction as collective nouns. Oftentimes, people think of an authoritarian regime or party as represented by the individual who heads it (such as Saddam Hussein in Iraq). In this paper, I always mean the group of people who not only lead a party or faction, but also the people who provide direct and indirect support for it.

Pre-Transition

Before the process of transition from authoritarian rule takes place, there must be some defining event or set of events that begins the process. This event or events can be the result of the authoritarian regime attempting to legitimise itself in the eyes of the governed[10] or it could be the result of a breakdown of the authoritarian state altogether. In either of these scenarios, the different orientations towards political order of hard-line and soft-line elements within the authoritarian regime cause the policies of the government, in some way, to foment dissent.[11]

Under Stalin, for example, there were no different orientations within the government (or what few that did exist were quickly squashed). Upon his death in 1953, a struggle between hard-liners and soft-liners broke out that put Khrushchev in charge. His visible softening at the 20th Congress of the Soviet Communist Party was shortly followed by the Hungarian Revolution of 1956. It was put down, of course, but set the stage for the eventual transitions in both Hungary and the Soviet Union.[12] It is these types of events that characterise the pre-transition phase.

Transition

Dissent leads to opposition. The difference between the two is in level of organisation. Whereas dissent is the grumbling of the man on the street, the organisation of that dissent is what characterises opposition. For me, what initiates the process of transition is the onset of opposition.[13]

The process of transition consists of eight distinct phases ('Phases' is an inaccurate word to describe the eight elements I see at play here. As a word, it implies sequence and a certain degree of order. These phases overlap each other, subsume each other, and provide context for each other. Despite this, a distinct set of actions takes place in each phase. For this reason, and lack of a better alternative, I use the word 'phase').

In addition, the process becomes iterative and, to a lesser extent, non-sequential.[14] By this I mean that the next eight phases repeat themselves until the transition is complete (I will define what I mean by 'complete' later). The process is somewhat non-sequential in that not all phases are always executed in each cycle and in that, under certain circumstances, a cycle may be involuntarily abbreviated.[15]

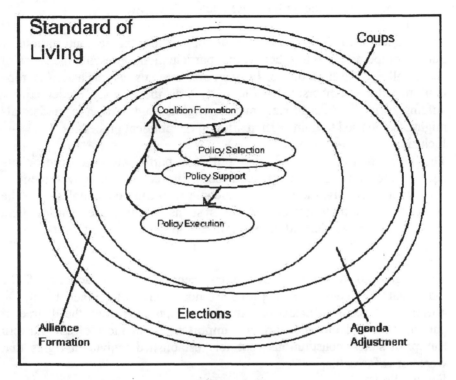

Figure 7

Figure 7 graphically displays the interrelationships between the eight phases. It is not designed to be understood at a glance. Instead it is a tool to help put the pieces together as I discuss them. In short, it may appear complex and obscure at first but should become understandable, even helpful, as I discuss each phase.

Phase 1 - Agenda Formation and Adjustment

Opposition to an authoritarian regime usually forms around one or more core

181

issues. It is, in fact, these core issues which allow the organisation of dissent in the first place. I believe there are five core issues. While I have not adopted directly the 'issue dimensions'[16] of other writers, these five represent a synthesis of the works of the authors cited below. They are:

a.   Participation

The degree to which a regime 'permits opposition, public contestation, or public competition'.[17] In other words, participation represents the types of people allowed to hold office. In one-party systems, as in Eastern Europe until recently, membership in the party was the primary credential for holding office.[18] Educational, racial, religious and economic credentials might also be used to limit participation in the political process.

b.   Inclusion

The 'proportion of the population entitled to participate in a more or less equal plane in controlling and contesting the conduct of government'.[19] This is, quite simply, the number of people who can vote coupled with the degree to which their vote counts (i.e. systems that give one man less than one vote, such as the old South African system, or systems that give multiple votes to the people, such the Hungarian system of the early 90's[20]).

c.   Civil Rights

The degree to which the government can control the actions of the individual.[21] If constitutional rights are not enforceable, either due to the power of unelected officials or external manipulation, then the degree of participation and inclusion are not important.[22] In most of the Eastern European states, constitutions routinely established individual rights that were not enforceable.

d.   Foreign Policy

The way the state appears to other states.[23] In other words, it is the degree to which a state has interventionist or non-interventionist policies. Whether a government seeks a defensive or offensive posture in relation to other states seems to be significant issue during the transition. One of the major problems during the transition process lies in dealing with old quarrels.[24] Many of these quarrels are border disputes that were, temporarily at least, resolved during the period of authoritarian rule, such as Russia and Moldova over the Trans-Dniestr; Serbia, Greece and Bulgaria over Macedonia; and Rumania and Hungary over Transylvania. Their re-emergence indicates the degree to which foreign policy is a core issue during transition.

182

e. Economy

    The degree to which the government controls the planning and execution of economic functions.[25] The inability of authoritarian economies, whether command or market based, to maintain pace with non-authoritarian economies is well documented.[26] In addition, the desire to achieve a western standard of living (realisable, as the conventional wisdom supposes, through a market economy) was one of the defining issues of the transition from authoritarian rule in Eastern Europe.[27]

f. Finally, the degree to which a government permits or participates in illegal activities (drug-smuggling, money laundering, etc) is yet another example of government control (albeit without a philosophical basis as cover).

Each of these five core issues provides a spectrum of advocacy. In other words, a person or party or nation can be thought to be strongly in favour of a command economy, the left-hand side of the spectrum, so to speak. Another could be in favour of a market-based economy, the right hand side of the economy issue. The same person might be on the left-hand side of the foreign policy scale, i.e. strongly pro-interventionist.

It is now a small step to go from using these five scales in a general sense to using them in a specific sense. It is theoretically possible to make a scale, say, from one to ten, and assign specific numbers on that scale to represent where a party or faction believes the country as a whole should be regarding that particular issue. In addition, it should be possible to determine where the country as a whole is, currently, regarding a specific issue. In other words, this set of scales would identify where the country's current set of policies and practices places it on each of the five scales. Obviously, this is largely the result of previous governments.

Thus it is possible to define a party or faction's agenda as the difference between where the country is on the five core issue scales and where the party or faction wants the country to be. An example might be useful. Assume a country with a low level of participation, a high level of inclusion, a command economy, few enforceable civil rights and a moderately interventionist foreign policy. On a scale from one to ten participation might be a three, inclusion a ten, economy and civil rights both threes and foreign policy a five. Compare this to a faction that wants a high level of participation as well as inclusion (say, a ten), a market economy (eight or higher), enforceable civil rights (nine or

183

higher), and a non-interventionist foreign policy (eight or higher). While each of the issues appears to be weighted equally, the system allows the opposition group's position to be defined in terms that would effectively indicate weighting.[28] For example, an opposition group that did not care about a country's foreign policy position might be represented quantitatively with any number higher than two but less than nine.

The advantage is parsimony. It is immediately obvious from such a system where lie the strongest disagreements as well as the areas of possible compromise between factions. In addition, policies of a government and pronouncements by both the opposition groups and the government could be seen as movement to the left or right on the scales.

The problem with the system is coding. It would seem impossible to determine with any degree of precision where a government or opposition group would lie on such a scale. This would be particularly difficult in the area of civil rights. Imagine a country that was relatively libertarian if you belonged to the 'correct' racial or religious group, but repressive otherwise. The countries of the former Yugoslavia are a good example of this; South Africa is another. The country's position is clearly not a one (completely repressive) or a ten (extremely libertarian). Other than that, arguments could be made for almost any position in between.

There are three counter arguments to this. The first is that the initial coding should be the result of interviews with experts. Finding suitable experts and forcing them to quantify their own judgements regarding particular factions is difficult but possible. More importantly, as more experts are consulted the results will inevitably begin to group themselves around certain variables (or a range of variables).[29] The second is technical. In recent years, mathematicians have developed a system called 'fuzzy logic'. The purpose of this system is to reproduce analysis based on best-guesses. It works like this: An analyst gives his best guess at where a certain variable lies on a scale as well as a high possible and a low possible value. A normal distribution of possible values is established between the two centred on the best guess. Mathematical functions then operate, not on the best guess, but on the probability curve in order to determine outcome. The result is that bad guesses are 'smoothed out' of the system, producing a better overall result at the end.

The final counter argument is that coding problems are inherent in all social science models. To eliminate an otherwise useful model because of coding problems seems counterproductive. The issue is to what extent can coding errors be eliminated and to what extent can error propagation be reduced.[30]

Up until now I have implied only two-tier system of government and opposition. This is clearly incomplete. There may, in fact, be several opposition groups, each with their own agenda (i.e. set of positions on the scales of each of the five core issues). The government may or may not be divided on its own agenda. The only thing that can be determined with any certainty seems to be where the country's policies and programs put it now on the five scales, and this is subject to change.

These complexities require the introduction of several new concepts, interest groups, parties and political power. Interest groups are groups of people united by a common set of priorities, desires and expectations.[31] Nationalists, feminists, warlords, ecologists, and the army are all examples of interest groups.

I have talked briefly about parties before, but in the specific sense that I use them in this model, parties represent the political interests of interest groups and individuals on a national scale.[32] This is the difference, for example, between Serbian nationalists and the party of Slobodan Milosevic that was the political instrument of those nationalists. Parties do not have to be legal to exist, nor do they have to have any place in the government. The interwar experience with the outlawed communist parties in Eastern Europe as well as the more recent experience with revolutionary parties such as Solidarity and Dobrislav Paraga's ultra-nationalist party in Croatia justify this broad definition.[33] In politically simpler countries, such as Afghanistan, making a transition from authoritarian rule, 'faction' would likely be a better word to describe what I mean by the term 'party'.

Government and opposition are composed of parties as I have defined them here. Each party thus has its own agenda and attempts to fulfil that agenda through the use of political power. A party's political power is defined as the quantitative and qualitative value of the party's people, leadership and ideas.

Political power is a relative concept. It is only valuable to the extent that it exceeds the political power of an opponent's political power. That there are different levels of power is obvious. In theory, the level of political power of each party should be measurable.[34] An authoritarian government may have so much political power (as in the case of the communists in Albania under Enver Hoxa[35]) that other parties have, effectively, no power at all.

Just as with the use of scales for the core issues discussed above, so should political power be subject to quantification. It requires the same kind of 'best guesses' as discussed before and is subject to the same arguments and counterarguments. I would like to add that this quantitative type of thinking seems to be prevalent among those actively involved in party politics. Politicians often talk of increases and decreases of political power due to a change in leadership or circumstances. Some rudimentary notion of how successful a certain position is or can be seems implicit in any political campaign. This notion of where one stands given one's political views would seem to be even more important in an authoritarian state since the consequences of failure are so much higher.

The final option in pursuit of political power, of course, is to change the agenda of a party. There is nothing inviolable about a party's agenda. Given that it represents fundamental beliefs of a group of people, I am forced to hypothesise that changing an agenda would be the last thing a party would want to do. Gorbachev tried to maintain the Communist party agenda while executing socio-economic change in the period from 1985-1991, thus exposing the party's weaknesses and ultimately contributing to its loss of power.[36] Parties can also change their agendas so much that they become indistinguishable from other parties. A good example of this is the six post-world War II parties of Czechoslovakia who rapidly became indistinguishable from the Communist Party itself.[37]

Thus, the first phase establishes the political status quo for the remainder of the cycle. Under this model, each party knows basically where the state is on each of the five core issues and to what degree it will have to change the policies of the state in order to fulfil its agenda.

Phase 2 - Alliance Formation

Alliances are formed between parties and interest groups. In some cases, the tie is so tight that the two are essentially inseparable. Solidarity in its early days might be an example of such a connection.[38]

The main reasons for these alliances are, for the interest group, to get access to the political power of the party and, for the party, to build its constituency which, in its turn, adds to its political power.[39] This is exactly the kind of pact that O'Donnell and Schmitter describe:

> *An explicit, but not always publicly explicated or justified, agreement among a select set of actors which seeks to define (or, better, to redefine) rules governing the exercise of power on the basis of mutual guarantees for the "vital interests" of those entering into it.*[40]

Interest groups provide an efficient way to bring people into a party. By allying oneself with an interest group, a party can effectively co-opt the group's constituency as its own. The only other way to build a constituency is to go directly to the people. This is less efficient and can incur the wrath of the interest groups that have been ignored. Parties also provide an equally efficient means for interest groups to get access to the political system.[41]

Since people normally fit into one or more interest groups, and the affiliation with one group may be stronger than the other, the party cannot expect to co-opt the entire group. It can, however, expect the interest group to deliver some portion of its constituency when the party needs it (e.g. during elections, coups, etc.).

Interest groups must be wooed and won by parties. Certain interest groups, however, can be seen leaning toward certain parties from the outset. The army, for example, normally sides with the government, while the intelligentsia normally sides with an opposition party in transitioning countries.[42] Thus, the process of incorporating them into some kind of party can happen so quickly that it is hard to determine which came first, the party or the interest group.

187

Other groups are approached later or not at all. These groups either do not add substantially to the party or they require extreme changes in the party's agenda to incorporate them. While it is not from Eastern Europe, the best example I can think of is the Ku Klux Klan. Though not actively approached these groups still lean towards one party or another. Because they are marginalised intentionally, their contribution is considerably less than those interest groups that are actively pursued.

Important interest groups are likely to be approached by a number of parties and it is not unlikely to see an interest group change its affiliation. One of the best examples of this is the Catholic Church's change of position towards authoritarian regimes. It had a tremendous influence in the recent Latin American transitions from authoritarian rule as well as in Poland.[43]

This is clearly an on-going activity for parties and interest groups. For purposes of this model I place it second only for the sake of logic. It and the first phase clearly provide the context, the backdrop, if you will, for the remaining phases.

Phase 3 – Coalition

Parties now make their second pact. This pact is a coalition that forms a government. In states that are just beginning the transition from authoritarian rule, the party that represents the authoritarian interests is very likely to have sufficient political power to control the government for a considerable length of time. A good example of this is Poland. It began its transition in 1980 but did not begin to openly share power with Solidarity until 1988.[44]

As time goes on and levels of political power change, coalition governments can emerge. These governments can be open coalitions as was the power sharing between Solidarity and the government in the last years of the eighties or covert coalitions as was the power sharing between Solidarity and the government in the middle eighties.[45]

Parties that are not in the government are in the opposition. These parties, while clearly not representing a majority of the political power available, can also work together to bring about the downfall of either the government or key governmental policies.

Because this is a pact, it is subject to dissolution. Upon dissolution, a new pact, a new coalition, must be formed in the context of constantly changing alliances and, to a lesser extent, agendas. Since nothing has been accomplished, the only thing lost has been time.

Time is not normally on the side of a state making the transition from authoritarian rule. Usually, in fact, the state is in an economic mess.[46] When parties waste time forming and reforming coalitions instead of going about the business of governing (as happened in pre-war Yugoslavia[47]), the standard of living begins to decline. As the standard of living begins to decline, people lose faith in the governmental process. Parties active in the process lose political power and may become marginalized.[48] Pre-war Yugoslavia and Germany are good examples of this.[49]

Thus, this process is not played out in a vacuum but against a populace that demands a better standard of living. Standard of living, in this model, represents the overwhelming non-political concern of parties. Certainly, the populace is willing to give governments some time to straighten out affairs, the experience in virtually all of the Eastern European countries shows this, but they will not give forever.[50] In short, parties must use their political power to form alliances and coalitions that will not only allow them to fulfil their agendas but also allow them to raise the standard of living (or, at least, not let it drop too low.)

Phase 4 - Policy Selection

Governments use policies to fulfil their agendas and to raise the standard of living. The nature of the policies depends on the country. Land reform, privatisation and disarmament are all policies that have been pursued, to one degree or another during the transition from authoritarian rule in the Eastern European states.[51] While the choice of policies is terribly important to a great number of people, it is only important in this model to the extent that it changes the standard of living and that it allows the parties in the government to fulfil their agendas.

The choice of specific policies is yet another pact that is executed internally among the members of the government and, to a lesser extent, externally with the opposition.[52] As such, their choice represents a compromise that revolves

189

around three concepts from this model: The effect that the policy will have on the standard of living, the degree of change that the policy will entail and the degree to which the policy will allow one or more parties to fulfil their agendas.[53]

Problems arising from policy selection may cause coalitions to dissolve. In Poland, Czechoslovakia and other Eastern European states, parties like Solidarity and Civic Forum can be viewed largely as anticommunist coalitions that splintered once the political power of the Communist Party was reduced enough to no longer be a threat.[54] The dissolution of governmental coalitions over policy selection without accomplishing anything, again pre-war Yugoslavia comes to mind, forces parties back into the context of agenda modification and alliance formation. The process begins again with only the loss of time and the possible reduction in the standard of living as a result.

Phase 5 - Policy Support

During this phase, parties use political power to either support or oppose specific policies. This phase overlaps the previous phase to a considerable extent. Despite this, I view support for a policy as a separate action from selection. There are several ramifications arising from this view.

First, small parties can use all of their political power to defeat or significantly modify specific, highly objectionable policies. Second, not all policies will get implemented. Parties may be so busy defending high priority policies that others are simply ignored. Finally, coalitions may dissolve over promised support that does not materialise.[55] The results of coalition dissolution are identical to the results in the last two phases.

Phase 6 - Policy Implementation

During this phase policies that were supported in the last phase are implemented. The success or failure of these policies depends on many things including, among others, the pre-authoritarian legacy with similar policies, the will of the people to execute the policies, the skill with which the policies are drafted, etc.

190

Three things can be said, in general, about policy implementation. The first is that only the probability of success or failure of a given policy can be assessed prior to implementation. Gorbachev's anti-alcohol campaign was designed to increase productivity by decreasing drunkenness on the job. It failed due to public backlash. The second is that the more radical the change in policy direction, the more there is at stake for the policy makers. It is probable that the failure of the radical economic change in Poland (initiated in January of 1991) to bring about equally radical change in the standard of living for the Polish people contributed significantly to the collapse of Poland's first post-communist government. The third is that, like the previous phases, policy implementation can result in the dissolution of a coalition. In this case something was accomplished (although the results were probably negative since the coalition is dissolving) and the parties find themselves, once more, back in the context of alliance formation and agenda adjustment.

The government can announce elections at any time. It is convenient to discuss them here because a logical time for a government to call for elections is after successful implementation of governmental policies.

Elections are held in a number of different ways. It can be highly inclusive with positions opened to everyone who cares to run. It can also be an instrument of repression in that it excludes certain minorities or parties from the process or in that it limits access to political positions. Elections can be one-party, two-party or multiple party. Political positions can be filled through a plurality system or a proportional system. The drawing of district lines can effectively isolate an interest group or party. In a state that is in transition, all of these considerations are subject to manipulation by the government that calls for elections.[56] In addition, all of these considerations can be subjugated to two core issues, participation and inclusion.

Participation and inclusion form a matrix that includes all possible forms of government.[57] Authoritarian regimes have low or little participation or inclusion, while more democratic regimes have higher levels of both. 'Polyarchies' have virtually unattainable levels of participation and inclusion.[58]

Since any form of government can be graphed onto this matrix, it is possible, theoretically, to resolve all the process related issues of an election into these two variables. As with all the variables in this model, the problem comes in

191

determining them precisely enough to be of some use. Also, as before, utilising fuzzy logic techniques and best guesses should provide some useful information.

Thus, rather than worrying about the exact rules of the election, this model focuses on how those rules make the system more or less participatory and inclusive.[59] The importance of this is, while the analyst will have to factor in all of the election variables into his conclusion, he will only have to come up with numerical values for two variables, participation and inclusion.

Elections are tools for the re-distribution of political power. Furthermore, the amount of power up for grabs depends upon how inclusive and participatory the elections are.[60] The sham elections of the communist Eastern European states are perfect examples of this. Although suffrage was general, important positions were given to party members, usually hand-picked by some committee. No real political power was redistributed as a result of these elections. On the other hand, many scholars have noted the effect of the first free elections, the founding elections, in a country. Redistribution of power can be immediate and overwhelming.[61]

Phase 7 - Coup / Military Action Phase

Coups or military action are means by which parties or individuals that currently do not have power or are in a risk of losing what they do have can seize power.[62] Like elections, coups can take place at any time. Logically, they would take place because of some expectation or event, such as the expectation of defeat in elections or successful policy implementation by another party.

Coups and military actions are normally quite risky and quite unlikely to succeed unless the groundwork has been carefully laid. In order to increase the probability of success, there seem to be certain key interest groups that can alter the outcome. The army is certainly the most important and neutralising or, preferably, having the army on your side is extremely important for a successful coup.[63] Other interest groups such as the media, bureaucrats, students, and the intelligentsia are important but have correspondingly less influence on the ability to successfully execute a coup.[64] Thus the coup provides the context for the political portion of the transition just as standard of living provides context for the entire transition process. In fact, the primary indicator that the transition process is nearing an end is when the chance for a coup nears zero.[65]

Phase 8 – Elections

Elections are the peaceful way to redistribute political power within a regime. While the announcement of elections is an activity that comes sometime earlier (I placed it in Phase Six for the sake of logic), the election itself normally occurs some time after its announcement.

The importance of the election depends, as I have stated, on the degree to which they are participatory and inclusive. In elections that are neither participatory nor inclusive, the stakes are small and the winners will be determined by the rules established by the government. In highly participatory and inclusive elections, typically called founding elections, the winners are more likely to be determined by the skill with which alliances were formed and people recruited prior to the elections. Founding elections, however, are highly unpredictable by their nature and no amount of politicking can guarantee the result.[66]

Thus, elections, while they exist within the context of the coup, provide the context for the other phases. Given the iterative nature of this model, everything political leads both to and away from elections.

Completion

The transition process is complete when the country achieves a stable form of government. This could be a democracy or another authoritarian regime, based on religious or ethnic ideas, perhaps. A government is stable when the risk of coup nears zero. Since coups override the rest of the political process, their elimination signals that the transition's redistribution of political power is complete.[67]

The Simulation

Simulations have proven to be extraordinarily successful as training devices and currently permeate virtually every technical field from aviation to auto repair. The relatively high cost to benefit ratio is the chief advantage offered by these simulations. For example, while a complete PC based aircraft simulator

193

will cost between 15 –39,000 US dollars, such a system is vastly less expensive than even the simplest propeller plane. Moreover, the level of realism in such a system is such that the Federal Aviation Administration allows some hours in a simulator to be logged toward a pilot's rating.[68]

The essence of simulation, and the reason why simulations are so pervasive in technical fields, is the existence of a reliable model. The physics of flight, for example, are generally well understood. Modelling a realistic simulation is more a matter of computer technology and programming ingenuity than of creating an accurate model. Even detailed military simulations depend more on accurately modelling the characteristics of various weapons systems than on attempting to model human behaviour. Human behaviour is the essence of politics and accurately modelling it is no easy task.

This is not to say that political scientists have not used simulations. Perhaps the oldest political science simulation in continuous use is the University of Maryland's International Communication and Negotiation Simulation (ICON).[69] Developed in the 1980's, it provides a framework for students and teachers to simulate the negotiation process on a wide range of international issues. Likewise, beginning in 1998, political science professors at the University of Melbourne began using a simulation to assess students based on their proprietary Fablusi role-play simulation generator.[70] Other simulators help students understand everything from the relative impact of various voting systems[71] to Middle Eastern politics.[72] None of these simulations, however, have explored the possibility of the simulation as a predictive tool, appropriate for intelligence analysis.

In 1993, I set out to test exactly such a hypothesis. Using the then transitioning country of Hungary as a test case, I developed a simulation based on the model described above. Data regarding Hungary was gathered exclusively from open sources, various experts and extensive field study conducted in the summer of 1993. Graduate and undergraduate students (mostly political science majors) from Florida State University participated in 14 iterations of the simulation. In all, nearly 150 students participated.

Students took on the role of the leader of one the eight major political parties in Hungary at the time. While the model dictated the rules which would define the interaction between the parties, outside of those rules, the participants were free

194

to interact in any way they saw fit. While the major goal of the simulation was to provide a concrete set of predictions regarding the outcome of the 1994 Hungarian general elections (still 6 months in the future at the time of the simulation), data was collected on a wide variety of variables each of which was subject to confirmation.

While the simulation was explicitly designed to generate predictive results that could be matched against reality, it turned out to have several additional interesting properties. First, when asked, students claimed that is was an effective way to teach about Hungary and Hungarian politics (8.52 on a scale of 1 to 10 with 1 being 'learned a little' and 10 being 'learned a great deal')[73]. Students also indicated that they were willing to participate in such a simulation again (9.36 on a scale of 1 to 10) and, in the strongest result, indicated that they had enjoyed the process (9.37 on a scale of 1 to 10). These results predict and compare favourably to the results found in other, more recent, political science simulations used exclusively for teaching[74].

The predicted results generated by the simulation correlate highly with what actually occurred in Hungary. First, the parties in power during the months between the playing of the simulation and the elections remained the same. The simulation predicted this result. In 91% of the turns played the ruling coalition stayed in power. Likewise, in 89% of the turns, the parties in power in the simulation formed a 'minimum winning coalition'. The theory of the minimum winning coalition is seen so often in real life that it has become a truism of political science, one that further indicates the validity of the model. Given that the coalition in power remained the same as in real life, one would expect that the policies selected by that coalition would mirror those chosen by the participants in the simulation. This occurred 80% of the time (despite having over 80 policy options from which to choose). Finally, with regard to the elections, the simulated range of results encompassed the actual results in approximately 85% of the cases.[75]

In preparing this chapter I began to examine the model in light of the most recent transition from authoritarian rule, that of Afghanistan. On its face there is little comparison between Hungary in 1993 and Afghanistan in 2002. Using the same criteria described in the model above, however, I was able to identify 11 politically active factions in Afghanistan compared to the 8 I found in Hungary.

195

Likewise, the number of interest groups vying for political power in the region appears to be significantly higher (68 vice 28). As a result of the increased political complexity in the region, the number of policy options available to leaders increased from 84 to over 150. Thus, despite the obvious increase in complexity, I found that the model seemed to fit nicely around the facts of the Afghani transition.

Based on these admittedly preliminary results, there seems to be more than adequate grounds for the continued exploration of the use of simulations by peacekeepers and others for predictive purposes. This technique is inexpensive, can be done using only open sources and has a proven training value. If the results described above can be replicated, it would be 70-90% accurate over the short to medium term and would involve no special equipment (though special training in using the technique would be necessary). Using the model above and with access to a handful of subject matter experts, a simulation of virtually any area in the world could be put together in a matter of weeks. Likewise, as new information comes in, the model can easily capture that knowledge within the structure of the simulation. This, in turn, could provide a sort of 'institutional knowledge' regarding the situation in the country (this last attribute is particularly useful for peacekeepers as they often rotate in and out of country).

Simulations have long served political scientists as useful teaching tools. Now, with the explosion of new thinking in the hard sciences about how to model complex systems, it appears that the simulation is ready to escape the classroom and become a useful tool in the hands of the peacekeeper.

Endnotes

---

[1] Guillermo O'Donnell and Phillipe C. Schmitter, *Transitions From Authoritarian Rule: Tentative Conclusions About Uncertain Democracies* (Baltimore: Johns Hopkins Press 1986) p.66.

[2] For an excellent introduction to site-swapping mathematics see 'Site-Swaps: How to Write Down a Juggling Pattern' at http://www.cix.co.uk/~solipsys/new/SiteSwap.html (accessed in January 2003).

[3] Peter J. Beek, and Arthur Lewbel, 'The Science of Juggling', *Scientific American* 5 (1995) pp.92-97

[4] Hartmut Jürgens, Heinz-Otto Peitgen and Dietmar Saupe, *Chaos and Fractals: New Frontiers of Science*, (New York: Springer Verlag 1992) pp. 255-257.

[5] Dankwart Rustow, 'Transitions to Democracy: Toward a Dynamic Model', *Comparative Politics* (April 1970) p. 344.

[6] O'Donnell and Schmitter, *Transitions* p. 6.

[7] This is not a common assumption. See the models discussed in David Collier and Deborah Norden, 'Strategic Choice Models of Political Change in Latin America', *Comparative Politics* 2 (1992) pp.229-243 and Samuel P. Huntington, *The Third Wave: Democratization in the Late Twentieth Century* (Norman, Oklahoma: University of Oklahoma Press 1991) pp.109-163 for examples of models that do not assume this. Despite this, it is often recognized. See Yossi Shain and Juan Linz, 'The Role of Interim Governments,' *Journal of Democracy* 1 (1992) p.75 and O'Donnell and Schmitter, *Transitions*, p.3.

[8] Joseph Held, The *Columbia History of Eastern Europe in the Twentieth Century* (New York: Columbia University Press 1992) p.269.

[9] Huntington, *The Third Wave*, p.75.

[10] O'Donnell and Schmitter, *Transitions*, 15; Yossi and Linz, 'Interim Governments,' p.75 and Klaus Von Beyme, 'Transition to Democracy or Anschluss? The Two Germanies and Europe,' *Government and Opposition* 25 (1990) p.172.

[11] O'Donnell and Schmitter, *Transitions*, p.17.

[12] Held, *History of Eastern Europe*, pp.xxxiv-xxxv and pp.219-222.

[13] Vladimir Tismaneanu, *Reinventing Politics* (New York: The Free Press 1992) pp.138-142. Compare with O'Donnell and Schmitter, *Transitions*, pp.6 and 26; and Gregorz Ekiert, 'Democratization Processes in East Central Europe: A Theoretical Reconsideration,' *British Journal of Political Science* 3 (1991) pp.286-287 and 312.

[14] Rustow, 'Transitions to Democracy: Toward a Dynamic Model', *Comparative Politics* 3 (1970) pp.337-363. The idea that transitions from authoritarian rule occur in phases is not new as evidenced by this chapter. The idea that these phases are iterative is.

[15] Herbert Kitschelt, 'The Formation of Party Systems In East Central Europe', *Politics and Society* 1 (1992) p.11.

[16] Arend Lijphart, *Democracies: Patterns of Majoritarian and Consensus Government in Twenty-one Countries* (New Haven: Yale University Press 1984) p.128.

[17] Robert Dahl, *Polyarchy: Participation and Opposition* (New Haven: Yale University Press 1971) p.4. What Dahl calls 'Liberalization', I refer to as 'Participation', since the primary liberalizing attribute is the ability for more and more people to participate as candidates for elected office.

[18] Held, *History of Eastern Europe*, pp.11-15 and S.N. Sangmpam, 'The Overpoliticized State and Democratization: A Theoretical Model', *Comparative Politics* 4 (1992), p.413.

[19] Dahl, *Polyarchy*, p. 4.

[20] Huntington, *The Third Wave*, p.7 and John Hibbing and Samuel Patterson, 'A Democratic Legislature in the Making: The Historic Hungarian Elections of 1990', *Comparative Politics* 1 (1992) p.433.

[21] Schmitter and T. Karl, 'What Democracy is...and is not,' *Journal of Democracy* 2 (1991), p. 81-82 and Kitschelt, 'Formation of Party Systems', p. 13.

[22] Ibid.

[23] Lijphart, *Democracies*, pp.138-139.

[24] O'Donnell and Schmitter, *Transitions*, pp.28-32 and Huntington, *The Third Wave*, p.169.

[25] Lijphart, *Democracies*, pp.129-132; O'Donnell and Schmitter, *Transitions*, pp.45-47 and Huntington, *The Third Wave*, pp.59-72 and Valerie Bunce, 'The Struggle for Liberal Democracy in Eastern Europe', *World Policy Journal* 3 (1990) pp. 405-406.

[26] David Lake, 'Powerful Pacifists: Democratic States and War,' *American Political Science Review* 1 (1992) 24-35.

[27] *Atlas of Eastern Europe* (Washington: Central Intelligence Agency 1990) pp.35-37 and Tismaneanu, *Reinventing Politics*, p.244.

[28] Lijphart, *Democracies*, p.144.

[29] Kristan J. Wheaton, *Modeling and Simulating Transitions From Authoritarian Rule* (Florida State University 1993) 55-56.

[30] For a general discussion of coding problems in the social sciences see Earl Babbie, *The Practice of Social Research* (Belmont: Wadsworth Publishing Co. 1989).

[31] O'Donnell and Schmitter, *Transitions*, p.58; Lijphart, *Democracies*, pp.141-143 and Tismaneanu, *Reinventing Politics*, p.177.

[32] Kitschelt, 'Formation of Party Systems', p.2 and O'Donnell and Schmitter, *Transitions*, p.58.

[33] Tismaneanu, *Reinventing Politics*, p.177; Held, *History of Eastern Europe*, pp.3-9 and 260; Sabrina Ramet, *Nationalism and Federalism in Yugoslavia* (Bloomington: Indiana University Press, 1992), pp.203-204.

[34] Kitschelt, 'Formation of Party Systems', p.28 and Figs. 4-7. Kitschelt tried, in a rudimentary way, to define the political power of a party. I am talking about a much more specific measure.

[35] Held, *History of Eastern Europe*, pp.34-53.

[36] Tismaneanu, *Reinventing Politics*, pp.179-191.

[37] Held, *History of Eastern Europe*, p.129.

[38] Ibid., p.260.

[39] O'Donnell and Schmitter, *Transitions*, p.58.

[40] Ibid., p.37.

[41] Ibid., p.58.

[42] Ibid., pp.39-40 and pp.49-50.

[43] Huntington, *The Third Wave*, p.75.

[44] Held, *History of Eastern Europe*, pp.263-264.

[45] Ibid., 263-264 and 274.

[46] O'Donnell and Schmitter, *Transitions*, p.46.

[47] Held, *History of Eastern Europe*, pp.318-319.

[48] Benjamin Franklin may have been thinking about this process when he said, 'Gentlemen, we must all hang together or, certainly, we will all hang separately.'

[49] Held, *History of Eastern Europe*, p.349.

[50] Huntington, *The Third Wave*, pp.292-294.

[51] Held, *History of Eastern Europe*, pp.liv-lxix.

[52] O'Donnell and Schmitter, *Transitions*, p.38 and John Sloan, 'The Policy Capabilities of Democratic Regimes in Latin America,' *Latin American Research Review*, 2 (1989) p.116.

[53] O'Donnell and Schmitter, *Transitions*, p.38 and Huntington, *The Third Wave*, pp.169-171 and Sloan, 'Policy Implications', p.124.

[54] Held, *History of Eastern Europe*, p.146 and pp.275-276.

[55] Huntington, *The Third Wave*, pp.290-292.

[56] Lijphart, *Democracies*, pp.150-168.

[57] Dahl, *Polyarchy*, p.6.

[58] Ibid.

[59] Kitschelt, 'Formation of Party Systems', p.9.

[60] O'Donnell and Schmitter, *Transitions*, pp.57-59.

[61] Ibid., pp.61-64 and Huntington, *The Third Wave*, pp.174-178.

[62] Gregor Ferguson, *Coup D'Etat: A Practical Manual* (New York: Sterling Publishing Company 1987) p.13.

[63] O'Donnell and Schmitter, *Transitions*, p.25.

[64] Ferguson, *Coup D'Etat*, p.20.

[65] O'Donnell and Schmitter, *Transitions*, p.25.

[66] Ibid., p.62.

[67] Rustow, 'Transitions', pp.358-360. Although Rustow is talking about transitions to democracy, I find that the idea compelling that some general, minimal level of satisfaction is the signal that the process is complete.

[68] For an excellent commercial website on flight simulation and simulators see: http://www.advancedsimulation.com/ (accessed in January 2003).

[69] See http://www.icons.umd.edu/about/history.htm for additional information about ICON (accessed in January 2003).

[70] See http://ts.mivu.org/default.asp?show=article&id=816 for additional information about the Fablusi generator (accessed in January 2003).

[71] See http://politicalsim.com/index.html for an example of such a simulation (accessed in January 2003).

[72] A. Vincent and J. Shepherd, 'Experiences in Teaching Middle Eastern Politics via Internet based Role Play Simulations', *Journal of Interactive Media in Education* 11 (1998).
[73] Wheaton, *Modeling*, pp.81-84.
[74] Albert Ip and Roni Linser, 'Evaluation of a Role-Play Simulation in Political Science', *Technology Source*, 1/2 (2001).
[75] Wheaton, *Modeling*, pp.84-95.

Information Peacekeeping & the Future of Intelligence

'The United Nations, Smart Mobs, & the Seven Tribes'[1]

Robert David Steele

Introduction

The future of global intelligence is emergent today. There are five revolutionary trends that will combine to create a global information society helpful to global stability and prosperity.

First, the traditional national intelligence tribe, the tribe of secret warfare and strategic analysis, will be joined by six other tribes, each of which will gradually assume co-equal standing in a secure global network: the military, law enforcement, business, academic, non-governmental and media, and religious or citizen intelligence tribes, the latter being 'smart clans' and 'smart mobs' challenging 'dumb nations' for power.

Second, in those specific areas generic to all tribes, collaborative advances will be made, and codified in 'best practices' defined by the International Organization for Standardization (ISO);[2] included will be shared competencies and standards related to global multi-lingual open source collection, massive geospatially-based multi-media processing; analytic toolkits; analytic tradecraft; operations security; defensive counterintelligence; and the capstone areas of leadership, training, and culture.

Third, multi-lateral information sharing rather than unilateral secrecy will be the primary characteristic of intelligence, we will still need and use spies, including spies skilled in offensive counterintelligence and covert action, not only clandestine collection, but fully 80% of the value of intelligence will be in shared collection, shared processing, and shared analysis.

Fourth, intelligence will become personal, public, & political. It will be taught in all schools and become a core competency for every knowledge worker; it will emerge as a mixed public-private good and a benchmark against which investments of the taxpayer dollar can be judged; and it will impact on politics as elected and appointed officials are evaluated by the voters based on their longer-term due diligence in applying intelligence to the public interest.

Fifth and finally, intelligence will transform peacekeeping by simultaneously making the public case for major increases in funding for 'soft power' instruments among the Nations, to include funding for permanent United Nations (UN) constabulary forces, as well as a United Nations Open Decision Information Network (UNODIN), itself a strategic and tactical intelligence architecture for multicultural policy, acquisition, and operational decisions having to do with global security.[3]

Seven Intelligence Tribes

First, the tribes. When it first became clear to me, around 1986, that no single nation and certainly no single intelligence organization, was capable of single-handedly mastering the data acquisition, data entry, and data translation or data conversion challenges associated with 24/7 'global coverage,' I initially conceptualized a global network of national-level agencies cooperating with one another.

However, in the course of sponsoring over fifteen international conferences, during which I have deliberately sought to bring before my national intelligence colleagues the best that the private sector has to offer, it has become obvious to me that there are seven tribes of intelligence, not one; that all of these tribes are at very elementary stages in their development; and that the tribes share some generic functionalities that lend themselves to burden-sharing, at the same time that the tribes also have unique conditions where they alone can excel.

For the sake of simplicity, and recognising that the evaluations will vary from nation to nation, I will tell you what I think of our intelligence tribes in relation to my concept of an objective or 'perfect' intelligence standard. On a scale where 100 is the achievable score, I see National at 50%, Military at 40%, Business and Academic at 30%, and the remaining three tribes, Law Enforcement, Non-Governmental Organisations (NGO), Media, and Religious-Citizenry, at 20%, as shown in Figure 1.

- National: 50   out of 100
- Military: 40   out of 100
- Business: 30   out of 100
- Academic: 30   out of 100
- Law Enforcement: 20   out of 100
- NGO-Media: 20   out of 100
- Religious-Citizenry   20   out of 100

Figure 1: Evaluation of the Objective Capabilities of Each Tribe[4]

So, only at the national level are we halfway competent, and we still receive a failing grade, 50%. The military, in part because of massive spending on targeting and virtually unlimited manpower, is close behind with 40%. Business is skewed upwards to 30% by the oil, pharmaceutical, and some financial or insurance companies, or it would be 10%. Similarly, academia has some centers of excellence that help the group achieve 30% but it too is closer to the 10% mark. Finally, in the lowest tier, are religions, clans, and citizens, although Opus Dei, the Papal Nuncio, B'Nai Brith, the Islamic World Foundation, and segments of the Mormon religion and certain cults are themselves in the 40% range, overall this group is at 20% and the masses are at 10% or less. The average performance level for all seven tribes in the aggregate is at the 30% level, this is probably too generous, but it will do as a baseline for our assessment.

It merits comment that the relative sophistication of the groups is going to change in inverse proportion to their current status. Religions and clans and citizens, the non-state groups, have fewer legacy investments in technology, and are much more likely to leap ahead of the government and business communities by making faster better use of wireless broadband smart tools, and by being less obsessive about old concepts of security that prevent burden-sharing.

In the new world order, unless governments get smart and deliberately nurture a new network that embraces all of the tribes and brings to the government all advantages from progress being made by the various tribes, I anticipate that this list will be turned on its head, non-state actors will be better at intelligence than governmental organizations, with business and academics remaining loosely in the middle. Law enforcement, unless there are strong business and public advocacy demands at the national level, is likely to remain severely retarded within the new intelligence domain.

Professionalisation through Standards

Second, the generic areas for progress. I listed these in the beginning and show them again in Figure 2. It is obvious to me that the single easiest place to begin is with a global web-based architecture for ensuring that all useful open sources are digitised, translated, and linked using the Open Hyperdocument System (OHS) conceptualised years ago by Doug Englebart, one of the pioneers of the Internet. You should visit him at www.bootstrap.org. A Digital Marshall Plan funded by the USA, and regional joint open source collection, processing, and translation centres, are an obvious and, one would think, non-controversial starting point for a global intelligence community.

- Open Source Collection (24/7 Global Coverage)
- Multi-Media Distributed Processing
- Generic Analytic Toolkits
- Analytic Tradecraft
- Defensive Security & Counterintelligence
- Personnel Certification
- General and Specialist Training
- Leadership & Culture Development

Figure 2: Generic Areas for Tribal Co-Evolution

In a related and equally vital area, I would note that the dirty little secret of all government and corporate Chief Information Officers is that they are only processing, at best, 20% of what they collect, and they are only storing perhaps 20% of what their people generate in the way of records. Electronic mail is rapidly becoming both the primary vehicle for communicating knowledge, and the primary vent for the loss of knowledge. Let me put this in a different way: by developing information technology without having an intelligence architecture in place, we have in effect, slit both our wrists in the bathtub, we do not know when we will die, but death is certain. Along with global coverage of all open sources, we urgently need to create the framework for a globally-distributed processing system that is not held hostage to proprietary vendor technologies. The Europeans are completely correct, especially the Germans, in pressing forward with Open Source Software. Now that the Chinese are also taking LINUX seriously, the way is open for global progress.[5] The sooner we neutralise Bill Gates, the sooner we will be free to develop a truly comprehensive European intelligence community as well as the integrated analytic toolkits that are vital to the intelligence profession.[6]

We have known since the 1980's that there are eighteen distinct analytic functionality's that must be available to every knowledge worker, regardless of tribe, as itemised in Figure 3. These include not only the standard desktop publishing, multi-media presentation, and real-time review and group editing functions, but the much more complex intermediate analytic functions such as collaborative work, structured argument analysis, idea organisation, interactive search and retrieval, map-based visualisation, and modelling or simulation using real world real time data. At the bottom level, fully half the functionality's deal with data entry and conversion, digitisation, translation, image processing, data extraction, data standardisation, clustering and linking, statistical analysis, trend detection, and alert notification. We are nowhere near achieving these integrated functionality's because our governments have failed to understand that national information strategies must provide for the co-ordination of standards and investments as a *sine qua non* for creating Smart Nations.

Functionality's for Finished Production
- Real time Tracking and Real time Group Review
- Desktop Publishing and Word Processing
- Production of Graphics, Videos, and Online Briefings

Functionality's in Support of Analytic Tradecraft
- Collaborative Work
- Note taking and Organising Ideas
- Structured Argument Analysis

- Interactive Search and Retrieval of Data
- Graphic and Map-Based Visualisation of Data
- Modelling and Simulation

Data Entry, Conversion, and Exploitation Functionality's

- Clustering and Linking of Extracted Data
- Statistical Analysis to Reveal Anomalies
- Detection of Changing Trends
- Detection of Alert Situations
- Conversion of Paper Documents to Digital Form
- Automated Foreign Language Translation
- Processing Images, Video, Audio, Signal Data
- Automated Extraction of Data Elements from Text and Images
- Standardising and Converting Data Forms

Figure 3: International Analytic Toolkit[7]

We *must* develop standards so that all data is automatically processable regardless or origin, or language, or security classification. XML Geo, for example, is an emerging standard for providing all data with a geospatial attribute or attributes, and is vital to international data sharing as well as global automated fusion and pattern analysis. The Americans are moving too slowly on this, I would like to see the Europeans press forward on this specific international standard. Mandating transparent stable Application Program Interfaces (API) is an obvious need as well, enabling European, Asian, Near Eastern, and other third-party software to mature together rather than in competition with one another.

I won't discuss analytic tradecraft, security, and counterintelligence here, but they are all important and they can all be developed in an unclassified generic manner that is beneficial to all seven intelligence tribes.[8]

Let me spend a moment on leadership, training, and culture. If there is one area where we must go in entirely different directions from the past, it is in this area of human management. Intelligence professionals are 'gold collar' workers, not factory workers or bank clerks or even engineers. Their job is to think the unthinkable, to make sense out of evil, to draw conclusions while blind-folded with one hand tied behind their backs. The Weberian model of bureaucratic management is simply not suited to the intelligence profession. Thomas Stewart, in his book *The Wealth of Knowledge: Intellectual Capital and the Twenty-First Century Organization* makes the point: 'All the major structures of companies, their legal underpinnings, their systems of governance, their management disciplines, their accounting, are based on a model of the corporation that has become obsolete.'[9] This is ten times truer for intelligence organisations.

In the 21st Century, the intelligence leaders that will succeed are those who break all the 'rules' of the past, they must confront their political masters instead of allowing policy to dictate intelligence; they must be public rather than secret; they must share rather than steal; they must think critically rather than silence critics. We must migrate our cultures to emphasise multilateral over unilateral operations; open sources over secret sources; human expertise over technical spending; analysis over collection; multi-lingual perspectives over mono-lingual; the acknowledgement of mistakes versus the concealment of mistakes, and finally, long-term thinking over short-term thinking. There is no training program for such a culture today, and in America, at least, we have no leaders committed in this direction.

OLD INTELLIGENCE PARADIGM	NEW INTELLIGENCE PARADIGM
Intelligence Driven by Policy	Policy Driven by Intelligence
Unilateral	Multilateral
Mostly Secret	Mostly Public
Technical Emphasis	Human Emphasis
Collection Emphasis	Analysis Emphasis
Mono-lingual focus & filter	Multi-lingual focus and filters
Mistakes hidden	Mistakes acknowledged
Short-term thinking	Long-term thinking

Figure 4: The New Intelligence Paradigm

Within the individual Nations, it is virtually impossible to find leaders who are skilled at working with more than one intelligence tribe, because that is not where we have placed our emphasis. Apart from obsessing on the national intelligence tribe alone, we have allowed the bureaucracy of intelligence to

207

further isolate individual leaders within the culture of an individual organisation with a functional specialisation, such as signals intelligence, imagery intelligence, clandestine intelligence, or analysis. We have also done badly at respecting the vital roles played by counterintelligence and covert action.

At the global and regional levels, while it might appear to be even more unlikely that we can identify, develop, and empower leaders able to work with all seven tribes across national boundaries, I believe it could in fact be easier, because at this level there are no pre-conceived bureaucracies, doctrines, or biases. In my view, if the financial resources can be made available by the United States of America, and key people can be seconded by the various Nations to regional as well as United Nations (UN) intelligence centers and networks, then new intelligence concepts and doctrine and management, and training, and culture, can be devised over the next twenty-five years.

There are three initiatives that can contribute to the accelerated development of intelligence professionalism to a new global standard. First, a project must be undertaken to interview international intelligence specialists in each aspect of intelligence, both functional and topical, with a view to documenting best sources and methods. Such a project is about to begin an initial two-year period, and I believe it will succeed because 9-11 has finally demonstrated that how we do intelligence now is simply not good enough, in combination with other non-traditional threats, e.g. from disease, I believe there is now a demand for new knowledge about the craft of intelligence.[10]

Second, and ideally with help from our European intelligence colleagues, we must convert what we learn from the first project, into International Organisation for Standardisation (ISO) metrics or measures of merit. An ISO series for intelligence will be revolutionary, in part as a means of sharing knowledge about the profession of intelligence; in part as a means of enabling an objective nonpartisan evaluation of the state of intelligence in any given tribe or nation or against a specific target of common interest; and in part as a means of accelerating the evolution of the intelligence discipline from craft to profession.

Third, and in tandem with the first two initiatives, we need both a web-based and a regional center-based approach to intelligence training that permits the best existing training programs from any nation or organisation to become

208

available more broadly, and by thus enabling savings, also permits varied nations and organisations to share the burden of creating new training, including distance learning, on all aspects of both the profession of intelligence, and the objects of its attention, the targets. I envision an Intelligence University with a small campus in each region, perhaps co-located with a major national university, where multi-national classes are offered to the very best candidates from each of the seven tribes, and where they can learn while also getting to know one another at the entry level, at mid-career, and at senior management levels. I also envision a global multi-lingual training curriculum for intelligence, both its practice and its targets, that is web-based, to include interactive video counseling and multi-media visualisation, and that fully integrates open sources of information, all of the elements of the analytic toolkit itemised in Figure 3, and direct access to experts at appropriate levels of availability and cost.[11]

Global Coverage through Multilateral Intelligence

In the third area, that of multi-lateral sharing, I will use both South Asia and Central Asia as examples. It is clear to me that Central Asia, the former Muslim khanates of Bukhara, Khiva, and Kokand, and an area inhabited by unruly Turkmen, today known as Kazakhstan, Kyrgzstan, Tajikistan, Turkmenistan, and Uzbekistan, we have an intelligence challenge of considerable proportions. When we combine that with three countries of Azerbaijan, Armenia and Georgia known as the Caucasus, and with the rest of the Muslim crescent from Pakistan through the contested areas of Kashmir, Nepal, Sri Lanka, and Bangladesh, down to Malaysia, portions of the Philippines, and Indonesia, what we have is a new form of 'denied area', one as complex and challenging as Russia and China have been in the past, and as Arabia and India remain today.

These areas are denied to us by our ignorance, not by any lack of access.

As I do my intelligence headlines every morning, and I select articles about new forms of joint military-police intelligence cooperation within individual countries, or a series of *bi-lateral* intelligence cooperation agreements between Australia and each of several different Asian countries, I keep thinking to myself, 'We need several regional intelligence centres that combine the resources of the many nations and the seven tribes to focus, respectively, on the Caucasus and Central Asia; on Afghanistan, Pakistan, India, and the contested

209

areas; and on the South Asian Muslim crescent.' It is clear to me that the time has come for both national and global revolutions in how we manage intelligence, and the figure below highlights key aspects of this.

NATIONAL REVOLUTION	GLOBAL REVOLUTION
One Leader, Three Deputies	Multi-Lateral Coordination Councils
Secret Collection	Collection
Open Collection	Processing
All-Source Analysis	Analysis
Unite the Seven Tribes	Unite the Seven Tribes
Pool Resources Across the Seven Tribes	Establish Regional Intelligence Centres
Serve the People	Serve the People

Figure 5: Key Aspects of the Revolution in Intelligence Affairs

I have written elsewhere[12] about the need to consolidate classified intelligence capabilities under the authority of one Director of *Classified* Intelligence (DCI); the need to create a counterpart Director of Public Information (DPI) who is empowered, at least in the United States of America, with a $1.5 billion a year Global Knowledge Foundation,[13] and the need for a National Intelligence Council at the Prime Ministerial or Presidential level which can fully leverage and integrate the expertise and access of all seven tribes of intelligence. Although not specified in Figure 5, it is also essential at the national level that there exists a National Information Strategy, and a single National Processing Agency that can be entrusted with the secure integration and exploitation of all information available to the national government, both secret and non-secret (e.g. immigration applications).

The global revolution in intelligence affairs should be manifested in the establishment of three multi-national co-ordination councils, each consisting of the respective Associate Deputy Directors of National Intelligence for Collection, for Processing, and for Analysis. An executive secretariat for each, and a secure web-based means of tracking requirements, data, analytic products, and individual experts, would complete this global partnership. At the same time, there must be at least six regional centres where multi-lateral intelligence co-ordination and co-operation becomes a reality.

210

Below is a depiction of one such centre, for South Asia.

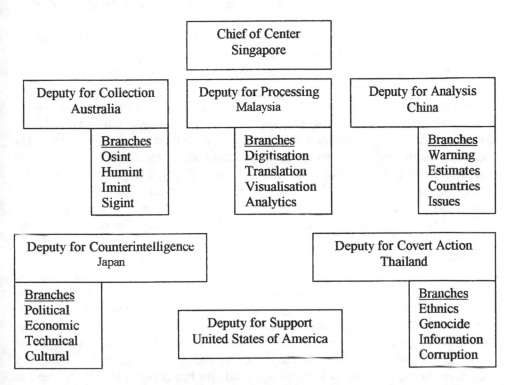

Figure 6: Regional Intelligence Center

It merits emphasis that the regional centres would have both management and staff that are truly international, with 'out of area' managers and staff being especially helpful in ensuring that 'localities' does not undermine the professionalism of the activity. Naturally there would be various means of carrying out quality assurance, and each Nation would retain the prerogative of managing its own unilateral collection, processing, and analysis. Each participating Nation would receive management positions commensurate with its financial or staffing contributions as well as its expertise, and every position would have both a primary and a secondary incumbent, with the secondary always being from a different nationality. Over time, each centre would strive to integrate managers and staff from all seven tribes, not only the national tribe,

211

and rotationals to at least one Centre would become a pre-requisite for promotion to the highest levels within any tribe but especially the national tribe.

The case of the United Nations, unlike the North Atlantic Treaty Organisation (NATO) or the International Committee of the Red Cross (ICRC) or INTERPOL, merits a brief comment. The UN is conflicted about intelligence, equating it with espionage instead of decision-support. Unfortunately, the UN approach now, one of classic denial, is to tip-toe toward 'information' functions in a vain attempt to achieve intelligence, while refusing to take seriously the value of intelligence as a craft, as a process, and as an emerging profession. On the one hand, despite the most recent commitment of the Secretary General to reform the Department of Public Information (DPI), that department remains a one-way highway from the UN to the Public, with 77 disparate 'lanes' (information centres) that are good at *dissemination* but not good at collection, processing, or analysis. Earlier, in 2000, the Secretary General created an Information and Strategic Analysis Secretariat within the Department of Political Affairs, in cautious recognition of the UN's deficiencies in strategic intelligence analysis.[14] This has not, however, resolved the urgent gaps in intelligence support for peacekeeping and humanitarian policy, acquisition, and operations, nor does it actually provide a full range of intelligence services, including tailored overt collection and massive multi-media processing, for political affairs. In this sense, it may be said that the Secretariat is a dangerous stop-gap, misdirecting UN 'intelligence' at this early point in the Secretary General's consideration of longer-term needs for broad reforms that will lead to strategic, regional, tactical, and technical decision-support for all UN policies, procurements, and programs.

It may be that the UN, NATO, ICRC, and INTERPOL should consider sponsoring both an intelligence-information 'audit' of their own organisations, and follow this with a joint two-week workshop with world-class intelligence authorities whose task it might be to educate senior managers about intelligence; to elicit from them their vision of emerging and changing requirements for intelligence from within their organisations; and to devise, in partnership with those senior managers, a campaign plan for both defining generic 'best practices' suitable for adoption by the UN, and establishing a program within each organisation that integrates overt, legal, ethical intelligence practices into every aspect of their operations.[15]

212

Intelligence as a Public Good

This leads to the fourth area of change, in which intelligence must become personal, public, & political. I believe that there is a proven process of intelligence that has extraordinary value, and that there are among us a few great practitioners, of intelligence collection, of intelligence analysis, of counterintelligence, of covert action in all its forms, whose best practices must be documented and standardised and taught to entire societies. In my view, national security and national prosperity in the 21st Century are absolutely contingent on our rescuing the population from its factory-era educational system that creates drones-slaves for machines. We must migrate the essence of the intelligence profession to the other six tribes, and make every citizen an 'intelligence minuteman', as Alessandro Politi put it so well in 1992. I believe that intelligence is a mixed public-private good[16] , and that our policy makers will not make intelligent decisions, nor respect intelligence, until we first establish our value in the minds and hearts of those who pay taxes and elect politicians, the citizens.

Especially important will be our establishment of longer-term perspectives that hold policymakers accountable for foolish decisions with very bad consequences far out into the future, and our provision of useful intelligence to the public that will help citizens demand responsible decision-making with respect to public health, the environment, water and energy scarcity, cultures of violence, and other non-traditional threats to the future of our children.

My concept for a global revolution in intelligence affairs restores the connection between taxation, representation, and action.

Information Peacekeeping from Public Intelligence

#1: Public intelligence will change <u>what</u> we spend money on.
#2: Public intelligence will change <u>when</u> & <u>how</u> we intervene.
#3: Public intelligence will change <u>who</u> does the thinking & deciding.
#4: Public intelligence will change who makes a difference & how.
#5: Public intelligence will change how the world views intelligence.
#6: Public intelligence will change the strategic focus of all organisations.

Figure 7: Public Intelligence and Information Peacekeeping

Alvin Toffler in his book *PowerShift* talked about how information is a substitute for both wealth and violence and of course Sun Tzu spoke centuries ago of how the acme of skill is to defeat the enemy without fighting. These and other ideas inspired me in the mid-1990's to focus on the concept of *information peacekeeping*, and I concluded then, both in a paper for the U.S. Institute of Peace subsequently published in the *Journal of Conflict Resolution*, and in a chapter for one of the *CYBERWAR* books, that information peacekeeping is both the purest form of war, and the best means of avoiding and resolving conflict.[17] But how, one might ask? I will answer.

First, as intelligence professionals we have to admit to ourselves that we have failed to impact on policy where it matters most: on how the national treasure is spent. In America we spend roughly $400 billion dollars a year on military 'heavy metal' that is useful only 10% of the time; and we spend roughly $40 billion a year on each of the three other major domains of national power: diplomacy including economic, educational, and cultural initiatives; intelligence; and homeland security or counterintelligence. We spend almost nothing, at the strategic level, on global public health or global environmental stabilisation, areas where some estimate that $100 billion a year is needed for each of these two challenges, modest sums, considering the replacement cost of an entire population or planet. As we move toward a future in which intelligence is very much a public good and labouring in the public service, I expect that we will spend less on conventional military forces, and more on 'soft power'.[18] At some point, if multi-cultural intelligence is effective and the seven tribes work together, I expect us to make the case for a global health service and universal health care; a fully-funded standing United Nations constabulary force with organic weapons, mobility, and communications capabilities; and also a fully-funded global 'rescue fund' for stopping environmental degradation.

This answers the question of *what* we must buy in the way of instruments of national power. It will take at least twenty years to achieve the influence that I believe we are capable of, and thus strike a better balance in how major Nations spend taxpayer dollars.

That leaves another question unanswered: *when* do we intervene in failed or rogue state situations or conditions? Intelligence has failed here as well. Kristan Wheaton, one of our most capable defence attaches, today supporting the

International Tribunal, has written a fine book called *The Warning Solution: Intelligent Analysis in the Age of Information Overload* (AFCEA International Press, 2002). He explains why we have failed and focuses on the simple fact that policymakers are overwhelmed with $50 billion dollar problems right now, and do not have the time to consider $1 billion or even $5 billion 'interventions'. Robert Vickers, the National Intelligence Officer for Warning, a man who did what he could to get the U.S. policymakers to focus on Rwanda and Burundi, on Bosnia and Kosovo, in time to prevent genocide, has coined the term 'inconvenient warning'. In England they speak of 'warning fatigue'.

In the aftermath of 9-11, when over 3.000 people died in a very dramatic way, there was much talk about how this would change our understanding of the world and our appreciation for how we must invest in alternative forms of national power. *Nothing has changed.* We have given billions of dollars to the same bad managers and old mind-sets that failed to protect America in the first place, and our President decided to pick a fight with Iraq while deliberately ignoring North Korean nuclear weaponization, possibly even keeping this information from the Senate[19], he also decided to support outrageous Israeli incursions on the Palestinians; to avoid confronting the Saudi Arabian financiers of global terrorism; to accept Pakistani and Chinese and Russian deceptions; and to shun his responsibilities for the 32 complex emergencies, 66 countries with millions of refugees, 33 countries with massive starvation issues; 59 countries with plagues and epidemics; the 18 genocide campaigns; and the many other issues of water scarcity, resource waste, corruption, and censorship that contribute to what William Shawcross calls a state of endless war among and within nations.[20] If intelligence is remedial education for policy-makers, as Dr. Gordon Oehler, one of the truly great CIA analyst-leaders has said, then we have failed here as well, over the course of many Presidents, not just the one we have now.

Norman Cousins, in his book *The Pathology of Power* (Norton, 1987), observes that governments cannot perceive great truths, only small and intermediate truths. It is the people that can perceive great truths, such as the need for massive new endeavours to stabilise our world and deal with what can only be considered global transnational multi-cultural issues under the jurisdiction of no one nation, and of vital importance to all nations.

215

Inspired in part by Cousins, and Shawcross, and many others who have spoken at OSS conferences over the years, or whose books I have read and reviewed on Amazon.com, I came to the conclusion after 9-11 that another 5.000 Americans will die, within the American homeland, before the people become angry enough to demand change.

Change is not going to come from the bureaucracy, nor from the politicians and their corporate paymasters, until the people are aroused.

I expect at least 5.000 *additional* deaths across Australia, Europe, and Russia, all are as much at risk as America, and all countries and organisations have every reason to take intelligence reforms as seriously as I do.

We must arouse the people, by informing the people, through public intelligence.

In the 21st Century, as Carol Dumaine from Global Futures Partnership[21] has noted, the lines among the various intelligence constituencies—I call them tribes—are blurring, and we are becoming, very slowly, a very large, informal, global network of professionals whose personal brand names matter more than our citizenship or specific responsibilities. We are, possibly, the first layer of what may become the World Brain.

The question of 'when' to intervene will be answered by the people once they become 'smart mobs' within a World Brain architecture that contains eight integrated web-based elements open to all tribes and all individuals, as listed in the figure below, together with web-enabled means for tracking political and economic decisions at every level (local through global), for communicating with policy-makers, and for dismissing rascals who fail to listen.

Weekly Reports	Distance Learning
Virtual Libraries	Expert Forums
Shared Directories	Shared Calendars
Shared Budget Information	Shared Geospatial Plot/Active Map

Figure 8: Changing How the World Views Intelligence

In my view, in the next five years, we have the following objectives:

First, to nurture and advance each of the seven tribes within each Nation.
Every Nation should manage an annual conference that brings the seven tribes together. I would be glad if each Nation sent a delegation of seven, one person from each tribe, to the annual OSS conference, and held their own national conferences two weeks later, as the Swedes do. Logically, there should be national security conferences at the local and provincial levels as well, and annual national and international meetings of each of the seven tribes.[22]

Second, to devise generic solutions to those intelligence challenges that are of common concern to the seven tribes and to all Nations. The Americans have the money, other nations underestimate their power to influence American spending, at least in this minor area for which there is no competing domestic constituency. If these issues are raised at the Ministerial level, eventually there will be a Global Intelligence Council, including all seven tribes, not only the national tribe, able to make decisions on co-ordinated standards and investments. There can be Regional Intelligence Centres. There can be ISO standards for every aspect of the intelligence profession.[23] There can be a generic analytic toolkit and a global program to ensure all information in all languages is available to every analyst. There can be a global grid that links sources, experts, citizens, and policymakers in an interactive structured credible manner not now available through the Internet.

Third, to support the establishment as soon as possible of the United Nations Open Decision Information Network, UNODIN. The Secretary General announced in late September that humanitarian affairs and public information were the two areas where he wishes to achieve substantial reform. There is much resistance to the Secretary General's desire to migrate from an archipelago of seventy-seven libraries and introspective research centres, to a global network that is capable of collecting, processing, and analysing multi-media information 'on the fly' in order to provide actionable intelligence decision-support to the United Nations leadership. Right now the United Nations relies for its intelligence on American secrets and academic processing of open sources, this is the worst of all possible worlds. Each Nation's delegation to the United Nations must be educated about this situation, and must work together to sponsor a proper plan for using funding from both the Member nations and from benefactors like George Soros and Ted Turner, to create a World Intelligence Centre, a global web-based UNODIN, and independent United Nations collection capabilities, perhaps developed in partnership with the emerging European intelligence community. We must not allow American mistakes and mind-sets to cripple or corrupt the future intelligence architecture of the community of nations.

Fourth, and last, to serve the citizen public. Policymakers will come and go, and often be corrupt, but the people are forever, and often ignorant. What we do is honourable, but we are in our infancy. We have a very long road ahead of us. If we evolve intelligently, by the end of this decade we will see a public intelligence network that empowers the citizens to the point that they will establish more balanced allocations of money across the varied instruments of national power; they will improve our responsiveness to early warning; and they will insist that we have the necessary investments in a global multi-cultural network capable of providing 24/7 intelligence support to diplomatic operations, to law enforcement operations, to ethical business operations, to academic and cultural outreach operations, and to humanitarian as well as environmental sustainability operations.

Only by earnestly supporting and educating the people, and by establishing international standards, can the profession of intelligence achieve its full potential.

The new craft of intelligence is the best hope for achieving global stability and prosperity though informed decision-making at every level of society, within each of the seven tribes that comprise the 'brains' of any nation. Millions more will die before we get it right. There is no time to waste; we must start now.

Endnotes

---

[1] This chapter was prepared for presentation as the keynote dinner speech to the annual conference on 'Peacekeeping and Intelligence: Lessons for the Future?' sponsored by the Netherlands Defence College (IDL) and the Netherlands Intelligence Studies Association (NISA), 15-16 November 2002 in The Hague, The Netherlands. An electronic copy of the latest available draft can be obtained at www.oss.net within Archives/Speeches. The term 'smart mobs' is attributed to Howard Rheingold, author

of *Smart Mobs: The Next Social Revolution—Transforming Cultures and Communities in the Age of Instant Access* (Perseus 2002) as well as brilliant earlier books on tools for thinking, virtual reality, and virtual communities. The distinction among the seven tribes (or 'communities of interest') is original to the author. Many books have contributed to my understanding of the nexus among intelligence as a craft, information technology as a tool, and communities as a state of mind-culture, and most of them are listed in the several hundred pages of annotated bibliography in each of my first two books, with details and core chapters available free at www.oss.net. Apart from all the books written by Rheingold, five in particular merit special mention here as fundamental references: Robert Carkhuff, *The Examplar: The Exemplary Performer in an Age of Productivity* (Human Resource Development Press 1984); Harlan Cleveland, *The Knowledge Executive: Leadership in an Information Society* (New York: Truman Talley 1985); Kevin Kelley, *Out of Control: The Rise of Neo-Biological Civilization* (Reading, MA: Addison-Wesley 1994); Paul Strassmann, *Information Payoff: The Transformation of Work in the Electronic Age* (New York: Free Press 1985); and Alvin Toffler, *Power Shift: Knowledge, Wealth, and Violence at the Edge of the 21st Century* (New York: Bantam 1990).

[2] The acronym ISO is based on the Greek for 'same' or 'standard' and does not correspond to the name of the organization in any language. My thanks to Col Walter J. Breede, USMC (Ret.) for pointing this out. The International Organization for Standardization and its new President-elect, Mr. Ollie Smoot, recently committed to furthering 'the role of open and global standards for achieving an inclusive information society.' In partnership with the United Nations Economic Commission for Europe (UN/ECE), the International Telecommunication Union – Standardization Department (ITU-T), and the International Electrotechnical Commission (IEC), they hosted a summit 7-9 November 2002 in Bucharest, Romania on the topic of 'Global Standards for the Global Information Society.' At this point in time only the original press release is available to the public, at www.iso.ch.

[3] While the author has a very strong interest in the future potential of the United Nations (UN) as a global intelligence *qua* decision-support network, and will continue to articulate views regarding the future of the United Nations, at no time should anyone construe statements by the author about the UN as being suggestive that any advisory relationship exists with that organization, or any of its leaders, either contractually or *pro bono*. The known antipathy of the UN to intelligence *qua* espionage and its existing problems (a one-way public information highway with seventy-seven lanes, multiple centers of influence with competing desk officers, and the absence of a global information strategy for external information acquisition, distributed processing, and web-based dissemination of all UN publications, both formal and informal), suggest that the UN is both a most worthy object of attention for intelligence reform, and

219

perhaps the greatest challenge, greater even than the U.S. Intelligence Community with its opposite obsession on secret technical collection to the detriment of all else. [4] Since I have written two books on the national tribe and have planned a book on each of the remaining six tribes (plus a book on Whole Earth intelligence and a final book on The Ethics of Intelligence), I do not want to go into great detail here on the nature of each tribe. Outlines and discussion groups for all eight new books are at www.oss.net. However, below is a table that provides a short description of the tribe, a representative professional association (or two), and representative books. There are no truly international associations for any tribe with the exception of the religious tribes—generally each tribe has national or industry associations, all of which would benefit from a new web-based federation of tribes that can be integrated geographically, functionally, and by industry or topic, while sharing generic open transparent standards and 'best practices.'

National Intelligence Tribe. Primarily comprised of the official intelligence agencies, but can and should include portions of the diplomatic and other government departments with international responsibilities.	Association of Former Intelligence Officers (AFIO) www.afio.org	Robert D'A. Henderson, *Brassey's International Intelligence Yearbook, 2002 Edition* (Washington DC: Brassey's 2002); Robert David Steele, *On Intelligence: Spies and Secrecy in an Open World* (Oakton, Va.: OSS 2002); Michael Herman, *Intelligence Power in Peace and War* (Cambridge: Cambridge University Press 1996); Robert S. McNamara and James G. Blight, *Wilson's Ghost* (New York: Public Affairs, 2001)
Military Intelligence Tribe. Primarily those serving directly in military intelligence occupational specialties but should include defense attaches, topographical and foreign area specialists, and direct liaison personnel.	National Military Intelligence Association (NMIA) www.nima. org	George W. Allen, *None So Blind: A Personal Account of the Intelligence Failure in Vietnam* (Ivan R. Dee, 2001); James J. Wirtz, *The Tet Offensive: Intelligence Failure in War* (Ithaca: Cornell University Press 1991); Samuel M. Katz, *Soldier Spies: Israeli Military Intelligence* (Novato, CA: Presidio Press 1992); Tom Mangold and John Penycate, *The Tunnels of Chu Chi* (Berkeley 1985)
Law Enforcement Intelligence Tribe. Ideally should include undercover officers, technical collectors, and managers, in reality tends to be limited to civilian police analysts. This is the weakest tribe, and the most important, the linch pin for global tribal change.	International Association of Law Enforcement Intelligence Analysts www.ialea. org	Peter Gill, *Rounding Up the Usual Suspects? Developments in contemporary law enforcement intelligence* (Aldershot: Ashgate 2000); Marilyn B. Peterson et al. (editors), *Intelligence 2000: Revising the Basic Elements* (IALEIA, 2000); Robert B. Oakley et al (editors(, *Policing the New World Disorder* (Washington DC: National Defense University 1998); Angus Smith (editor), *Intelligence-Led Policing: International Perspectives on Policing in the 21st Century* (IALEIA, 1997)

Business Intelligence Tribe. Primarily comprised of business or competitive intelligence practitioners but should include strategic planners, market research, scientific & technical or private investigators, information brokers and special (business) librarians.	Society of Competitive Intelligence Professionals (SCIP) www.scip.org Association of Independent Information Brokers www.aiip.org	Babette E. Bensoussan and Craig S. Fleisher, *Strategic and Competitive Analysis: Methods and Techniques for Analyzing Business Competition* (Upper Saddle River NJ: Prentice Hall 2003); W. Bradford Ashton and Richard A. Klavans, *Keeping Abreast of Science and Technology: Technical Intelligence for Business* (Columbus: Batelle Press 1997); Ben Gilad, *Business Blindspots* (Cambridge: Probus Publishing Company 1994); Sue Rugge and Alfred Glossbreener, *The Information Broker's Handbook* (New York: McGraw-Hill 1992)
Academic Intelligence Tribe. Ideally should include all subject matter specialists; in reality tend to be limited to those with an international affairs or comparative politics interest.	International Studies Association (ISA) www.isanet.org	David L. Boren and Edward J. Perkins (editors), *Preparing America's Foreign Policy for the 21st Century* (Norman: University of Oklahoma, 1999); Richard H. Shultz, Jr., Roy Godson, and George H. Quester (editors), *Security Studies for the 21st Century* (Washington DC: Brassey's 1997)
NGO-Media Intelligence Tribe. Should include members of major non-governmental non-profit associations with interests in global security and assistance, as well as investigative journalists, computer-aided journalism, and watchdog journalism.	Union of International Associations www.uia.org International Consortium of Investigative Journalists www.icij.org	*Non-governmental Organizations Research Guide* (Duke University 2002), at http://docs.lib.duke.edu/igo/guides/ngo; *Non-Governmental Organizations at the United Nations* (Information Habitat, 2002), at http://habitat.igc.org/ngo-rev; Charles Lewis et al, *The Cheating of America: How Tax Avoidance and Evasion by the Super Rich Are Costing the Country Billions - and What You Can Do About It* (Center for Public Integrity, 2002)
Religious-Clan Intelligence Tribe. Some religions are very well structured (Papal Nuncio with Opus Dei, B'Nai Brith), others more informal but still penetrating (Mormons, Islam), and some simply committed to creating havoc. Clans, such as the Armenians, Chinese, Kurds, also have networks.	Catholic Opus Dei www.opusdei.org Jewish B'Nai Brith www.bbinet.org	Canadian Security Intelligence Service, *Doomsday Religious Movements* (Report 2000-3), 18 December 1999; outside of those publications focusing on faith-based terrorism, there is almost nothing substantive on religious intelligence and influence operations beyond the obvious. This area can also include neighborhood groups, citizen intelligence, online protection societies (including cell phones wired to instantly summon citizen 'angels' in bad neighborhoods, i.e. virtual self-protection societies).

[5] German and Chinese commitments to LINUX, as well as emerging U.S. Department of Defense recognition of the enhanced security that open source software provides in comparison with proprietary software, have been reported in the OSS.NET headlines, and primary research citations can be found at www.oss.net using its search engine.

[6] *Cf.* Lawrence Lessig, *The Future of Ideas: The Fate of the Commons in a Connected World* (New York: Vintage Books 2002), is a seminal work in this area. There are at least two major areas of law to be re-crafted in the 21st Century: the laws of software

regulation, focusing on making software interoperable while leaving content relatively free to move about; and the laws of privacy versus security, requiring stricter controls at the personal datum level, while making possible more robust mining of data in the aggregate to identify and monitor terrorism and crime personalities.

[7] These are as devised by Diane Webb, with the assistance of Dennis McCormick and under the supervision of Gordon Oehler, then Director of the Office of Scientific & Weapons Research in the Central Intelligence Agency. Their approach, reported in *Catalyst: A Concept for an Integrated Computing Environment for Analysis* (CIA DI Publication SW 89-10052 dated October 1989) was destroyed when CIA information technology managers decided to settle on the PS 2 as the standard CIA workstation, and ordered the termination of all funding for object-oriented programming and UNIX workstations—this was the equivalent of an intelligence lobotomy from which CIA has still not recovered almost fifteen years later.

[8] It merits comment that during the recent conference on 'Peacekeeping and Intelligence: Lessons for the Future?', 15-16 November 2002, in The Netherlands, a number of speakers with deep peacekeeping experience emphasized the need to restore the primacy of human collection and human analysis, while noting that intelligence as a specialization must be reintegrated down to the team or squad level, and analysis must be reintroduced down to the lowest level at which there is an organic intelligence unit. The conference was sponsored by the Netherlands Intelligence Studies Association (NISA) and the Netherlands Defence College. A brief summary and highlights from three speakers are provided at www.oss.net within the headlines for Sunday, 17 November 2002. It merits *strong emphasis* that for the first time in history, there is a common understanding cross at least ten key nations most experienced in peacekeeping operations, that the UN must—it has no choice—devise official intelligence concepts, doctrine, tables of equipment and organization, and early warning methodologies. There is also general consensus that sensitive *national* collection methods aside, the UN *itself* can create an intelligence architecture that is legal, ethical, and open, relying exclusively—in meeting its own needs—on open source intelligence (OSINT) and commercially-provided secure communications.

[9] Thomas A. Stewart, *The Wealth of Knowledge: Intellectual Capital and the Twenty-first Century Organization* (New York: Currency, 2001) p.19.

[10] National Security Strategy Center (NSIC), sponsor of the earlier Consortium for The Study of Intelligence and the *Intelligence for the 1980's* series, has conceptualized and obtained funding for a new endeavor whose details will be announced in due course by Dr. Roy Godson, the leader in this area.

[11] Among several distinguished authorities speaking at the conference on peacekeeping intelligence, *supra* note 8, two in particular discussed both the deep problems with UN and member nation leaders who do not understand the value and nature of intelligence, and the need for training programs at the executive level to overcome these gaps in

knowledge. MajGen Frank van Kappen, Marine Corps Royal Netherlands Navy, retired, served as the Military Advisor to the Secretary General of the United Nations; Mr. Jan Kleffel, retired from the national intelligence service of Germany, served for five years in the United Nations.

[12] *On Intelligence: Spies and Secrecy in an Open World* (Oakton, Va.: OSS 2002); Chapter 13 available as a free download from www.oss.net, or the book by purchase from Amazon.com.

[13] The budget for this organization would fully fund regional multi-lateral open source intelligence centers as well as distributed multi-lingual processing capabilities and shared global geospatial information. Separate arrangements would have to be made for multi-lateral classified centers and networks, but here also the United States of America would have much to gain from offering full funding in return for local knowledge and access.

[14] Martin Rudner, 'The Future of Canada's Defence Intelligence,' in *International Journal of Intelligence and Counterintelligence* 4 (Winter 2002-2003) p.555 within pp.540-564. The three classic publications in an all too sparse literature on UN intelligence are Hugh Smith, 'Intelligence and UN Peacekeeping,' *Survival* 3 (Autumn 1994); Paul Johnston, 'No Cloak and Dagger Required: Intelligence Support to UN Peacekeeping,' *Intelligence and National Security* 4 (1997); and A. Walter Dorn, 'The Cloak and the Blue Beret: Limitations on Intelligence in UN Peacekeeping,' *International Journal of Intelligence and Counterintelligence* 4 (Winter 1999-2000).

[15] It may be that the United Nations simply cannot be helped, in part because the most powerful member nations do not want it to have an independent intelligence capability, and the level of ignorance about the craft of intelligence *sans* espionage is so low among UN and humanitarian officials as to represent a generational issue that will require completely new blood, over the course of 20 years, before progress can be entertained. In the interim, new forms of multinational intelligence cooperation have already emerged. Denmark, Finland, Norway, and Sweden have perfected integrated intelligence centers and integrated use of their respective tactical military intelligence collection capabilities, in some cases also integrating capabilities from other countries such as Estonia. Their success has been so remarkable that there is now talk of trying to replicate their model among Belgium, the Netherlands, and Luxembourg. Authorities on the Nordic model include Col Odd Egil Pedersen, Royal Norwegian Army; Col Jan-Inge Svensson, Royal Swedish Army; and Dr. Pasi Välimäki, National Defence College, Finland, all speaking at the conference cited in *supra* note 8. Especially noteworthy was the Finish discussion of the new Nokia telephone with embedded encryption that is 'good enough' for peacekeeping operations security, and extremely valuable because it allows any individual or organization to join the commercial cell phone network without requiring special equipment or security clearances from the North Atlantic Treaty Organization (NATO) or any member

country. Whatever the obstacles, and perhaps by focusing on intermediate regional solutions first, the UN requires new forms of open, legal, ethical intelligence. MajGen Tony van Diepenbrugge, deputy chief of the Netherlands Army, and MajGen Patrick Cammaert, Marine Corps Royal Netherlands Navy, and the military advisor (designate) to the Secretary-General of the UN, are among the foremost authorities on military information and military intelligence shortfalls and successes in peacekeeping operations, and both, speaking at the same conference, believe that progress can be made over time.

[16] I am indebted to Michael Castagna, former Marine and now a mid-level manager in the National Aeronautics and Space Administration, himself an emerging leader in the valuation of intangible goods including knowledge, for his careful examination of whether intelligence is solely a public good (nonrival and nonexclusive) or a private good (rival and exclusive). On the basis of his thoughtful examination, I have concluded that it is both—mixcd. On the one hand, it must be regarded as a public good in that, like national defense, the country at large cannot do without it and there are aspects of intelligence, especially national but also state and local, that must be funded by the application of taxpayer dollars. However, it is also a private good in that there are low barriers to entry and many situations where individuals and organizations can discover, discriminate, distill, and disseminate intelligence of extraordinary value, in an exclusive and competitive manner. Indeed, a major challenge facing future leaders of intelligence will be that posed by those who champion false savings and the elimination of a national intelligence budget and national intelligence capabilities, in favor of out-sourcing and 'pay as you go' forms of national intelligence. As with most great issues, when the matter of choice comes up, between capitalism or controlled economics, between conservatism and libertarianism, between intelligence as a public good or intelligence as a private good, the best answer is usually 'both.' Intelligence leaders of the future must guard and nurture the public good aspects of intelligence, while taking care to give free rein to and respect the private good aspects as well.

[17] *Cf.* 'Creating a Smart Nation: Strategy, Policy, Intelligence, and Information' in *Government Information Quarterly* (Summer 1996); 'Virtual Intelligence: Conflict Avoidance and Resolution through Information Peacekeeping', *Journal of Conflict Resolution* (Spring 1999) first presented as a paper at Conference on Virtual Diplomacy, U.S. Institute of Peace, 1-2 April 1997; and a chapter in each of the first two *Cyberwar* books edited by Dr. Douglas Dearth and published by AFCEA International Press. More recently, *The New Craft of Intelligence: Achieving Asymmetric Advantage in the Face of Nontraditional Threats* (U.S. Army War College, Strategic Studies Institute), February 2002 and *The New Craft of Intelligence: Personal, Public, & Political* (Oakton, Va.: OSS, 2002), with a Foreword by Senator Pat Roberts (R-KS), have explored the extraordinary value of public intelligence.

---

[18] For a book-length examination of this issue, see Dr. Joseph S. Nye, Jr., *The Paradox of American Power: Why the World's Only Superpower Can't Go It Alone* (New York etc.: Oxford University Press 2002), reviewed by the author at Amazon.com.

[19] A Congressional authority has told me privately that the North Korean information was briefed to the Senate Select Committee on Intelligence (SSCI), but neither the White House nor the SSCI appear to have promulgated the information to the Senate at large during the debate going on with regard to declaring war on Iraq.

[20] William Shawcross, *Deliver Us from Evil: Peacekeepers, Warlords and a World of Endless Conflict* (New York etc.: Simon & Schuster, 2000).

[21] Although Ms. Dumaine is a CIA employee from the analysis side of the house, and her small (less than 3 full-time employees) element is part of CIA, it is, like In-Q-Tel, completely independent and striving to bring into CIA the kinds of new ideas that are available in the private sector but have not been realized within various governments.

[22] Business intelligence in the US and France, and to a lesser extent in some other countries, maintain moderate tribal training and conferencing. Academics and journalists are too fragmented, and the religious tribes too secretive. The NGOs reject intelligence as a concept alltogether, and need to learn the lessons of this book.

[23] The top headline at www.oss.net for Wednesday, 13 November 2002 contains the full text of the press release announcing the beginning of the campaign to achieve ISO standards for intelligence. The first step is for individual nations to establish Technical Advisory Groups for Intelligence (TAG-I), ideally including representatives of each of the seven tribes. Such groups are subordinate to the national standards organization in every case. Once a critical mass has been achieved at the national level, multiple national standards organizations can petition ISO for the creation of an ISO Committee and an international intelligence standards series. The Committee would be comprised of national representatives, generally the chairperson for the TAG-Is that choose to be actively involved. Any TAG-I may propose a standard to the ISO Committee, and all TAG-Is would have an opportunity to suggest modifications to the standard as part of the international approval process.

Part IV provides six seminal past publications and two extracts, each of which is reprinted with the kind permission of the editors, publishers, or authors. We urge our readers to note the one-page advertisements for the several journals that are leading providers of information about the art and science of peacekeeping intelligence (PKI), in order of appearance here: *Survival, International Peacekeeping, Intelligence and National Security,* and the *International Journal of Intelligence and Counterintelligence.*

The first article, by **Hugh Smith**, is a broad overview suitable for Force Commanders, Special Representatives of the secretary-general, and senior UN and Member Nation policymakers. It lays out in broad strokes three main points: 1) it is not possible for the UN to be effective without institutionalised intelligence at both the strategic and operational levels; 2) most of the intelligence that the UN needs to be effective, and certainly all of the intelligence the UN itself actually collects, can be derived from open or passive sources that are legal, ethical, and not intrusive on any party; and 3) one aspect of a future solution may possibly be the creation of regional intelligence centres, much as Europe is considering, that can serve as operational intelligence centres in support of UN missions in their region.

The second article, by **A. Walter Dorn** and **David J. H. Bell**, complements the brilliance of the first by providing an extraordinarily well-rescarched look at the first effective United Nations intelligence organisation, the somewhat make-shift Military Information Branch of the Operation des Nations Unis au Congo (ONUC) in the 1960-1964. Working with original files from the Departmental Archive Group at the UN Archives in New York, the authors provide a superior account of the failures, the successes, and the issues surrounding the vital matter of intelligence support for UN peacekeeping missions in the field, at both the operational and tactical levels.

The third article by **Sir David Ramsbotham** emphasises in its opening that intelligence is about comprehension and knowledge or understanding, intelligence is, in essence, a *process* for collecting, analysing, and disseminating information that is *vital* to the success of any peacekeeping operation. Analysis in support of peacekeeping, Sir Ramsbotham notes, can in fact be the most important contributor to preventive action. He goes on to discuss the Commanders Critical Intelligence Requirements (CCIR) process used by the North Atlantic Treaty Organisation (NATO) and its application to UN operations. Sir Ramsbotham concludes in full agreement with Hugh Smith as to the need for strategic, operational, and tactical intelligence elements in support of UN decision-making and UN operations, and ends with some attention to the importance of focusing on post-conflict reconstruction or peace rebuilding, an aspect of UN operations that itself has considerable requirements for intelligence.

The fourth article by **Per Eriksson** advances for the first time a moral argument for over-turning the UN's traditional antipathy to intelligence of any sort. He says, '…it is not morally acceptable to send soldiers to a war zone without proper knowledge of the situation'. Having said that, he then goes on to advance, with excellent details, the many reasons why and how intelligence can be vital to successful UN operations as viewed from the strategic, operational, and tactical points of view.

The fifth article by **Paul Johnston** tackles the UN aversion to 'intelligence' head on. The author does a fine job of discussing the reasons the UN continues to resist the concept of structured intelligence, and he does an equally fine job of specifying why all of those reasons are invalid. As he observes, 'Intelligence is not about secrecy; it is about learning what is going on by the rigorous analysis of all available information, and, most importantly, by the active tasking of information collectors to confirm or deny what one thinks one knows'. The author concludes: 'None of this need violate neutrality, impartiality, or political sensitivity. For the most part it would simply be the rationalisation of the information that the UN is already collecting in any case. There should be no reason why the UN cannot provide effective intelligence support to its own peacekeeping mission.'

The sixth article by **A. Walter Dorn** is a modern-day tutorial on the limitations as well as the possibilities for intelligence in UN peacekeeping. He discusses the advantages of openness versus secrecy, and goes on to review the purpose, methods, UN limits, and UN issues associated with planning, gathering, processing, and disseminating information. Of particular interest is his figure on the information-gathering spectrum from what is permitted (white) to what is prohibited (black). Most of the potential gains in UN intelligence for peacekeeper force protection can be found in the middle or grey area.

The seventh item is an eight-page extract from **Loch Johnson**'s latest book, *Bombs, Bugs, Drugs, and Thugs*. Professor Johnson, arguably the 'dean' of American intelligence reformers, one of just two individuals privileged to serve on both the Church and the Aspin-Brown Commissions focused on US intelligence reform, has some relatively critical things to say about America's intelligence liaison with international organisations. He also has some thoughts on possibilities for improvement on both sides.

The eighth and final item is an eight-page extract from **Martin Rudner**'s article in the Winter 2002-2003 issue of the *International Journal of Intelligence and Counterintelligence* on the topic of 'The Future of Canada's Defence Intelligence'. From within that article, we have extracted the portion that specifically addresses the strategic challenges facing both the UN and NATO.

Intelligence and UN Peacekeeping

Hugh Smith

An old United Nations hand once observed that 'the UN has no intelligence'. Putting aside the deliberate ambiguity of this remark, it is certainly true that the UN does not collect, process and disseminate intelligence in the directed and comprehensive way that major powers do as a matter of course. The UN is reluctant even to use the word 'intelligence', preferring the term 'information' in order to avoid the usual connotations of subterfuge and secrecy.[1] 'Intelligence' also implies the existence of enemies or, at least rivals, a suggestion that the UN is naturally anxious to avoid. For these and other reasons that are discussed below, the role of, and need for, intelligence capabilities in peacekeeping operations is rarely debated in either UN documents or the public literature.[2]

Whatever terminology is used, the problem of determining what information is required, collecting and assessing this information, and disseminating the resultant intelligence is of growing importance to the UN in its peacekeeping activities. During the Cold War, peacekeeping was, by and large, a matter of monitoring agreements or stable cease-fires that had already been negotiated between the contending parties. Apart from the Congo operation (1960-64), peacekeepers were seldom directly involved in military action. While the UN would have liked better intelligence in its peacekeeping activities, it was able to get by with *ad hoc* and inadequate arrangements. The situation has changed markedly in recent years.

A second generation of peacekeeping operations has emerged in response to a wide range of difficult problems, particularly internal conflicts or the breakdown of law and order.[3] Peacekeepers are liable to find themselves in countries in which no government is in undisputed control, special order has broken down or is on the point of collapse, hostilities are actually under way or imminent and the use of force against UN personnel is a distinct possibility. In these circumstances, roles such as protecting humanitarian aid, disarming factions, monitoring fragile cease-fires, preventive deployment and negotiating agreements among reluctant players have made the requirement for good and timely intelligence overwhelming.

The need for intelligence is being increasingly felt both by the UN and by states contributing to peacekeeping operations. Particularly in more complex and fluid situations, intelligence will be crucial in achieving the goals of the mission laid down by the UN Security Council. Intelligence may also be important for the lives and well being of UN personnel on the ground. With more than 200 peacekeepers killed in 1993 alone, the greater hazards of contemporary peacekeeping have led governments to demand better intelligence both prior to making a commitment to an operation and during its deployment.[4] The anarchical or near-anarchical situations that have created this demand for improved intelligence, however, will also usually make such intelligence more difficult to obtain, keep current and disseminate effectively.

The UN must come to terms with intelligence. But the problems are not easily resolved. Traditionally, intelligence has been produced and used by a particular state for its own purposes. Much of the intelligence is gathered without the consent or even knowledge of the Target State. Intelligence, too, is normally retained under national control, although it may be shared with friendly governments, up to a point. In the UN, however, intelligence takes on a very different shape. It is gathered not in order to be used against enemies, the UN has no enemies of the kind that national imtelligence thrives on, but for the purposes of the international community. It is gathered more openly than national intelligence and is unlikely to remain secure in the medium or long term.

The concept of 'UN intelligence' promises to turn traditional principles of intelligence on their heads. Intelligence will have to be based on information that is collected primarily by overt means, that is, by methods that do not threaten the target state or group and do not compromise the integrity or impartiality of the UN. It will have to be intelligence that is by definition shared among a number of nations and that in most cases will become widely known in the short or medium term. And it will have to be intelligence that is directed towards the purposes of the international community. Such a system is unlikely to emerge of its own accord. The UN needs to establish a clear conception of how it wants intelligence to develop in the context of peacekeeping, and perhaps also, of preventive diplomacy.

The Need for Intelligence

Intelligence is required at all levels and is needed in both the planning and deployment of peacekeeping. Strategic intelligence is obviously required to understand the political situation between the parties to a conflict prior to UN involvement and, once peacekeepers are deployed, to anticipate the political moves of governments or factions, especially if there is a risk of violence.[5] The fundamental importance of political intelligence is self-evident, for the UN is seeking to produce a desired political outcome. Information about the economy and society of the country will also be valuable.

Operational intelligence is required to plan the most effective deployment of resources and to carry out the UN mandate. It will be particularly important in fluid military and political situations. The ability to assess the level of armaments, and the movements, strategies, military potential of and likely threats to peacekeepers by the contending factions is obviously vital. The security or insecurity of transport and supplies is also crucial. In addition, there is the vast array of information that military forces need in order to deploy to and maintain themselves in a given country: terrain, weather, transport routes and their usability, water and electricity supplies, hospital and medical resources, risks from disease, communications facilities and local infrastructure. All of these may affect the viability of the mission in general.

Tactical intelligence is needed by troops on the ground to support peace-keeping activities, such as monitoring cease-fires or border areas and to alert personnel to potential dangers. The identification of breaches of cease-fires, unauthorised troop and weapon movements, the level of demobilisation and the existence of weapons caches can be critical to the maintenance of peace. Such tactical information is liable to pose difficult political problems for the UN and has the potential to take on strategic significance in delicate situations. The management of intelligence at the tactical level, moreover, can be influential in maintaining or losing the UN's credibility among the parties to the conflict. If intelligence is not deftly handled, it is easy for the organisation to gain a reputation for being slow to react and for gullibility and political partiality. At

231

the tactical level, too, counter-intelligence may be necessary if there are elements hostile to the UN.

Current Deficiencies and Partial Remedies

The existing structure of intelligence in peacekeeping operations is largely *ad hoc* at both the planning and deployment stages. The UN's inability to conduct adequate advance planning is one of the acknowledged defects of peacekeeping and is one of the areas currently being strengthened.[6] Some of the problems are inherent, such as the suddenness with which some crises arise, but a weakness is often the lack of relevant intelligence. In some instances, the UN is able to send fact-finding missions or reconnaissance and advance parties (as with the UN Advance Mission in Cambodia (UNAMIC)), but the scope of these missions is usually limited by a lack of time and resources. More often than not, the UN can provide only minimal information to peacekeepers before they are deployed.

In some instances, states are able to provide their own contingents with the necessary intelligence prior to deployment. Some countries will have extensive knowledge of the area concerned, especially if they have been a colonial power there or are regional neighbours. More likely, however, the contributing state will have had time or no connection with the area concerned. Most participants in peacekeeping operations find themselves operating well outside their area of direct military and political interest. Small and even middle powers simply cannot maintain accurate and current intelligence on every part of the world where they might be called upon to take part in peacekeeping operations.

On deployment, peacekeeping missions will establish some kind of headquarters that will have at least rudimentary facilities for receiving and processing what is called 'military information'. In most cases, the intelligence function must be built up over a period of time with the personnel that are available end can be spared from less pressing tasks. Even in major operations, such as the UN Protection Force (UNPROFOR), raw information often had to substitute for intelligence, at least in the early phases when collection plans were lacking and no capacity existed for processing the data gathered. The mixture of nationalities involved also makes for difficult communications as well as revealing national differences in operating procedures and significant variations in the level of training and expertise.

232

There are also differences in attitude between the various nationalities. Some countries will reject the development of an intelligence capacity because they do not appreciate its significance, because they consider it inappropriate for the UN, or because they see their role as simply collecting data without providing analysis.

National contingents, of course, may partly overcome these problems by receiving intelligence directly from their own governments. Again, the ability of countries to do this varies and difficult situations may arise. Same contingents may be better supplied with intelligence than others or, more significantly, better supplied than the force commander. One UNPROFOR commander, Lieutenant-general Satish Nambiar, for example, could not, as an Indian national, receive intelligence from NATO sources. In these circumstances, the principle of exclusive operational command by the UN may be undermined and the risk of contingents following orders only from their national authorities heightened.[7]

The ability of national contingents to collect and process intelligence within their area of operations will also vary. Some, perhaps most, will simply lack the resources, expertise and experience to conduct intelligence activities, while some may lack an interest in doing so. A number of countries, however, will incorporate an intelligence capacity into a contingent as a matter of routine. Their doctrine for national defence may also focus on the collection of information and the preparation of intelligence in low-level conflicts. Australia and Indonesia, for example, have concentrated on collecting intelligence for low-level conflicts, although for rather different reasons.

The pooling of intelligence in the course of peacekeeping operations is to be welcomed, but there are limitations Such dissemination normally requires the approval of national headquarters and may require the sanitising of information. A further distinction may be drawn between intelligence that can be retained by other states and intelligence that can be shown to, bot not retained by, other states.[8] Existing intelligence links among NATO countries and between the US and other states have proven particularly useful in allowing information to be shared among the countries concerned. In practice, too, contingents may use their own discretion in passing on information and informal networks will develop among some of the contingents.

In some circumstances, the force commander may be able to receive intelligence from a friendly nation that is not available to other national contingents. In the case of the UN Transitional Authority in Cambodia (UNTAC), for example, the Force Commander, Lieutenant General John Sanderson, was no doubt provided with intelligence not only by his own government in Australia, but also by the United States. From the military perspective, this is unlikely to cause problems since commanders are frequently privy to information that their subordinates are not. The problem is, rather, a political one. As an Australian, General Sanderson could receive intelligence from the US in a way that, for example, an Indian or a Brazilian force commander could not. Countries might thus be denied the command of peacekeeping operations because of their political alignment.

Against this background of partial, *ad hoc* arrangements, there will be intelligence failures, usually minor, but sometimes disastrous. An example was the attempt by US Army Rangers to capture General Aideed in July 1993. A carefully-planned raid was executed on a suspected hideout, only to discover that the building was the office of a UN agency.[9] This failure of intelligence was due in part to a refusal by US forces to share information with the UN. In the subsequent handover to the UN Operation in Somalia (UNOSOM II), by contrast, it was the UN that displayed initial reluctance to accept intelligence support from the United States, because of the organisation's distrust of military intelligence and of US intelligence in particular.[10]

In the face of this patchwork of capabilities and *ad hoc* arrangements, the force commander must do what he can to hold the intelligence function together. The idea of one state playing the lead role in intelligence has been suggested, but this is likely to run into the expected political objections unless one state is playing the lead role in the mission as a whole. In the case of UNPROFOR, the establishment of a headquarters was certainly assisted by a common NATO background, but this is not likely to be a frequent occurrence. In general, an improvement in intelligence capabilities is more likely to occur as part of a wider process of professionalising the military side of peacekeeping in areas such as planning, logistics, training, communications, and command and control.[11]

An important step in this direction was the creation in 1993 of a Situation Centre at UN headquarters to monitor peacekeeping operations. The Centre gathers and processes information from the field on a continuous and systematic basis. The Centre functions for 24 hours a day and seven days a week, a major improvement on the previous arrangements whereby UN headquarters was accessible to peacekeepers in the field for only five days a week from 9 AM to 5 PM. With a staff of about 24, the Centre maintains two officers on duty at all times to receive communications from any UN peacekeeping operation.[12] The Centre produces reports on the major operations under way that are then forwarded to the UN secretary-general, via the under-secretary-general for Peacekeeping, by noon each day or more frequently as required.

The Centre, however, does more than simply pass on information received from various transmissions to the UN Secretariat. The Centre has a research and information cell that interprets information received from the field and combines it with data obtained from a wide variety of other sources. The Centre is not a comprehensive intelligence unit, a command centre or a 'war room' (as some US Congressmen call it). It does, however, systematise data and has begun to provide an institutional memory.[13] The Centre is also going some way towards meeting the growing demand from the UN leadership and from contributing states for intelligence about ongoing operations. It is apparent that, once the benefits of timely and accurate intelligence are understood, both national and international decision-makers will tend to seek even more intelligence.

The UN's intelligence efforts in peacekeeping operations have thus been limited both in terms of planning and of conducting peacekeeping operations. Some improvements have been made, but the further development of intelligence capabilities raises a number of important issues that point to major constraints and possible inherent limits on what the UN can achieve.

Intelligence and the Impartiality of the UN

The collection of information is a normal part of any operation involving military personnel. The value of locally gathered intelligence from civil disorders, tenuous cease-fires or armed factions has already been emphasised. Bot the collection of information is an activity that is fraught with political difficulties. The principal concern is that the collection of intelligence by the UN in the course of peacekeeping, whether it is operating within a state or between states, could be seen as compromising the organisation's traditional impartiality towards the contending parties.[14]

It is possible that one or more sides will be reluctant for the UN to acquire information about their activities. One reason for this, of course, is that a party to a conflict has something to hide. It may wish to conceal the fact that it has breached a cease-fire, has moved troops and weapons in contravention of an existing agreement, has evaded undertakings to demobilise forces or simply wishes to feed the UN with false information. It has been a common claim in the former Yugoslavia, for example, that attacks on civilians have been staged by the victim in order to win international sympathy and to denigrate the other side. Unless the UN has same idea's of what is actually happening on the ground, it will find that its role as an impartial monitor may be politically compromised or revealed as ineffective.

It is possible, too, that all parties to the conflict will be suspicious of the UN in its gathering of information. Even if one side has scrupulously observed the terms of an agreement, it may still be anxious that information about its positions or activities will be leaked from the UN to its opponents. This is not an unreasonable fear. Some contingents in UNPROFOR, for instance, appear to have provided information, which was acquired through the UN, to the side the contingent favoured. The UN, moreover, normally ensures that its signals are non-secure.[15] This caused much anxiety, for example, for the Israelis during their presence in Lebanon since they feared that signals could be intercepted by their opponents. There may also be a concern that national contingents in a peacekeeping operation could collect information for their own purposes, whether for commercial or security reasons. Everything the UN does in a particular country, moreover, is liable to be observed and, perhaps, bugged by local factions.

In addition to organisational deficiencies and differences of approach, the means available to the UN to acquire reliable and timely information will vary from mission to mission. In some situations, the mere presence of observers and reports from the local population will be extremely useful. The value of patrol forces has also been frequently stressed by experienced peacekeepers.[16] Effective patrolling will potentially reduce risks to peacekeepers rather than expose them to danger. The scope for collecting human intelligence will, of course, depend on local conditions. In parts of Somalia, for example, a friendly population, freedom of movement of forces and support from non-governmental organisations provided favourable conditions.[17] A significant, but by no means total, limitation on the value of patrols may be the lack of knowledge of the local language.

Technical means of collecting information may also be available and appropriate. Where hostilities are under way, the widely taught techniques of crater analysis may reveal the locatioas of weapons and the origins of munitions employed. In the former Yugoslavia, aerial reconnaissance and mortar-locating radar's *(Cymbeline)* have also proved effective.[18] Aerial photography is often an attractive option, having the advantages that it is cheap, simple and, compared to satellite photography, requires little interpretation. It is also a capability possessed by over 50 states.[19]

There are limits, however, to these techniques. UN personnel may be refused total access to this technology on the grounds, for example, that there is a danger from snipers or mines, or that their safety cannot be guaranteed. The technical means of gathering information may suffer not only from a lack of the relevant resources, but also from inherent problems. Crater analysis, for example, will be less valuable when the same kinds of munitions are used by all sides in a conflict, which is the case, for example, in the former Yugoslavia. (where most munitions come from a once-united national army) and Cambodia (where same weaponry dated back to the Second World War). Mines, too, are eminently difficult to track to their source. The use of a mortar-locating radar near Sarajevo by a Ukrainian detachment also ran into particular problems when both sides made it an object of attack and killed eight personnel.

Ideally, of course, clear and agreed rules for the UN to collect information, whether by human or technical means, will be established. But in practice, the UN will commonly be faced with numerous problems that place it squarely in the political arena: should the UN seek out the required information more vigorously and thus risk alienating one or more sides to a conflict? Should information collected about one party be made available to the other, which may happen surreptitiously in any case? Should the UN seek to ensure that information made public does not assist one side or the other? Is it consistent with impartiality for the UN to threaten to publicise information about, say, 'breaches of a cease-fire'? Should the UN ever publicly denounce the offending side by, for example, the release of aerial photography as in the Cuban missile crisis of 1962? Should the UN admit its incapacity to determine who are the perpetrators of significant breaches of a cease-fire or of blatant attacks on civilians?

The political problems of intelligence become greater the more pro-active the UN's role becomes. The intention may be to prohibit factions from deploying forces in prohibited areas or to push an offending party towards compliance with the terms of an agreement, but there is a risk that the effect will be to alienate or provoke the party concerned. If the UN is contemplating even more vigorous action, such as air strikes, the political impact will be even greater and the need for intelligence imperative. Clearly the possession of information is never a neutral fact. It makes the UN a player in the politics of the country concerned and it leaves the UN more dependent than ever on intelligence of the highest quality.

It is also important to remember that the UN will not necessarily be able to act on the information it has and that this, too, may carry political disadvantages. It may be clear to the world, for example, that the UN is aware of terrible events occurring before its very eyes, yet the organisation can only look on impotently. Erskine Childers recounts the bitter words of one Bosnian who looked up at a UN aircraft and said 'there goes the UN, monitoring genocide'.[20] In the case of the UN, knowledge also implies responsibility.

The Security of UN Intelligence

The security of UN intelligence, or, more accurately, the lack of security, is a political minefield and underlies some of the problems discussed in the previous section. Traditionally, intelligence is kept from hostile powers and is confined to those who need to know. Both of these principles are challenged by intelligence in UN operations. It must be reasoned that any information provided to the UN will sooner or later become public knowledge. There are inevitable political reasons for this release of information.

A wide range of parties is interested in information relevant to peacekeeping. All of these parties, UN military personnel in the field, UN civilian and military staff, states participating in a peacekeeping operation, as many as 30 or 40 in a single mission, and members of the Security Council, the principal decision making body for peacekeeping, have some claim upon this information.

Peacekeeping does not involve security of information in the conventional sense.

The fundamental reason for the openness of UN intelligence is the fact that the organisation is international and its personnel are multinational, first, on the political level, states tend to have diverse interests in any peacekeeping operation. Once states acquire information that can promote their own interests, the temptation to exploit this information will be strong. Second, the loyalty of personnel working directly and indirectly for the UN will tend to lie, in the last analysis, with their own country. This is not to deny that many individuals can and do maintain a strong loyalty to the UN, but the security of information must always be in some doubt.[21] It is simply impossible to conduct security clearances on UN personnel, a situation that will be exacerbated as more personnel are assigned to intelligence tasks and the numbers of civilian staff and private contractors increase. Fears that the UN could not keep information secure and that UN staff had been infiltrated by supporters of Aideed, for example, apparently contributed to the failures of communication that led to the fire-fight that killed 18 and wounded 78 US soldiers in October 1993.

It can be legitimately asked: whose side are UN intelligence personnel on? The UN Situation Centre provides an interesting case study. In late 1993, the Centre comprised 24 staff, headed by a Canadian civilian with a Belgian Lieutenant-colonel as deputy. A total of 16 different nationalities were represented, from Australia to Zimbabwe, Norway to Pakistan, Jordan to Russia. It is to be expected that many of these personnel will be under instructions to report any significant information that goes through the Centre to their national authorities. In the most obvious case, staff who learn of an impending threat to their country's personnel in a peacekeeping force could hardly be expected to hold back such information from their government.

It is worth noting that as far as military personnel are concerned, it is US policy to instruct officers assigned to the UN to put the organisation before their country. This is not so much a conversion to internationalism on the part of the US, but rather the result of a long-term political calculation. The US hopes to avoid awakening suspicion of its motives while encouraging other states to contribute intelligence to the UN. The US can also afford to serve the UN first because its own intelligence sources and agencies are far more numerous and effective than those available to the UN. Most countries are not so fortunate.

Another factor contributing to the openness of UN intelligence is the transparency of peacekeeping operations, which are normally accessible to the world's media in a way that national military operations are not. Since peacekeeping operations are rarely as dangerous, and hence as inhibiting to reporters, as actual hostilities, peacekeeping operations tend to attract media attention.[22] The UN finds it very difficult to prevent reporters from moving around an operational area, the result of a lack of authority as well as a lack of resources, so that the media is often only limited in their access by the unavailability of transport. National contingents, moreover, may actively encourage the media to report on their activities. Peacekeeping operations are thus liable to be compromised, by, for example, the premature disclosure of movements, the revelation of problems and limitations on UN forces, or the exaggerated reporting of risks and casualties with a consequent undermining of morale.

Despite the many problems in the security of intelligence, there are two compensating factors. First, is the short lifespan of much intelligence. Once it becomes widely known, most intelligence ceases to be sensitive because the event has already occurred or relevant action has been taken. Provided that sources are not compromised, which is generally less of a problem in the case of the UN, subsequent disclosure is not necessarily undesirable. Second, is that the insecurity of intelligence is more likely to prove inconvenient than fatal. Most peacekeeping operations, most of the time, do not involve the use of force by or against the UN. Nonetheless, it is precisely in the most dangerous situations that secure intelligence is most needed.

Sources of Information

The sources of information available to the UN are in principle as diverse as those open to states, although differences naturally exist. It is not expected, for example, that the UN will make use of spies or agents or resort to bribery and blackmail in its quest for information. Such covert information gathering is seen as contrary to the ethic of peacekeeping and as a breach of the sovereignty of the targeted nations. It also leaves all parties to a conflict suspicious of what the UN might know or what the UN might mistakenly believe about them. The subsequent revelation of covert activities would also prove highly embarrassing and counter-productive. Nonetheless, the UN may receive unsolicited information from all kinds of sources, including individuals and organisations.

In some cases, national laws will have been broken by the informants. The UN Special Commission on Iraq, for example, received secret tip-offs. Unsolicited documents and many other kinds of information about Iraqi weapons capabilities.[23] Such informal sources clearly require delicate handling.

The principal sources of intelligence open to the UN, however, are essentially 'above board'. This does not mean that they rely purely on the Cupertino of the parties to a conflict, but that the methods of collection are overt. Indeed, there are many sources of information that can be turned into intelligence for peacekeeping purposes and access to them is perhaps the least of the difficulties surrounding UN intelligence. Nonetheless, each source has its own special characteristics.

Member-States

The UN can call upon any of its over 180 members to provide information and since the end of the Cold War there are signs that member-states are increasingly willing to respond. The intelligence-rich members of the UN, notably the US, Britain and France, have become significant participants in peacekeeping, while Russia has been actively supporting the UN in certain operations. Even if the major powers do not have personnel in a particular mission, they *may* well be willing to assist the operation by providing intelligence. At the same time, the contributions of middle and small powers should not be overlooked. There are many areas of the world that do not attract much attention from the major powers, Central Africa, for example, where neighbouring countries may be best placed to provide information for the UN.

In encouraging member-states to contribute intelligence for peacekeeping, the UN can take various approaches. One useful strategy is to play off one state against another. It can be argued that a UN operation should not rely on information provided by only one or two states and that other states should ensure that their data are also given to the UN. Another strategy is to establish permanent channels of communication with member-states. The Situation Centre, for example, has acquired a computer-based system for transferring information known as the Joint Deployable Intelligence Support System (JDISS).[24] This allows the Centre to talk to databases in other countries that have the same system, notably the US and one of two NATO countries. The interchange of information is, of course, closely controlled by each state, but the basis for greater collaboration has thereby been established.

The principle long-term approach must be to accustom States to sharing information and to establish confidence in the ability of the UN to use information effectively and discreetly. This will be greatly enhanced by political support at the highest level. In January 1993, for example, President Bush set out US policy:

> To the extent prudent, US intelligence today is... being used in dramatically new ways, such as assisting the international organisations like the United Nations when called upon in support of crucial peace-keeping, humanitarian assistance and arms control efforts. We will share information and assets that strengthen peaceful relationships and aid in building confidence.[25]

This sort of commitment, which can he maintained even if the US does not send personnel, is essential to help the UN price information out of national intelligence agencies that are unaccustomed to sharing information with international organisations.

The genuine difficulties that exist for member-states in providing information to an international organisation cannot be ignored, especially by an organisation that does not have effective security classification procedures or security practices. The UN has not needed such procedures and practices in the past and may, as suggested above, find it impossible to implement them fully. National agencies are, therefore, likely to retain their natural concern with compromising sources, national-security classification requirements, sensitivity towards neighbours and allies, third-party restrictions, information that has been illegally obtained and domestic political factors.[26] Giving away hard-won information goes 'against the grain'.

These same organisations, however, are also facing the challenge of diminishing resources. A number of governments, especially in the West, have come to see cuts in intelligence as part of the peace dividend. One consequence may well be less support for the UN, but an alternative response could be a search for new roles. Support for UN peacekeeping might prove an attractive budget-enhancing or, at least, budget-protecting option for national intelligence organisations.

Open Sources

National sources of intelligence are not necessarily reliable or appropriate for the UN's needs. To reduce reliance on member-states, the UN can make use of open sources that are becoming increasingly varied and accessible. There are traditional pubic sources used by journalists, scholars and other investigators, books, journals, magazines, industry publications, government documents, legislative reports and records (notably the US Congressional Record), commercial registers, such as the Lloyd's Register of Shipping, and the data collected by institutions, such as the Stockholm International Peace Research Institute and the International Institute for Strategic Studies.

For current information, the most accessible open sources are television and radio networks. While CNN, for example, can arouse public concern over humanitarian issues, it is also invaluable in providing continuous information on many conflicts around the world and is keenly watched in the Situation Centre. There are also numerous national and international news services available and it is politic for the UN to subscribe to a wide range of these, if only to allay suspicions that it is reliant on one or two agencies identified with particular countries.

In recent years, the world information market has grown even wider as certain governments have sought to make money through the sale of information. Russia has opened its archives to raise hard currency, while the Central Intelligence Agency is also declassifying material for sale. Satellite data are also increasingly available.[27] The Situation Centre already buys information from the French SPOT satellite, which has a resolution of 25 meters (OSS Note: Actually 10 meters). A recent entrant to the satellite data market is Russia, which is reported to be willing to sell imagery with a resolution of two metres.[28] While low-resolution imagery is primarily of background value, the signs are that better-quality imagery will soon become readily available to the UN, as it will to any interested party.

Other International Agencies

In principle, the UN has access to information from a great variety of intenational agencies and organisations that could be of relevance to peacekeeping. Its own specialised agencies, such as the World Health Organisation, the UN Educational, Scientific and Cultural Organisation, the International Labour Organisation, the Food and Agriculture Organisation and the UN Industrial Development Organisation, together with programs such as the United Nations High Commission for Refugees, the United Nations Development Program and the United Nations Environment Program, all gather information on population, health, economic development, refugees, educational and scientific programs, and environmental issues for their own particular purposes. Outside the UN itself there are various international regimes dealing with such matters as nuclear non-proliferation, the control of chemical and biological weapons and the transfer of conventional arms and missile technology.

The use by the UN of information acquired by such organisations, however, raises problems of principle and practice. Data are provided by a state or collected by an agency for the purposes of that agency. Should such information be made available to the UN for peacekeeping operations (or any other purpose for that matter)? There is a risk that the integrity of an agency will be questioned and the flow of information to it compromised if it supplies information to other organisations, even the UN.

On the other hand, could information gathered by the UN in the course of peacekeeping be properly put to other purposes? In some instances, such a purpose may be directly related to the peacekeeping operation, for example war-crimes trials arising from a conflict in which the UN has been involved through peacekeeping. This may create reluctance among states opposed to such trials to supply information to the UN. There is also the concern, manifest in the case of the former Yugoslavia, that the threat of war-crimes trials will cause local military and political leaders to resist a negotiated settlement. Further questions would arise over the transfer of information gained during peacekeeping to other international agencies for entirely unconnected purposes.

UN-Owned Sources

Apart from collecting information through its own officials and through peacekeeping forces on the ground, the UN can make use of its own technical means to gather data. This has already been done on a small scale in some peacekeeping operations in which UN forces have already made use of some fairly sophisticated technologies. Night-vision binoculars, for instance, have been used by peacekeepers in Lebanon, Kuwait and Western Sahara, although they are expensive at over $3.000 each and may be limited by ground haze. Attention has also been given to the prospect of the UN acquiring advanced technology for information gathering. At the top of the range of options for new technology are observation and communications satellites that would be owned and operated by the UN. These would certainly prove an expensive undertaking and a source of disputes over funding, the areas to be targeted, access to the data collected and the staffing of the agency.

There are more down-to-earth, less contentious technologies, however, that have a range of possible uses.[29] The Synthetic Aperture Radar, for example, can be employed to search for weapons caches under a jungle canopy and is potentially useful when peacekeepers have the responsibility of disarming factions in a civil war. Passive ground sensors can pick up vehicle movement and, in favourable conditions, human activity. Low-altitude drones, which are difficult to detect on radar and pose no risk to pilot's lives, could be of particular value when the UN is monitoring a cease-fire or contested territory and is constrained in its movements.

Some of these technologies, however, have drawbacks as means of collecting intelligence. Such technologies are liable to be expensive, to suffer technical limitations and to require skilled operation and interpretation. To secure maximum value from technical methods, moreover, the UN would need to develop a body of expertise among its own personnel or gain access to such expertise from member-nations. Both options pose difficulties. Nonetheless, the attractiveness to the UN of control over its own assets is likely to be high, primarily to reduce reliance on information provided by national governments that may not always be forthcoming. In theory, too, the wider use of such technology could reduce the cost of peacekeeping or allow the UN to use its limited manpower more effectively.[30]

245

Technology, of course, will never remove the need for other sources of intelligence. It cannot provide the political knowledge essential to peacekeeping. It cannot substitute for the operational and tactical intelligence that can only be obtained by human contact on the ground. Nor will technology fill the gap left by the UN's substantial inability, for practical and ethical reasons, to gather secret information by covert means. As with any other organisation that makes use of intelligence, the UN will have to combine its sources of information as best it can and exploit to the full those in which it has an advantage.

Institutionalising UN Intelligence

The desirability of a co-ordinated and comprehensive intelligence capability in UN peacekeeping operations badly needs demonstration. The barriers to developing such a capability are equally self-evident, the political sensitivity of acquiring and exploiting information, the lack of security of information and problems of access. Nonetheless, certain steps have been taken towards the development of an intelligence capability in some areas. How far can this process go? Can UN intelligence for peacekeeping be institutionalised?

One important factor will be the natural pressure for the UN to establish its own intelligence system, with its own means of collection, analysis and dissemination. It is a trend encouraged by the prospect of reduced reliance on national sources of intelligence and by the potential for the UN to gain access to data from other international agencies and to acquire its own information-gathering technology. The major Western powers appear to support such a development, or at least not to oppose it, but this is in doubt based on the assumption that the West will be able to retain a dominant role in any UN intelligence function.

A further pressure for the creation of a UN intelligence system is the attraction of preventive diplomacy, which requires a strong information base. This led to the establishment in 1987 of an Office of Research and Collection of Information in order to provide an early warning of conflicts and to suggest options for dealing with them to the UN secretary-general.[31] The Office was abolished in 1992 following the reorganisation of the Department of Political Affairs, but the need for early warning still remains. Boutros Boutros-Ghali's

246

An Agenda for Peace, published in 1992, asked member-states to 'be ready to provide the information needed for effective preventive diplomacy'.[32] In the following year, the UN secretary-general pointed out that the UN had set up more fact-finding missions in 1992–93 than in any other year.[33] The thirst for information in the field of preventive diplomacy may thus provide a continuing basis for intelligence in peacekeeping

Proposals have been made for the establishment of a permanent intelligence unit within the UN. The Australian Foreign Minister, Senator Gareth Evans, for example, has suggested that 'a group of professionals from various countries with expertise in intelligence... be recruited and approved by the Security Council'.[34] The group, it was suggested, would have access to classified information in order to provide independent advice to the Council. Several concerns exist about this and similar proposals. Could military or civilian officials sever their national connections and become genuinely independent? Would such impartiality be given credibility by member-states? There are also organisational difficulties. Could the UN provide adequate training for its staff or keep abreast of current expertise? How would the UN deal with the recurrent problems of recruiting high-quality staff while satisfying demands for national representativeness?

The institutionalisation of UN intelligence also raises questions about effectiveness. How efficient would such a bureaucracy be? A large and expensive organisation might produce little in the way of results, especially as far as peacekeeping is concerned. Such an organisation might also become prey to the defects common to intelligence agencies in general, such as rigidity, narrow views of the world or obsessive concern with secrecy. The organisation might also fall into the temptation of using agents and other covert means of information gathering, or be suspected of doing so. Any process of institutionalisation is liable to entrench undesirable as well as desirable features.

The task of establishing an effective UN intelligence function might be eased by the development of information centres based on regional organisations. Centres of this kind would gather data on a wide range of topics of concern to regional states. In Europe, for example, there are plans to establish a Western European Union Space Centre to collect and co-ordinate satellite data and make it available to member-states.[35] The function of this Centre would be to assist in the monitoring of arms control agreements, regional crises, environmental change and other agreed purposes, but the relevance to peacekeeping is apparent. Proposals have also been put forward for the European Union to establish an intelligence organisation.[36]

In Southeast Asia, there has been widespread discussion about confidence-building measures and transparency as part of a common effort to improve mutual security.[37] A regional data centre has been mooted and it would be a logical step forward for the states of the region. Centres of this kind would avoid the political difficulties entailed in establishing UN-owned agencies in a region, while being able to provide information to the UN for a wide range of purposes. Nonetheless, any agreement between a regional agency and the UN on how and when to provide information would entail a delicate balancing of interests.

Prospects and Pressures

It is apparent that any development of UN intelligence will be heavily shaped by a small group of Western nations. They, almost exclusively, have the knowledge, experience and global reach that is required. In the UN Situation Centre, for example, 17 of the 24 staff were drawn from Western Europe, North America and Australia and generally occupied the senior positions. Procedures in the Centre are based on Western practice, while English is spoken and used for all written reports. Any extension of the use of technology in intelligence gathering for the UN, moreover, would only reinforce the dominance of Western powers, both practically and symbolically.[38]

Such developments will serve to emphasise the hegemony of the major Western powers, in terms not of military power, but of information. Substantial reliance on Western intelligence by the UN could well produce an adverse reaction from the majority of its members outside the club. It is already a common complaint among Third-World nations that they provide the majority of peacekeeping personnel, but play relatively little part in the direction and management of peacekeeping operations. These complaints will only grow louder if the UN increases its reliance on Western powers for intelligence. The reality is, however, that it may have little other option.

The development of an intelligence function by the UN, if it is to occur at all, will have to observe these and other political constraints. It is not a matter primarily of financial and personnel resources, much less of technology. Nor will the future of intelligence in UN peacekeeping operations be determined by bureaucratic pressures, favourable as they may be, or by the growing desire for intelligence by the UN leadership. Nor will the domination of particular powers in itself produce an intelligence capacity. In the final analysis, it will be a matter of politics. The principal determinant will be the role of the UN relative to the interests of its members and the commitment members are prepared to make to the organisation.

Nonetheless, it might be supposed that intelligence could have a certain life of its own. States are losing control over the creation and transfer of information, just as they have lost, to some degree, their monopoly over the means of violence and their ability to regulate national economics. If we are entering the 'information age', greater opportunities may exist in the future for the UN to enhance its influence through peacekeeping, and other activities, by controlling and managing intelligence.

Endnotes

Acknowledgements. The author is grateful to a number of military personnel and civilian officials for helpful discussions on this topic. An earlier version of this paper was presented at a conference on 'Intelligence and Australian National Security Policy', held at the Australian Defence Studies Centre, Canberra, 2S – 26 November 1993.

[1] Intelligence is a 'dirty word' according to the International Peace Academy, *Peacekeeper's Handbook* (New York: Pergamon Press, 1984), p. 39.

[2] The topic is barely mentioned in the UN secretary-general's report, *Improving the Capacity of the United Nations for Peace-keeping*, A/48/403, 14 March 1994. Some discussion is contained in International Peace Academy, *Peacekeeper's Handbook*, pp. 59–62, 120-21, which notes that 'the intelligence concept' may be required in certain future operations.

[3] For discussions of the nature of contemporary peacekeeping, see John Mackinlay and Sarat Chopra, *A Draft Concept of Second Generation Multinational Operations 1993* (Providence, RI; Thomas J. Watson Institute for International Studies, Brown University, 1993); Cathy' Downes, 'Challenges for Smaller Nations in the New Era of UN and Multinational Operations', in Hugh Smith (ed.), *Peacekeeping – Challenges for the Future* (Canberra: Australian Defence Studies Center, 1993), and

249

'Demobilization after Civil Wars', in IISS, *Strategic Survey 1993-1994* (London: Brassey's for the IISS), pp. 25-31.

[4] For the British position, see British reply to the Secretary-General, *United Nations Peacekeeping* (London: HMSO, July 1993), pp. 4 and 7–8.

[5] For an example of timely information passed to the UN Special Representative in the United Nations Transition Assistance Group (Namibia), see Margaret Thatcher, *The Downing Street Years* (London: Harper Collins, 1993), pp. 528-29.

[6] The report of the UN Secretary- General, Improving the Capacity of the United Nations for Peacekeeping, pp. 36-37.

[7] On the importance of this principle, see *ibid.*, pp. 25-27.

[8] See Joint Chiefs of Staff, *Joint Doctrine for Intelligence Support to Operations* (Washington DC: Joint Publication 2-0, Joint Staff. 1993), pp. VII, 1-2.

[9] Ruth Sina, 'Warlord Slips Through Wide Intelligence Net'. *The Australian*, 7 October 1993, p. 6.

[10] Lieutcnant-Colonel David J. Hurley, 'Operation Solace', *Defence Force Journal* (Australia), no. 104, January/ February 1994, p, 33.

[11] See the report of the UN secretary-general, *Improving the Capacity of the United Nations for Peace-keeping*, pp. 28-39.

[12] Staffed initially through the voluntary secondment of staff by member-states, an establishment of 15 has recently been approved. Supplementation by member-states will, therefore, still be needed.

[13] Mats R. Berdal. 'Fateful Encounter: The United States and UN Peacekeeping', *Survival*, vol. 36, no. 1, Spring 1994, p, 46.

[14] Mats R. Bordal, *Whither UN Peace-keeping?*, Adelphi Paper 281 (London. Brassey's for the GSS, 1993), p. 43.

[15] Ibid., p. 8. See also International Peace Academy, *Peacekeeper's Handbook*, pp. 39 and 120.

[16] The scope for using patrols to collect information is emphasised in International Peace Academy, *Peacekeeper's Handbook*. pp. 105-14.

[17] Lieutenant-Colonel Geoffrey Peterson, 'Human Intelligence and Somalia – A Cost Effective Winner for a Small Army'. *Defence Force Journal* (Australia), no. 104, January/February 1994, p. 37.

[18] General Rose. 'Looking for a Return to Normality', *Jane's Defence Weekly*, 1 June 1994, p. 5.

[19] Michael Krepon and Jeffrey P. Tracey, 'Open Skies' and UN Peacekeeping', *Survival*, vol. 32, no, 3, May/June 1990, pp. 261-62 and 263.

[20] 'The United Nations in the 1990s: Restoring the Vision', a seminar at the Peace Research Centre, Australian National University, 26 August 1993.

[21] The possibility also exists that UN personnel could use information for private gain and would be susceptible to blackmail or bribery.

[22] On procedures for dealing with the media, see International Peace Academy, *Peacekeeper's Handbook*, pp. 76 – 78 and 340-42.

[23] Remarks by Timothy T. Trevan, in United Nations, 'Disarmament- New Realities: Disarmament, Peace-building and Global Security', excepts from panel discussions at a conference held at the United Nations, New York, 20-23 April 1993 (New York: United, Nations, 1993), p. 262

[24] Berdal, 'Fateful Encounter', p. 46.

[25] George Bush, *National Security Strategy of the United States* (Washington. DC: White House, January 1993 p. 8.

[26] In Bosnia-Herzegovina, for example, the UN command received no intelligence from national sources because of the lack of security and the reluctance of nations to supply intelligence. See Brigadier Roderick Cordy-Simpson, 'UN Operations in Bosnia-Herzegovina', in Smith (ed.), *Peacekeeping*, p. 106.

[27] General Lewis Mackenzie indicated the potential value of satellite data when he remarked that 'Sarajevo cried out for things like satellite imagery'. Cited in Peter Saracino, 'Polemics and Prescriptions', *International Defence Review*, vol. 26, no. 5, May 1993, p. 370.

[28] Bhupendra Jasani, 'The Value Of Civilian Satellite Imagery', *Jane's Intelligence Review*, vol. 5, no. 5, May 1993, p. 235. [OSS Note: As of 2003, 1 meter imagery is commonly available from the US Space Imaging Corporation, and Russian military combat charts with contour lines and all cultural features, at the 1:50.000 scale, with ports and cities at the 1:10.000 and 1:25.000 scale, all generally updated in the late 1990's, have become easily available through such organisations as East View Cartographic—at prices as low as $135 for a Russian tactical military map of a specific African area.]

[29] Details are taken from Krepon and Tracey, 'Open Skies', and. William J, Durch, 'Running the Show: Planning and Implementation', in Durch (ed.), *The Evolution of UN* Peacekeeping (New York: St Martin's Press, 1993), pp. 69-71.

[30] Krepon and Tracey, 'Open Skies', p. 251. This is disputed in a Canadian study. See Stephan B. Flemming, *Organizational and Military Aspects of High-Tech Surveillance and Detection Systems for UN Peacekeeping*, Project Report 535 (Ottawa: Operational Research and Analysis Establishment, Department of National Defence., 1992), p. 3.

[31] Gareth Evans, Co-operating for Peace: The Global Agenda for the 1990s and Beyond (Sydney: Allen and Unwin, 1993), p. 65.

[32] Boutros Boutros-Ghali. *An Agenda for Peace: Preventive Diplomacy, Peacemaking and Peace-Keeping* (New York; United Nations, 1992), p. 14.

[33] Boutros Boutros-Ghali, 'Agenda for Peace–One Year Later', *Orbis*, vol. 37, no. 3, Summer 1993, p. 325.

[34] Evans, *Cooperating for Peace*, p. .163. See also remarks by William Colby, former Director of Central Intelligence, in *Disarmament—New Realities'*, pp. 254-55.

---

[35] Jasani, 'Civilian Satellite Imagery', p, 235.

[36] Jaap Donath, 'A European Community Intelligence Organisation', *Defence Intelligence Journal,* vol, 2, no. 1, Spring 1993', pp. 15 – 33.

[37] Desmond Ball, 'Arms and Affluence: Military Acquisitions in the Asia-Pacific Region', *International Security* vol. 1 8, no. 3, Winter 1993/94, pp. 105-12.

[38] Flemming, Organisational and Military Impacts, p. 9.

Intelligence and Peacekeeping:
The UN Operation in the Congo, 1960-64

A. Walter Dorn and David J. H. Bell

Effective peacekeeping required the proactive acquisition and prudent analysis of information about conditions within the mission area. This is especially true if the operation is conducted in a hazardous and unpredictable environment and the lives of peacekeepers are threatened, as was the case with the UN operation in the Congo (ONUC). A Military Information Branch (MIB) was established as part of ONUC to enhance the security of UN personnel, to support specific operations, to warn of outbreaks of conflict and to estimate outside interference (for example, the importation of armaments). The MIB employed signals intelligence using a wireless message interception system, photographic intelligence using aeroplanes equipped for the purpose, and human intelligence from lawful interrogations of prisoners and informants. A detailed description of the activities of the MIB is provided here for the first time, using newly uncovered archival files. The study points to some of the difficulties and benefits of developing dedicated intelligence gathering bodies.

> *We are fully aware of your long-standing limitations in gathering information. The limitations are inherent in the very nature of the United Nations and therefore any operation conducted by it.* Secretary-general U Thant to Lt-Gen. Kebbede Guebre, the Commander of the UN Operation in the Congo, 24 September 1962 (Code Cable #6780)

The United Nations has always been sensitive about the issue of intelligence gathering. UN officials fear that Member States, many of whom possess their own powerful and established intelligence networks, would accuse the UN of violating national sovereignty if discovered probing into their affairs without invitation. They also fear that the UN's integrity would be compromised if it were discovered to be engaged in intelligence activities, since some habitually employed intelligence techniques, such as theft, eavesdropping, surveillance and bribery, are often sinister elements of the international conflicts that the UN is committed to resolving.

Such reasoning doubtlessly underlay Secretary-general Hammarskjold's refusal in 1960 to support the establishing of a permanent UN intelligence agency and his conviction that the UN 'must have clean hands'.[1] Similarly U Thant was vigilant about maintaining strict limits on the scope of information gathering. That the UN today lacks a formal intelligence body shows that such views continue to prevail.

The UN's opposition to founding an intelligence network also carried over to resistance to the establishment of intelligence operations in its peacekeeping missions. Out of necessity, however, the UN has embraced at least some intelligence-gathering techniques and, on occasion, has established dedicated intelligence bodies. This chapter describes the first such organisation set up by the UN: the Military Information Branch of the UN Operation in the Congo (ONUC).[2] This early attempt at intelligence gathering demonstrates both the benefits and problems of such bodies.

The ONUC Precedent

While the UN's experience in the Congo (now Zaire) has been the subject of numerous memoirs and academic works, no study has ever been devoted to ONUC's extensive intelligence operations. The fact that the UN possessed an advanced intelligence component in the Congo is not known, even to many that have studied the operation in detail.[3] This case history merits attention, considering that the most recent peacekeeping operations are facing similar challenges as ONUC, including the need for intelligence gathering.

ONUC foreshadowed the current direction of peacekeeping operations in many ways. It was a large and complex operation, numbering about twenty thousand personnel at its peak, the largest peacekeeping operation prior to the end of the Cold War. Two hundred and thirty-four ONUC personnel perished in the Congo, the highest number of fatalities of any UN peacekeeping operation.

ONUC's mandate not only covered traditional peacekeeping between belligerents, such as interposition between hostile parties and the maintenance of neutral zones, but it also included elements of policing, disarmament and enforcement. ONUC provided security for technical aid personnel, senior Congolese officials, refugees (including 30.000 Balubas in one camp) and for important installations, including major airports and certain mines. It had responsibilities for restoring law and order, preventing civil war, training Congolese security forces, and ultimately, for securing the withdrawal of foreign mercenaries, by force if necessary. In its campaign against Katangese mercenary forces, ONUC carried out air attacks, the only UN peacekeeping force to do so to date. Lastly, the problems that attended UN efforts in the Congo, especially the absence of central government and the frequent hostility of various factions towards the UN, seem to presage the difficulties which the UN has encountered in Somalia and the former Yugoslavia.

Background

The Congo was left totally unprepared for its independence from Belgium on 30 June 1960. Even on the even of independence, Africans were excluded from government administration and from the officer corps of the Force Publique (the predecessor to the Congolese National Army or ANC).[4] The latter difficulty sparked a series of mutinies by Congolese soldiers beginning on 5 July. In an effort to protect European residents, Belgium deployed its troops in the Congo, in contravention of the Treaty of Friendship, which was supposed to form the basis for post-independence relations between the two countries. The Belgian action led the Congolese government to appeal to the UN secretary-general for military assistance. Fearing superpower intervention if the request went ignored, Hammaskjold obtained Security Council approval on 14 July 1960 to send such a force, which became known as ONUC.

The mutinies not only destabilised the political system and precipitated lawlessness, but they also represented the catalyst for the secession of Katanga province. Immediately following the mutinies, the government of Katanga, the mineral-rich province of the south, became frustrated over the poor prospects of settling its political and economic claims with the central government. Katangese independence, proclaimed on 11 July by Katangese President Moise Tshombe, was not formally sanctioned by the Belgian government but was nevertheless supported by Belgium through military aid and by Belgian mining

255

interests eager to retain control of the province's mining industry. In addition to supplying armaments, Belgium also assisted Katanga in the recruitment of European mercenaries for the latter's army. Katangese succession relied on approximately 500 well-trained and disciplined foreign mercenaries for leadership of its army (the Gendarmerie) of under ten thousand. A constitutional crisis emerged in early September after President Joseph Kasavubu dismissed Prime Minister Patrice Lumumba, who refused to step down and attempted to flee to Stanleyville where his deputy Antoine Gizenga has established a rival regime. When, in August 1960, the Baluba of South Kasai also proclaimed independence, the country was divided into four camps. Into this quagmire the UN found itself thrust under the dynamic and ambitious leadership of secretary-general Dag Hammaskjold, who lost his life in a plane crash on 17 September 1961 while on his way to meet with the Katangese leader. His successor, U Thant, led the Operation out of its impasse and brought stability to the country before finally overseeing the withdrawal of UN forces. The last UN peacekeepers left the Congo on 30 June 1964.

Uncertain Mandate for Intelligence Gathering

In the initial period of ONUC's existence an ideological fray developed between the Force's military and civilian leadership.[5] The source of this friction was ambivalence over ONUC's role, including the role of intelligence gathering within the operation. The military elements were accustomed to military operations in which organised intelligence gathering was an accepted practice. They were critical of the lack of any comparable structures in ONUC and were concerned about the threat that this posed to ONUC personnel. The civilian leadership justified the absence of an intelligence system on the grounds that ONUC military forces were mandated to perform a strictly peacekeeping and training role. Hammarskjold stated at an early meeting of the Congo Advisory Committee that ONUC could not afford to engage in secretive practices habitually associated with intelligence services, even through he admitted that the lack of an intelligence network was a serious handicap for the operation.[6] According to military leaders, principles of war and basic tactical conceptions were deliberately ignored by ONUC's civilian leadership in the control and deployment of the Force.[7] Thus, despite the demands of ONUC's first Force Commander, Major-General Von Horn of Sweden, who urged at the end of 1960 'the setting up of an information gathering and processing agency'[8] in addition to an enormous increase in ONUC personnel and firepower, the absence of an organised intelligence structure persisted for over a half year into its mission.[9]

Creation of the Military 'Information' Branch

Two months of relative calm after ONUC's deployment were followed by a rapid decline in the political situation in the Congo. Civil war erupted in North Katanga and South Kasai, with the central government, the artificiality of its authority growing apparent, powerless to act. The 'Congo crisis' reached its climax after the death of Lumumba in February 1961, at which time ONUC's mandate was transformed to include an enforcement dimension to take 'all appropriate measures to prevent the occurrence of civil war...including...the use of force, if necessary, in the last resort'.[10] It was at this stage, when ONUC acquired a more ambitious mandate, that the need for an intelligence structure was accepted by ONUC's civilian leadership and an intelligence organisation was established. It was particularly important since none of the countries with embassies and intelligence officials in the Congo were willing to supply intelligence, even through many of them supported the operation in principle and voted for it in the Security Council.[11] If the UN was to obtain any information on sensitive political and security matters in the Congo, it would have to be through their own intelligence apparatus.

As a reflection of the UN's mindfulness of the shady connotations stemming from the term 'intelligence', ONUC's intelligence operation was known euphemistically as the 'Military Information Branch'. Memos were circulated requesting that the Branch be alluded to in ONUC correspondence as the 'Information' Branch as opposed to 'Intelligence' Branch. Force Commander Von Horn suggested that the later term was 'banned' outright from the UN lexicon.[12] The reality is that the term persisted to an extent throughout the operation: Lnt.Col. Bjorn Egge and N. Borchgrevink, the first Chiefs of Military Information, addressed themselves using the title 'Chief of Military Intelligence'; and documents were occasionally labelled as being produced by the 'Military Intelligence Branch'.

The Role of the Military Information Branch

The Military Information Branch (MIB) was established in order to accumulate and collate information, evaluate it, and disseminate intelligence. Its duty was to provide intelligence for four purposes:

1. *Enhanced Security of UN Personnel.* ONUC forces operated in a volatile political environment, in which their relations with various factions frequently changed from amicability to animosity. In this setting, a principal task of the MIB was to recognise the prevailing attitudes of Congolese factions toward UN personnel, both military and civilian, so as to forewarn Military Operations, specifically the Force Commander, of security threats.

2. *Support for Specific Operations.* The potential for disaster was great if the deployment of UN forces was to be based on erroneous or insufficient awareness of the activities and capabilities of non-UN military forces. MIB was required to provide the Force Commander with intelligence prior to undertaking military actions.

3. *Warning of Possible Outbreaks of Conflict.* Factional strife could threaten the security of ONUC personnel, even if harm to UN forces was unintended by the belligerents. For example, UN personnel could be harmed in crossfire, and ONUC's mission could be impaired by disruption of its transportation routes. Moreover, since any threat of atrocities against the European population might spark a mass exodus of inhabitants with essential skills, averting a breakdown of public services depended on early warning by ONUC of threats to the peace.

4. *Estimations of Outside Interference.* Information on arms traffic and the number of foreign mercenaries entering the Congo was especially important in order for ONUC to estimate the military capabilities of secessionist Katango province.[13] As part of this mandate, the Branch monitored supply routes into the Congo from bordering countries.

It was reasoned that failure to adequately and effectively gather intelligence would risk the safety of both ONUC personnel and Congolese civilians. If a tragedy occurred, the UN would inevitably be challenged by world opinion over why it had not been prevented. As an international organisation still in its formative years, already a magnet of controversy and increasingly financially constrained, the UN would ill-afford to be accused of lack of foresight, efficiency and professionalism in a major peacekeeping operation.

The Evolution of the MIB—Revamping and Amalgamation

Criticism, however, rapidly emerged. In September 1961, ONUC embarked on implementing SC Resolution 161 (1961) by staging a dragnet operation designed to round up and expel foreign mercenaries in the Katangese Gendarmerie. The operation illustrated the unpreparedness and lack of organisation of ONUC forces to perform their enforcement mandate, and exposed the UN to international reproach. As Chief of Military Information, Lt-Col Borchgrevink maintained that a 'main shortcoming' of the operation was inadequate intelligence. This resulted in a 'failure' by the MIB to estimate the capabilities of the Katangese Gendarmerie'.[14]

The military leadership, which had earlier demanded the establishment of MIB, now began urging its restructuring and requested a dramatic increase in its resources. The Military Advisor to the secretary-general, General Indar Jit Rikhye of India, agreed in November 1961 that it was 'urgently necessary to establish an efficient intelligence service which is totally lacking at the moment'.[15]

Information Chief Borchgrevink provided a scathing assessment of the capacity of the Military Information Branch in his report of 7 March 1962 to the Military Advisor in New York. He noted that the MIB 'does *not* have proper control of the intelligence situation'.[16] At the time, the Military Information Branch at ONUC Headquarters, Leopoldville numbered nine officers: a Chief of Military Information, an executive officer, five desk officers and two interrogators.[17] Some of the staff lacked intelligence training; and in a setting in which bilingualism was imperative for an effective information-gathering system, not all of MIB headquarters staff could speak both French and English. ONUC did not possess the capability for systematic interception of wireless radio messages and for routine aerial photography.[18]

Borchgrevink also complained that the ONUC procedural practices often ignored the MIB. He alluded to instances in which intelligence passed from the Force Commander to UN headquarters in New York without evaluation by the MIB, and the practice of the Operations Branch, the main division of ONUC, of not consulting MIB prior to the deployment of UN forces. He also cited the lack of contact between ONUC's Political/Economic Branch (mandated to keep abreast of the political and economic matters) and the MIB.[19]

A few days later, the secretary-general's Military Advisor approved a proposal to revamp the MIB.[20] The plan foresaw a heightening of the organisation's resources, an increase in MIB personnel, and changes in ONUC procedure regarding intelligence flows. New MIB sections were added, including photo-interpretation and wireless monitoring. The creation of the positions Counter Intelligence Officer (CIO) and Provincial or Field Liaison Officer (PLO, and also called 'Field Intelligence Officer') was accepted. A PLO was designed for each of the Congo's six provinces in order 'to collect and collate military, political and tribal information'.[21] By 17 September 1962 there were 27 intelligence officers either stationed at the various provincial headquarters or posted with national brigades.[22] An intelligence officer was to be assigned to the Political/Economic Branch to ensure quick exchange of intelligence. Procedures were tightened to give MIB the exclusive authority to prepare intelligence reports for New York. The structure of the overhauled MIB is shown in Figure 1 (next page).

The new structure remained in place until after ONUC's December 1962-January 1963 campaign in Katanga, in which UN forces successfully occupied most of the secessionist province and forced Tshombe to capitulate.[23] Soon afterwards ONUC command was instructed by UN Headquarters to effect a 30 per cent reduction of its staff.[24] This led the Force Commander Kebbede Guebre in March 1963 to amalgamate the Military Operations and Military Information Branches, reducing the total number of officers, secretaries and non-commissioned officers in Leopoldville headquarters from 36 to 26.[25] A further abatement was the abolishment of the PLO post in August 1963.[26] Similar reductions to ONUC's intelligence component continued until the UN operation concluded in 1964.

MILITARY INFORMATION BRANCH

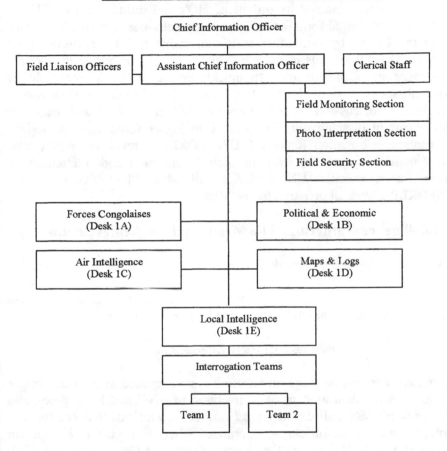

Figure 1: Military Information Branch

Reporting Methods

From the advent of the MIB, information was disseminated within ONUC through a formal process involving four types of reports. The principal means was the daily Situation Report (SITREP), issued by units in the field to the Operations Branch of ONUC's provincial headquarters, and submitted by the provincial HQ to ONUC headquarters in Leopoldville. Information Summaries

(ISUM's), prepared by the MIB, provided a telegraphic summary of important items of intelligence obtained by provincial HQ's and military units. ISUM's summarised in condensed form the recent military activities of non-UN military forces in the Congo by estimating their armaments and by outlining their movements. They also discussed the prevailing political situation in the Congo. ISUM's were intended primarily to quickly inform units in the field of changing situations. Periodic Information Reports (PERINFOREP's) presented a more lengthy discussion of the topics covered in ISUM's and were the primary means of disseminating intelligence to higher formations in ONUC. Supplementary Information Reports (SUPINFOREP's) reviewed a particular aspect of non-UN forces, for example their organisation and/or strength, in readiness for a specific UN operation. ISUM's, PERINFOREP's and SUPINFOREP's were all prepared by the MIB.[27]

Intelligence Gathering: The Means and the Achievements

As ONUC's intelligence system developed, a variety of intelligence-gathering techniques were introduced, continued and/or expanded. These techniques were characteristic of conventional intelligence operations. They included wireless message interception, aerial intelligence, and human intelligence.

Wireless Message Interception

No permanent wireless message interception system existed in the early stages of ONUC.[28] A minimal amount of interception of ANC and Katangese radio sets was nevertheless utilised on an *ad hoc* basis with positive results. For example, an intelligence officer was surprised when on a visit to Kabalo (in northern Katanga) he discovered the Ethiopian battalion Commander, Lnt-Col. Alemu, had established an improvised interception service. Messages were intercepted using a commercial receiver, while a local Baluba took down messages in Swahili and translated them into French.[29] Security of Katangese radio nets was found to be 'extremely bad'.[30]

In February 1962 the secretary-general's Military Advisor agreed to the establishment of a broad radio-monitoring organisation for the MIB. Rikhye justified such a monitoring system on the grounds that it was an 'invisible' activity and therefore did not violate ONUC's agreement with various Congolese factions, notably its cease-fire agreement with Katanga.[31]

The service was authorised to monitor broadcasts of foreign radio stations, Radio Katanga, and radio stations in Leopoldville and Stanleyville. This provided forewarning when Tshome and his Interior Minister, Godefroi Munungo, used public radio broadcasts to incite violence against ONUC and even to call for the death of the UN representative in Elisabethville.[32] ONUC soldiers could thus prepare themselves for threats from both Katangese civilians (including children) and military and paramilitary personnel.

ONUC was also authorised to monitor the operational and administrative wireless nets of the ANC in Leopoldville and Stanleyville, and of the Gendarmeries in Katanga. The structure provided for a staff of seven at ONUC HQ Leopoldville, including one cipher operator for breaking codes, and four operators in Elisabethville, Stanleyville, Bukavu and Lulubourg.[33]

By May 1962 ONUC HQ in Katanga had established a system to monitor the Katangese military radio net on a 24-hour basis. In the one-month period between 30 March and 30 April 1962, for example, Katanga headquarters intercepted 382 messages.[34] Katangese radio security measures were again found to be poor, with even the most sensitive military information going on the air in the clear.[35]

The use of ciphers and codes by the Katangese Gendarmerie in some of their communications complicated the ability of the MIB to gather intelligence from radio intercepts and to do so rapidly (that is, before the information became antiquated). In early September 1962, Ulrie Lindercrona, who had the task of cracking codes, determined the key to a substitution cipher, known as 'Charlie', which was used primarily by Katangese forces in Kamina sector.[36] He was also able to break the code frequently used in messages between Kongolo and Elisabethville.[37] With other ciphers Lindencrona was less successful. In his submission to MIB HQ Katanga of 11 October 1962, he reported that all the keys to the 'Cessar' cipher had eluded him. This cipher was used by all Katangese units and was regarded by Lindencrona as 'probably the most important of all types'. While he believed that there was a possibility of breaking Cessar, the lengthy amount of time required to produce sufficient statistics to determine the system had left him unable to produce the keys.[38] This problem persisted during the Katanga operation in December 1962-January 1963[39] in which UN forces successfully rounded up the majority of foreign mercenaries and eliminated Katangese air capability. Given that the monitoring service was a casualty of the cutbacks effected after this campaign, it is likely that efforts to decrypt Cessar stopped at this time.

Radio intercepts provided voluminous intelligence, and were particularly useful during ONUC's December 1962-January 1963 Katanga campaign ('Operation Grand Slam') to remove foreign mercenaries, gain complete freedom of movement in the province, and bring about the end of the Katangese secession.[40] While many messages stated mere trivialities and irrelevancies of minimal use to ONUC, some described important facts and details crucial to its operations. ONUC learned of orders from Katangese authorities for bombardment missions and reconnaissance missions, and obtained information regarding troop movements, arms shortages, and hidden arms caches. For example, knowledge that the Katangese Gendarmerie Commander had ordered his air force Commander to bomb the Elisabethville airfield during the night of 29 December, which was obtained by radio interception, triggered the final military push into Katanga.[41] ONUC learned on 5 January 1963 of discussions being made for a possible attack by Gendarmeries on Albertville.[42] On 10 January ONUC discovered, again through a radio intercept, that 1,200 gendarmes had arrived in Luena and that they were awaiting new heavy guns.[43] Since some of these messages were sent in code, this intelligence could not have been procured without MIB's code-cracking capabilities.

Aerial Intelligence

For much of its operation, ONUC possessed insufficient aircraft and photographic equipment to provide photographs and photo-interpretation of strategic installations and positions in the Congo. A minimal amount of air intelligence was gleaned in the early period of ONUC from aircrews of UN and commercial transport aircraft working for the UN and from their stops at Congolese airfields.[44] Mandatory debriefing of all military transport and charter company aircrews was later instituted when MIB suspected that these personnel were making important observations and not reporting them.[45]

The absence of jet fighters left ONUC severely handicapped in its September 1961 Katanga campaign. A lone Katangese Fouga Magistère jet almost paralysed ONUC forces,[46] and compelled UN headquarters to consider adding to ONUC a fighter aircraft dimension. This was instituted in October 1961, when four Ethiopian F-86 and five Swedish J-29 fighter jets, and four Indian B-

1 Canberra light bombers, entered service to become the 'UN Air Force'.[47] The primary task of the fighter force was to incapacitate the Katangese Air Force (FAK). Its secondary tasks were to provide aerial reconnaissance and air support during hostilities.[48]

ONUC's increased reconnaissance potential did not trigger a substantial augmentation in aerial intelligence, much to the chagrin of ONUC's military leadership. In November 1961 a memo circulated by ONUC Air Operations alluded to a continued 'lack of air intelligence; not even for fighter operations' and declared that 'officers have not got nearly as much information as needed to operate in a proper way'.[49]

To correct this deficiency the Chief of Military Information requested in January 1962 that Fighter Operations Branch initiate an extensive air 'recce' (reconnaissance) programme.[50] Such an undertaking, however, was inhibited by ONUC's limited aerial photography capabilities. The only aircraft available for photoreconnaissance were two Canberra's of the No. 5 Indian Squadron and the odd transport plane. The cameras on the Canberra's left much to be desired for effective photo work, since they could only take vertical photographs and were primarily designed for photographing bombing results. Photos from transport planes were of limited usefulness because they were taken through aircraft windows using ordinary hand-held cameras. These restrictions led Chief of Fighter Operations, Col. S. Lapel, to assert that 'it is not possible to carry out such an extensive air recce programme with the aircraft available'.[51] But even if such an ambitious recce operation had been possible, ONUC would still have faced difficulties in converting photographs into reliable intelligence; ONUC lacked photo-laboratory resources, including processing and interpretation equipment, and personnel.[52]

Aerial reconnaissance was especially imperative since detailed maps of the Congo were unavailable, and because ONUC communications was poor in much of the country.[53] This meant that the UN often had no other means of obtaining information except by continuous visual and photoreconnaissance from the air. The confined use by ONUC of ground radar facilities also translated into a necessity for air intelligence. Because of the 'exorbitant expense'[54] of radar, ONUC possessed only two radar sets: one at Kamina, with a maximum range of 200 miles;[55] and one at Elisabetehville, with was installed in August 1962.[56] The shortage of radar made it difficult for ONUC to track and intercept airborne Katangese aircraft. Destruction of FAK aircraft thus depended on following up reports by ONUC troops of aircraft movements, and on frequently combing airfields.[57] This fact was demonstrated in ONUC's December 1961 Katanga operation: all the Katangese aircraft destroyed were located on the ground, whereas those that were airborne evaded their UN pursuers by disappearing into the clouds.[58]

Poor reconnaissance capabilities hindered the MIB's efforts to estimate the strength of the Katangese Air Force (FAK). This is reflected in the Supplementary Intelligence Report in which the Branch states that collection of accurate information on Katangese air capacity was hampered because 'ONUC has no dedicated air photo-reconnaissance facilities...and lacks surveillance radar to detect or follow all aircraft movements in Katanga'.[59] According to the report, the implication of this was that 'due to lack of complete information, there is *no* alternative but to consider FAK as a dangerous enemy in the air'.[60]

UN Headquarters in New York was able to secure improved aerial intelligence resources after the Swedish government agreed to send two Saab 29C aircraft equipped for photoreconnaissance and a photo-interpretation detachment.[61] Their arrival in November 1962 signalled a considerable improvement in ONUC's ability to collect aerial intelligence,[62] and supplied ONUC with vital information prior to its campaign in Katanga during the next month. The aerial intelligence that they provided led the MIB to reappraise its estimation of Katangese air capability. Many FAK planes which had previously been cited by ONUC were found to be unserviceable, and it was also determined that Katangese ammunition stockpiling was occurring only at several airfields. Due to the new photo-interpretation facilities, reports of anti-aircraft batteries and underground aircraft shelters at some Katangese airfields were rejected.[63]

Human Intelligence—Prisoners, Informants and Agents

Captured or suspected mercenaries detained by ONUC Forces underwent a formal interrogation procedure. While this term is used sometimes to imply brutality, there is no indication that 'interrogations' conducted by MIB officers were anything but scrupulous. Memos were distributed by ONUC Command instructing UN forces to comply with the 1949 Geneva Convention on the treatment of prisoners.[64] The Convention text itself was widely circulated among UN personnel.

Staging 'detailed interrogations' (as opposed to 'preliminary interrogations') was the responsibility of MIB officers. Three hundred interrogations were conducted from the beginning of the operation in July 1960 until March 1962 alone.[65]   Given the shortage of MIB officers and the fact that many interrogations took days, the procedure placed considerable strain on MIB resources.[66]   The exercise, however, sometimes led to positive results. For example, the interrogation of several suspected mercenaries in March 1962 was particularly helpful to evaluate FAK air capacity. The intelligence obtained pointed to the presence of modest numbers of small aircraft in Katanga, and to vigorous efforts by Katanga to purchase transport and fighter aircraft.[67]   In his recent account of the Congo operation, General Rikhye states that interrogations 'proved invaluable' and that updated lists of mercenaries, so obtained, aided O'Brien in his negotiations with Tshombe for the removal of the European advisers and mercenaries.[68]

MIB officers also conducted interrogations of asylum-seekers from the Katangese Gendarmerie and bureaucracy. On occasion this was an invaluable way of gathering intelligence. For example, Cleophas Kanyinda, a clerk with the Katangese government who was responsible for paying the salaries of mercenaries, fled to the Tunisian camp of ONUC on 25 November 1962. He divulged to ONUC the names and whereabouts of several dozen mercenaries.[69] David Sutherland and John Franklin, vehicle mechanics for the Katangese Gendarmerie, sought asylum with the UN in late summer 1962 after they were ordered to participate in transport convoys. The two disclosed the names of 52 mercenaries and revealed the location of several large weapons dumps near Jadotville. They also informed ONUC of the import of 600 Landrovers into Katanga from N'Dola, Rhodesia.[70]   On the basis of this information, MIB instructed officers to make 'discreet inquiries' (presumably with contacts in Rhodesia) in order to confirm these details. An inquiry was urged because premised on the fact that Government permission would be required for their import, confirmation of this information may even lead to our knowing if the Rhodesian Government helped Katanga in securing this deal.[71]

ONUC's use of informants has been portrayed as a 'comic' and rather scanty enterprise.[72]   In 1962, Conor Cruise O'Brien, who has served as the ONUC representative in Elisabethville, suggested that this activity was restricted to the employment in Elisabethville of 'one Greek ex-policeman with an imperfect knowledge of French' (who was known by the Katangese Gendarmerie as

'Chief of the United Nations Intelligence Services in Katanga') and 'a few Baluba houseboys'.[73]

Informants, both paid and unpaid, were utilised more extensively than this account suggests. For example, in 1962 an intelligence officer (IO) with the Irish Battalion kept a mercenary 'on tap' in order to glean information. At the same time the Tunisian battalion IO maintained a Belgian contact in Kipushi (on the Katangese border with Northern Rhodesia) to learn of troop and arms movements.[74] The IO also had several contacts in the Elisabethville post office, which he regarded as a 'very useful method of collecting information'.[75] Using these contacts, ONUC was able to locate a box of detonators consigned to a Belgian mining company and to intercept a letter to a Katangese Government minister.[76]

One notable and successful use of informants was the search on 6 April 1962 of an Elisabethville warehouse which uncovered 40-50 aircraft engines and a wealth of other aircraft parts. The search was conducted after an inside source informed ONUC HQ Elisabethville of the location of this cache and noted that it was set to be shipped elsewhere for assembly.[77] The source thus enabled ONUC to thwart an escalation in FAK's air capability.

ONUC also possessed informants within the Katangese government and contacts outside the Congo. The MIB based its April 1961 estimate of foreign mercenaries in the Katangese Gerdarmerie ('between 400-550') on 'informants in Katangese Government circles', in addition to statements by mercenaries.[78] MIB's July 1962 assessment of Katanga Military forces was based in part on information provided by 'five regular European sources all with indirect access to military information', each of whose information was corroborated by the others.[79] In March 1962 informants carried out an investigation (without any positive results) in Congo (Brazzaville) of a report that six FAK Fouga Magistère's were stationed at Pointe Noire.[80]

Information provided by informants was a mixed basket, as were details dispensed by prisoners and asylum-seekers. MIB had no means of confirming or denying much of the information provided by these sources. Informants sometimes only reported on statements made by others, for example, Katangese politicians, or Genarmerie officers. The information they provided was consequently not as accurate as the information provided to them. Since it was in the Katangese interest to provide assurances of safety to its residents (not to mention to keep informants in Katanga misinformed), it is not surprising that information provided by some informants grossly exaggerated Katangese military capacity. For example, Jean Pignorel and Corey de Vries were each told repeatedly and separately that FAK had assembled 20-30 Fouga jets at Kolwezi by late 1962.[81] As already discussed, however, aerial intelligence suggested and FAK capabilities were minimal, an opinion that was ultimately verified during ONUC's December 1962-January 1963 Katanga operation.

The use of agents by MIB touches upon the issue of the limits by the UN on intelligence-gathering techniques. Chief of Military Information, N. Borchgrevink, noted in 1962 that 'UN agents have…been used on a very limited scale', and further stipulated that the 'field of work for UN agents was in the Congo and in its neighbour states, from which arms supplies and mercenaries enter the Congo'.[82]

There is indication that contributing states were extremely reluctant to accept the use of agents, particularly outside Congolese borders. On one occasion, the MIB was instructed by the Force Commander to conduct a 'special mission' to gather intelligence on surrounding African countries. The Branch nominated a French-speaking Canadian officer to undertake this mission. The Canadian contingent Commander, however, refused to accept the request, stating that Canadian personnel could not participate in missions outside the Congo without the approval of the Canadian government, and that approval was unlikely to be forthcoming considering the 'covert' nature of the task.[83] The Branch was unable to carry out this mission because suitable mission personnel were not available.[84]

There is also evidence that within ONUC itself there was a reluctance to accept the use of agents. ONUC Force Commander Kebbede Guebre, for instance, thought it 'not advisable' at all for the UN to employ professional intelligence agents.[85] Fear of a fall from grace if the UN were discovered employing 'spies' in the Congo and elsewhere seemed enough to outweigh the benefits that such exercise might have provided.

MIB: The Shortcomings

The MIB was established in an effort to institutionalise within ONUC a formal information-gathering programme. An *ad hoc* and haphazard approach to intelligence procurement and dissemination, however, persisted to a degree even with the MIB. While MIB's structure was impressive on paper, some of the duties and personnel it envisioned were never realised. Such was the case with the Provincial Liaison Officers. In July 1962 three of ONUC's six provincial command headquarters did not possess PLO's, and this probably continued to the end.[86] The intelligence effort in these provinces thus depended upon the priority and importance that the commanding officer gave to intelligence. Furthermore, the frequent turnover of intelligence staff was not conducive to the development of a systematic intelligence structure; nor was the inadequate intelligence training of many officers assigned to the Branch.[87]

Established procedures for intelligence dissemination were often ignored, impairing MIB HQ in Leopoldville from having an accurate and up-to-date intelligence picture. For example, in November 1961, Katanga province's intelligence staff consisted of 'one-half man'.[88] SITREPS contained precious little intelligence and Katanga Command neglected to submit to Leopoldville fortnightly Printer's.[89]

The timidity of the UN's civilian leadership toward intelligence precluded MIB's establishment until after ONUC's statutory authority was transformed to include an enforcement dimension. The late start was not without serious implications. A twelve-man patrol from ONUC's Irish contingent was ambushed on 8 November 1960 by bow-and-arrow-wielding Baluba tribesmen near Niemba, in Kivu province. Only two of the soldiers survived. While it has been suggested that a Swedish officer warned the officer in charge of the patrol to exercise caution in dealing with Baluba of this isolated area,[90] there is no indication that ONUC Command was aware of the warning. The warning was not taken seriously by the patrol: one of the survivors explained that the patrol was under the false impression that the tribesmen were friendly.[91] It was later determined that the tribesmen could not distinguish ONUC from other military forces who were hostile to them.[92] Had ONUC possessed a well-equipped intelligence organisation that oversaw a structured intelligence procurement and dissemination process, these killings might have been prevented.

In numerous instances, inadequate information on deteriorating political conditions exposed ONUC troops to extreme hazards. A bloody example is the Port Francqui incident of 28 April 1961. The incident was precipitated by the visit of the Congolese Interior Minister to Port Fancqui, in the north-western Kasai province. During a public speech the minister accused the local ANC of being the cause of trouble rather than a deterrent and denounced them for being anti-Lulua. He also threatened that the UN would disarm them if their attitudes did not change. The minister was under UN escort. The ANC troops were offended by these comments, and believed that the UN shared the same partiality towards the Luluas in the tribal conflict in northern Kasai as the Interior Minister. The next evening, ANC forces attacked UN troops stationed at Port Francqui.[93] The ninety-man Ghanian garrison was clearly unprepared for the attack. Dispersed in six different places in town, the UN troops were quickly overpowered.[94] According to UN records, 47 UN personnel were killed.

The official report of the incident concluded that the direct cause of the incident was the speech and attitude of the Interior Minister. What is striking about this is that the minister's UN escorts did not make the connection between the minister's threat and the potential for a violent reaction against the UN; nor did they report the information on the minister's visit to intelligence-trained officers who could have made the connection and alerted command of the possible threat. As the report suggests, the principal weakness of ONUC that was evident in the Port Francqui incident was that there was 'no system of alert to warn troops against any aggressive action by ANC'[95], in sum, poor procedures leading to no intelligence.

The arrival of jet fighters and light bombers in late 1961 constituted a mighty increase in ONUC firepower. Unfortunately, ONUC's aerial intelligence capabilities remained meagre and this meant that there was a high likelihood of mishap during jet attack missions. ONUC's December 1961 campaign in the Elisabethville area of Katanga demonstrates this.

Flight Operations Branch lacked 'attack photographs' of many of the intended targets prior to this campaign.[96] These photographs were intended for briefing pilots on the location and appearance of targets before an attack mission. Among the targets in Katanga for which there was no photograph was the airfield at Shinkolobwe, located Northwest of Elisabethville. Unfortunately during an attack sortie on this airfield the Shinkolobwe hospital was attacked by UN jet fighters. The Chief of Fighter Operations, Col. S. Lampell, said afterwards that the lack of these photographs made it difficult for pilots under attack conditions to distinguish between targets and non-targets. He noted that if such photos had been available during the Katanga campaign it is most likely that the regrettable attack on the hospital could have been avoided.'[97]

The addition to ONUC of two photo-reconnaissance aircraft and a photo-interpretation unit was a decisive factor contributing to the success of the UN operations in Katanga in December 1962-January 1963. During the weeks preceding this operation, these aircraft undertook continuous reconnaissance flights, giving information before the operation began on the whereabouts and numbers of FAK fighter aircraft, two Vampire and eight to ten Harvard aircraft, according to Force Commander Guebre.[98]

Conclusions—Lessons for Today

The Military Information Branch that was established as part of ONUC represents a major precedent for a variety of reasons. The MIB was the UN's first intelligence body. In its systematic information gathering, it employed such means as radio message interception, aerial reconnaissance and human intelligence. The Congo operation revealed the necessity of including an extensive intelligence element in a sophisticated UN military operation.

The initial absence of an intelligence structure placed the Force in a dangerously handicapped position which threatened the lives of UN personnel, the success of ONUC operations, and the reputation of the UN itself. Too often in this period ONUC was unaware of deteriorating conditions until after violent incidents occurred. When its mandate was transformed to include enforcement elements, ONUC's intelligence capacities, institutionalised with the establishment of the MIB, were significant but still insufficient, leading at times to trouble.

The reluctance of the UN's civilian leadership to embrace intelligence gathering in the Congo operation was a manifestation of a broader concern about the future of the UN in a polarised world. At the peak of Cold War acrimony, there existed no shortage of vehement opponents to the UN's increasing authority, especially that of its secretary-general. The UN could not afford to be seen engaging in sinister activities commonly associated with intelligence gathering. For political reasons, the UN thus could not institutionalise a permanent agency to collect sensitive information.

The end of the Cold War signals an important opportunity for the UN to increase its information-gathering capacity. There is no reason why the UN should not institutionalise a sophisticated information gathering and analysis system operating within the bounds of international law. This holds especially true if the UN wants to improve its early warning and preventive diplomacy abilities.[99] Clearly, today's UN peacekeeping operations must not be burdened with the intelligence handicap that ONUC faced on many occasions. The UN can also draw from the Congo experience as it considers adding new technologies, including aerial and satellite reconnaissance,[100] to its information-gathering repertoire.

There exists a principled basis for such an expansion in UN capability. Information gathering is hardly an anathema to UN policy. On the contrary, it is more in accordance with UN practice that the use or threatened use of bombers, guns and tanks. Information gathering can help defuse an incipient crisis that might otherwise only be responded to by brute force later. Such activity therefore must be seen not only as a practical, worthwhile exercise but also an application of the principles for which the UN stands.

The establishment of the Situation Centre at the UN Secretariat in 1993 reflects and effort within the UN to expand its information capacity. The Centre, part of the Department of Peacekeeping Operations, manages the dissemination of information reports from governments and the UN's peacekeeping operations on a 24-hour basis, and also performs limited analysis of information. While peacekeeping operations have proliferated, the number of personnel engaged in these operations has increased from 15 to 75 thousand personnel in three years, there has not been a correspondingly large increase in support-level staff at UN headquarters. In a setting where decisions must be made rapidly by the UN's leadership, the information and research capacity of the Secretariat must be sufficient to meet the task of instructed decision-making. The Congo operation demonstrated this and current experience renders the same conclusions.

Future studies could examine the extent to which the information-gathering techniques employed by ONUC have been used in contemporary peacekeeping operations. The larger UN forces have at times monitored radio communications of the belligerents (for example, in the former Yugoslavia and Cambodia).[101] In Cambodia, peacekeepers gathered intelligence on a battalion level. During raids of the SOC party headquarters, UNTAC teams were able to obtain documentary evidence of non-compliance with provisions of the peace treaty.[102] In Rwanda, officers with the poorly equipped and understaffed UN force unsuccessfully attempted to corroborate allegations made by moderates in the Rwandan military that a plan for mass genocide was being developed. According to Force Commander Romeo Dallaire, information was bought apart of the effort to become informed about deteriorating conditions.[103] The information-gathering and analysis capability of the force, however, was far from adequate: without intelligence, Daillaire lamented, the peacekeepers were operating 'deaf and blind'.[104]

It would be unwise for the UN to employ full-time 'agents' to conduct covert investigations, and it is doubtful that Member States would permit such a practice, but local civilians in areas where peacekeeping operations are conducted, will always be an important source of information. Covert methods are not necessary for the UN to keep informed of most conditions in its peacekeeping operations, and for the UN to identify potential political hotspots. ONUC showed how open information sources, or 'high intelligence', were invaluable for the conduct of a dangerous peacekeeping operation. Even today, most information on such matters is procurable from open and in-confidence sources. Moreover, according to staff at the Situation Centre, a great deal of information is available that is not being exploited.[105]

It is true that some vital information may need to be targeted using dedicated resources; but UN methods should always operate within the bounds of international law and common sense. The UN should not carry out any intelligence work that involves disguising or misrepresenting its activity.

An increase in resources dedicated to UN information-gathering services, such as those in the Situation Centre, will leave the UN better equipped to face its challenges. That there existed in the formative years of UN peacekeeping an extensive information-gathering network might make it easier to accept a more far-reaching network in the future.

The Congo experience demonstrates that knowledge is power for the UN. It shows the UN can still have clean hands and engage in extensive and necessary information gathering for the prevention and management of conflict.

Endnotes

The authors benefited greatly from discussions with Sir Brian Urquhart, General Indar Jit Rikhye and F.T. Liu. They gratefully acknowledge the assistance of Marilla S. Guptil, Deputy Chief Archivist, and the other staff at the UN Archives, New York. Funding from the Department of Foreign Affairs and International Trade Canada is also gratefully acknowledged.

---

[1] Conor Cruise O'Brien, *To Katango and Back* (New York: Grosset & Dunlop, 1962), p. 76.

[2] The acronym ONUC is from the French title: Operation de Nations Unis au Congo.

[3] For example, Anthony Verrier states: 'Neither in New York nor in Leopoldville was there a staff which dealt with information and intelligence', in *International Peacekeeping* (London: Butler & Tanner Ltd., 1981), p. 48. Similarly, Peter Jones states: 'there is no evidence that any of ONUC's aerial assets were every dedicated to aerial surveillance', in his paper on aerial surveillance in *Peacekeeping and International Relations*, March/April 1993, p. 4. Both statements are incorrect.

[4] The acronym ANC is from the French title: Armee Nationale Congolaise.

[5] Interview with Sr. Brian Urquhart (UN Representative in Elisabethville, Nov. 1961-Jan. 1962), 24 Aug 1994.

[6] O'Brien, p. 76 (see note 1 above).

[7] Chief of Military Operations, 'A Review of ONUC Military Operations in the Congo and its Future Deployment and Organization', 16 March 1962, DAG-13/1.6.5.4.0:17—Reports General [Citations beginning with DAG rcfcr to papers in the Departmental Archive Group at the UN Archives in New York. DAG-1 contains the archival files of the Office of the Secretary-General; DAG-13 contains the files of UN Missions and Commissions; DAG-13/6 contains ONUC's files.

[8] Major-General Carl von Horn, 'Congo Lessons: Special Report on ONUC operations up to 31 December 1960', p. 83, DAG-1/2.2.1:64.

[9] For a detailed account of the disagreement between ONUC's military and civilian leadership over ONUC's mandate and intelligence and military capabilities, see von Horn's *Soldiering for Peace* (London: Cassell, 1966). Rikhye's memoire gives valuable insights into the personality of General von Horn, *Military Advisor to the Secretary General* (London: St. Martin's Press, 1993).

[10] SC Res. 161 (1961), 21 Feb. 1961.

[11] Interview with General Indar Jit Rikhye, Trinity College, University of Toronto, 7 Feb 1995.

[12] Von Horn, 'Congo Lessons', p. 10.

[13] Chief of Military Operations, N. Borchgrevink, 'Study on Intelligence in the Congo: Annex B—The Intelligence Problem', 7 March 1962, pp. 3-4, DAG-13/1.5.4.0:1—ONUC Operations.

[14] Chief of Military Operations, 'A Review of ONUC Military Operations', p. 2 (see note 7 above).

[15] 'Military Advisor's Comments on General Observations of the Force Commander and Dr. O'Brien on the implementation of the Security Council Resolution of 24 November 1961', p. 4 DAG-1/2.2.1:64.

[16] Chief of Military Information, Annex A, p. 2 (see note 13 above).

[17] Ibid., Annex B, p. 15.

[18] Ibid., Annex B., pp. 9, 12 and 14.

[19] Ibid., Annex A, p. 2.

[20] Memorandum, Chief of Military Information, N. Borchgrevink to Military Advisor New York, 17 March 1962, DAG-13/1.6.5.4.0:1—ONUC Operations. The decision was made in an environment of great fiscal restraint at the UN. It was facing near bankruptcy when a campaign was launched to sell bonds in order to keep it afloat financially.

[21] Military Information Branch (MIB), 'Terms of Reference: Provincial Liaison Officers'. 15 July 1963, DAG-13/1.6.5.4.0:1.

[22] MIB, 'Nominal Roll—Intelligence Officers Stationed throughout the Congo', 17 Sept. 1962, DAG-13/1.6.5.4.0:1—Organization and Functioning of MIB.

[23] The operation was based on SC Res. 169 (1961), 21 Nov. 1961, which authorized 'the use of the requisite measure of force' to apprehend and depot all foreign mercenaries from the Congo.

[24] Memorandum to Chief of Military Information from Chief of Civilian Personnel, 5 July 1963, DAG-13/1.6.5.4.0:4—Civilian Operations.

[25] Memorandum, Force Commander Guebre to Dr. Ralph Bunch, 5 April 1963, DAG-13/1.6.5.4.0:1—Organization and Establishment of MIB.

[26] Memorandum, Chief of Staff B.A.O. Ogundipe, 20 Aug. 1963, DAG-13/1/6/5/4/0:1—Organization and Functioning of MIB.

[27] See Memorandum, Chief of Military Information, Lt-Col. Bjorn Egge, 'Collection of Military Information', 22 April 1961, DAG-13/1.6.5.4.0:14—Collection of Information.

[28] Chief of Military Information, Annex B., p. 10 (see note 13 above).

[29] 'Report—Liaison visit Katanga-Orientale', 27 Nov. 1961, DAG-13/1.6.5.4.0:17, Reports General

[30] Ibid.

[31] Ibid.

[32] Rikhye, pp. 25-89 (see note 9 above).

[33] Chief of Military Information, N. Borchgevenik, 'Proposed Organization and Function of Monitoring Section Military Intelligence Branch', 17 Feb. 1962.

[34] Chief of Military Information, Katanga HQ, 'Monitoring of Katangese Military Radionet from 30 March to 30 April 1962', 1 May 1962, DAG-13/1.6.5.7.2.0:18—HQ Katanga Command Radio Intercept.

[35] Ibid. There exists some doubt as to how institutionalized the MIB's monitoring service became, even in Katanga where the most developed service was established. In his 'Report on Completion of Assignment' to Secretary-General, Force Commander Guebre suggested that during the December 1962-January 1963 Katanga operation, MIB in Katang possessed only 'improvised interception'. DAG-1/2.2.1:36.

[36] Ulrie Lindencrona, 'Report on Ciphers and Codes used by the Katangese Forces', 11 Oct 1962, DAG-13/1.6.5.4.0:16—Monitoring General.

[37] Ibid.

[38] Ibid.

[39] The intercepted radio transmission from Baudouinville on 15 January 1963, which stated (uncoded) that 'the most important messages passed in Cessar code cannot be broken yet', obviously could hardly have been a revelation to Lindencrona. DAG-13/1.6.5.7.2.1:1—Misc: No. 28 Intercept.

[40] See Force Commander, Lt-Gen. Kebbede Guebre, 'Report on Completion of Assignment to Secretary General', Aug. 1963, DAG-1/2.2.1:36.

[41] Rikhye, p. 304.

[42] 'Secret Intercepts', 5 Jan. 1963, DAG-13/1.6.5.4.0:16 685—Monitoring Katanga.

[43] 'Secret Intercepts', 10 Jan. 1963, DAG-13/1.6.5.7.2.1:1—Misc. No. 28 Intercepts.

[44] Chief of Military Information, Annex B, p. 10 (see note 13 above).

[45] MIB, 'Debriefing of Aircrews', 9 March 1962.

[46] Force Commander, 'A Review of ONUC Military Operations in the Congo and its Future Deployment and Organization', 16 March 1962, p. 2.

[47] Memorandum, 'Command and Control—Fighter Operations Group', 13 Oct. 1961, DAG-13/1.6.5.8.3.0:1 6600/F-OPS Policy, October 61-March 63.

[48] Air Commander, H. A. Morrison, 'Command and Control—Fighter Operations Group', 13 Oct 1961.

[49] Memorandum, 'Statement Regarding Cables No 7741-7757 from New York', 6 Nov. 1961, DAG-13/1.6.5.4.0:1.

[50] As discussed in Memorandum, Chief Fighter Operations, S. Lampell to Chief of Military Information, 'Aerial Photography: Intelligence Collection Programme', 3 Feb. 1962, p. 2.

[51] Ibid.

[52] Ibid.

[53] MIB HQ, 'Katangese Air Capability: An Appreciation', 30 May 1962. DAG-13/1.6.5.8.4.0:1.

[54] Fighter Operations, 'Enemy Opposition and the Task of Fighter Force', April 1962, p. 2, DAG-13/1.6.5.8.3.0:1 F-Ops Policy.

[55] Ibid.

[56] Memorandum, Chief Fighter Ops Officer, Kanva Singh, to Air Commander, 'Debriefing and Radar Reports,' 8 Sept. 1962, DAG-13/1.6.5.8.3.0:1.

[57] Fighter Operations, 'Enemy Opposition and Task of Fighter Force', p. 2 (see note 54 above).

[58] Ibid.

[59] MIB HQ, 'Katangese Air Capability', (see note 53 above).

[60] Ibid., p. 9.

[61] Cable #6120, Dr. Ralph J. Bunche to Force Commander Guebre, 24 Aug. 1962; Force Commander Kebbede Guebre, 'Report on Completion of Assignment', p. 15 (see note 40 above).

[62] MIB, 'Report on visit to Kolwezi and Jadotville Airfields 25-29 Jan. 1963', 22 Feb 1963, p. 9, DAG-13/1.5.8.4.0:1.

[63] Ibid.

[64] Chief of Military Information, G. Samuelson, 'Administrative Regulations for ONUC Detainees', MIB Leopoldville, 17 Dec. 1962, DAG-1/2.2.1-37.

[65] Chief of Military Information, N. Borchegrevink, 'Study on Intelligence in the Congo: Annex B—The Intelligence Problem', p. 10, DAG-13/1.6.5.4.0:1.

[66] Chief of Military Information, N. Borchgrevink, Annex B, p. 10.

[67] MIB HQ, 'Katangese Air Capability', p. 2 (see note 53 above).

[68] Rikhye, p. 253 (see note 9 above).

[69] 'Report No. 1, KAYINDA, Cleophas', 25 Nov. 1962, DAG-13/1.6.5.4.0:8—Mercenaries Source Reports.

[70] 'Operation Stag-Hound: Summary of Interrogation in Respect of Sutherland and Fanklin', MIB, 25 Oct. 1962, DAG-13/1.6.5.4.0:11.

[71] 'Ref. ONUC 7361', 30 Oct. 1962, DAG-13/1.6.5.4.0:14—Arms Traffic.

[72] O'Brien, p. 76 (see note 1 above).

[73] Ibid.

[74] 'Minutes of Intelligence Conference No. 4', 12 March 1962, p. 2, DAG-13/1.6.5.7.2.0:18—HQ Katanga Command.

[75] 'Minutes of Intelligence Conference No. 3', 5 March 1962, p. 2, DAG-13/1.6.5.7.2.0:18

[76] Ibid.

[77] 'Summary No. 43', 6 April 1962, DAG-13/1.6.5.8.4.0:3.

[78] Chief of Military Information to Force Commander, 'Information Acquired at Elisabethville, 5 April 1961, p. 1, DAG-13/1.6.5.4.0:8—Mercenaries/Source Reports.
[79] MIB, 'An Assessment of the Katanga military forces', 15 July 1962, DAG-13/1.6.5.8.4.0:3.
[80] MIB HQ 'Katanges Air Capability', p. 7 (see note 53 above).
[81] 'Interrogation Summary', Nov. 1962, DAG-13/1.6.5.8.4.0:3.
[82] Chief of Military Information Borchgrevink, Ammenx B, p. 12.
[83] Memorandum, MIB, 'Area of Responsibility', 6 March 1962, DAG-13/1.6.5.4.0:18.
[84] Ibid.
[85] Force Commander Guebre, 'Report on Completion of Assignment', p. 14 (see note 40 above).
[86] Memorandum, MIB. 6 July 1962, p. 2, DAG-13/1.6.5.4.0:1; Chief of Military Information N. Borchgrevink, Annex B, p. 9.
[87] Force Commander Guebre, 'Report on Completion of Assignment', p. 15.
[88] 'Report—Liaison Visit Katanga-Orientale', p. 2 (see note 29 above).
[89] Ibid., p. 63.
[90] Ernest W. Lefever and Joshua Wynfred, *United Nations Peacekeeping in the Congo: 1960-1964—An Analysis of Political, Executive, and Military Control*, Vol. 1 (Washington: Brookings Institute, 1966), Appendix P7.
[91] Verrier, p. 62 (see note 3 above).
[92] Ibid., p. 63.
[93] Operations Officer, 'Report on Incident at Port Francqui', 3 May 1961, DAG-13/1.6.5.4.0:12.
[94] Lefever and Wynafred, Appendix P18 (see note 90 above).
[95] Operations Officer, 'Port Francqui', p. 3.
[96] MIB, 'Target Folder Katanga: Description of Fixed Targets: Nov. 61-April 62', DAG-13/1.6.5.8.4.1:4.
[97] Chief Fighter Operations to Chief of Military Information, 'Aerial Photography', p. 2 (see note 50 above).
[98] Force Commander Guebre, 'Report on Completion of Assignment', p. 27 (see note 40 above).
[99] The UN Declaration on Fact-finding, approved by the General Assembly on 9 Dec. 1991in Res. 46/59, reflects this sentiment. The Secretary-General's *An Agenda for Peace*, section III, and subsequent General Assembly resolutions also prescribe increased monitoring for early warning and preventive diplomacy.
[100] Walter H. Dorn, 'Peace-keeping Satellites: The Case for International Surveillance and Verification', *Peace Research Reviews*, vol. X, parts. 5-6 (Dundas: Peace Research Institute-Dundas, 1987).
[101] Interview with anonymous official involved in UN peacekeeping operations.

---

[102] The authors are grateful to the referees who supplied this information. See also Michael Doyle and Nishkala Suntharalingam, 'The UN in Cambodia: Lessons for Complex Peacekeeping', *International Peacekeeping*, Vol. 1 No. 2 1994, p. 125.

[103] Romeo Dallaire, 'Our Man in Rwanda', presentation at Trinity College, University of Toronto, 15 March 1995.

[104] Ibid.

[105] Interview: Mr. Stan Carlson, Chief UN Situation Centre, 18 Aug. 1994.

Analysis and Assessment for Peacekeeping Operations

Sir David Ramsbotham

There is a need, however, to strengthen arrangements in such a manner that information ... can be synthesised with political indicators to assess whether a threat to peace exists and to analyse what action might be taken by the United Nations to alleviate it.[1]

The need to satisfy the UN's requirement for reliable information and intelligence gathering capability is important if peace enforcement operations are to be successfully carried out.[2]

Of all the producer policy-maker relationships discussed in the original volume, none are more fraught with difficulty than those connected with peacekeeping. Behind the two statements quoted above lies the paradox that, for all too long, because of its association with secret services and covert activities, 'Intelligence' has been regarded as a 'dirty word' in UN parlance.[3] To a soldier this is quite extraordinary, because, in military doctrine and practice, intelligence is a significant, vital and basic ingredient of every operation. Moreover, peacekeeping missions include military operations for which the forces involved require an understanding of those people who wish to maintain and those who may wish to disturb, the peace and why. Some may call that information, and some intelligence, but it is *fact*, and it is no coincidence that the chapter from which UN secretary-general Boutros Boutros-Ghali's quote is taken is headed 'Fact Finding'. Without such basic facts at their fingertips, peacekeepers cannot hope to be able to carry out their tasks in an impartial and progressive way. Therefore, to regard 'intelligence' as a dirty word in relation to peacekeeping, when the information gained is essential for those who have to conduct peacekeeping missions, is to be blind to both necessity and reality.

281

The dictionary definitions of the word intelligence could be said to satisfy all parties, depending on what one wants to read into them. Intelligence, as a noun, is 'The action or fact of mentally comprehending something, understanding, knowledge: mutual conveyance of information, communication: a piece of information or news, the obtaining of information, the agency for secret information'.[4] Intelligence, as a verb, is 'To bring intelligence of (an event, etc,), to inform (a person), to convey intelligence: to tell tales'.[5] For the purpose of this article an intelligence operation will be defined as 'the collection, analysis and dissemination of information relevant to the peacekeeping mission between all interested parties'.[6]

The aim of this article is to examine the role of intelligence analysis and assessment in support of peacekeeping operations in a changing world. Necessarily, this means the article will focus on what I perceive to be the intelligence needs of the United Nations, because its global responsibilities 'to maintain international peace and security'[7] make it the primary 'employer' of peacekeeping forces. That said, a 'health warning' is necessary because it is essential to examine any issue involving the UN against the background of two major deficiencies that affect its operational ability: the lack of political will in the global community to provide the organisation with what it needs to enable it to act effectively on the community's behalf and an inadequate and fragile internal co-ordinating machinery. It is not useful to consider any one part of the UN in isolation, because each function and element impacts on others.

This article will attempt to suggest what policymakers, both at UN Headquarters and UN missions in the field require in the light of the demands that this imposes on the possible producers. Because this is a rapidly developing subject, and outsiders can only be as up-to-date as their latest information, some of what is treated here as desirable may already have been implemented. But that does not affect the utility of an overview of the requirement for a coherent and robust intelligence system, capable of satisfying the needs of all involved in peacekeeping, before, during and after each mission.[8] The article will examine the intelligence needs of the three types of missions included under the generic term peacekeeping: preventive action, conflict resolution (whether traditional peacekeeping or peace enforcement), and post conflict reconstruction (or peace-building), each of which will be examined in turn.

Preventive Action

In peacekeeping, there is much to be said for the saying that 'a stitch in time save nine', Early, or preventive deployment, such as that intended by NATO's multi-national Allied Mobile Force, is the best example of what I mean in military terms. UN preventive action includes both 'Preventive Diplomacy', the title of the relevant chapter in *Agenda for Peace,* which also mentions 'Preventive Deployment'. The early arrival of a representative body, ostentatiously making the point that any threat to peace in a particular area is a threat against all members of the global community, accompanied by a vigorous public relations campaign amongst the people in the threatened area, is an outward and visible symbol of international resolve, particularly if it is mandated by the Security Council. An example of the efficacy of such action was the preventive deployment of UN troops to Macedonia under Security Council Resolution 795 of December 1992, made possible by the fortuitous, temporary availability of Canadian troops. Subsequently staffed by an American battalion from July 1993 and a mixed force of UN observers, this operation thus far, has prevented the trouble in Bosnia spilling over that emotive border.[9]

However, preventive action can only be taken following early warning, and early assessment of that warning, which requires the willingness and co-operation of member states to make essential information available. It also requires the recipients of such information to be willing to listen to and act upon it. As Boutros Boutros-Ghali puts it 'Preventive steps must be based upon timely and accurate knowledge of the facts'. Beyond this, an 'understanding of developments and global trends, based on sound analysis, is required'.[10] The UN should not develop its own intelligence *gathering* machinery, or put its own satellites up into space, not only because of the expense involved, but because member nations already possess what is required. What the UN needs is an effective intelligence co-ordination mechanism, capable of analysing what it is given or is gleaned on its behalf, informing the decision making process, and passing essential information to all UN departments and agencies who have functional responsibility in any possible operation. The mention of member states brings into sharp focus the principal problem faced by the UN, namely that of *obtaining* intelligence, or information, from them. For entirely understandable reasons, governments are unwilling to release information about themselves that might fall into what they regard as wrong hands, or which

283

might be used, to alleged advantage, against them. Traditionally, national intelligence services collect, analyse and use intelligence for their own national purposes, retaining it under national control, and sharing it only with those whom they wish to share it.[11]

The UN, however, which ought to qualify as a friendly government, requires intelligence for the good of the international community, and, in the spirit of that integrity and impartiality that it seeks to maintain, must be quite open about what it needs, and why. If there are no secrets about what is required and why, then in theory, there should be no reason why member nations should withhold information, because no member state need feel threatened by a UN acting on its behalf. But as Hugh Smith points out, 'such a system is unlikely to emerge of its own accord. The UN needs to establish a clear conception of how it wants intelligence to develop in the context of peacekeeping, and (perhaps also) of 'preventive diplomacy'.[12] I would argue that there is no 'perhaps also' about the need to develop a concept of intelligence in the context of preventive action, because it is so essential if such action is to be successfully triggered. Preventive action needs should establish the credibility of the development of a coherent UN intelligence operation, because, although it is only one element in the peacekeeping continuum, its intelligence needs are the same as those of the other two, only more acute in terms of time. But how could the UN convince the global community of the integrity and impartiality of a UN intelligence operation? The answer may lie in a practical suggestion based on experience in another field.

Commanders Critical Intelligence Requirements (CCIR)

In the early 1980's, when NATO faced the Warsaw Pact across the German border, commanders at all levels became increasingly concerned at the amount of information available, from a wide variety of sources, and how it could be prioritised and filtered.[13] Accordingly an exercise called the 'Commanders Critical Intelligence Requirements (CCIR)' was initiated, in which they were invited to think through each phase of war, relating it to the ground over which they might have to fight, and determine what information they regarded as critical to the success of their particular operational aim within the overall operational context. Such an appreciation was carried out at each level of command, because triggers or indicators were different for each level, Commanders also needed to know the operational aims of their superior commanders, because their own appreciation had to be related to them, to ensure coherence of the overall intelligence plan. Each CCIR list was used, by intelligence staffs, to filter that part of the take which had to be passed immediately to their commander, thus preventing him from being swamped. The process also helped to refine collation, and prioritise the tasking of surveillance.

But the key word in the whole process is the first one, commander. Each CCIR list is a commander's personal assessment of what he needs to know in order to carry out his mission, resulting from his analysis of the situation with which he is faced. To achieve this he needs to ensure that all necessary intelligence is made available to him, from whichever source is capable of providing it. If such a source is not under his command or immediately available to him, it is up to an immediate superior to obtain what a subordinate requires. Although designed for a very different purpose, I believe that this process could be the key to helping the UN overcome the reluctance of national governments to provide intelligence support to the international organisation.

CCIR application in UN operations

Although it may be, and seem, *ad hoc,* there is a command and control structure for each and every UN operation, starting from the Security Council and the Secretariat and spreading down to individual units on the ground, be they civil or military. The nature of modern peacekeeping requires that, included within it, there must be a properly structured, trained and equipped intelligence staff at each level.

The Security Council establishes the aim for every mission. It is then the responsibility of the force commander, and subordinate commanders at all levels, to determine their own intelligence requirements, and draw up their own CCIR list related to it. Requests for mission elements should be passed back up the chain to UNHQ in New York, which would be responsible for obtaining it from wherever it is available, including member nations. The tag 'Mission Specific' or 'Mission Critical' attached to these requests, emphasising that the information is critical to the success of a mission being carried out for the global community, should (in theory) satisfy those governments and intelligence services who may be concerned about any altruistic intentions amongst those seeking information that they regard as sensitive to their own

285

national interests. The procedure has the additional merit of putting commanders through the discipline of thinking through, and asking only for what they need for the execution of their mission. It also provides a disciplined framework within which intelligence staffs can work, which in turn must help those working in *ad hoc* environments.

The only way that the intelligence needs of a preventive action mission will differ from any other is in terms of time. Early warning of possible threats to peace, particularly forecasting communal or intra-nation conflict, may prove to be the most sensitive area of all for individual nations when it comes to releasing information about themselves for someone else to analyse. However, for the global community preventive action represents the cheapest and most timely action that the UN can take on its behalf, and it should encourage all to co-operate.

But the process of keeping a UN 'intelligence watch' on potential trouble spots is as much political, economic and social as military in direction. 'Threats to the security of a nation must now include anything, anywhere on the globe, which threatens the health, economic well-being, social stability and political peace of its people.'[14] That is not to say that the military should not be included in the analysing process, but that the 'intelligence watch' should be conducted by the UN Department of Political Affairs (DPA), in concert with the Department of Peacekeeping Operations (DPKO) and the Department of Humanitarian Affairs (DHA), on the assumption that they work closely together anyway. The UN will always seek a long-term political solution to a problem, although deliberately tasked military and humanitarian means may be the short-term expedient by which this is achieved. Relating this to the CCIR process, it should be the DPA, under direction from the secretary-general, that determines what particular factors should be watched in which countries, and what circumstances warrant information being laid before the Security Council. This requires a properly established and structured analysis and assessment staff, in New York, international in content, working on the input from all sources, including member nations. This 'internationalisation' is a key ingredient in satisfying national sensitivities.

There is, of course one wild card in all this, which is the ability of the media to pre-empt preventive action by emotive presentation of situations of alleged crisis or near chaos. Graphic images of tragedy can provoke 'Do Something' cries from the global community, prompting a knee-jerk UN response that is reactive rather than preventive in content. In the conclusions to an important 1994 study, Nick Gowing, the Diplomatic Editor of the UK's Channel 4 News, makes the point that:

> It is estimated there is the potential for 2000 ethnic conflicts in Africa and 260 conflicts in the Russian 'Near-Abroad'. If the battle lines of the future are being already drawn and the 'bloody conflicts' have already begun, is real-time television merely highlighting conflicts, which western governments ultimately have no ability to prevent, or political will to solve? The evidence is not encouraging. The answer is probably yes.[15]

Those horrendous statistics alone suggest that the UN needs a monitoring system, to ensure that preventive diplomatic or deployment action, humanitarian and/or military can be considered and possibly taken in time, with the media being encouraged to publicise what the UN is doing rather than not doing.

Preventive deployment can be either humanitarian or military in content, since the early introduction of specifically required aid may be just as appropriate in some situations as the arrival of troops in others. This highlights another and significant part of the intelligence debate, namely that information provision and dissemination is not solely the business of member states. Both UN Agencies and Non-Government Organisations (NGO) have a significant part to play as well. They too need early warning of what is required of them, and were information exchange a more accepted activity, the delivery of aid would be more effective. Moreover, during their activities, routine and on missions, humanitarian agencies also gather information that could be useful to others. Culturally and procedurally they are not good at passing this on, which is not only inefficient but, on occasions, dangerous to others. Not only should all agencies, UN and NGO, be given the necessary information on which to prevent action, but they should also be prepared to make available to the UN analysts any indicators of possible trouble that they come across, to ensure that the preventive action which they applaud may be mounted in time to be successful. They point, quite understandably, to the number of times that warnings from them have been ignored by UN officials and others who were not prepared to listen let alone act. But both the need and their concern suggest that a change of culture is essential and will have to be encouraged.

Conflict Resolution

When the focus of discussion shifts to conflict resolution, one is on more fertile ground from an intelligence operational perspective, because some of the necessary conditioning material already exists in published *Mission Analyses* and *Lessons Learned by Force Commanders*. These invariably mention the need to improve peacekeeping intelligence operations. The comment arising from the operation, quoted at the outset of this essay, is a case in point.

Within the UN

The basic relationship between UN Secretariat policy makers and the member state producers remains the same as for preventive action, but there is a curious paradox contained in a UN as opposed to a national chain of command. At the strategic level, UNHQ is the overall policy maker, and a force commander is both an intelligence producer and an operational executive. At the mission level, however, the force commander is the operational policy maker, and UNHQ one of the intelligence producers. In national operations, or those conducted by an operational alliance such as NATO, a force commander receives strategic direction *and* intelligence down a clearly defined command chain. UN Security Council resolutions, however, tend to contain neither strategic direction, nor intelligence, not least because the Military Staff Committee, which the UN's founding fathers intended should provide this, does not exist. As a result, force commanders have to carry out their own analysis and risk assessment, which is not satisfactory when global issues are at stake, as several of them have testified.[16]

Recent and current experiences demand that the UN must improve its ability to respond to crises, as well as to determine when to refuse to do so. As part of this process it needs, in particular, to improve its contingency planning capability, as well as its ability to mount and sustain operations. The UN's initial task is to determine what assets will be needed to execute a possible mission, for which very specific intelligence is required, Contingency planners need to know details of the infrastructure of any country in which an operation may be being considered, road, rail, air and port capacity, the availability of vital items such as food, water and fuel, communications structures and medical services.[17]

Rather than having to obtain this information afresh for each mission, it could be held in a database, built up from answers to requests put by the UN to each member state in the form of a questionnaire. On mounting and sustainment there is a need to know what military and logistics forces nations may be able to provide. Thanks to the recently completed Stand By and Logistics studies, the UN staffs are now better placed to assist this phase of planning. Of course, each mission is subject to the recommendations of a detailed reconnaissance, but the subsequent and inordinate time it takes to establish UN contingents could be reduced by better contingency planning. The spectre of national sensitivity can be mitigated if every member state is invited to make available the same type of information about itself.

Within UNHQ, peacekeeping operations need to be monitored, with an intelligence staff available to process requests from force commanders. In 1993 a Situation Centre was established. It operates round the clock, seven days a week, with a staff of 24. Two officers are on duty at all times. A DHA desk is included. Although it has a research and information cell that interprets data obtained from a wide variety of other sources, the centre is not a 'comprehensive intelligence unit' in its own right. Its task is to provide information about current operations,[18] which is particularly timely and useful to those responsible for conflict resolution, and hopefully will become more and more part of the UN culture. But it does not obviate the need for a proper analysis and assessment capability to serve the policy-makers, and provide the secretary-general and the Security Council with a UN overview, to supplement the national views that will be reflected by national Permanent Representatives.

UN Mission requirements

In his article about the need for UN peacekeeping intelligence, Hugh Smith includes specific requirements for:[19]

> Strategic intelligence is obviously required to understand the political situation between the parties to a conflict prior to UN involvement and, once peacekeepers are deployed, to anticipate the political moves of governments or factions, especially if

289

there is a risk of violence. The fundamental importance of political intelligence is self evident, for the UN is seeking to produce a desired political outcome. Information about the economy and society of the country will also be valuable.

Operational intelligence is required to plan the most effective deployment of resources and to carry out the UN mandate. It will be particularly important in fluid military and political situations.

Tactical intelligence is needed by troops on the ground to support peacekeeping activities, such as monitoring cease-fires or border areas and to alert personnel to potential dangers. The management of intelligence at the tactical level, moreover, can be influential in maintaining or losing the UN's credibility among the parties to a conflict. At the tactical level, too, counter-intelligence may be necessary if there are elements hostile to the UN.

The credibility issue lends weight to Smith's argument that 'the concept of UN intelligence promises to turn traditional principles on their heads. Intelligence will have to be based in information that is collected primarily by overt means, that is by methods that do not threaten the target state or group and do not compromise the integrity or impartiality of the UN'.[20]

At the head of every mission will be a Special Representative of the secretary-general (SRSG), with a team of political and economic advisers. The SRSG is supported by a military force commander, with a headquarters into which all military elements will be linked, and a DHA humanitarian co-ordinator, with a headquarters linking all of the humanitarian agencies. The SRSG, who is responsible for implementing the overall aim of the mission, delegating particular operational responsibilities to his military and humanitarian commanders, will need an intelligence staff to analyse political, economic and social affairs. The force commander requires a more military intelligence staff, including trained analysts, as well as collators and collectors. The efficacy of the military intelligence operation will depend on the quality of the force commanders' CCIR assessment.

In peace enforcement operations, proven operational intelligence operational procedures should be followed, possibly under a 'lead nation' to ensure commonality. 'Desert Storm', for example, was essentially a US-led operation, with NATO procedures predominating. UNOSOM II was, in many respects, an example of how not to do it, with specific intelligence deliberately being denied to certain partners, encouraging resentment and suspicion.[21] However, the most important result of these experiences has been the application of the 'lessons learned' process, with wide circulation of analyses of the deficiencies, illustrated by practical examples. It is now up to the international community to rectify these to ensure that they are not repeated in future operations.

In all peacekeeping operations, every national contingent can be expected to bring its own intelligence staff to handle national matters, and through whom information will be passed up and down the command chain. This is important, as often the Humint that national contingents gain, as part and parcel of their day-to-day responsibilities, is an important contribution to the overall picture. National contingents can also act as information exchanges for UN Agencies and NGO's operating with them, and with whom mutual operation, because it is locally focused, is often easier and closer.

However the DHA should be encouraged to develop its own intelligence or information gathering capability. Frequently, it is those engaged in humanitarian activities who are in closest touch with indigenous people, and their analysis of the situation, and warning of likely problems, is therefore a vital part of the whole. Their contribution needs to be handled sensitively, quickly and efficiently. Sensitivity is vital because of the need to convince NGO's and others that their knowledge is valuable to the achievement of the mission, and will not be used for other purposes. That is why it would be better for the humanitarian operations co-ordinator to conduct his/her own collection operation, passing what has been gathered and analysed both upward to the SRSG and sideways to the force commander. That way functional sensitivities can be dealt with up functional chains, co-ordination taking place where most appropriate. But, having said that, it must be made quite clear what items are critical to the mission as a whole, as well as critical to each part of it.

For practical illustration of the need for this the report on UNOSOM II offers another significant observation:

Many senior political advisors, especially on sensitive political issues, lacked experience and knowledge of UN peacekeeping practices and were insensitive to the local culture's requirements.[22]

Local cultural information, so vital to the success of a mission, should be disseminated to all participants, military and humanitarian. But all this activity depends on communications, an essential of any C3I process. This has become much more efficient with the acquisition of the American Joint Deployable Intelligence Support System by the UN's Situation Centre.[23]

Post Conflict Reconstruction or Peace Rebuilding

These tasks are included in the continuum in order to complete an overview of the whole UN Policy Maker/Producer relationship. The Security Council should mandate post-conflict reconstruction just as it does preventive action or conflict resolution. There is, after all, no clearer expression of international commitment to assist a country emerging from conflict or chaos than the help given to enable it to take up or resume its place in the international community. As with conflict resolution, this requires the international community to establish what needs to be done and then enable it to happen with appropriate aid. In order to determine what is needed both to restore a damaged infrastructure and to regenerate a damaged economy, policy makers require a political, social and economic intelligence operation, quite separate from any associated conflict resolution operation in content, but not in time. Concurrence is the key, so that purposeful reconstruction can start the moment conflict is ended. That is why I advocate the appointment of a third co-equal subordinate to an SRSG, namely a Director of Post Conflict Reconstruction, from either the DHA or the UN Development Programme (UNDP), to supervise the analysis and assessment.

A principal part of this whole process will be an appreciation of which agency can do what, in the best interests of the country concerned. In the case of Mozambique,[24] for example, the UN needed to know, among other things, what was required to clear minefields and to rebuild the internal communications system so that normal economic life could resume. It also needed a financed plan for demobilising and disarming the assessed numbers of former combatants, who will remain a threat to peace until something is found for them to do and they can be reintegrated into normal society. Job creation is the key to this and one source of employment involves the sugar industry, a major contributor to the Mozambican economy before the war. The estates on which this sugar was grown are now derelict and the selection and training of several thousand former combatants to restore the infrastructure to the estates is the first step to the rehabilitation of the ex-soldiers. Then the private sector will come in to start up production, requiring the training of many more former guerrillas to work on the estates. This process will fulfil a double mission: providing constructive work for idle armed combatants and helping to 'kick start' the economy. Money from the World Bank and the International Monetary Fund is required to prime the process, as well as national aid. But the important point is that such a plan can only be determined if all potential participants are brought into the reconstruction assessment and analysis process, another UN policy maker/producer relationship, to establish what is best for the country and what it will cost.

Conclusion

What I have tried to illustrate is that the continuum of peacekeeping presents the international community with an increasing number of intelligence tasks and priorities. These may seem obvious when examined against needs, and none of them are new to national intelligence authorities, because they replicate what is demanded of them in their day to day responsibilities. But the concept of mounting intelligence operations is new to the UN, as is the need for national communities to meet their responsibilities to the international community by providing essential intelligence resources. It was mentioned at the outset that lack of national political will and a fragile and inadequate co-ordination machinery were the biggest single factors preventing the UN from fulfilling its unique global responsibilities. It can, after all, only do what the resources it is given will allow. Hitherto resources have always been discussed in terms of men, money and machines. The producer policy maker relationship for peacekeeping described above demonstrates that planning for peacekeeping must also include intelligence analysis and assessment, an essential ingredient for success.

Endnotes

---

[1] Boutros Boutros-Ghali, *An Agenda for Peace* (NY: UN, 1992), p.15.

[2] UN S/1994/653, 1 June 1994, p.47. Report of the Commission of Inquiry established pursuant to Security Council Resolution 885 (1993) to investigate armed attacks on UNOSOM II personnel which led to casualties among them.

[3] Hugh Smith, 'Intelligence and UN peacekeeping', *Survival*, 36/3 (Autumn 1994), pp.174, 190 n.1, citing Int. Peace Academy, *Peacekeeper's Handbook* (NY, 1984), p.39.

[4] *The Shorter Oxford Dictionary* (Oxford: Clarendon Press, 1978), p. 1089.

[5] Ibid.

[6] This is consistent with standard definitions of intelligence, which emphasise the several phases of intelligence production. See Abram Shulsky, *Silent Warfare: Understanding the World of Intelligence* (NY: Brassey's, 1991), p.2.

[7] *Charter of the United Nations and Statute of lhe International Court of Justice* (NY Dept of Public Info.), p, 1,

[8] On this, see Mats R. Berdal, *Whither UJV Peacekeeping?* Adelphi Paper 281 (London: IISS, Oct. 1993), p.44; John MacKinlay and Jarat Chopra, *A Draft Concept of Second Generation Mullinational Operatians1993* (Providence, RI: Thos. J. Watson. Inst. for Int. Studies, 1993), pp.37-38.

[9] Canada, Senate, *Meeting New Challenges: Canada's Response to a New Generation of Peacekeeping: Report of the Sandieg Senate Committee on Foreign Affairs* (Ottawa, Feb. 1993), p.45.

[10] Boutros-Ghali (note 1) p. 14.

[11] E.g., Lt. Gen. Satish Nambiar, the commander of UNPROFOR, was not cleared for intelligence from NATO Sources: Smith (note 3), p.177.

[12] Smith (note 3), p.175.

[13] On this see, Paul B. Stares, *Command Perforrnance: The Neglected Dimension of European Security* (Washington, DC; Brookings, 1991), pp.87, 90–4, 98–9.

[14] Quoted in *The Independent* (London) 24 March 1994, p,11.

[15] Nick Gowing, *Real time television coverage of armed conflicts and diplomatic crises: does it pressure or distort Foreign Policy decisions?* John F. Kennedy School of Government Working Paper Series 94-1 (Cambridge, MA: Harvard Uni,, June 1994), p.85.

[16] Smith (note 3), p. 177.

[17] Ibid., p.176.

[18] Ibid,, pp. 178 – 9.

[19] Ibid., pp. 175 – 6 (my emphasis).

[20] Ibid., p.175.

[21] Ibid. p.178; Dent Ocaya-Lakidi, 'UN and the US Military Roles in Regional Organisations in Africa and the Middle East', Dennis J. Quinn, (ed.), *Peace Support*

Operations and the US Military (Washington DC: National Defence Uni. Press, 1994), p. 158.
[22] UN S/1994/653, 1 June 1994, p.47.
[23] Smith (note 3), p. 184.
[24] The author is currently involved in reconstruction in Mozambique.

Intelligence in Peacekeeping Operations

Par Eriksson

A common view within the United Nations system has been that intelligence and an intelligence service are illegitimate elements in a UN context, even in field operations. An organisation like the UN has to be completely open and transparent, according to this view, and must not involve itself in any intelligence activities, which may hurt its relations with the local parties. This attitude, sometimes summarised as 'intelligence is a dirty word,' is strange, considering that traditional peacekeeping, emphasising observations and reporting, actually consists mainly of surveillance. In today's peacekeeping operations[1] this approach could very well jeopardise both the life of the peacekeepers and the success of an operation. Let me emphasise that peacekeeping organisations (especially the UN) *as they exist today* cannot realistically maintain an advanced, comprehensive and combined intelligence service of their own at a strategic level. Thus, the focus here is on operational/tactical level intelligence and, to some extent, on the national strategic level. Furthermore, the chapter is written from a Swedish perspective: a small, non-aligned state with a rather extensive experience in UN peacekeeping.

Conflicts and Peacekeeping in the 1990's[2]

The peacekeeping operations that have emerged since the end of the Cold War are more complex, compared with the traditional interposing operations. They often deal with conflicts characterised by civil war with strong national and ethnic overtones, and involve intentions, overt and covert motives and a sheer number of actors that are extremely hard to survey. Bosnia provides an excellent example. In March 1993, Lewis MacKenzie, UN commander of Sector Sarajevo at the beginning of the conflict, said:

> *Now the world is sanctioning Serbia for its alleged actions, but no one has confirmed any direct involvement of Serbia in the war. Croatia has very large forces and a large number of units fighting in Bosnia, yet so far there has been very little condemnation of the Croatians. Presumably the reason why there is so much talk and so little action is that the situation is so complicated. No one knows what to do, other than try to feed some of the innocent victims.*[3]

Furthermore, as is often the case in civil wars, the civilian population is a prime target. The war is hence fought over wide areas, without any clear front lines, featuring large-scale massacres, rapes, and destruction of cultural heritage. Sometimes the work of 'armed bandits,' sometimes of the 'regular' armies, it is often difficult to distinguish each force from the other.

The most important features, however, are probably the volatility and dynamics of the conflict. The peacekeepers often have to balance an extremely sensitive status where a, single shot in the area of operation may acquire a strategic importance, and a statement from the White House may cause shots to be fired. The tactical commander must consider more than the situation in his area, such as what is going on at the higher levels (peace negotiations, the international political game at regional and global levels, etc.), a condition which puts great demands on him and his staff.[4]

Most peacekeeping operations have interpreted 'impartial behaviour' as allowing the use of violence only in strict self-defence. Otherwise, the task has been to monitor, observe and report with the consent of at least a, majority of the important actors.[5] During recent years, a more active behaviour has developed, including inter alia direct actions against the parties, without a claim of self-defence.[6] This is reflected in the development of doctrines and mandates, which more and more frequently allow the use of force to accomplish an operation's[7] vital tasks. The consent of all involved parties (which indeed can be very difficult even to discern) is hence no longer an unconditional prerequisite. It is also reflected in a will to possess sufficient protection and firepower to guarantee the security of the peacekeeping force's soldiers, thereby improving the chances of carrying out the operation in a partially hostile environment, and to give the parties confidence in and respect for the peacekeeping units' will and abilities.[8]

298

Hence, there is a need for a different interpretation of the impartiality of an international peace operation. One suggestion is the impartiality of the police officer: identical transgressions suffer identical sanctions, regardless of who is the perpetrator. This is impartiality in relation to a set of rules rather than to the parties of conflict. Confidence, in the sense that the parties must believe that the peacekeeping units are present to enable a long-term peaceful solution and not to pursue the interests of certain states or parties, and respect are necessary features to make this kind of impartiality meaningful.

Respect in this context means first of all that the parties accept the peacekeeping force as a legitimate representative of the world community. Secondly, if one or more parties do not acknowledge this legitimacy, the peacekeeping force must be able to use armed force and act with firmness while it simultaneously, by impartiality and confidence, seeks to create a space for constructive actions or negotiations. Of course, as a prerequisite, the peacekeeping organisation must possess an overall legitimacy and integrity, otherwise its actions may be only force, not peacekeeping.

Intelligence in Peace Support Operations Today

The traditional view on UN peacekeeping operations is that they do not need an intelligence service that provides long-terms predictions.[9] Their 'information service' mainly compiled and presented reports on whatever events that had occurred. Analysis was often limited to pointing out whether the activities and tension in the area had increased or decreased. In matters of security, the operations relied mainly on information provided by the great powers and/or the competing parties themselves.

This kind of information service is hardly sufficient today. Firstly, since the great powers do not control the clashing parties as much as they used to, and since the peacekeeping forces now often deploy in the middle of an on-going, volatile conflict, the risk of attacks on the peacekeepers has increased and, for the sake of their own safety, they therefore need to know more about the situation in the area. Secondly, the more complex tasks, involving ethnic, social and nationalist factors, as well as difficulties in trying to identify the combatants, demand a profound insight in the parties' nature, interests and activities. Thirdly, the UN and other international organisations cannot afford to have less knowledge of the parties' intentions and activities than the parties themselves if the organisations desire to achieve any political tasks at the negotiating table. At the very least, the peacekeeping organisation must not invite the use of bluffing tactics, and must also be able to prove responsibility and/or intent behind events. Fourthly, considering the great powers' vast intelligence capacity, the parties may actually believe that the world community knows more than it really does. For instance, a party might then interpret a lack of reaction to a massacre in progress as a carte blanche rather than just ignorance.[10] Finally, an intelligence service is needed to predict conflict creep/leap, that is, when the nature of the conflict and the means and methods of the parties evolve due to fluctuating fortunes on the battlefields, the changing composition of the belligerent forces, new peacekeeping tactics, etc.

Intelligence and The Credibility of the Peacekeeping Units

When fighting a regular war, the intelligence service's choice of methods is determined by what it is looking for, the time available and the resources available. It does not, unlike a peacekeeping force, need to concern itself with the reactions of the adversary, apart from certain tactical and operational considerations.

The peacekeeping force, on the other hand, must protect both its integrity vis-à-vis the fighting parties and the organisation's (e.g., the UN or OSCE) ability to achieve political successes in negotiations. At the same time, it is not morally acceptable to send soldiers to a war zone without proper knowledge of the situation.

The essential concepts should still be impartiality, confidence, and respect. Using the police again as a simile: as long as the public knows that the police will not use surveillance for blackmail or to pass information about one's business to competitors, it accepts that police officers carry out surveillance. Police surveillance is considered a prerequisite for effective law enforcement, which requires both the prevention and the investigation of crimes.

The peacekeeping force must make clear to the parties that collected intelligence does not reach their adversaries, that the main purpose of this intelligence is to facilitate peace negotiations and the successful execution of the peacekeeping operation, that it is the right and duty of the peacekeeping force to carry out intelligence collection, and finally, that the other parties are subjected to an identical scrutiny.[11]

This does not mean, however, that the parties need to accept any method, just as a citizen would not accept that police officers let the ends justify the means or indulge in the registration of the citizens' political preferences. The limit is emotional rather than rational. That a faction would accept a UN reconnaissance patrol consisting of special forces with blackened faces in its area is hard to believe, but it would be less upset by the use of an unmanned reconnaissance aircraft (UAV), even though such a device probably is able to collect more intelligence than the patrol.

There will, of course, always be individuals who accuse the peacekeepers of espionage and partiality, usually those who in one way or another have been criticised by the world community or have reasons to suspect that intelligence may cause such criticism, or those who simply feel that the activities of the peacekeeping force run counter to their interests. This is a serious matter only when a common view develops that the peacekeeping organisation is treating the parties in a biased way[12] or when the peacekeeping force is too weak to resist such pressure. It is worse if some parties think that they have good reasons to believe that the peacekeeping organisation is leaking information to their adversaries.

Intelligence and The Troop-Contributing Nations

Understandably, states hesitate to hand over intelligence or intelligence assets to organisations like the UN, these organisations leak, they lack routines to handle sensitive material in a proper way (at least at the tactical/operational level), they consist of a large number of member states which may not all be friends, etc. Furthermore, the troop quality varies greatly from contingent to contingent in matters of discipline, training and economic conditions. Certain units may even contain individuals who are ready to sell or swap information.

Occasionally, the troop-contributing nations may have interests and ties that go against the explicit aims of the operation's mandate (and sometimes even against the official rhetoric of the country in question). Such nations will hesitate to supply the operation with any (or at least any correct) intelligence. Nor will they wish to see efficient 62/S2 cells or units.

Certain small nations may also be concerned that an expanded intelligence function in an international organisation will endanger their national integrity particularly if the intelligence aspect is dominated by personnel from a few nations. On the other hand, the Western nations and Russia are generally those able (and willing?) to provide a qualified intelligence capability.[13]

The conflict in the former Yugoslavia during the UN operation there demonstrated that some countries do not hesitate to attach well-developed national intelligence assets, outside the UN's control, to their contributions to the UN. These nations consider it absurd to send troops to a sensitive area without the capability to analyse the situation properly. They furthermore co-operate in unofficial 'clubs,' often founded on traditional alliances. 'Membership' is earned by proof of the ability to contribute useful information and capability for handling the information in a responsible way.

The current structure of the UN operations, which consist mainly of national contingents, creates almost by necessity unclear chains-of-command. The contingents, technically under UN command, are in reality controlled by their national governments in certain matters.[14] But national control is not always an evil; the UN's own control system does not always function in a wholly rational manner, so outside influence is sometimes necessary.

National control will greatly affect the intelligence function. For instance, the intelligence needs determined by the UN system are not always accepted by the individual contingents: a national government may interpret the mandate differently, a contingent may wish to avoid disputes with one of the parties involved in the conflict, or control by foreigners may be unacceptable to the contingent in question. A contingent commander will occasionally decide that the UN's intelligence is insufficient for the safety of his unit, or he will initiate independent intelligence operations.[15]

The UN's systems for intelligence management are weak in that the organisation actually relies on being supplied with intelligence collected by the great powers in one way or the other. This becomes a problem only when the intelligence collected under a peacekeeping pretext actually is directly intended to satisfy national needs, it is however difficult to prevent the national use of intelligence collected for peacekeeping operations, particularly since national knowledge is used to support the operations.

On the other hand, the IFOR operation has, due to the overwhelming NATO dominance, a clearer chain-of-command and more adequate security routines than many other peace operations. The UNPROFOR also had a NATO command structure, but at the same time consisted of a large number of non-NATO contingents. The replacement of UNPROFOR by IFOR thus meant an increase of information/intelligence coming down through the system. This intelligence is, of course, dominated by the Great Powers, which means that smaller countries will always have an uneasy feeling of not being told the whole story.

The Intelligence Process Adapted To Peacekeeping Operations

The intelligence process in a peacekeeping operation differs in important ways from the one in traditional warfare, including certain limitations on the choice of collection methods; an international context which might create problems regarding co-operation and dissemination, etc.

However, the intelligence as such may also differ significantly, making it necessary to deal with information on the economy, the ethnic situation and so on. This is often something new to the officers assigned to the tactical level intelligence cells, and they therefore need help when phrasing the questions as well as when analysing the answers.

Planning

Peacekeeping units, mainly for political reasons, are usually more independent than units in regular war, and do not always accept orders in general, and demands for intelligence in particular, from the superior staff. However, they may also have additional intelligence requirements originating from their semi-independent position or from national needs.

Furthermore, intelligence requirements, regardless of who decides them, will have more in common with the requirements of the low-intensity conflict than with those of conventional war. Intelligence on, for instance, the well being of the civilian population or the local economy will be at least as important as intelligence on the number of tanks in an area.

303

The objectives and character of a peacekeeping operation naturally vary, depending on the nature of the conflicts and the aims of the mandating organisation. In some cases, the main task is to deliver relief in a non-hostile environment (e.g. Bangladesh), sometimes in an environment that has 'gone bad' (Somalia). In other cases, the objective is to separate two armies that stand head-to-head at a confrontation line (the Sinai operations), sometimes the line of confrontations is blurred, with barely controllable ethnic and criminal groups warring over a large area (Bosnia). Finally the peacekeepers could be deployed prior to any armed conflict, serving as a 'tripwire' and, no less important, as an intelligence collector for the world community (UNPREDEP in Macedonia). All these operations have had their own specific set of intelligence requirements.

It is, however, not sufficient to have read the mandate and its interpretations when planning the collection of intelligence. Necessary also is an understanding of what phase the operation is in. The peacekeeping operations that have emerged since the end of the Cold War are dynamic and often quickly change character, almost from day to day. The intelligence requirements change equally quickly.

Intelligence Requirements

Listing the requirements is often easier than explaining how they are to be translated into correct tactical intelligence questions. Three specific intelligence needs of a typical peacekeeping situation can be explored here: the ethnic situation, the socio-economic situation and the attitudes of local leaders and civilians.

1. Knowledge of the *ethnic situation* can, of course, be used to avoid cultural blunders (e.g., by knowing that it is not proper to offer local Muslim leaders a sumptuous buffet during Ramadan), but that is more a matter of common sense than of intelligence. Intelligence proper, however, comes into play in order to correctly assess to what level and extent the conflict has ethnic and nationalist dynamics. It is important to understand that an isolated Muslim-dominated village inside Croatian territory may be a hotspot, or why certain areas react more adversely than others to the presence of alien ethnic groups. Some examples of tactical intelligence questions: what are the historical and current ties between the area in

304

question and other groups, states or alliances? What was its experience in World War II? Have religious or nationalist fundamentalists been active in the area? If so, how were they received? Which group torched the church? Should we expect an ethnic cleansing in the area?

2. The *socio-economic factor* is frequently a crucial element for proper understanding of low-intensity internal conflicts. Conflicts that on the surface possess nationalist or religious traits may prove to have significant social and/or economic factors when scrutinised closely. The Lebanese civil war is a double example of this. The social stratum of the influential and rich was almost identical to the urban Christian population, while the poor stratum consisted of the Shia Muslims. The social conflict therefore had the appearance of a religious struggle, or at least overlapped that struggle. Traditional clan and group leaders (zuama) held, as a group, a firm grip on power and were willing to ally with yesterday's enemy if that would favour the zuama's interests. The old power elite directed the war in the way that was most favourable to it. Accordingly, knowing who has traditionally held power and influence in the area is vital. Is it still possible to utilise this structure? Who profits from the war? Who controlled last year's harvest? Who controls local trade? Where does the flow of funds end up? Who' influences the inhabitants' voting? Is there government law enforcement in the area or is this handled by an irregular 'police force'?

3. The attitudes among the civilian population and local civilian officials are of decisive importance for the peacekeeping operation's structure and execution. Is the international force viewed as a friend, a foe, or just an outsider? Is the war perceived as an international or domestic conflict? What does the civilian population consider as being a famine (this could, of course, differ greatly between, for instance, Somalia and the former Yugoslavia)?

Intelligence Collection

The border between what is or is not politically acceptable in collection methods in peacekeeping operations is, as noted earlier, fairly vague, and often seems founded more on emotions and traditions than on rational considerations. The UN has certain limitations and could hardly accept the presence of murderers or ministers on a UN 'payroll' as part of the general methods of collection.

The following arguments attempt to define some principles the parties might consider acceptable:

- A passive intelligence service is preferable to an active one. To have something listening all the time means avoiding the escalating act of turning something on, for instance sending out a patrol. Artillery-spotting radar is one example of such a device.[16]

- An invisible collection method is better than a visible one. Concern for prestige and prides characterise this attitude. No one wants to have his intentions and weaknesses revealed, particularly in public, in front of one's peers. Satellites and UAV's are examples of less visible collection means.

- Intelligence intended for the protection of the peacekeepers is fairly uncontroversial. Few parties would, at least not openly, question the peacekeeping unit's right to locate minefields.

These arguments lead to three main conclusions.

> First, the peacekeeping operation should have access to systems consisting of passive and less visible sensors, satellite and aerial photoreconnaissance, UAV sensor platforms, etc.

> Second, the operation should use the most visible resource available, i.e. national processing and collection at home.

> Third, the operations should make better use of the intelligence collected by OP's and patrols/convoys. If the parties have accepted the presence of a peacekeeping unit at a certain locations, they can hardly prevent its personnel from being alert.

These three conclusions are applicable under 'normal' conditions. Under worse conditions (e.g., the peacekeeping units have been threatened or there is a risk of massacres or a full-fledge war), the peacekeeping organisations should assume the right to carry out intelligence operations by almost any suitable method, regardless of political constraints. Also, in certain other situations, that is, when the UN has decided to carry out a particularly important operation, satisfaction of the intelligence service's *requirements* should have a greater priority than usual.

While reviewing some collection methods, human intelligence, technical intelligence and traditional UN methods, open sources in this context will be bypassed.[1] Nevertheless, these are obviously of fundamental importance, not only as providers of background knowledge but also, as the media have a high degree of access to the area and as the global corrupter networks grow faster and bigger, as providers of information on the development down to the tactical level.

Human Intelligence

One of the major advantages of a peacekeeping operation is direct access to the specific area and its inhabitants. Important information can be acquired by listening and seeing, by chatting with the women of the village, by establishing relations with vendors in the marketplace. This information is hard to acquire by the traditional means of military intelligence, the use of which could give rise to tension. Close and friendly relations with the local civilians and the local military and civilian officials provide not only a continuous input of the moods, but also more solid pieces of intelligence. Such information is often not furnished in return for money, but because groups or individuals are fed up with the conflict. The Somalia experience shows that women and children generally provide more accurate information than do paid professional informers. Women and children, who generally suffer the worst from the conflict, have also proven to be less inclined to hand over fabricated intelligence. [17]

---

[1] Editors' Note: Leadership Guide 1.0 addresses open sources of intelligence (OSINT) and points to the three North Atlantic Treaty Organisation (NATO) guides to OSINT in support of operational planning and execution: *NATO Open Source Intelligence Handbook* (November 2001); *NATO Open Source Intelligence Reader* (February 2002), *and Intelligence Exploitation of the Internet* (October 2002). All are available for free download at www.oss.net in Archives/References.

Refugees, both those who remain in areas near the conflict zone and those who have fled to distant countries (e.g., the troop-contributing countries), frequently possess information on the current situation, on what happened earlier and occasionally on what may happen. The exploitation of these groups, for intelligence purposes has not been especially systematic, neither in the traditional operations nor in the new ones. The Hague Tribunal's preparation for its trials of war criminals and certain European countries' debriefing of Bosnian refugees are two of only a few existing examples.[18]

As always when using Humint, protection of the source's identity is essential. Furthermore, in conflicts where some of the parties do not hesitate to kill civilians, as in the former Yugoslavia or Rwanda, protecting the method of collection may be necessary to avoid the possibility that someone may decide that it is better to kill the civilians than to let them flee.

Strictly speaking, the Non-Governmental Organisations (NGO's) are not 'Humint'. Regardless of their varying quality, they often run extensive activities in the area in question, and therefore possess quite a lot of knowledge about the current situation. They are, however, frequently reluctant to be associated with the peacekeeping operation's military operations, partly to avoid being compromised in the eyes of the competing parties and partly, in some cases, to avoid sharing the credit for its relief effort with someone else, or perhaps because their ethos includes a reluctance to things military. The peacekeepers should respect the first reason, an organisation like the Red Cross is successful due to its reputation of complete impartiality.[19] Regardless of this obstacle, there are still opportunities to conduct some sort of dialogue between the military branch of the peacekeeping operation and an NGO within the framework of exchanging information on the current security situation. Each organisation will at least be able to improve on its own security through such a dialogue.[20]

Technical Intelligence

Today's advanced sensor systems that can pinpoint a vehicle from hundreds of miles away are obviously of great interest to the peacekeeping operations. But it seems unlikely that the UN would acquire its own satellites or sophisticated radar systems within the foreseeable future. It is, first of all, a political problem, many states are reluctant to give the UN large independent surveillance resources. Furthermore, it is unlikely that any country is willing to sell its most sophisticated systems to the UN or similar international organisations. It is, however, also an economic problem: satellites and JSTARS are immensely expensive. Alternatives include the leasing of resources for particular operations, and the lending of equipment to the UN, as has been the case with the US's U-2 aircraft patrolling northern Iraq.[21] Another option is for a state to collect information with its national assets and then hand it over. If and when this is not possible, the UN is relegated to less advanced and more conventional methods, those that many states all over the world are able to perform. These include Sigint, artillery-spotting radar's, small aircraft air surveillance and UAV's.

The Swedish UN battalion in the Congo used signals intelligence (Sigint) with great success in 1961-1962. The Katangese units often spoke openly when using radio communications, believing that the UN forces did not understand Swahili. The Swedish battalion, however, included several interpreters who were able to translate the broadcasts, which on many occasions provided information of decisive importance.[22] Even though this may have been a particularly fortunate case, Sigint continues to prove itself very useful today: at the strategic/operational level, to find out whether atrocities such as ethnic cleansing were carried out under orders from superior commanders or what kind of contacts there are between the two conflicting parties; at the operation/tactical level, to predict the parties' actions, to find out whether a weapons firing was intentional or not, to locate combat units, and so on.

The first task may require the use of devices that usually are present only at national peacetime Sigint establishments. On the other hand, the regular wartime operational/tactical Sigint/EW equipment should suffice for the second set of tasks. Artillery-spotting radar's have been used with varying success in Bosnia during the days of UNPROFOR. The radar equipment is a complex system that must be handled by qualified crews.[23] A radar unit may also become a primary target for those who desire to act clandestinely.[24]

Despite these problems, the radar units in Bosnia did provide the UN with information on which side really fired the shells during particular incidents. This information has provided a decisive advantage in numerous negotiation sessions.

309

The United States uses UAV's (Predator) as a national asset in the former Yugoslavia with apparently satisfying results. France has also deployed UAV's in Bosnia. Besides the price, another advantage is that the UAV can keep its position above the surveillance target for a long time and thus monitor a chain of events. There is clearly a potential to develop UAV's as an integral part of the intelligence assets of a peacekeeping force, since both individual troop-contributing nationals and the US are able to afford them.

UN Peacekeeping Methods

The United Nations' traditional methods of collecting intelligence in peacekeeping operations were developed during an era when the peacekeepers usually had the parties' more or less reluctant consent and when they, by operating on both sides of the line of confrontation, were able to acquire a fairly complete picture of the situation. Still, if carried out properly and wisely, they can be efficient even today when collecting particular information and when building trusting relations with officials and civilians in the area of operations.

The methods are, however, easily interfered with, and freedom of movement is a crucial prerequisite. The location of observation posts (OP's) and checkpoints (CP's), as well as the route of patrols, may, if the peacekeeping force is weak, be controlled by the stronger parties' wishes rather than by the peacekeepers' requirements.[25]

Liaison officers attached to the peacekeeping units to handle relations with local groups and units, military as well as civilian, generally have somewhat sensitive relations with the intelligence component. Both need to access each other's information, but the liaison officer also needs assurance that the parties do not regard him as primarily an intelligence officer. Doing so could disturb negotiations and relations.

UN Military Observers (UNMO's) are unarmed officers who are supposed to monitor the developments, establish contacts with and between the parties, and act as the UN's feelers in what are often the world's most troubled areas. They generally provide valuable information, both because they develop close contacts with the parties and because they get to know their area well. They are unfortunately also an exposed group that may become incarcerated, kidnapped or hampered in other simple ways by the parties.

310

Processing and Analysis

A peacekeeping operation contains a lot of information, which, if properly used and processed, could provide a significantly better picture of the operation, particularly at a tactical/operational level. Intelligence is unfortunately very fragmentary, since the peacekeeping units often have neither complete control of their area of operations, nor a wide range of collection methods to choose from. A tank is observed here, famine there, and troop movements at a third place.

The intelligence is not only fragmentary, it does not adhere to the rules of regular war. An example: a report about four tanks on a road, if analysed in the traditional way, would be interpreted as a reinforced platoon or a company that would constitute 'only' a reconnaissance patrol. In Bosnia in 1995, the same four tanks would have heralded a major offensive.

Obviously, awareness is needed about which criteria should be used for the interpretation of events. Likely to vary significantly from one operation to another, they must therefore be continuously updated and developed. The close ties between the political/strategic level and the operational/tactical level must also be considered.

Frameworks to Create Patterns

The parties' intentions in a low intensity conflict, much harder to discern than in a conventional war, are often difficult to understand. Who is allied to whom? What are the parties' goals? Which groups belong to a certain party? What axe the parties' relations to other states/actors outside the area of conflict?

In peacekeeping operations, intelligence analysts at the battalion level[26] therefore need a framework to which they are able attach and test their pieces of intelligence in order to identify a pattern in the fragmentary information. This framework would consist mainly of assessments of the impact of different strategic/operational developments on an area.

One way ahead is to work with scenario creation. By role-playing the conflict's leaders, and delving into their main goals and how much they are ready to pay in cash, lives and international notoriety, analysts can get surprisingly close to

311

the real developments. This method presupposes the joint effort of many skilled individuals: operational researchers, behaviour scientists, experts on security politics, and area specialist's as well as military men. They must view the conflict in a broad geographic perspective and consider not only the actors in the conflict's vicinity but also the great powers.[2]

But it is not sufficient to create and game such scenarios. The results of the games must be presented in such a way that they are relevant to the units in the field; the scenarios should also be handed over face-to-face in the field to secure their understanding while the scenario-makers simultaneously acquire information and feedback to help them in a new round of scenario-making.

Indicators and Concepts

Traditional military intelligence processing is focused on war materiel that is typical for certain branches (e.g., artillery-towing vehicles), other materiel (e.g., 20 tanks assembled at X) or activities (the enemy dispatches combat patrols at Y). This information, the indicators, is continuously compared to what is known of the enemy's behaviour or to a hypothesis of what is the enemy's intentions. Several indicators may be put together as a concept, the presence of a certain number of indicators may lead to the conclusion that the concept 'mechanised division' is, with a certain probability, located south of Z.

To apply this method to the peacekeeping operation could help the intelligence group to handle both the strategic/tactical interaction and the need for 'unconventional' intelligence. Indicators in an international context would of course differ from those of a conventional war, and they might also vary between operations and between the different phases of an operation. The concepts would frequently consist of a great number of indicators and sub-concepts as outlined on the next page:

---

[2] Editors' Note: Kristan Wheaton, in Chapter 12, 'Modeling and Simulating Transitions from Authoritarian Rule', provides a 'field expedient' means of scenario development.

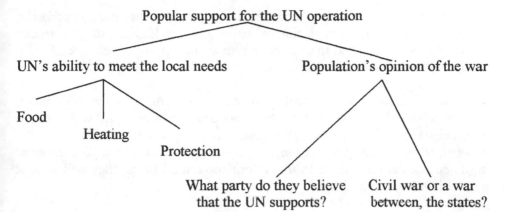

The creation and development of these indicators and concepts, as well as the frameworks, should be a continuous process, to be carried out by the national intelligence service to maintain continuity.[27] That service also has the advantage of possessing a perspective of the conflict that is probably absent among those working in the operation. The work should, however, be performed in close co-operation with the units in the field.

Dissemination

The security problem of dissemination has at least two aspects: the risk of revealing one's sources and methods to possible competitors when handing over national intelligence to the operation or to another national contingent and the risk that the information in the international organisation is leaked to the conflicting parties. The leaking could be done for political or economic reasons, but also sometimes more or less unintentionally, e.g., when using insecure communication lines. Both may hurt the peacekeeping operation's relations with the troop contributors as well as with the opposing parties.

Since the UN system lacks a strategic level intelligence service, and since it will hardly acquire any sophisticated operational level collection means as satellites and JSTAR's, its peacekeeping operations will have to rely on nationally controlled assets for these two features. Strict security regulations, training, and sanctions against transgressors are needed to raise confidence in the peacekeeping operation's ability to handle sensitive material.

313

The superior staffs need intelligence to be able to assess the situation properly, while the soldiers need it to be able to collect more intelligence, to act correctly in sensitive situations and to counteract rumour-mongering. These needs could collide with other security aspects.

One way of dealing with this collision could be to compress the information already collected at a low level. Each battalion would be provided with detailed instructions on what kind of intelligence it is supposed to collect, e.g. the number of heavy weapons in the area, troop movements, etc. The superior staffs do not demand access to this information at all times; they will instead ask for it only when necessary.

The system presupposes two types of intelligence reports. The first, with a high level of compression, describes the local situation in fairly general terms, and includes only particularly important details. The other is a complete report that, for instance, specifies the movements of troops and heavy weapons in detail. The first report is disseminated among superior staffs, subordinate units and individual soldiers. The second is disseminated on a regular basis to only a small circle within the battalion staff; it may also be disseminated orally to a superior staff.

This approach would put high demands on the battalion's intelligence section, which will utilise a compression level normally found at the divisional or higher levels. It also requires that the superior staffs be able to trust the ability and loyalty of their battalions. Otherwise, the staffs will demand raw data or create their own collection system.[28]

Overcoming Intelligence Absence

In today's complex peacekeeping, the need for intelligence is rather clear, both to ensure the safety of the troops and to improve the chances of a successful operation. This can be done within the mandates and without corrupting the integrity of the peacekeeping force.

Certain political and economic limitations are imposed on a peacekeeping intelligence group. Yet, the peacekeeping operation has certain advantages compared to other types of low intensity operations, as, for instance, access to the disputed area and the interaction with the parties.

For intelligence cells to become really efficient they need improved security routines. This may raise not only the troop-contributors' will to supply intelligence and intelligence assets, but also the parties' confidence in the operation and then, perhaps, their will to share some of their intelligence and intentions.

Even though a lot of the advanced analysis is done nationally at home, today's peacekeeping operations put new and higher demands on their intelligence cells.

There might be less counting of the number of wheels on the APC, and possibly more finding out from which country one side got the APC, or if the unit, can be linked with any specific ethnic or economic group. This implies that the intelligence units, even at the battalion level (which is a normal size contingent, and thus the highest national level within the operation) must include a broad spectra of qualifications, military as well as academic, to be able to pose the relevant questions.

Intelligence in peace operations is a serious, and complex, matter that should not be taken lightly. However, once in the field, the lack of intelligence may very well prove to be even more serious.

Endnotes

This chapter is based on the author's contributions to a joint Swedish-Norwegian study on intelligence in peace support operations. The author gratefully acknowledges the helpful comments contributed by the co-researchers in this study, Senior Analysts Nils Marius Rekkedal and Wegger Strommen of the Norwegian Defence Research Establishment. The author is also deeply in debt for the help and comments from two senior colleagues at FOA [National Defence Research Establishment, Sweden], Senior Analysts Anders Almen and Robert Dalsjo.

---

[1] When, in this context, I speak of 'peacekeeping' I do it in a broad sense, including such different operations as UNFICYP, UNOSOM, and IFOR, as well as other types of peace support operations, such as conflict prevention. On the other hand, I exclude operations that are more to be seen as regular war, for instance, Operation 'Desert Storm.' The main reason for this is the different and less significant (at least at a

315

tactical level) political dimension in these types of operations.

[2] I appreciate the input I've received from senior analyst Robert Dalsjo when writing this section. He has written several papers concerning the political implications of peacekeeping in the new world era, for instance 'Sweden's Interest and Role in Peace-support Operations' (FOA pre-print FOA-D-95-00184-1.4 – SE) and 'Sweden and the Balkao Blue Helmet Operations' (article in the book *Solidarity and Defence,* ed. Lars Ericson, Stockholm 1995, Svenska Millitarhistoriska Kommissionen).

[3] Lewis MacKeazie, *The Changing Face of Peacekeeping* (Ed, Alex Morrison), Toronto, The Canadian Institute of Strategic Studies, 1993.

[4] In Bosnia information on strategic level peace plans on several occasions resulted in almost immediate offensives as the parties tried to capture and pacify such areas that the plan would give them. One interpretation of this is that they wished to secure 'what is theirs', while they expected the enemy to have less inclination to defend these areas. In Somalia, the death of American soldiers caused immediate demands at home for a withdrawal.

[5] One example is the reaction of UNIFIL at the Israeli invasion of southern Lebanon in 1982: the Israeli forces were allowed to pass through the UNIFIL's lines, encountering only a very small, sporadic and symbolic resistance from the UN forces.

[6] One example is the French battalion's actions against snipers in Sarajevo. The maintenance of a reasonably secure environment for Sarajevo's civilians was deemed so important that the UN soldiers fired back at snipers even when they did not fire directly at the personnel of the UN forces. This is not actual self-defence; the UN forces instead used violence within the framework of a peacekeeping endeavour to resolve its task.

[7] For a further investigation of the development of matters of doctrinal development for the peace support operations after the end of the cold war, see for instance Niklas Granholm, 'International Operations, A Preliminary Typology', FOA-B--9S-00099-1.4-SE, Nov. 1995.

[8] For instance, a peacekeeping operation can hardly be regarded as impartial by any standards if it is unable to see to that all parties follow an agreement on disarmament. Of course, there are historic exceptions to the typical 'weak' peacekeeping force, for instance in the Congo.

[9] Not all UN peacekeeping operations have completely ignored the importance of intelligence but the use of it has been somewhat complicated and surrounded with more or less strange taboos: for instance, it was called information, not intelligence assets.

[10] [On the other hand, we have seen in both Somalia and Bosnia how groups insensitive to the reactions of the world community have attacked the UN forces.

[11] If all parties are under the same scrutiny they would also know that the other side cannot do anything without being surveyed by the international community. This could help to stabilise the area. One example of this is the surveillance systems supplied by

the USA to the Sinai after the Camp David agreement. Dr. John Macartney, Syracuse University, 'Peacekeeping with Intelligence,' paper presented at the 37th annual International Studies Association (ISA) Convention, San Diego, 1996, page 16.

[12] This condition existed to some degree in Bosnia during the UNPROFOR days. The UN seemed to react less harshly to crimes against 'safe areas' when they had been carried out by Sarajevo forces than by Pale forces. The fairly mild criticism levelled by the UN at the Croatian injustices against civilians when the country recaptured Krajina is another example.

[13] Hugh Smith, 'Intelligence and UN Peacekeeping,' *Survival,* autumn 1994, p. 189. This article, one of the first on the subject, was a bright light in a time when intelligence and the UN was seen as an impossible combination. The comprehensive article is still highly recommended reading for anyone interested in the area.

[14] For instance the Swedish cabinet blocked the transfer of a part of NORDBAT 2 from Tuzla to Srebrenica in October 1993.

[15] It is a public secret that France and Great Britain had special units in former Yugoslavia ready during the UNPROFOR days to carry out *inter alia* intelligence missions.

[16] It is hard to justify why one prevents the UN's control functions while simultaneously claiming innocence. Despite this, such acts do occur.

[17] Dr. Bruce Hoffman, St. Andrews University, at a FOA seminar 4 May 1995.

[18] Refugees from ex-Yugoslavia have been asked to provide information to the Hague Tribunal on what they know of atrocities in camps and during ethnic cleansing.

[19] It is hardly a coincidence that the headquarters of the International Red Cross is located in Switzerland, a country so neutral that it has abstained from joining the United Nations.

[20] In Somalia, despite some difficulties in relations between NGO's and the military operation, the NGO's indeed proved their value by providing important information and insight to the military peace operation, not only on the humanitarian situation but also on the political situation and the security situation.

[21] John Macartney, Syracuse University, 'Peacekeeping with Intelligence,' paper presented at the 37th annual ISA Convention, San Diego, 1996, p. 16.

[22] Jonas Waern, 'Katanga,' Kristianstad, *Atlantis,* 1980, p. 296 (in Swedish), 1980.

[23] The Jordanian radar company did not have a satisfactory technical performance, due mainly to a shortage of skilled personnel.

[24] The Ukrainian artillery-spotting radar unit in Sarajevo was a primary target for both sides during a period. Hugh Smith, 'Intelligence and UN Peacekeeping,' *Survival,* Autumn 1994, p. 181.

[25] This is, for instance, applicable to the location of the OP' in the NORDBAT 2 area. The battalion was more or less confined to its camps by the Sarajevo forces during early 1995, after which the OP's were established by negotiation. The UN's lack of

clout at the negotiating table affected their location – they were frequently at places of minor importance to the conflict.

[26] In most peacekeeping operations the battalion level is the highest national level within the operation – the IFOR operation is in this aspect an exception.

[27] Of course some work of this kind is done by the superior commands of the operation. Despite that, I believe that as long as these staffs are not fully 'combined' and do not meet the necessary security requirements, and as long as not all contingents are able to handle the information in a proper way, each country will be more or less on its own when it comes to advanced intelligence analysis.

[28] The JCO (Joint Commissioned Officers) in Bosnia worked in small groups collecting information and, at least in the beginning, reported directly to the BHC.

No Cloak and Dagger Required: Intelligence Support to UN Peacekeeping

Paul Johnston

Ever greater numbers of blue helmets under hostile fire around the world have finally produced something of a long overdue interest in the intelligence requirements of UN military missions. Indeed, retired Canadian major-general Lewis MacKenzie, the first UN commander into Sarajevo, once described his greatest regret from that mission as:

> Not knowing what was really going on. The UN treats intelligence gathering with great suspicion, because it is deemed to be spying on member states. We once found ourselves in a situation where the BBC World Service was telling us what was happening 200 metres away from our own headquarters. That was really frustrating.[1]

The difficulties of peacekeeping and the various causes of 'peace missions' failures are many and complex, but one of the root causes, as General MacKenzie's words make clear, is often a lack of understanding on the part of UN missions of 'what was really going on'. Peacekeeping and peacemaking missions have foundered on difficulties with everything from assessing factional respect for zones of separation in Bosnia, to the failure to identify and locate factional leaders such as Muhammed Farrah Aideed in Somalia. Yet ironically, as General MacKenzie alludes in his remark, it is precisely the UN's own reluctance to countenance 'intelligence' that leads to many of these difficulties with 'knowing what was really going on' in the first place. But it need not be this way. Effective military intelligence can be conducted on UN missions without compromising political sensitivities, so long as proper

319

intelligence fundamentals are respected. And the UN need not fear any of this intelligence work, no cloak and dagger are required, just the efficient management of the information which UN missions are already collecting in any event.

UN Aversion to 'Intelligence' ...

Hugh Smith, an Australian defence academic, began a 1994 article on intelligence support to UN peacekeeping missions with the quip that 'the UN has no intelligence'.[2] While meant somewhat tongue-in-cheek, it does make a serious point: the UN has a great aversion to 'intelligence' with a capital 'I'. The UN maintains that as a strictly neutral world-wide organisation, it does not conduct intelligence operations. Indeed, the quasi-official *Peacekeeper's Handbook* goes so far as to state:

> The UN has resolutely refused to countenance intelligence systems as part of its peacekeeping operations; intelligence, having covert connections, is a dirty word.[3]

The UN's reasoning for this is that:

> ...any form of covert intelligence is liable to create prejudice and suspicion ... Trust, confidence and respect form the essential fabric on which a successful peacekeeping operation needs to be based. 'Spying' does not help towards this end.[4]

This represents a muddled conflation of intelligence with espionage, but nevertheless, in deference to this sensitivity Canadian military doctrine actually states:

> The term 'intelligence' carried negative and covert connotations. To ensure the operations of the peacekeeper appear to be impartial, trustworthy and overt, the term 'information' will be used in place of 'intelligence'.[5]

In a similar vein, US doctrine states that 'In Peace Keeping, the terms *information* and *intelligence* are synonymous.'[6]

... But the Very Essence of Peacekeeping *Is* 'Intelligence'

If the UN seriously wishes to pursue peace missions they must get over this sensitivity about 'intelligence'. As recent history makes so clear, no UN force can operate effectively in darkness.[7] If blinded to the situation, a peacekeeping force will not only be ineffective in its mission, but eventually it will place even its own members' lives at risk.

Even if the UN's political leadership in New York has been reluctant to accept this, the UN's peacekeeping forces themselves have realised the significance of intelligence for some time. For instances, a study produced by UNPROFOR (United Nations Protection Force) headquarters in 1993, signed by Lieutenant General Wahlgren himself (the Force Commander) and forwarded to UN headquarters in New York[8] stated that:

> Great care is taken in the mission to refer to information gathering as opposed to intelligence gathering. Indeed, we refer to information officers vice intelligence officers and avoid any overt actions that might raise suspicions that we are in fact involved in the intelligence function. However, while this may be appropriate for a relatively benign mission such as UNFCYP (United Nations Force in Cyprus), it is not appropriate in missions such as UNPROFOR.

> Peacekeeping in a theatre such as UNPROFOR, where the opposing forces are constantly manoeuvring, demands an intelligence function. There have been several instances where an advance knowledge of probably intention would have been extremely helpful (e.g. the Croatian offensive of 23 January 1993), yet the lack of authority to conduct a proactive intelligence function makes this extremely difficult to do. UNNY (United Nations New York) must 'rethink' the entire approach to information versus intelligence gathering. The authority to proactively conduct an intelligence campaign should be given to the Force Commander with the caveat that limitations may be applied by UNNY.

In fact, an examination of the UN's own definitions and vocabulary reveals that not only does the UN conduct 'intelligence' by any other name, but most of what UN forces actually do is 'collecting intelligence', whether they want to admit it or not. Sir Brian Urquhart, the former British soldier and Second World War veteran who went on to do much work for the UN and has been involved in peacekeeping since its invention, offered the following definition of peacekeeping:

> The use by the United Nations of military personnel and formations not in a fighting or enforcement role but interposed as a mechanism to bring an end to hostilities and as a buffer between hostile forces.[9]

Commenting on this definition, John Ruggie, of the Institute for Strategic Studies at the US National Defence University added that peacekeeping forces have an 'umpire' role, and 'toward that end, they observe and report'.[10]

Indeed, words like 'observe', 'report', 'monitor' and 'fact-finding' appear often in peacekeeping literature and the UN's own documents.[11] John Mackinlay, a British academic, divides peacekeeping operations into three 'levels': level one which encompasses observation missions and 'traditional' peacekeeping operations (those in which all parties to the dispute agree to the UN presence); level two which is characterised by 'preventive deployments' (missions where a peacekeeping force is interposed between warring factions without their full consent), or 'internal conflict resolution measures' (such as overseeing the cantonment and disarming of warring factions); and level three, which is characterised by active measures actually to roll-back aggression, either with sanctions of some form or outright war against a state or entity which the UN has ruled to be an unlawful aggressor.[12] Considering the thrust of the literature, it seems clear that a common thread runs through all of this terminology, the central requirement to observe, collect and report information.

Consider the terms 'United Nations Military Observer', *'Observation Force'*, and *'United Nations Patrols'*. These are the terms the UN itself uses to describe what most Blue Berets in practice actually do. And what is the product of all this observation and patrolling? Information, the UN stoutly maintains, certainly nothing so distasteful as intelligence. However, collecting information on military forces and processing it in order to assess what those military forces are doing is, of course, the very essence of 'military intelligence'.

The Information/Intelligence Distinction

All of this bears upon the distinction between *information* and *intelligence*. While it does not really matter if many feel that the term 'information' is more appropriate to the UN context than 'intelligence', this should not be allowed to obscure the fact that there is an important point buried beneath this semantic slight of hand. Classic Western military intelligence doctrine defines information as raw data, whereas intelligence is the end result of processing this raw data and drawing pertinent conclusions.[13] Use of the term 'military information' as a euphemism for military intelligence glosses over this important distinction. And it is an important distinction.

Suppose an individual UN Military Observer (UNMO) spots a large column of troops moving through one faction's area towards the line of confrontation. Perhaps he notes that it is a battalion of T-55 tanks. This is information. Probably critical information, but only information. What does it mean? In isolation, it is difficult to say. The tanks could be defensive reinforcements, part of a unit rotation, they could be associated with routine training, or it could be a concentration of forces presaging an attack. These examples illustrate just a few of the possibilities that spring immediately to mind. How does one know? Fundamentally there are two ways.

First of all, one collates and cross-references all available information. Perhaps it is known that a certain unit regularly conducts road move training through that area. Perhaps it is known that that faction's unit rotation schedule calls for a relief in place at this time. Perhaps other indications that preparations are underway for an offensive have been noted.

The other way one knows the significance of that raw information is by further exploration of the issue, that is to say, by sending out further observers and patrols to *confirm* or *deny* whatever working hypotheses were formed in the first step. This is critical and really cuts to the heart of the issue, for it demonstrates that real intelligence is *interactive* and must be integrated into the operation itself. Intelligence *must* be able to task collection assets, albeit through the operations staff and ultimately the commander.

These two steps, and especially the second one, namely, the tasking of collection assets, are the *sine qua non* of effective intelligence work. This interactive cycle is what General Wahlgren and his staff were referring to above in the remark 'the authority to *proactively* conduct an intelligence campaign should be given to the Force Commander'.[14] Without this systematic and rigorous approach to information, UN missions have no way of really knowing what any warring factions are up to.

UN Collection Difficulties/Sensitivities

Because of the political sensitivity on many UN missions, limitations are often placed upon the collection of information. Indeed, Canadian doctrine specifically states that this will often be essential for maintaining the credibility of the force. Generally, one finds the following sorts of restrictions, which are drawn from Canadian doctrine:[15]

a. Only overt methods may be used,
b. Information should be collected and used impartially,
c. No information about belligerents will be revealed to other belligerents, and
d. Collection will be directed only at the capabilities and belligerents' armed forces.

All too many seem to believe that since restrictions on intelligence collection are necessary, *ipso facto* there is no room for military intelligence on UN operations. The UN, and Canadian peacekeeping doctrine, would certainly appear to feel this way.

Yet nothing could be further from the truth. As argued above, the real essence of military intelligence is not, as it appears to be commonly thought, secrecy. The real essence of military intelligence is simply the rigorous processing of all available information, married with the process of actively seeking to confirm or deny one's hypotheses. This can be done within the confines of these, or nearly any other, collection limitations. To refuse to 'do intelligence' is merely to manage one's information poorly. If there really is no intelligence being done in the UN, then just who is deciding where to send all those UN patrols and UNMOs, and what are they being asked to look for?

New Enthusiasms

In this brave new age of more aggressive UN peacemaking and peacekeeping, there has been some dawning of awareness of the importance of intelligence (by any name) to peacekeeping. Broadly, most of this interest falls into two camps, enthusiasm for new monitoring technologies and enthusiasm for the creation of some form of 'intelligence directorate' within the UN body itself.

Of the two, enthusiasm for new monitoring technologies may be the most widespread. Jeffery Tracey, for instance, a Canadian scientist who has working in the technical support to arms control verification,[16] has argued for the use of commercially available satellite-imaging systems in support of the UN generally and peacekeeping in particular.[17] This, Tracey argues, would be overt and cost-effective. As Tracey's background in arms control verification suggests, his approach builds upon a long history of success in developing technical means of verifying compliance with international agreements. Significantly, Tracey's article only mentions the world 'intelligence' twice, once to claim that intelligence 'does nothing to build confidence and trust between multinational regimes'[18] and once to stress that surveillance of the sort he is advocating 'must not be perceived as a covert means of intelligence gathering'.[19] Undoubtedly, this reflects the UN's (and like-minded individuals') negative attitude towards 'intelligence', but all these proposals for new monitoring technologies, many of which in and of themselves have great merit, in essence amount only to sources of information. Like all raw sources of information they really become useful only when processed, and of course the act of doing so is the act of 'doing intelligence'.

As mentioned above, there is also a new enthusiasm for doing precisely that: many writers and pundits have argued for a formally institutionalised intelligence office in the UN, generally as part of some reorganised and revitalised UN staff in New York.[20]

Levels of Intelligence

The enthusiasm for new monitoring technologies and new UN intelligence agencies is commendable, but some order needs to be brought to the debate. In fact, between open sources and the information being generated by the sources currently available to the UN, there is probably enough information out there to provide whatever intelligence the UN needs. The primary requirement is to organise this so that it can be properly processed to produce the finished intelligence that the UN and its peacekeepers need. A necessary first step towards this is to be clear about the intelligence requirements, and perhaps the first point to be made in this area is to understand the various levels of intelligence.

Classically, military thought distinguishes three 'levels' of analysis: strategic, operational, and tactical. In the UN's case, the strategic level would equate to UN Headquarters in New York, where the secretary-general and his staff sit with the General Assembly, the Security Council, and the headquarters of most UN organisations. For the UN, the operational level equates to the 'theatre' headquarters of the various missions around the world, for example, the old UNPROFOR headquarters in the Balkans or UNTAC headquarters in Cambodia. These headquarters are integrated civil/military organisations, with a mission commander[21] who reports to the secretary-general in New York. Finally, the tactical level comprises the units on the line, doing the actual peacekeeping.

Hugh Smith makes the point that the UN needs good intelligence at all levels, and this is certainly true, but most discussions of forming institutionalised intelligence seems to have concentrated on what we would call the 'strategic' level, that is an office in New York to advise the secretary-general and the Security Council, to the detriment of attention to the operational and tactical levels.

This is unfortunate, because it is probably at the operational level that the greatest weaknesses lie, and the greatest potential. Major General Dallaire, the UN Force Commander in Rwanda during that country's recent civil war, has pointed out that 'It is this type of intelligence (operational) which is absolutely essential to the force commander in order to enable him to fulfil his mandate.'[22] General Dallaire argued that 'the UN's primary intelligence requirement is for *operational* intelligence'.[23]

Strategic intelligence for the UN is clearly important, but the lack of a UN intelligence directorate notwithstanding, there is little shortage of 'strategic intelligence' for the UN. Academics, the media, and other open sources provide a wealth of analysis and background to all the disputes ongoing and looming

326

around the world. It should also not be forgotten that the UN can do nothing until the member states in general and the Security Council in particular decide to do something. And the Security Council members all have their own strategic intelligence sources.

Likewise, intelligence shortcomings at the tactical level are not quite as pressing as those at the operational level. Since member nations contributed formed units (generally battalions) to UN peacekeeping missions, these units generally come with their own organic intelligence sections. Furthermore, a well-organised intelligence effort at the operational level would tend to produce a great deal of the intelligence needed at the tactical level as a by-product.

The real problem lies at the operational level. Because UN peacekeeping missions are formed on an *ad hoc* basis, the mission headquarters are not formed units that have trained and worked together, they are cobbled together from the individuals of many nations. Furthermore, forming an effective headquarters' intelligence section has generally not been mission commanders' highest priority, attention has tended to fixate on the administrative and logistic task of simply getting the force together and in place. Experience also suggests that member states contribute a very mixed bag of personnel to headquarters intelligence billets; some are highly qualified and some are elder officers with absolutely no intelligence training or experience who have been sent on the mission essentially as a *sinecure*.[24]

The egregious difficulties or outright failures that UN peacekeeping missions have experienced have not been because of a lack of strategic intelligence in New York, they have been because of a lack of operational intelligence at the mission level.

The UNPROFOR Example

UNPROFOR's bittersweet experience in the Balkans is a classic example of all this. The original peacekeeping mission to the former Yugoslavia consisted of 12 battalions sent to the breakaway republic of Croatia in 1992, under the auspices of UN Security Council Resolution 743. These battalions were grouped into four sectors (each with a sector headquarters) which in turn reported to UNPROFOR headquarters in Zagreb. The mission subsequently expanded to include Bosnia-Herzegovina, which became known as the 'B-H

Command', and Macedonia. In keeping with classic UN practice, the sector headquarters and UNPROFOR headquarters were no formed units, but *ad hoc* groupings of individuals from many nations.

UNPROFOR headquarters did form an intelligence section, or 'military information' section as they called it, but in compliance with UN tradition it was weakly staffed and formed the smallest staff branch in the headquarters.[25] Furthermore, in practice it restricted itself to simply consolidating all the incoming unit situation reports in order to produce a daily summary for the commander. According to the testimony of various Canadian officers who where there early in the mission the UNPROFOR military information cell did not form a collection plan, it did not send out information tasks to the units or the UN military observers roaming the area, and it did not produce a formal estimate of the situation, in short, it was not doing military intelligence.[26] It was simply working as something of a duty centre, producing a daily summary from unit reports.

Dissatisfied with this state of affairs, various commanders took the initiative to form their own intelligence sections.[27] The result is that over time the UNPROFOR intelligence section grew and came to have qualified personnel, but there was also a proliferation of 'national' intelligence sections within UNPROFOR, as each troop contributing nation formed a G2 section at its own national contingent headquarters. This can create some real complications, since troop contributing nations are not always willing to share all of their intelligence with all other troop contributing nations. This tended to produce a tangled web of intelligence sharing within UNPROFOR with different national unit's privy to different intelligence. In the worst case this could conceivably have led to units in the field receiving intelligence that UNPROFOR headquarters itself was unaware of.[28] The obvious solution to this problem is to give the UN force itself a credible intelligence capability, so that troop contributing nations do not feel obliged to send their own national intelligence cells to support their own national contingents. Because of the hard work and sometimes-inspired improvisation of many officers on UN duty, UNPROFOR eventually achieved a fairly comprehensive and smoothly working intelligence organisation, but none of this has been institutionalised within the UN generally. The next peacekeeping mission the UN creates will have to start all over again.

Possible Solutions

So what is to be done? Surely the first order of business on UN peacekeeping missions is to form a clear and detailed picture of the warring factions, and what their dispositions, capabilities and intentions are. How can this be done? By applying the discipline of intelligence to the vast pool of information already being collected from all sources in any event, not least of which are all the UNMOs, military monitors, and UN patrols out there. Where does one do this? In a proper, all-source analysis intelligence cell, co-located with the force commander. This is the first and fundamental need: to create proper intelligence cells with proper mandates in all UN headquarters. Failure to do this merely blinds the commander and the whole UN force.

A Permanent Staff in New York

In order to effect all these measures in the organisation of peacekeeping missions, some form of a permanent 'intelligence' (or 'military information' if they prefer) staff will probably be required at UN headquarters in New York. However, the main role for this organisation would not be the provision of strategic intelligence to the secretary-general, the Security Council, or anyone else at UN headquarters, but rather to serve as an institutional memory and planning staff for future UN missions.

This staff could ensure that sound intelligence doctrine was institutionalised within the UN, and perhaps even more importantly it could ensure that when new peacekeeping missions are planned, their headquarters includes a proper intelligence section right from the start. So long as UN mission headquarters are formed only as missions are established, without such a permanent intelligence staff in New York there will be little opportunity for continuity between missions, and every new mission will be forced to start almost from scratch and suffer its own growing pains.[29]

Conclusion

The UN is not currently organising its information requirements very rationally. Like it or not, what they are doing is military intelligence. A rose by any other name may smell as sweet, but use of the euphemism 'military information' is muddying the process. As the UN's own definitions and vocabulary makes clear, most of what peacekeeping is about is the collection and processing of information. 'Intelligence' is simply the discipline of doing this in the most effective way possible, and to wilfully refuse to countenance intelligence is merely to insist on going about the business in a muddled way.

Intelligence is not about secrecy; it is about learning what is going on by the rigorous analysis of all available information, and, most importantly, by the active tasking of information collectors to confirm or deny what one thinks one knows.

None of this need violate neutrality, impartiality, or political sensitivity. For the most part it would simply be the rationalisation of the information that the UN is already collecting in any case. There should be no reason why the UN cannot provide effective intelligence support to its own peacekeeping missions.

Endnotes

[1] Major General (retired) Lewis MacKenzie, quoated in 'MacKenzie: Disappointed by Lack of "inter-National Self Interst" ', *The Gazette*, Saturday 12 Feb 1994, p. B2.
[2] Hugh Smith, 'Intelligence and UN Peacekeeping', *Survival* 36/3 (Autumn 1994), p. 174.
[3] International Peace Academy, *Peacekeeper's Handbook* (NY: Pergamon Press, 1984), p. 39.
[4] Ibid.
[5] Canadian Forces Publication 301(3) *Peacekeeping Operations*, 1992, Section 618, para. 1, sub-para e.
[6] United States Army FM 100-23 *Peace Operations*, Dec. 1994, p. 45.
[7] Although not a UN peacekeeping mission *per se*, perhaps the best example of this is the ill-fated US-led mission to Somalia, where a lack of knowledge of the factions in general and Muhammed Farrah Aideed in particular was a major factor in the eventual collapse of the mission there.
[8] 'UNPROFOR One Year Later', op cit.
[9] Brian Urquhart, 'Thoughts on the Twentieth Anniversary of Dag Hammerskjold's Death', *Foreign Affairs* 60 (Fall 1981), p. 6.
[10] John Ruggie, 'The UN: Stuck Between Peacekeeping and Enforcement', *Peacekeeping: The Way Ahead*, McNair Paper 25 (Washington, DC: Institute for National Strategic Studies, NDU 1993), p. 3.

[11] For example, the *Peacekeeper's Handbook*, or secretary-general Boutros-Ghali's original *An Agenda for Peace* (NY: UN Department of Public Information, 1992).

[12] John Mackinlay, 'Defining a Role Beyond Peacekeeping: Military Implications of United Nations *Peacekeeping Operations*. McNair Paper 17 (Washington DC: Institute for National Strategic Studies, NDU 1993), pp. 32-37.

[13] See, for example, Canadian Forces Publication 315(2), *Combat Intelligence*, 1988, Ch. 1, para. 3.

[14] Emphasis added.

[15] Canadian Forces, *Peacekeepign Operations*, Section 618, para. 1.   See also *Peacekeepers's Handbook* (note 3), pp. 39 and 59.

[16] This is a field in which Canada has been a leader. The Department of Foreign Affairs and International Trade maintains a Verification Research Unit (VRU) to encourage and co-ordinate this.

[17] Jeffery Tracey, 'The Use of Overhead Surveillance in United Nations Activities' in Alex Morrison (ed.), *The Changing Face of Peacekeeping* (Toronto: Canadian Institute of Strategic Studies 1993), pp. 107-142.

[18] By which he presumably means *different* regimes, Ibid., p. 108.

[19] Ibid., p. 111.

[20] For an example of the literature in this vein, see Bruce Poulin, 'An Early Warning Apparatus for the United Nations', *The McNaughton Papers*, Vol. VI (Toronto: Canadian Institute of Strategic Studies, 1994), pp. 9-13.

[21] That is *Mission* Commander, not *Force* Commander. Often given the title of 'Special Representative of the secretary-general (SRSG), this individual is generally a civilian and is the one who represents the secretary-general in the theatre and reports to him in New York. The military commander is generally known as the 'Force Commander' (FC) and he usually reports to the SRSG. However, in practice the FC usually has considerable independent stature and a direct line to the UN in New York himself.

[22] Major General Dallaire, 'Briefing on Intelligence and Lessons Learned in Rwanda', unpublished, August 1994, p. 3.

[23] Ibid., p. 28. Emphasis added.

[24] Interviews with Nick Ward, UNPROFOR Canadian Contingent G2, 1993; and Capt. Richard McRae, UNPROFOR and B-H Command intelligence staff officer, 1994.

[25] Ibid.

[26] Ibid.

[27] Or Deputy Commanders.   Canadian Major General Gaudreau, who was the UNPROFOR Canadian Contingent Commander and UN Deputy Force Commander, instigated a significant increase in the intelligence staff.

[28] This problem could be worse were it not for the common practice of 'double-hatting' contingent commanders.   For example, Canada provided a major-general to UNPROFOR as the Deputy Commander, and also made this same individual, as the

senior Canadian officer in theatre, the Canadian contingent commander. This meant in effect that the UNPROFOR Deputy Commander was privy to whatever Canadian and allied intelligence Canada possessed on the Balkans, even if this material was not provided to UNPROFOR headquarters *per se*. Since senior UNPROFOR commanders generally came from Western nations (primarily Britain and France), UNPROFOR itself indirectly benefited from the Western intelligence community's product.
[29] Of course, this same problem applies equally to the operations and logistics staffs. A full UN general staff in New York would probably solve a myriad of problems.

The Cloak and the Blue Beret: Limitations on Intelligence in UN Peacekeeping

A. Walter Dorn

In 1960 it was suggested that the word 'intelligence' should be banned from the lexicon of the United Nations.[1] Indeed, the UN continues to shy away from official use of the term because of its association with illegal or undercover activities, such as spying, theft, and distortion, with which the UN would not (and should not) be involved. Nevertheless, intelligence, in its pure sense of processed information, both open and secret, relating to security, is an essential part of UN peacekeeping, and is recognised as such by UN staff, both civilian and military.[2] Peacekeeping operations (PKO's) have sometimes included 'information units' or 'Military Information Branches' (MIB's) in their structures. Thus, the UN has officially side-stepped the term 'intelligence,' though some staff members of these units unofficially called themselves intelligence officers, and many have been drawn from the ranks of various professional military and police intelligence organisations.[3]

Many failures in the history of UN field operations might have been avoided had the UN taken a more forthright approach to intelligence and possessed a stronger mandate to gather information and improve its information-gathering systems.

The list includes outbreaks from the distant past, such as the Korean War of 1950 (witnessed but not foreseen by the UN Commission on Korea), and more recent ones, such as the incursion of SWAPO guerrillas into Namibia (1989), the Iraqi attack on Kuwait (1990), the renewal of civil war in Angola (1995), and the genocide in Rwanda. (1994), all of which occurred in or near areas of United Nations operations. UN Force commander Romeo Dallaire complained of being 'deaf and blind' in Rwanda without a substantial intelligence capability.[4] Many UN force commanders, past and present, would echo his remarks.

The UN's information branches and units, both in the field and at UN headquarters, when they are created, are merely small parts of a vast network of international and national bodies engaged in information-gathering and sharing during a peacekeeping operation. While the UN information units are dwarfed by national intelligence bodies, they can gain much useful information using a variety of means to help the UN's mission. Unfortunately, with the exception of a few articles, little attention has been paid to intelligence-gathering peacekeeping.[5]

The Secrecy Dilemma

One of the first stumbling blocks that the United Nations encounters in intelligence gathering is the issue of secrecy. Secret intelligence (i.e., intelligence that cannot be divulged except to specifically authorised individuals or organisations) has been used by the UN regularly, though hesitatingly and inconsistently, over the years. For the UN, a great dilemma arises when the information is gathered secretly, since the world body is officially dedicated to transparency, impartiality, and the rule of law. On the one hand, the UN recognises that secret information-gathering and handling is often required to achieve its noble ends (e.g., the protection of its forces and the success of its missions); on the other, this sometimes questionable means carries great hazards, even if legal. UN officials have seen that even open, passive information collection, such as taking photos with an unconcealed camera, can raise the hackles of a conflicting party, who might consider it a hostile act and may suspect (wrongly in most cases) that the UN will use it in a way that will hurt its cause. (In the former Yugoslavia, UN peacekeepers have been prohibited from carrying cameras except by special authorisation from the force commander). The UN cannot afford to lose credibility or tarnish its image as an honest broker and impartial mediator by having competing parties accuse it of using covert methods to gather information. Moreover, the UN must seek to maintain high moral and ethical standards. According to an earlier secretary-general, Dag Hammarskjold, the UN must have 'clean hands'.[6]

The first multidimensional peacekeeping effort, the UN Operation in the Congo, created by Hammarskjold in 1960 and described in detail here, shows the difficulty and the importance of finding the proper limits for secret information-gathering.

Under certain circumstances, secrecy of information is unarguably essential. A case in point was UN monitoring in Bosnia. Scandinavian soldiers in the UN Protection Force (UNPROFOR) carefully observed the impact of mortar fire from Serb units outside a besieged Muslim town. The peacekeepers immediately reported by radio the locations of the hits to UN force headquarters. But unknown to the peacekeepers, the Serb soldiers were monitoring the UN radio communications and using this information to correct their fire. By sending messages 'in the clear,' the UN was inadvertently helping one party to commit aggression. In this case, secrecy of information, (through secure communication lines or other methods) was clearly called for.

More generally, the success of a UN PKO may depend on secrecy and intelligence gathering. This is true for both classical PKO's tasked with monitoring cease-fires and those interposed in a demilitarised zone between opposing forces, where 'quiet diplomacy' behind closed doors and quick pre-emptive (secret) deployment is often the best means to address observed or potential violations. Often, moving peacekeepers into a position desired by one or more conflicting parties is necessary to prevent them from fighting for it. For this kind of rapid and undeclared preventive action, early warning about the actions and intentions of the parties is needed. This involves unobtrusive and keen observation of their troop dispositions.

Secret intelligence is even more important in modern multidimensional PKO's with their expanded responsibilities: elections monitoring, where individual votes must be kept secret - arms control verification, including possible surprise inspections at secret locations - law enforcement agency supervision (to 'watch the watchmen') – mediation where confidential bargaining positions that are confidentially shared by one party with the UN should not be revealed to the other - sanctions and border monitoring, where clandestine activities (e.g., arms shipments) must be uncovered or intercepted without allowing smugglers to take evasive action. When forces are operating in hazardous or potentially explosive areas, such as the former Yugoslavia, Rwanda or Somalia, secret intelligence takes on added importance and calls for special skills in

335

intelligence gathering. For instance, clandestine arms shipments, secret plans for aggression or ethnic cleansing or genocide, and threats to the lives or the mission of the peacekeepers should be uncovered as quickly as possible.

While secrecy can often be justified as essential, there are also many reasons to support openness. Table 1 provides a list of the advantages of openness, as well as the requirements for secrecy. The list shows the complex dilemma the UN (and, indeed, any organisation that tries to live up to high ethical standards) faces when it tries to determine the degree of secrecy it will employ.

Advantages of Openness	
More acceptable/desirable morally	Positive example to conflicting parties
Less threatening ('nothing to hide')	Reduces suspicions of covert operations[1]
Less potential for misunderstanding	Demonstrates lack of self-interest
Builds confidence	Increases knowledge (info to right hands)
Permits greater feedback (internal/ext.)	Less costly in time, money, people, equip.
Facilitates accountability (credit/blame)	Reduces compartmentalisation[2]
Advantages of Secrecy	
Better protection of sources & methods	Increases secret inputs from others
Prevents disclosure of weaknesses[3]	May reduce information misuse (or not)
Provides competitive advantage	Permits selective information exchanges
Allows better timing/amount of release	Permits time for authentication/correction
Factors Influencing the Degree of Secrecy Required	
'Need to know' for mission success or safety of personnel	
Political approval of UN member states[4]	
Approval (tacit or explicit) of host state or parties observed	
Legal implications (violations of national or international laws?)	
Operational considerations (technical and human means of information gathering)	
Cost in time, manpower, money	

Table 1. Secrecy versus Openness: Advantages and Factors

---

[1] AWD Note: Including use of the UN as a front or source for foreign intelligence services.

[2] AWD Note: Reduce compartmentalization contributes substantially to team spirit and a sense of integration among the multinational contingent commanders and staffs.

[3] AWD Note: Can also reduce disclosure of embarrassing facts, and reduce accountability.

[4] AWD Note: The following is the order, for better or worse, by which approval is usually sought: P5 (the Permanent Five members of the Security Council, starting with the S1 – the only superpower, the US), SC15 (the 15 members of the Security Council), TC20-30 (troop contributing nations to the PKO, whose number may vary) and MS185 (all the UN Member States).

Unfortunately, the UN has not adequately prepared itself to deal with secret intelligence in a systematic fashion. In comparison with nation states and military organisations (such as NATO), little consideration has been given to the matter. The UN does not have guidelines to govern the methods of information-gathering, to determine which material is to be kept secret, at what classification level and with what means, to uphold rules of secrecy or workable procedures for declassification. Often the character of a PKO's information policy is decided by the commander in the field or by each contingent, or even each individual, differently.

The tension between secrecy and openness, between information ends and means, makes a study of the problem not only interesting academically, but also potentially useful in practice. As background, Table 2 describes the basic components of the 'intelligence cycle': planning, gathering, processing, and disseminating. With each stage, the UN has requirements and limitations that need to be reconciled, as well as secrecy issues to be addressed. This conceptual, staged view of the intelligence process provides a logical manner to study the major issues. In detail and examine the balance to be achieved. While the planning stage is important, the major issues are found in the other stages, starting with information gathering.

	Purpose	**Methods**	**UN Limits**	**UN Issues**
Planning	Decide needs, methods, limits, and limitations.	Prioritise needs, key sources, key targets.	Complaints from nations about infringement.	Secrecy helps prevent detection or manipulation.
Gathering	Obtain raw data, learn history, have situational awareness.	Obtain information from multiple open, gray, and covert sources.	Abide by international laws, avoid association with Intel. orgs.	Active vs. passive monitoring; avoid cover, distortion; protect sources.
Processing	Understand actors, create contextual understanding, develop scenarios, policy options.	Corroborate, synthesise, analyse. Identify gaps, apply creative thinking.	Avoid partiality, excessive criticism, over or under-prediction.	Degree of openness about results of analysis.
Dissemination	Take action, demonstrate competence in field and at HQ.	Communicate to right person in time—uni, multi, broadcast.	Sharing with other parties (equally?), sensitivity to parties concerns.	Protect sources & methods, honour security guidelines from members.

Table 2. Stages in the Intelligence Cycle

Information-Gathering

Often the United Nations must engage in information-gathering activities that could be termed 'borderline' or in the 'grey zone.' What are the limits of this intelligence grey zone, in theory and practice? The balance point is, obviously, dependent on the situation, but some basic principles can be established. The wide spectrum of intelligence, gathering activities is illustrated schematically in Figure 3. On the left are the non-controversial (white) activities and on the right those which are prohibited and generally associated with more secrecy (black), Even in the white area, the UN PKO's must generally have the approval of conflicting parties, or at least that of the host state. These include setting up permanent observation posts, installing sensors, and overseeing certain areas for reconnaissance purposes. The black areas are 'out of bounds' for the UN, for example, hiring of agents who misrepresent themselves to authorities, theft of documents, extortion to obtain information, etc. Since such activities can be categorically dismissed, the most interesting studies can be made in the grey area. The limitations on intelligence gathering are legal as well as moral, political, and practical.

Permitted	**Questionable**	**Prohibited**
(White)	(Grey)	(Black)

Visual Observation
- Observation posts   - Observation after forced entry
     - Vehicular observation   - Observers concealed or camouflaged
        - Aerial reconnaissance   - Observers out of mission area

Sensors
- Visible (video) - Infrared (IR), radar, X-ray, satellite
     - Ground sensors (acoustic/seismic)

Human Communications
- UN personnel: - Clearly, identified   - Unidentified   -Undercover/disguised
- Informants: - Unpaid   - Rewarded   - Paid (agents)
       - Radio message interception (SIGINT)   - wiretaps
         * clear and encoded message's

Documents (read/copy/distribute)
- public   - private   - confidential   - stolen

         Passive   **Active**

◄———————— **Overt** ——————————— **Covert** ———————►

Figure 1. Information-Gathering Spectrum from Permitted to Prohibited

The UN, being a law-abiding, as well as partly law-creating, organisation, pays careful attention to the legal limits placed upon its field missions. To begin with, the UN Charter in Article 2(7) states that:

> Nothing contained in the present Charter shall authorise the United Nations to intervene in matters which are essentially within the domestic jurisdiction of any state ... except for the enforcement measures under Chapter VII.

While this provision is often interpreted as a prohibition, it is in fact, neutral. The Charter itself may not be used as a basis to authorise intervention (except for UN enforcement measures), but one can argue that the UN acting on its own authority or based on customary international law (e.g., the implied powers doctrine accepted by the International Court of Justice [7]) may selectively make such interventions (including information–gathering at an early stage). This is an important argument, since modern conflicts are largely internal in character,[5] and UN intervention is becoming increasingly significant and frequent in such important areas as human rights and preventive action, which require in-depth monitoring of domestic affairs and early intervention.

A significant legal and political constraint on UN behaviour arises from the mandate of the mission, usually supplied by the Security Council, and the Status of Mission Agreement (SOMA) or the Status of Forces Agreement (SOFA) into which the UN enters with the host state and/or the local authorities, including the combatants. The agreement almost always stipulates that the UN PKO and its members will 'respect all local laws and regulations' (which could presumably include laws on monitoring of military activities). The standard SOMA/SOFA also requires that they 'refrain from any action or activity incompatible with the impartial nature of their duties.'[8] PKO's are usually exceedingly careful not to wander too far from the mandate or original

---

[5] Editors' Note: For the year 2002, the *Map of World Conflict & Human Rights* published by the PIOOM Project of Leiden University included 175 violent political (internal) conflicts, 79 low intensity conflicts (<1000 dead per year) and 23 severe low intensity conflicts (>1000 dead per year). Millions of displaced persons across 66 countries, plagues and epidemics in 59 countries, food scarcity in 33 countries, and water scarcity as well as crime issues across many countries required UN recognition of 20 declared complex emergencies across 32 countries in the year 2002.

agreement, either in their monitoring or other actions, for fear of jeopardising the consent or co-operation of the parties.

An excellent, but tragic, example of the 'sovereignty constraints' on information gathering and sharing was provided by the UN Iran-Iraq Military Observer Group (UNIIMOG), prior to the Iraqi invasion of Kuwait.[9] The mission was mandated in 1988 to monitor the cease-fire between Iran and Iraq. Since the July 1990 movement of Iraqi troops was southbound toward Kuwait rather than eastbound toward Iran, the UN observers could not officially report on them. UNIIMOG monitors saw plenty of evidence of an Iraqi build-up far in excess of that required for training or exercise purposes. Housed at the Shatt Al Arab hotel, beside the southern terminus of the main Iraqi railway, UN team number 6, for instance, obtained a clear view of extensive Iraqi preparations, including the establishment of third–line maintenance and supply depots, and the steady flow of tons of military equipment (including tanks, trucks, and rockets) and thousands of personnel. But the UN mission headquarters, located in Baghdad, had imposed a reporting ban on any activities and equipment directed toward the south, The Iraqi government threatened to expel the UN if it did not comply.[10]

The then-UN secretary-general Javier Perez de Cuellar would later write: 'The major powers knew in advance that a very large Iraqi force was moving towards the Kuwaiti border. I did not have such knowledge...I failed to anticipate Saddam Hussein's aggressive intent'.[11] While Perez de Cuellar fails to mention the evidence in the possession of UN peacekeepers that could have been sought, he does draw an important lesson:

> The United Nations and the secretary-general, in particular, should have better sources of information on developments such as large troop movements that pose a threat to the peace, And the United Nations, as much or more than national governments, should have the skill and insight to understand the import of such information and take appropriate preventive action.[12]

Information about armaments, their movements and sources, is a common need in proactive PKO's. In some cases, the importation of weapons constitutes a violation of peace agreements or Security Council resolutions. In most cases, they are destabilising to the peace and even threatening to the UN personnel. The UN faced this challenge as early as 1962 in the Congo, when the UN Force Commander asked the Military Information Branch (MIB) to conduct a 'special mission' to gather intelligence from surrounding African countries. The Branch nominated a French-speaking Canadian officer to undertake this mission. The Canadian contingent commander, however, refused to accept the request, stating that Canadian personnel could not participate in missions outside of the Congo without the approval of their government, and that approval was unlikely to be forthcoming considering the covert nature of the task.' In the Congo operation, more peacekeepers were killed than in any other venture (until the ongoing UN operations in the former Yugoslavia), thus making the development of the MIB a critical requirement even at that time. Many lessons on the opportunities, uses, and limitations of UN intelligence-gathering can be learned from this early experience.

Case Study: The UN Operation in the Congo[6]

In other PKO's, the UN fared better, in terms of the amount of US imagery data shared: for instance, satellite photos were shown (not given) to the Force Commander of the UN Emergency Force in the mid-1960's, U-2 aerial photographs of Cuba were given to the secretary-general's Military Adviser during the Cuban Missile Crisis of October 1962 and satellite imagery was shared with selected personnel (mainly from NATO countries) in the UN Protection Force in the former Yugoslavia during 1993 – 1995. In the Somalia operation in 1993 – 1994, the United States provided a great deal of information through its Intelligence Support Element (ISE). Indeed, modern peacekeeping in the 1990's has experienced a revolution in intelligence sharing, as well as intelligence gathering.

Information-Gathering in Modern Peacekeeping Operations

The end of the Cold War gave rise to an expansion in the mandates, scope, and capabilities of United Nations peacekeeping operations. Until 1992, the largest and most complex such operation had been ONUC, with nearly 20.000 peacekeepers at its maximum. The UN force in the former Yugoslavia

---

[6] Editors' Note: As Chapter 15 provides the original case study with full details and notes, four pages of replicative material have been deleted.

(UNPROFOR, 1992–1995) employed at one point more than 40.000 troops. The mandates for most modern peacekeeping operations are broad, and have included sanctions monitoring, the protection of so-called 'safe areas,' ensuring the delivery of humanitarian aid, support to refugees, elections monitoring, infrastructure development, etc. Today, the peacekeeping forces employed are not drawn merely from the usual 'middle powers' and non-aligned states, which were the staple of the classical peacekeeping, but now include major powers such as Britain, France, and, to some extent, Russia and the United States (which has supplied US/UN peacekeepers in Macedonia and Somalia, and civilians in other operations, such as in Cambodia, Angola, Mozambique). These technologically advanced nations brought in new means and methods. Also, the end of Cold War rivalry reduced the fear in the UN Secretariat of the previous criticism from major powers (especially the USSR) that the UN peacekeepers were overstepping their bounds.

Another impetus for intelligence–gathering in the new world of internal, ethnic conflict was that the UN often found itself in a vulnerable position where conflicting parties would take advantage of the naivete or vulnerability of the UN. In the former Yugoslavia, Serb, Croatian, and Muslim forces have frequently probed the UN to uncover and benefit from the UN's knowledge gaps and other weaknesses. (On several occasions the Serb forces actually took UN peacekeepers hostage and used them as human shields against bombing raids by NATO.) In traditional peacekeeping, the policy and practice of troop contributors was to minimise or ignore the military intelligence component because of the belief that intelligence gathering could undermine or compromise the principle of impartiality. But in the 1990s, with the PKO's functioning under more trying circumstances, the attitudes have changed. Intelligence personnel from the middle powers (e.g., Canada) and major powers (e.g., France, UK) were increasingly sent to dangerous places such as Croatia, Bosnia, Kosovo, Iraq, Haiti, and Somalia. Interestingly, UN headquarters in New York City rarely or never asked for such personnel, but once in the field, intelligence officers were much used and appreciated by colleagues, both in the field and at UN headquarters. It was found, for example, that professional intelligence officers had better knowledge of intelligence procedures and better access to foreign intelligence sources and agencies. Those who had security clearances were able to obtain information that otherwise would not have been available. This gave rise, on occasion, to some awkward, if not ridiculous situations. For example, in UNPROFOR, a Canadian peacekeeper with NATO

342

clearance received U.S. satellite photographs (useful to determine his operational deployment) but he was not permitted to show the images to his UN commander, who was a French officer.

The incorporation of military information/intelligence units became common in modern PKO's. In several recent operations, these sections have been labelled as G2, in accordance with standard military practice.[13] In the Rwanda operation (UNAMIR) in 1995, after the genocide, the G2 incorporated six intelligence officers. The Haiti operation was among the best-staffed operations in terms of intelligence, where there were 29 such officers, all Canadian. In Somalia, the UNOSOM 'Information Management Office,' referred to as 'U2' by U.S. forces, was significant, with over a dozen personnel, but was dwarfed by the US's own information collection agencies there.[14]

After the Cold Wax, the UN still had many challenges and limitations in dealing with secret intelligence. In a lessons-learned seminar on Somalia in 1995, participants suggested that 'the United Nations must continue to move beyond its earlier attitude and reluctance with respect to the propriety of 'intelligence.'[15]

In large field operations, major troop contributors sometimes took matters into their own hands, after finding that the United Nations was too limited or slow in intelligence gathering. One such example is an undercover operation in Bosnia-Herzegovina (B-H), where UN peacekeepers were under constant threat.[16] In March 1994, troop–contributing nations to UNPROFOR deemed it important to learn about territory and terrain in 8-H areas where the UN was not present–about 70 percent of the country at the time. While the UN had, in theory, complete freedom of movement, its vehicles and personnel were routinely prohibited from proceeding through the array of checkpoints. An 'intelligence gap' endangered the safety of peacekeepers, because of possible weaponry, forces, and supplies in the restricted areas. To gain this information, several European troop contributors to the UN force (including Britain and France) assembled a group of individuals and put them under cover.

The group presented themselves to various Bosnian authorities as members of a European tourist association. They explained that the war would eventually end and that Yugoslavia would once again become a major tourist centre, potentially the 'playground of' Europe.' They needed to scout out various possible resort centres, survey the landscape (including climbing hills and following hiking trails), examine the state of repair of buildings (which future tourists mould presumably inhabit), check the conditions and capacities of the roads (to see if buses (or tanks) could travel on them), etc. While under this cover, they moved about B-H, adding greatly to their knowledge and intelligence.

This operation was almost certainly done without the UN's authorisation. The UN has a policy of not carrying out undercover activities, but nation states can assume the responsibility themselves. Under certain specific circumstances, when lives are threatened, this practice can be tolerated by the UN. There have been, for example, many special forces and undercover units in the former Yugoslavia, numbering in the hundreds or perhaps thousands of personnel and presumably many intelligence-gathering operations undisclosed to the UN.

The PKO's in Somalia (UN Operations in Somalia: UNOSOM I, II, and III) bad an even greater intelligence component. Somalia was called a 'Humint rich' environment. In the UN's first operation (UNOSOM I, 1992–1993), some fifty UN military observers (UNMO's) were deployed. The Somali people offered much information in casual conversation. While the force commander did not authorise payments to locals by UNMO's, he did suggest that, as an expression of gratitude, the UNMO's could present tea bags or similar gifts to those who had been helpful.[17] The United States intervention (UNITAF) led to the mounting, under US auspices, of an enormous intelligence effort.

At one point, the major target was the leader of one faction, Mohamed Farah Aideed, who, after declared a 'wanted' criminal by the United States and the UN, went into hiding to avoid arrest. Despite much technology and the deployment of its specially trained forces (a Ranger battalion), the United States was not able to find, let alone apprehend, Aideed. In the UN's second Somalia operation (UNOSOM II, 1993 – 1995), the UN did, in fact, pay informants and agents for the regular provision of information. The chief administrative officer kept a list of such persons in his safe, along with amounts paid to each.[18] Thus, the UN may well have crossed into the 'black zone' of prohibited activities, but a, final judgement of its action would entail a more careful examination of the UN's circumstances, needs and methods.

'Human Rights Monitoring': An Important New Information Source

One of the most important expansions in modern peacekeeping has been the monitoring of human rights within states, which necessarily involves a certain degree of secrecy. UN human rights investigators, often part of a larger PKO, must encourage their witnesses to describe horrible acts they saw, experienced or even committed. Often, they must assure the witnesses that their names and identities will be kept confidential. In Guatemala, two UN bodies were created to oversee human rights: a Truth Commission,[19] whose mandate was to investigate atrocities committed during the 36 days of civil war (up to 1994), and MINUGUA, which investigates current abuses (since 1994). Both bodies had to take precautions to ensure that witnesses willing to provide information not be identified. For example, human rights observers/investigators had to make sure they were not being followed before attending meetings with witnesses and informants. In fact, the Truth Commission hired carefully-selected Guatemalans, who made themselves inconspicuous by driving in their own unassuming pickup trucks, dressing in ordinary Guatemalan fashion and blending into the crowd, Many of the meetings were conducted at bars and at night, a far cry from the traditional UN observer patrolling under a UN flag and in conditions of maximum visibility.

The Guatemalan military has kept not only the UN monitors under surveillance but also officials of the Guatemalan government. While peace was being negotiated in the early 1990s, UN secretary-general Perez de Cuellar recalls, the Guatemalan President 'found it necessary to communicate with my representative, Francesc Vendrell, through a used car dealer because he knew that all of his telephones were tapped' by the military.[20]

The Truth Commission had a stronger mandate than MINUGUA for investigation: it could exhume bodies, while MINUGUA could 'look at but not touch' the evidence supplied to it. But because the Truth Commission was not allowed to assign blame to individuals ('name names') in its reports, it often employed a system of pseudonyms in its internal documents, and still keeps the links to real names carefully secured in safes.

In Haiti, UN human rights monitors had the difficult task of monitoring the local police units to which they were attached. Naturally, the Haitian police officers were wary about talking about the beating of detainees and other forms

345

of abuses they may have witnessed or committed. But by combining confessions with a system of support, rehabilitation, and confidentiality, UN officials found that 'the police were dying to talk.... We just had to create a space where they felt comfortable.'[21]

Human rights NGO's have often supplied the UN with important information. Perez de Cuellar recently revealed that before making each trip abroad to countries known to commit human rights violations, 'I was briefed confidentially by Amnesty International on individual cases of' human rights abuse on which I might usefully intervene, It was my practice to take along a list of such cases on my travels ...'[22] He also highlighted the importance of secrecy:

> The secretary-general can quite often intervene confidentially
> with a regime and gain the freedom, or at least an improvement
> in conditions, of individual political prisoners. Yet a critical
> public report can jeopardise his ability to perform this useful
> service.[23]

The element of secrecy became very important when Perez de Cuellar had to deal with the murky and tense world of hostage takers as he attempted to gain the release of those held in the Middle East. For example, a UN peacekeeper, Lt. Col. William Higgins of the U.S. Marines, was abducted in 1988 by an unknown group calling itself the 'Organisation for the Oppressed of the World.' Under-Secretary-General Philip Goulding met secretly with senior Arab officials but was unable to obtain the officer's release. A videotape, which was eventually released to a newspaper in Beirut, Lebanon, was analysed to reveal that it was indeed Colonel Higgins's body hanging from a scaffold.[24]

In dealing with hostage taking, it is important for the UN to know what governments are doing to save their nationals who are being held hostage, but, as might be expected, governments are reluctant to reveal their intelligence sources (for fear of compromising them) or their actions (for fear of exposing them, such as deals with terrorists). A case in point concerned VN efforts to release British hostages, including Alec Collett, a British journalist writing for the UN Relief and Works Agency in Palestine, who was taken hostage in 1985. Perez de Cuellar notes in his memoirs: 'We kept in close touch with British authorities who were making their own efforts to free Collett although they never informed the United Nations of what they were doing.'[25] Like Higgins, Collett is thought to have been murdered. The hostage takers claimed that Collett was a British spy, working for the United States on behalf of Israel, a lethal combination of allegations. This highlights how the UN must be ever-so-careful in permitting even the perception of intelligence agency complicity in sensitive mission areas such as the Middle East.

A more successful and encouraging outcome was obtained with the release of other hostages (including British citizen Terry Waite, and American Terry Anderson) in the fall of 1991. In top secrecy, Perez de Cuellar sent his 'special adviser,' Giandomenico Picco, to meetings with Iranian and Libyan leaders, as well as to engage in secret negotiations with underground groups in Lebanon. While enduring blindfolds, endless car rides, and a risk of himself being taken hostage, Picco was the channel for the exchange of secret information between Israel and Iran, as well as others during the episode. His efforts proved quite successful.

Information Analysis and Dissemination

As information is gathered, it must be analysed for purposes of verification, corroboration, and extraction of the most important details, as well as to identify new requirements and information methods. Even the analysis of open information occasionally needs to be, in hazardous conditions, a secret activity. For one, keeping secret the lists of open sources and names of people might be required to prevent others from tampering with them. More importantly, nations or conflicting parties could object if they found out that the United Nations might be analysing their behaviour. Should the analysis involve scenario building, including worst-case estimates, prediction, and passing judgement on a leader's character (which is often necessary to make realistic assessments and predictions), conflicting parties would find this activity offensive. Some governments might object, based on fears of UN interference, and label the activity as UN spying.

For instance, when the Office for Research and the Collection of Information (ORCI) was established in the UN Secretariat in 1987, a group of nine conservative United States senators openly objected to its creation and proffered a bill in the Senate to withhold more US dues in the amount that the office would cost.[26] They claimed that ORCI would be used as a base for

Soviet espionage, even though the office was placed under an African (James Jonah from Sierra Leone), and its information gathering was basically limited to taking newspaper reports from the wire services. But more amenable leaders in the U.S. government prevailed. State Department officials convinced the senators of the lack of foundation for their fears, and the bill was dropped. Still, the UN has to take into account such domestic concerns, especially when those maintaining the fears have their hands on the national purse strings.

Yet, the UN has little competency in analysis, scenario building, and prediction. Desk officers do virtually none of this, being overloaded with simple information gathering and a minimal of organising. The strongest analytical capacity exists within the Information and Research (I&R) Unit of the Situation Centre, which is part of the Department of Peacekeeping Operations (DPKO). Though small, with only four 'intelligence' officers, it has the greatest 'reach' in terms of information gathering and analysis because these individuals are 'connected' to national intelligence systems, having been seconded from them. Created in 1994 with one US intelligence officer, the unit grew to include four officers drawn from four of the five permanent members of the UN Security Council (France, Russia, UK, and the United States).[27] The analysts who work there unashamedly, though unofficially, call themselves intelligence officers, which is not surprising since they are mostly drawn from the intelligence branches of their militaries. They have produced important information/intelligence reports that have gone well beyond the scope of regular UN reports, including information on arms flows and covert assistance from states to the conflicting parties and leaders. They have evaluated the motivations of contending parties, prepared threat assessments, and made other forecasts.

With the UN's decision to phase out from service in DPKO the gratis officers (whose salaries are paid by their national governments), the future of this important unit is in doubt. Many developing nations, which could not afford to send gratis officers, were resentful of the over-representation of Western governments in the Department. Secrecy in the workings and deliberations of the Security Council, the body primarily responsible for guiding UN peace operations, is a matter of contention in the UN. The five permanent members (China, France, Russia, United Kingdom, and the United States) began in 1988 to engage in intensive and frequent private consultations. This process, while welcome as a measure of cooperation between them, became formalised with

348

frequent closed-door meetings, freezing many UN members and the world public out of the picture. The Security Council currently meets far more regularly in closed, rather than open, sessions in a private room next to the Council chambers. Non-Council members cannot attend unless they are specifically invited or involved in the conflict. This practice of strict secrecy naturally creates suspicion and apprehension among other UN members, who remind the Security Council that, according to Article 24 of the Charter, the council 'acts on their behalf', but, ironically, doesn't let them know what they are planning. Countries like Canada, which often have military and civilian personnel in the field under UN command, feel that the information sharing is inadequate.[28] UN members, including General Assembly itself, have repeatedly called for more transparency in the Security Council's deliberations. Gradual improvements, such as more frequent briefings of non-members and more publicly available documentation, have been made.

Confidentiality

The ability to carefully and wisely distinguish between what should be open and what should be secret (and for how long) is the key to creating confidence within both the UN and the international community. An effective confidentiality system is necessary to maintain the proper balance, whether in the Security Council, at UN headquarters, or in held operations. In this regard, the UN system is weak in comparison with that of most governments, and devotes few resources to it. While the UN Secretariat has 'categories' of information confidentiality (UN-restricted, confidential, secret, and top secret), specific means for handling of information in these categories is not recognised or followed, in terms of either physical security (locks) or dissemination and declassification procedures. Some PKO's instituted their own classification systems with more than the four categories. Sometimes the UN is overly secretive (even about trivial documents over forty years old) and sometimes-sensitive information is shared indiscriminately. Numerous leaks have caused some governments to consider the UN as a sieve, Javier Perez de Cuellar, from his vantage point atop the UN hierarchy from 1981 to 1991, admits to this:

> The diplomatic missions have always felt that security in the Secretariat is lax and that any confidential information provided to the Secretariat would quickly be widely circulated, In general, this is true...[29]

That the Soviets, as well as other employees, at the UN reported regularly to their national governments on important developments was well known. Perez de Cuellar notes: 'As long as the Cold War continued, Soviet staff members, whether KGB or not, owed their first loyalty to Moscow rather than to the United Nations ... As a result, and to their understandable frustration, the Soviet nationals in my office were excluded from sensitive functions.'[30] Twenty years earlier, secretary-general U Thant sometimes purposefully used his Soviet Under-Secretary-General to convey selected information to the Soviet government, rather than going through official channels.

Within the Executive Office of the secretary-general, confidential information is usually handled more carefully. Perez de Cuellar reports that 'in dealing with sensitive problems, I relied on the support of a very small staff in whose loyalty I had complete confidence.'[31] He adds that his record of keeping secrets helped gain the confidence of the US government, which occasionally provided his office with intelligence assessments.

> One such incidence occurred in early April 1988, when a representative of the Bureau of Intelligence and Research of the US Department of State provided my chef de cabinet, Virendra Dayal, with a comprehensive assessment of the status of the conflict between Iran and Iraq. The information provided gave me reason to think that just possibly, after months of frustration, the time might be approaching when a cease-fire could be obtained.[32]

The question has been raised in the UN whether it should undertake formal agreements with governments for the regular sharing of information/intelligence,[33] thereby increasing the amount of information that the UN could count on. Governments currently share information with the UN on a 'need to know basis,' for example, when the governments think that the UN needs to know. Some UN officials would prefer a pipeline of regular information, so that they could depend on a constant input from various sources and make the choice themselves as to which information is useful. The UN could then better corroborate information among different sources and decrease the danger that information is provided in a partial, biased form with interpretation and fact combined. The disadvantage could be that the UN might be formally restricted on how it shares this information, once received. Also, the UN could suffer from information overload (perhaps deliberately by the supplier), given the secretariat's lack of staff and expertise in intelligence management.

What, then, should be the UN's policy on secrecy? A balance between secrecy and openness obviously needs to be achieved. While information secrecy should be situation-dependent, guidelines for the classification of information are valuable. The emphasis should be on openness,[34] but, in cases where secrecy is warranted, it should be strictly maintained. One approach or 'rule' is suggested here.

Information should be open unless by divulging it, the UN would:

    a. result in death or injury to individuals;
    b. bring about failure of a UN mission or mandate;
    c. violate the right to privacy of one or more individuals; or
    d. compromise confidential sources or methods .

The degree of secrecy (restricted, confidential, secret, top secret) would depend on the extent of the threat of information release. With each higher category, the degree of security is increased through better physical security (e.g., using safes, restricted areas, etc.), closer monitoring of documents (e.g., by numbering each copy), and routine checks by an authority made responsible for the confidentiality system (something that has been done in the newly-established Organisation for the Prohibition of Chemical Weapons, located in The Hague).

The UN should also have a smooth procedure for declassification. Currently, the UN archives have a 20-year rule, though any information marked secret or top secret must be reviewed by all the relevant departments (DPKO, DPA, etc.) even after that period has passed. In practice, this system has many failings, and requests for the declassification may take years to wind through the system. Many national government models could be reviewed by the UN as it seeks to establish a more robust and yet flexible confidentiality regime.

UNSCOM

The United Nations Special Commission (UNSCOM) was the most intrusive

351

and extensive monitoring operation in UN history, with a substantial intelligence component. Although not a peacekeeping mission but a disarmament operation established under the enforcement provisions of the UN Charter (Chapter VII), it shared many features in common with PKO's. In particular, it conducted monitoring in accordance with Security Council resolutions and with written agreement from the host state, for example, the cease-fire agreement which included Iraq's pledge to destroy all its weapons of mass destruction. To carry out in-country monitoring by international (UN) officials, UNSCOM needed, as do peacekeepers, at least a minimum of cooperation and consent from the host state. This was not always forthcoming. In the end it was denied.

The UNSCOM experience provides many examples and lessons in intelligence directly relevant to peacekeeping. UNSCOM demonstrated several new and ambitious means of information gathering, analysis, and dissemination. In pushing the limits of the grey zone of UN information gathering, it helped clarify some of the boundaries between recommended and prohibited behaviour. Many novel features and significant pitfalls of the Iraq operation were revealed by a former UNSCOM Chief Inspector, Scott Ritter, after his resignation in August 1998.[35]

One area of UNSCOM innovation was the extensive use of high technology to gather information. High-tech surveillance devices helped considerably to find hidden weapons systems and components in unlikely buildings and locations, both above and below ground and even under water. Some UNSCOM missions included US Navy divers who scoured the bottom of certain Iraqi rivers to find weapons components. UNSCOM used US high-altitude U-2 planes to cover vast tracks of Iraqi land, an activity that helped spot suspicious sites and vehicle movements.[36] UNSCOM also received high-resolution US satellite imagery, which helped to provide an estimate (downwards) of the number of undeclared mobile missile launchers and to discover camouflaged roads to sensitive sites. Germany provided helicopters with ground penetrating radar in an effort to discover Iraqi SCUD missiles and metal components buried under sand, though no missiles were found.

UNSCOM installed video cameras at sensitive dual-use sites (like foundries) to make sure that no undeclared activities (e.g., missile fabrication) were taking place. These cameras and other unmanned sensors transmitted information continuously to the Baghdad Monitoring and Verification Centre (BMVC) to permit surveillance of key alarm indicators, such as sound and heat from machine operation. Video cameras were also employed during inspections, and even in negotiations with Iraqi authorities, as a manner of recording personal responses and remarks for later playback. In one inspection, UNSCOM personnel filmed a convoy of heavy tractor-trailers leaving a site that m as about to be inspected. These transports carried the unmistakable forms of Calutrons, proving that Iraq had sought to produce highly enriched uranium.

Signals intelligence also became a part of the UNSCOM effort. Britain supplied sensitive communication scanners for surveillance of Iraqi military communications, in an effort to reveal the Iraqi weapons concealment mechanism. The BMVC itself employed a variety of high-tech counterintelligence measures, including electronically swept facilities with double-door access and encrypted telephone links to UN headquarters.[37] Inspection teams in the field also had satellite telephones for direct communications to New York, which were particularly useful during tense stand-offs with Iraqi authorities. An early incident occurred when a group of UNSCOM inspectors were immobilised in a Baghdad parking lot after they had uncovered secret files on Iraq's nuclear capability. A US national, David Kay, fearing the confiscation of documents, faxed revealing documents directly to Washington, thereby bypassing the UN in New York. Iraq used this instance, and others, to assert that UNSCOM was providing a cover for US espionage, and Kay was later reprimanded by UN officials.

On-site inspections were the backbone of UNSCOM's investigations and international inspectors had unprecedented rights. Based on Security Council resolutions, which invoked the enforcement provisions of the UN Charter, UNSCOM could conduct inspections virtually anywhere, anytime, without right of refusal. In practice, UNSCOM had to be sensitive to Iraqi sovereignty and requests. A cat and mouse game was played, with Iraq usually losing out. From inspections, for instance, UNSCOM exposed Iraq's undeclared chemical weapons and facilities, its nuclear weapons program, and significant elements of its biological weapons program.

UNSCOM also demonstrated the great utility of document searches. Initially the Iraqis were caught off guard, not having sequestered documentation, as it had with the actual weapons and other hardware. The examination of secret

353

documents and correspondence in government files (especially those found in the Agriculture ministry) were especially valuable in tracing Iraq's clandestine nuclear weapons program. Such Iraqi paperwork also helped reveal the nature of Iraq's concealment effort, which had to be carefully co-ordinated among various Iraqi organisations. From vehicle manifests, for example, the movements of certain illicit cargo were tracked. On several occasions, UNSCOM inspectors successfully pursued men fleeing with large bundles of documents (labelled 'Top Secret') under their arms. In addition to translators, UNSCOM employed computer experts to recover deleted files from Iraqi hard drives, an activity that proved especially useful in uncovering information on Iraqi ballistic missile programs.

The greatest revelations, however, came from several high-level defectors, especially Hussein Kamal, a son-in-law of Saddam Hussein, who was in charge of the Military industrial Commission. In August 1995 meetings in Jordan with UNSCOM head Rolf Ekeus, he described key elements of Iraq's concealment mechanism, and told of previously unknown bioweapons projects, hidden ballistic missiles, and large document caches. As a result, UNSCOM obtained at his chicken farm 1.5 million pages of hidden documentation (for which the Iraqi government blamed Hussein Kamal, saying he was acting without authorisation or government awareness in carrying out the programs described therein) and later found missile production tools at another farm.

Through the process of information sharing and cooperation with national intelligence agencies, UNSCOM found itself in the black (prohibited) zones. As an operation run by the UN, it had to maintain objectivity and impartiality, in both fact and international perception, in carrying out a specific mandate. But, one of Iraq's key allegations was that the UNSCOM employed CIA agents. This was consistently discounted in the West, but subsequently revealed to be true by Inspector Ritter. In fact, during one inspection directed at the Special Presidential Guard, UNSCOM was said to have on its inspection team nine CIA paramilitary covert operators who were alleged to have supported a failed coup plot by units of the Guard.

UNSCOM had to be careful not to be too closely associated with the United States because it was routinely called an American pawn by the government of Iraq, on whom it depended for inspection privileges and cooperation. The US domination also boded poorly with Russia and France, who thought that UNSCOM was being used as a tool of US foreign policy. Indeed, on several occasions overly intrusive UNSCOM inspections were apparently designed to serve as a pretext for US military attacks. Yet, some association with the United States was inevitable. Many UNSCOM inspectors and its deputy head were from the United States, and UNSCOM relied heavily on the United States for technology, inspection personnel, and funding.

A more obvious transgression of UN impartiality was the sharing of UNSCOM intelligence with the military intelligence service of Israel, Iraq's mortal enemy. Ritter himself originally proposed making contact with Israel. The idea was dismissed in 1992, but by 1994 the Executive Chairman of UNSCOM had a channel to the Israeli military intelligence service, Aman, which produced a subsequent stream of information. Ritter arranged for US U-2 images to be delivered to Israeli intelligence through UNSCOM in exchange for Israeli help in interpreting them, so that inspection targets could be more accurately identified. This imagery could potentially be put to other uses by Israel, for example, for future targeting during military operations, or for espionage and sabotage. Indeed, Israel was eager to monitor Saddam Hussein's movements and even passed this information on to Ritter. It also tipped off UNSCOM about an illegal shipment of gyroscopes, enough to provide guidance systems for a dozen missiles, leading to their interception in Jordan with the help of the Jordanian government.

UNSCOM also developed a substantial analytical capability. After its creation in 1991, it initially depended heavily on U.S. information analysis. But after the establishment of an Information Assessment Unit (IAU), it was able to rely more on its own facts and estimates, and those from alternate intelligence sources and agencies. The United States then increasingly sought information from UNSCOM. Secrecy measures were adopted by UNSCOM, not only in its dealings with foreign intelligence agencies, but also in its relations with Iraq itself. Two secret agreements were negotiated between the UN and Iraq on the modalities and limits of UN inspections: the agreement of 21 June 1996 negotiated by Rolf Ekeus, and a secret protocol of 23 February 1998 resulting from the trip of Kofi Annan to Baghdad.[38] As an organisation devoted to transparency, and with a UN Charter that provides that all international agreements should be open, the use of secret memoranda and agreements seems highly duplicitous and easily leads to a loss of credibility in the UN when exposed.

UNSCOM's experience shows the many pitfalls of overly aggressive intelligence-gathering. It also allows some general rules to be proposed.

First, the UN should preferably not use deception in its information gathering, though surprise plans and non-identification of inspectors can fall in the acceptable (grey) zone. (Under most arms control verification regimes, the host state has the right to reject certain inspectors.)

Second, the UN should be open to receiving information from defectors but should not be encouraging them.

Third, signals intelligence should be used only to the extent justified by the inspection mandate. Inspections should be restricted to its mandate, and member states not be allowed to use inspections for other objectives.[7]

Fourth, and finally, while the UN nay retain secrets, it should not make secret agreements with governments, especially the inspected state.

Information for International Security

Analysed information, of both a secret and open nature (i.e., intelligence), is required in UN peacekeeping operations. Yet, severe limits and many shortcomings impede the present system for information gathering, analysis, and dissemination. Some limits are for valid ethical reasons. The United Nations should avoid 'black' areas, the covert activities that are sometimes associated with national intelligence agencies. These include a wide range of nefarious actions, such as the use of fronts, covers, and deception (i.e., the common elements of spying). Bribery, blackmail, distorted propaganda, and

---

[7] For example, inspection targets should be chosen to meet valid inspection goals and not for other national or international purposes. UN bodies, when co-operating with major powers, should not be dominated by them, and instead always remain at arms length in perception and reality. Editors' note: we understand this to mean an absolute prohibition against any covert operatives from any country being part of the UN team.

double agents are similarly not to be considered.[39]   Immediately dissociated should be offensive covert operations, such as sabotage and character or person assassination, which are not part of the information/intelligence spectrum, but which are sometimes performed by some aggressive intelligence agencies.

The grey areas are harder to analyse and are situation dependent (see Figure 3). In threatening circumstances (e.g., the Rwandan genocide of 1994), the UN should be free to receive information volunteered by informants. While offering regular payments to them would be unwise, the UN should look seriously at helping to provide protection and asylum in a willing third state for important informants whose lives are at risk. In Rwanda, the UN ignored this possibility to its own detriment and disgrace, and to the unimaginable suffering of the Rwandese people.

Much information needs to be kept secret for a period of time. But secrecy for valid reasons (see Table 1) must be divorced from secrecy for other reasons (i.e., cover-ups). The UN can still have 'clean hands' while maintaining a secrecy regime, so long as it maintains high ethical principles. While deciding on the level of secrecy to be applied and for how long is sometimes difficult, the UN must face this important challenge.

With the end of the Cold War, an ironic situation developed in the intelligence field. The UN moved to centre stage in world affairs, with missions of greater scope and authority, and its need for accurate and timely intelligence increased proportionately. National intelligence agencies, on the other hand, became less crucial to international affairs, as the traditional Cold War spy games became less important. But the UN's intelligence function did not substantially expand, and the intelligence agencies in the West did not undergo a substantial contraction. At present, the United States government employs an intelligence community of over 40,000 persons in over a half dozen intelligence bodies. By comparison, the United Nations has only four full-time 'intelligence' officers[40] and these are not even on the UN payroll.[41]

The major nations have been reluctant to give the UN a greater intelligence mandate because to many of them, intelligence is power, and they believe their own power would be threatened by a UN that possessed real intelligence, especially intelligence they may themselves not have. But, an enlightened view would see international security as an essential prerequisite to national security

357

and the UN as an international institution that needs to be strengthened.[42]

Ultimately, more resources must be devoted to strengthening the UN's information/intelligence capacity if it is to engage in proactive peacekeeping and conflict resolution to prevent future wars, genocide's, and other crimes against humanity. The UN must be given the means, including information-gathering and analysis, to make manifest its goal, as stated in the opening words of the UN Charter, of 'saving succeeding generations from the scourge of war.'

Endnotes

[1] Major-General Carl von Horn, Commander of the UN Operation in the Congo (ONUC), made this remark in 1960. However, the term persisted informally in the operation, and the heads of the Military Information Branch (MIB) of the ONUC frequently called themselves Chief Intelligence officers. Source: UN archives, 'Congo Lessons: Special Report on ONUC operations up to 31 December 1960,' p. 83. [UN Archives, DAG-I /2.2.1:64]

[2] The definition of peacekeeping currently used by the UN is: 'the deployment of international military and civilian personnel to a. con6ict area, with the consent of the parties to the conflict, in order to: stop or contain hostilities or supervise the carrying out of a peace agreement.' (Source: http://www.un.org/Depts/DPKO). The definition of intelligence, as suggested here, indicates that national intelligence relates to national security and UN intelligence relates to international security, which is a broader concern but has a strong overlap with national security.

[3] While the term intelligence has not been used in the title of any official posts within the UN Secretariat, an indication of its greater acceptability is shown by the creation of the position 'Intelligence Analyst' in the Office of the Prosecutor of the International Criminal Tribunal for the Former Yugoslavia in 1997. The functions include 'in-depth research and analysis regarding criminal investigations of' the conflict of information obtained from multiple sources, ... preparing strategic or tactical level reports relating to the criminal aspect on persons under investigation, ...' Job Vacancy Announcement, ICTFY, The Hague, 24 November 1997.

[4] Dallaire was prevented by UN headquarters officials from using informants to their maximum. For instance, he was prohibited to grant asylum to a key informer who had offered to reveal Hutu plots *in extenso* in January 1994, three months before the slaughter of close to a million people (mostly Tutsis) in Rwanda, Dallaire, Boutros Boutros-Ghali (the secretary-general at. the time) and Kofi Annan (current secretary-

general and then Under-Secretary-General for Peacekeeping Operations), have said that a well-informed, rapid, and strong UN force might have saved the country from its horrible fate. [See Philip Gourevitch, 'The Genocide Fax: A Warning That Was Sent to the UN That Might Have Saved Rwanda. Who Chose to Ignore it?', *The New Yorker* 11 May 1998, p. 42.).

[5] Previous articles on the subject in the academic literature are: Hugh Smith, 'Intelligence and UN Peacekeeping,' *Survival*, Vol. 36, Autumn 1994, p. 174; 'Intelligence and Peace-Keeping: The UN Operation in the Congo 1960-64,' A. Walter Dorn and David J, H, Bell, *International Peacekeeping*, Vol. 2, No. 1, Spring 1995, p. 11; Per Eriksson, 'Intelligence in Peacekeeping Operations', *International Journal of intelligence and Counterintelligence*, Vol. 10, No. 1, Spring 1997, p. 1.

[6] Quoted from Conor Cruise O'Brien, *To Katanga and Back*, New York: Grosset and Dunlop, 1962, p. 76.

[7] In the *Reparation* case, the World Court stated: 'Under international law, the [UN] Organisation must be deemed to have those powers which, though not expressly provided in the Charter, are conferred upon it by necessary implication as being essential to the performance of its duties,' *ICJ Rep.*, 1949, p, 182. The doctrine of implied powers was also adopted in the *Certain Expenses* and the *Namibia* cases. Indeed, peacekeeping, with soldiers under the command of the UN secretary-general, is not explicitly provided for in the UN Charter either.

[8] The provisions on respecting local laws and refraining from incompatible activities is contained, for instance, in paragraph 6 of the 'Draft Model Status-of-Forces Agreement and Host Countries,' which is in circulation at the UN. The relevant rights granted to the UN under the model SOFA includes 'freedom of movement throughout the territory' (paragraph 12), freedom to import equipment (to be used exclusively by the PKO (paragraph I5), unrestricted communications (paragraph 11), and non-interference with mail (paragraph 11).

[9] This information was drawn from an interview with Reg Fountain, a Canadian military officer who served with UNIIMOG, Pearson Peacekeeping Centre, 11 February 1998.

[10] Once the invasion had begun, Iraq imposed a ban on UN military observers: they could not leave the country (from 2 August for a month or so), and no phone calls were permitted to arrive or be sent to Muslim countries. Conversations (such as those to Canada) were closely monitored.

[11] Javier Perez de Cuellar, *Pilgrimage for Peace: A secretary-general's Memoir* (New York: St. Martin's Press, 1997) pp. 237–238.

[12] Ibid.

[13] This convention is based on the Continental Staff System, where the headquarters is divided up into 6 branches, numbered one through six. One is personnel, two is intelligence, three is operations, four is logistics, five is civil/military affairs, and six is

communications and computers, The letter designator could be A, 6, J, N, or U, which designate the headquarters as either Air Force, Ground (or Army), Joint, Naval, or United Nations. Therefore, the G2 is army intelligence, the N3 is navy operations, and U2 would be UN peacekeeping force intelligence.

[14] An example of the use of the term 'U2' for UN intelligence and the U2 interaction with the U.S. information centre is provided in an After Action Report (AAR) by the Chief of Staff of the 10th Mountain Division dated 1 February 1993, available on the Centre for Army Lessons Learned (CALL-TRADOC, Ft. Leavenworth), Lessons Learned Information Warehouse (LLIW on CD ROM) on peace operations.

[15] Information obtained at the 'Comprehensive Seminar on Lessons Learned from United Nations Operation in Somalia (UNOSOM)' organised by the UN DPKO Lesson Learned Unit, 13 – I5 September 1995, Plainsboro, New Jersey.

[16] This description draws upon a conversation on 10 February 1998 with a senior Canadian peacekeeper who had served as Force Engineer in UNPROFOR.

[17] Ibid.

[18] Information provided by Douglas Mason, former UNOSOM Chief Administrative Officer, at the Comprehensive Seminar on the Lessons Learned from the United Nations Operation in Somalia (UNOSOM), held in 13–15 September 1995 in Plainsboro, New Jersey.

[19] The Truth Commission in Guatemala was created and organised by the UN, unlike the South African Truth Commission, which is purely national in origin and composition.

[20] Perez de Cuellar, *Pilgrimage*, p. 438.

[21] UN Department of Communications and Public Information. 'Two civilian missions: Monitoring human rights ... and a humanitarian mission distributing essential goods,' obtained from www,un.org/Depts/dpko/yir97/civilian.htxn on 2 April 1998.

[22] Perez de Cuellar, *Pilgrimage*, p. 6.

[23] Ibid., p. 407.

[24] Ibid., p. 104.

[25] Ibid., p. 100.

[26] *The New York Times*, 18 April 1987, p, 4.

[27] The composition of the I&R unit, consisting only of seconded nationals from the permanent five members of the Security Council, does create the potential problem that incoming information may be biased toward the interests of the UN's most powerful states. In practice, however, such natural biases can be taken into account and found acceptable because more information is generally better than less.

[28] Ambassador Robert Fowler, remarks at the Leger Seminar on 'The UN Security Council in the 1990s,' Department of Foreign Affairs and International Trade, 20 September 1996.

[29] Perez de Cuellar, *Pilgrimage*, p. 168.

---

[30] Ibid., p. 8.

[31] Ibid., p. 168.

[32] Ibid.

[33] A Memorandum of Understanding (MOU) would outline the procedures for information sharing and handling. For sensitive and secret information, this would require an upgrade of its confidentiality system. Such an MOU is being considered by staff in the UN's Situation Centre.

[34] Secrecy begets more secrecy, as exemplified by the phrase: 'O what a tangled web we weave once we begin to practice to deceive!'

[35] The information and allegations of Scott Ritter are described in detail in an article 'Scott Ritter's Private War,' *The New Yorker*, 9 November 1998, p, 54, and in his book, *Endgame: Solving the Iraq Problem—Once and For All* (New York: Simon & Schuster, 1999). Though the interpretative and prescriptive elements of Ritter's analysis are questionable, his detailed description of his own UNSCOM experiences and its information-gathering methods appear to be valid, and are corroborated by other sources.

[36] At first the United States maintained strict control over the U2 operation and image development, and the photographs stayed with the U,S. government. Later, UNSCOM took control over U2 operations, deciding on mission tasking and, with CIA approval, the handling and sharing of imagery.

[37] Ritter further comments that even with the counterintelligence measures, 'still we didn't trust it completely. We had the air conditioner running as loud as we could and repeatedly used the large white marking board instead of talking.' Ritter, *Endgame*, p. 25.

[38] Ritter, *Endgame*, p. 141 and p. 181, respectively.

[39] The UN cannot afford to engage in extensive counterintelligence efforts because these would affect the atmosphere of the organisation and could result in 'witch hunts,' such as those that the UN experienced in the McCarthy era in the early 1950s.

[40] These 'intelligence' officers are in the Information and Research Branch of the Situation Centre in the Department of Peacekeeping Operations.

[41] The practical reason for this irony is clear: the UN has been able to secure neither funding nor mandates from member states for the much-needed expansion. In fact, the financial squeeze, imposed largely by the United States, has forced it into a contraction: it has 2,000 people fewer than it did in 1985 (out of a total of some 10,000, covering all areas of international affairs, from human rights to environment to peacekeeping). By contrast, the national intelligence agencies did not contract: huge sources of funds continued to flow into them (roughly $26 billion annually in the United States alone). It appears that the capacity for the institutional survival of intelligence agencies in the United States and other Western countries remains great.

[42] Statists may argue that with an independent and effective intelligence capability the intergovernmental UN would begin to become a super-governmental organisation. But there is no reason why an intergovernmental organisation cannot have the capacity to monitor compliance with the rules that are collectively established. On a more practical basis, many states feel that the UN is inherently insecure and any intelligence it came into possession of would inevitably leak back to their 'enemies.' This is a good reason to devote more effort and resources to developing the UN's confidentiality system.

America's Intelligence Liaison with International Organisations

Loch K. Johnson[1]

During the cold war, the United States faced one major threat: the bloc of communist countries led by the Soviet Union and mainland China. With the break-up of the Soviet Union in 1991 and the drift of China toward a stronger interest in commercial relations with the United States and the rest of the world, America's threat assessment changed. As former DCI R. James Woolsey famously put it, 'we live now in a jungle filled with a bewildering variety of poisonous snakes.'[2] Highest among the new threats were, initially, the proliferation of weapons of mass destruction and 'rogue' nations like Iraq and North Korea, along with international drug dealers, organised crime, and terrorism. With the September 11, 2001, attacks against the United States, global terrorism (and especially the al-Qa'eda organisation) jumped to the top of the list, accompanied by Iraq in particular (as war plans heated up against the regime of Sadam Hussein) as well as a more assertive North Korea seemingly bent on developing an arsenal of nuclear weapons. The drug dealers and international criminals did not disappear, however; nor did the need to keep an eye on countries like Russia and China, which maintained a sobering military the capacity to inflict great damage on the United States. All these threats summed to a simple truth: even the wealthy United States needed help from allies and international organisations to maintain a global watchfulness against what seemed to be a rising tide of new threats in place of the highly dangerous but more focused threats of the cold war. Since the end of the cold war, international organisations, especially the United Nations and the North Atlantic Treaty Organisation, have played an important part in America's foreign policy. During the Persian Gulf War, the United States relied heavily on the UN as a framework for building a coalition of forces to repel the Iraq army from Kuwait. In the pursuit of this military objective, the US intelligence community shared information and assessments with coalition members as the war unfolded. Even before the end of the cold war, the United States had been sharing intelligence with NATO members 'for many years on a classified basis, albeit within established limits.'[3]

As a larger organisation with less well formulated security procedures (and with some members hostile toward America), the UN has received less information over the years than has NATO from the U.S. intelligence community, although, according to the Aspin-Brown Commission, the United States still provides the majority of information used by the UN in support of its world-wide activities (contrary to a CIA officer's claim to a reporter that 'we don't get involved with international organisations'[4]). When UN and NATO missions overlap, as they did in Bosnia in the early 1990s, the intelligence community provides one level of classified information to NATO participants and a more filtered version to UN participants.

Most of the US intelligence shared with the United Nations is quite low-grade in classification, a special category of 'UN Use Only,' not to be distributed to the media or anyone else outside the framework of the United Nations. This means that the information can go to 185 nations, including a number of America's adversaries. As a result, the information is unlikely to stay secret. With this in mind, the intelligence community provides to the UN what one of its representatives has called 'vanilla' information: somewhat bland, highly sanitised documents which, after various interagency 'pre-dissemination reviews,' are usually less than timely in their arrival to consumers at the United Nations. Nevertheless, the information is still considered useful by UN officials, for often it is the only reliable source of analysis on some global issues.[5]

If asked, the United States will sometimes provide information on specific topics of interest to the United Nations, at a somewhat higher level of classification than normal, although still carefully sanitised to remove signs of sources and methods before being passed along. A recent example was an analysis of military, political, and economic developments in a war-torn developing nation. As a rule, the United States does not provide classified documents to the UN, with the occasional exception of tactical battlefield information in times of crisis for the UN's 'Blue Helmet' troops.

Another venue of 'information-sharing' (the term the UN prefers over the more intrusive sounding word 'intelligence'), and one that avoids giving sensitive documents to the United Nations, is the timely oral briefing. When the intelligence community determines that the Blue Helmets are in jeopardy, a member of the US Mission to the United Nations will (with clearance from the Department of State) present valuable battlefield information orally to the appropriate UN officials, possibly saving lives but without leaving any intelligence documents behind.

The question of intelligence sharing with international organisations is complex and nuanced, depending on the kind of organisation (its size and whether its members are U.S. allies, for example) and America's experience with the organisation. Whoever the recipient may be, the sharing of information by the United States is carried out through the most exacting procedures. Usually the intelligence is given in a highly diluted fashion; and when more sensitive information is disseminated, it goes only to a small group of consumers. There have been mishaps. In Somalia, UN officials poorly handled US intelligence documents and, worse still, left some behind during the withdrawal in 1994.[6] Subsequent inquiries into this case revealed, however, that the documents were less sensitive than initially feared. More importantly, as a result of this experience security procedures have been tightened by UN administrators to better safeguard intelligence documents in the field.

In all instances of US information sharing with the United Nations, the purpose is to advance America's national security interests, not to achieve some ill-defined goal of enhancing good feelings among UN officials toward Washington. Information that uncovers transgressions by Saddam Hussein, protects peacekeepers in Bosnia, provides a realistic understanding of events in Rwanda, or proves acts of atrocity by Serbian or Albanian soldiers, all are illustrations of information shared with the United Nations that benefits the United States as well. As a general proposition, America's best interests are served when the United Nations is in possession of accurate information about world affairs.

In many cases, UN officials are already well informed. As a result of their diplomatic contacts, world travel, and perusal of the standard sources of public information, most perceive no great pressing need for secret information (short of tactical military intelligence when Blue Helmets are under fire). These officials would like, nonetheless, to receive from reliable member states more studies produced by their individual intelligence agencies on the issue of human rights, as well as on such broad topics as world population growth and global food supply.

The extent of US liaison involvement with international organisations raises the significant question of the degree to which Washington's secret agencies undermine their credibility by making them appear lackeys of American foreign policy. This risk came to the public's attention in 1999, when news reports revealed that the CIA and the NSA had assisted the UN Special Commission (known as UNSCOM) in eavesdropping operations against some of Iraq's most sensitive communications. In this case, the United States had decided to go far beyond its normally low-level intelligence activities with respect to the United Nations.

The UN commissioned UNSCOM, a team of arms inspectors, to monitor Iraqi compliance with a 1991 cease-fire agreement requiring it to dismantle its program for strategic weapons. The team was nothing less than what one reporter called An international intelligence service for the new world order . . . the first of its kind . . .,' adding: 'More than 7,000 weapons inspectors from around the world served UNSCOM over seven years, spying on Iraq, surveying its military and industrial plants, trying to do what smart bombs could not: destroy nuclear, biological, chemical and missile programs hidden by Saddam Hussein.'[7] Germany provided helicopters to UNSCOM, for instance, with special radar to penetrate Iraqi sand dunes in search of buried weapons; Britain contributed sensitive scanners to intercept Iraqi military communications; and the United States loaned U-2 spy planes and even Navy divers to probe Iraqi lakes and rivers for submerged weapons.[8] In the description of another reporter, 'The spirit of post-Cold War co-operation promised a miracle: UNSCOM, operating on behalf of the UN Security Council, would utilise the secret intelligence agencies of its members states, Communist and non-communist alike, to investigate the Iraqi arsenal.'[9]

Information acquired by the NSA, which has the capacity to unscramble encrypted telephone conversations between Saddam and his aides, could assist the UN's search for weapons of mass destruction inside Iraq. At the same time, UNSCOM could be used by the US intelligence community for its own agenda: namely, ridding the world of Saddam Hussein. Under UNSCOM cover, the NSA apparently had even wired a UN microwave transmission system (without the knowledge of UN officials), which allowed the eavesdropping agency to monitor a wide range of secret Iraqi military communications.[10]

'The UN cannot be party to an operation to overthrow one of its member states,' complained a confidant to UN secretary-general Kofi Annan, when the US intelligence ties to UNSCOM became a matter of public knowledge. 'In the most fundamental way, that is what's wrong with the UNSCOM operation.'[11] Had the

UNSCOM weapons inspectors restricted their activities solely to its non-proliferation agenda, which had widespread support in the world, they could have preserved the high esteem in which most member states held them. Instead, news leaks and speculation from one of the inspectors (a former US Marine intelligence officer by the name of Scott Ritter) raised suspicions that UNSCOM had gone beyond just trying to find Saddam's weapons. According to these reports, the CIA had used UNSCOM in 1996 as an umbrella for its own intelligence collection operations, as well as for covert actions designed to topple Saddam Hussein.[12] The Clinton administration conceded that the CIA had been assisting UNSCOM 'through intelligence, logistical support, expertise, and personnel,' but denied using the team as a medium for coup plotting against the Iraqi leader.[13]

Wherever the truth may lie, UNSCOM had been fatally tarred by these charges. The independence of the United Nations was severely compromised, in perception if not in reality. In order to advance its plans to destroy Saddam Hussein, the UN liaison operations of the US intelligence community (presumably acting under White House orders) had instead destroyed the most important international effort in the modern era to halt the proliferation of dangerous strategic weapons.

To avoid the problem of national bias that comes with reliance on individual national intelligence services for its information, the UN will need to create its own intelligence capabilities, a professional corps of intelligence officers with a commitment to making the UN work (with all the necessary safeguards against the misuse of shared information). The UN is already taking some steps in this direction. It has set up a Situation Centre, which is building up a computer infrastructure for the collection, storage, and retrieval of open-source information on world affairs. Its modest resources, though, make this endeavour limited in scope.

The United Nations has also recently acquired authority to start up a satellite surveillance system that would allow its International Drug Control Program to monitor the cultivation of illegal drug crops in the major source countries. In this manner, the UN can establish an internationally accepted benchmark for measuring the faithfulness of promises by countries to reduce their production of drugs. 'For the first time the international community will have a very reliable instrument to measure the extent of illegal crops,' according to the executive director of the program.[14] The

European Space Agency is contributing the necessary satellites and technical expertise to support the operation.

These experiments in international intelligence remain alive, despite the UNSCOM setback. Still, it has been difficult to overcome the old mentality of viewing the UN as either a target or a cover for intelligence operations, rather than a customer for information and insight gathered by the secret agencies of member nations for the benefit of the whole world. This change in attitude is 'ill thought out and haphazard,' in the words of a former British Ambassador to the United Nations.[15] The relationship between international organisations and intelligence raises a paradox: how can these organisations be effective if they are so poorly informed about the outlaw nations they are expected to tame? The UN is meant to engage in conflict resolution, peacekeeping, peace enforcement, economic sanctions, controlling the spread of large-scale weapons, combating organised crime, fighting drugs, and bringing to justice war criminals and human rights violators. All of these tasks require intelligence, yet the UN has little at its disposal. International organisations cannot afford to develop their own full-service intelligence agencies. Besides, member nations are unlikely to tolerate the risk that the UN might end up peering into their own backyards. Member states could provide more intelligence assistance themselves, but they fear leaks of sensitive sources and methods. Further, the UN must worry about the national biases of intelligence emanating from member states.

Despite these dilemmas, one can envision nations and NGOs providing to the UN and other international organisations additional, second-hand satellites and other surveillance equipment for watching global environmental conditions, refugee flows, arms-control monitoring, and suspicious military mobilisations. Satellites can even track mosquito populations around the globe, by focusing on vegetation patterns and breeding grounds that attract the disease-bearing insects.[16] The UN could establish an Assessment Board comprised of retired senior intelligence analysts from member states: men and women with extensive analytic experience, known for their fierce independence and wisdom, who could evaluate the quality and objectivity of member-state intelligence reports solicited by the Secretary General of the UN.

International organisations require reliable information on global conditions. As a specialist on the United Nations notes, The UN must be given the means, including information-gathering and analysis, to make manifest its goal, as stated in the opening words of the UN Charter, of 'saving succeeding generations from the scourge of war.'[17] So far members of the UN have fallen far short of satisfactory intelligence cooperation, although some individual nations (like Great Britain) have been responsive to requests from UN officials for intelligence assistance. Increased intelligence burden sharing within the framework of the United Nations would allow an opportunity for global dissemination of information to all member nations, carefully reviewed by an esteemed Assessment Board to filter out national biases. This would be a valuable contribution toward the search for solutions to the challenges that confront all the world's people.

Certainly as nations continue to face a steady flow of illegal drugs across their borders, the spread of weapons of mass destruction, a growing presence of international criminal activities within their cities, and rising terrorism, they urgently need to identify and react to renegade behaviour in the world. The simple truth is: the planet is too vast for nations to cope with these threats alone. All civilised nations have a natural self-interest in dealing with these problems not just the United States. The time has come for the globalisation of intelligence. Here is something that France, Germany, Russia, China, the United States, and many other countries should be able to agree upon and work together toward, even if they have differences on the proper approach to the regime in Iraq and other specific topics. If the world fails to work together to share information about and control the proliferation of weapons, drugs, and crime, they shall find themselves separately engulfed and overwhelmed by these destructive forces.

Endnotes

[1] Editors' Note: at our request, the author was good enough to extract and tailor for this collection a section from his most recent book, *Bombs, Bugs, Drugs, and Thugs: Intelligence and America's Quest for Security* (NY: New York University Press, 2000), pages 167-172.

[2] Testimony, Hearing, U.S. Senate Select Committee on Intelligence, 103d Cong., 2d. Sess, March 6, 1993.

[3] Aspin-Brown Commission, *Report, op.cit.*: 129.

[4] Aspin-Brown Commission, *ibid.*; the quote is from Seymour M. Hersh, 'Saddam's Best Friend', *The New Yorker* (5 April 1999): 35.

[5] Author's interviews with UN officials (29 November 1995), New York City.

[6] Bill Gertz, 'Clinton Wants Hill Off His Back', *Washington Times* (1 November 1995): A1.

[7] Tim Weiner, 'The Case of the Spies Without a Country', *New York Times* (17 January 1999): E6.

[8] Scott Ritter, *Endgame* (New York: Simon & Schuster, 1999); A. Walter Dorn, 'The Cloak and the Blue Beret: Limitations on Intelligence in UN Peacekeeping', *International Journal of Intelligence and Counterintelligence* 12 (Winter 1999-2000): 437-38.

[9] Hersh, *op.cit.*, 36.

[10] Barton Gellman, AU.S. Spied on Iraqi Military Via U.N.', *Washington Post* (2 March 1999): A1.

[11] Quoted in 'Inspectors 'Helped Washington', *New Zealand Herald* (7 January 1999): B1, citing a *Washington Post* report.

[12] Ritter claims that CIA paramilitary officers were placed on the UNSCOM inspection team beginning in 1992, growing to nine members by 1996, *op.cit.*

[13] 'Intelligence Ties with UNSCOM Defended', *Otago (New Zealand) Daily Times* (8 January 1999): 8, citing *Washington Post* and *Boston Globe* reports.

[14] Quoted by Christopher S. Wren, 'U.N. to Create Own Satellite Program to Find Illegal Drug Crops', *New York Times* (28 March 1999): A10.

[15] Remarks (25 September 1999), Oxford University, England.

[16] ABC News Report, Discover News Channel (8 October 1999).

[17] Dorn, *op.cit.*, 442.

Canada, the UN, NATO, and Peacekeeping Intelligence

Martin Rudner

Intelligence Capabilities for Peace Support Missions

The Canadian experience demonstrates that Information and Intelligence capabilities for peace support and other non-war-fighting operations must relate to operational situations of far greater complexity and indeed ambiguity compared to the tradition combat situation for which these systems were designed.[1] For one thing, in peace support situations the potential adversaries (and their forces) are usually ambiguous, and often obscure and elusive as well. For another, the intentions of belligerents are typically volatile, and may not always be indicated by the positioning and activity of military or paramilitary forces. In such circumstances, highly sophisticated technical means of intelligence collection may be less relevant than the balanced application of all Information and Intelligence capabilities, and especially Humint. Moreover, the conventional principles of offensive, target-oriented tactical and operational intelligence may have to be modified in order to achieve a nuanced and accurate assessment of the peace breakdown/peace support situation. Based on their experience in Somalia, Haiti and Bosnia, the US Military Intelligence community discerned the following imperatives for future peace support Information and Intelligence capability planning:

(1) Intelligence support to force protection as the foremost priority;

(2) Human intelligence (Humint) as the paramount requirement;

(3) Technical means of collection to be utilised reservedly and appropriately to ensure synergy and balance with Humint;

371

(4) The architecture for Information and Intelligence to be modified so as to incorporate both political and military factors in every assessment, and to sustain interoperability and commonality with coalition partners and non-governmental organisations.[2]

The intelligence architecture of the Canadian Forces (CF) in operational contexts will generally be subordinated to Allied, and especially American, systems in terms of information and intelligence capabilities, particularly sophisticated sensors, processors, automated analysis tools, and supporting dissemination networks. While sophisticated sensors, imagery and signals technologies may well serve as force multipliers in peace support operations, experience indicates that they are generally of more limited operational effectiveness than in conventional combat situations. Similarly, high-capacity information processors and analysis tools tend to be of more limited applicability in the contexts of peace support missions. This is principally because the bulk of information collected (predominantly Humint) in these more ambiguous situations must be treated to qualitative analysis (characterisation of intent) that does not easily lend itself to machine-formatted data fields or reporting. Certainly, the future development of CF information and intelligence capabilities must certainly retain a capacity to interface with these advanced technologies. However, it would be distinctly advantageous and appropriate for Canadian Defence Intelligence to focus its own endogenous efforts on developing complementary talents, perspectives and Humint-centred capabilities.

Future peace support scenarios suggest that Canada's Information and Intelligence architecture will be impelled to accommodate, process, and effectively deal with substantial Humint input of military, political and increasingly also economic/humanitarian bearing.[3] To effectively perform these functions, Defence Intelligence will have to interact with the information-gathering capabilities of local authorities and non-governmental organisations. The implications for the future are clear: the more complex, fluid and dynamic the peace support context, arguably the more Humint oriented the supporting intelligence architecture must become.

This inclusion of Humint may pose certain conceptual challenges for the architecture of Defence Intelligence. The current architecture is shaped by an automated analytical process designed to input data, apply logical algorithms to it, and then produce an artificial real-time intelligence-based result for dissemination to forces in the field.

This design is optimised for responding to empirical facts and things, and not the subtleties of context. It is the essence of the so-called 'sensor-to-shooter' process. While this sensor-to-shooter capability should be retained, in particular for force protection, it requires enhancement to accommodate more subtle, context-based Humint apropos situations where complexity of the mission environment is much greater. Defence Intelligence architecture will have to be modified (and soldiers trained) to incorporate assessment of both a political and military context with every analysis, adding a very important human dimension to powerful, but limited, technology-based systems.[12]

The Intelligence Challenges of UN Peace Support Operations

Peace support operations, whether undertaken for classic peacekeeping missions or more contemporary preventive action, peace enforcement or peace-building objectives, demonstrate their own distinctive requirements for Information and Intelligence. Although there tends to be a large element of improvisation in peace operations, they seem to be guided by three salient principles: the importance of impartiality and transparency of policies; the exercise of control by an accepted international authority; and the need to ensure effective military and political command and control in an otherwise complex multilateral operating environment.[4] Experience indicates that the place of Defence Intelligence in peace operations tends to vary according to whether these missions were mandated under United Nations or North Atlantic Treaty Organisation auspices. Since peace support may be expected to remain a major and indeed pre-eminent international commitment for the CF for the foreseeable future, it is appropriate the development of force capabilities and doctrine be closely attuned to the attributes of the international operational framework(s) within which these operations are likely to be conducted.

UN peace missions display considerable ambivalence about Information and Intelligence.[5] In as much as the UN considers itself an essentially neutral, multilateral organisation, 'intelligence systems' were not countenanced as part of UN mandated peace operations, ostensibly due to their covert, sinister connotations.[6] So far as the UN was concerned, intelligence was equated with espionage, and therefore considered a betrayal of the 'trust, confidence and respect' deemed necessary for effective UN peacekeeping. Reflecting this view, Canadian military doctrine rejected the term 'intelligence' as being 'negative and covert', insisting instead that peacekeeping operations rely on a more principled access to 'information' that was 'impartial, trustworthy and overt.'[7]

Be that as it may, a review of UN peacekeeping operations undertaken at the behest of the secretary-general and published in August 2000 proposed a radical reconfiguration of the role of intelligence in the framework of UN peace and security. The Report of the Brahimi Panel determined that UN peace operations require a more robust military doctrine and a realistic mandate, including a preparedness to apply military force as appropriate to achieve mission objectives. Towards this end, the Panel concluded that 'United Nations forces for complex operations should be afforded the field intelligence and other capabilities needed to mount an effective defence against violent challengers.'[8] To put these capabilities in place, the Report recommended that the secretary-general establish an Information and Strategic Analysis Secretariat (EISAS), to be administered jointly by the Departments of Political Affairs and Peacekeeping Operations, and which would serve as an information gathering and analysis unit to support the UN's Executive Committee on Peace and Security.

By way of response, the Secretary General decided to establish an Information and Strategic Analysis Secretariat within the Department of Political Affairs, solely, as 'the focal point for the application of modern information systems and technology to all parts of the UN system engaged in peace and security activities.[9] As implemented, EIAS consists of three component units: a Strategic Analysis Service, a Peace-Building Unit, and an Information Management Service. Its prescribed functions included creating and maintaining an integrated database on peace and security issues, disseminating that knowledge within the United Nations system, generating policy analyses, providing early warning of impending crises, and formulating long-term strategies for the UN Executive Committee of Peace and Security. Thus, this new Information and Strategic Analysis Secretariat combines a strategic intelligence function along with policy planning functions. While this duality of functions may become problematic in and of itself, it is clear that strategic information, or intelligence, has now acquired a new legitimacy within the framework of UN peace support planning. This new found acceptability of Information and Analysis at the strategic policy level will doubtless resonate downwards to the development of Defence Intelligence capabilities, to gather, process and disseminate 'strategic information', also at the tactical and operational levels of UN peace mission planning.

The Intelligence Challenges of NATO Peace Support Operations

Since the end of the Cold War NATO, for its part, has undertaken peace support operations in the Gulf, in Somalia and in the former Yugoslavia.[10] These activities were not only 'out of theatre', but also engaged NATO forces in an entirely new genre of missions, for the Alliance, as such, aimed at conflict prevention, peacemaking, peacekeeping, humanitarian aid, peace enforcement and peace building.[11] As a result of recent experience, especially in Bosnia, NATO military planning for peace support operations is now prepares itself for a continuum of contingencies in which low-intensity monitoring may escalate into high-intensity peace enforcement. Moreover, NATO has also recognised that the intelligence requirements for peace support missions extend beyond Defence Intelligence as narrowly defined to also embrace the pertinent political, social, cultural, and economic dimensions of intelligence. Contingency planning for peace enforcement generates a powerful imperative for robust Information and Intelligence capabilities at the very outset of NATO-led peace support operations. Perceptions of impartiality and intelligence sharing will perforce be affected by this war preparedness. The Alliance's approach to peace support may well serve to undercut the effectiveness of the intelligence function, which may in turn constrain NATO's leadership role in peace support just a time when this mission is becoming salient on the Alliance agenda.

NATO does not possess an intelligence collection and analysis capacity of its own. Ordinarily, all of NATO's intelligence requirements are met from intelligence products supplied by member countries for the exclusive use of the Alliance itself and for its constituent governments. It is a fundamental principle of NATO intelligence sharing that none of the intelligence supplied to the Alliance can be shared with non-member countries or to any international organisation composed of non-member countries. This fundamental principle applies also on peace support missions involving NATO in partnership with other countries and organisations, notwithstanding operational requirements for intelligence sharing.

While providing some intelligence input into NATO, the United States tends to rely on its own very sophisticated C4ISR capabilities to acquire high-quality imagery, Sigint, and other elements of information superiority to support American forces engaged in NATO-led peace support missions. The American military often discriminates even between allies in allowing access to these intelligence products, so as to protect classified capabilities or methodologies. Thus, some of the highest value components of information superiority are reserved for US users and are not generally shared even with other NATO countries on the same NATO-led missions. However, Canadian Forces reportedly have enjoyed privileged access to this intelligence.

NATO military planning is, of course, cognisant of this tension between the security principle governing access to Alliance intelligence, on the one hand, and the operational principles of transparency and integrated command and control, which imply intelligence sharing among partners and international authorities involved in peace support coalitions, on the other.[12] Nevertheless, NATO insists that it cannot countenance any sharing of Alliance intelligence products with non-member countries or with international organisation of which they are a part. As a result, the intelligence architecture for NATO-led peace support missions has tended to assume the characteristics of a three tier, differentiated apparatus, with a top tier consisting of US forces and their most intimate allies who share access to American ISR capabilities to the fullest; a second tier composed of other NATO allies who may obtain Information and Intelligence made available through the Alliance, but which may exclude access to some reserved American-generated products; and a third tier consisting of all other country or international components.

This compartmentalisation of the NATO intelligence architecture militated against the effective command and control of peace support operations involving the Alliance, and sometimes produced grave deficiencies in the availability of tactical and operational intelligence even to Canadian participants. Thus, in 1992, General Lewis Mackenzie, commander of UN Forces in Bosnia, found the deficiencies of intelligence preventing the forces under his command from responding to hostile fire from positions ostensibly under UN control, complaining 'there was no way we could know ... we had absolutely no intelligence.'[13] Since ad hoc coalitions with non-NATO partners have become characteristic of peace and humanitarian missions, Canada, as a NATO member, intimate US ally and frequent coalition partner with non-members may well find itself on the fault lines between the three tiers of intelligence compartmentalisation.

Lessons Learned and Future Requirements

In order to ensure the effectively respond to the requirements for Information and Intelligence in the context of UN or NATO-led peace and humanitarian missions, future Canadian Forces operational capabilities will have to seek a closer interoperability and fusion in the production and dissemination of Defence Intelligence. Interoperability with allies and prospective coalition partners will remain a *sine qua non* for the operational integration of C4ISR capabilities on peace support missions. However, technical interoperability will not suffice. Structural impediments confronting both the UN and NATO systems, which prevent the effective deployment of Defence Intelligence capabilities in a coherent, integrated manner for peace support must likewise be addressed. To enable Canadian Forces on UN or NATO-led peace support operations to achieve information superiority, the future development of Information and Intelligence capabilities for Canadian Forces will have to promote a more balanced integration of technical and Humint sources, along with a closer fusion of the strategic, tactical and operational dimensions of Defence Intelligence. It seems clear that Canadian Forces commanders on peace missions will demand greater attention to the scope, depth and relevance of Defence Intelligence.

Endnotes

[1] Col. H. Allen Boyd, 'Joint Intelligence Support of Peace Operations', *Military Intelligence*, Vol. 24, No. 4 (October-December, 1998).

[2] *Vide*. Boyd, 'Joint Intelligence Support of Peace Operations'; U.S. Army, Headquarters, XVIII Airborne Corps Deputy Chief of Staff for Intelligence Briefing 'Joint Intelligence Operations: Operation RESTORE DEMOCRACY', U.S. Army World-wide Intelligence Conference, Fort Huachuca, Arizona, January 1995; Pick, "CI and HUMINT in Multinational Operations: 'The Lessons of Vigilant Blade 97'; David Rababy, 'Intelligence Support During a Humanitarian Mission', *Marine Corps Gazette* (February 1995), pp. 41-2; Alastair Duncan, 'Operating in Bosnia', *RUSI Journal* (June 1994), pp 12-15; Thomas Wilson, 'Joint Intelligence and UPHOLD DEMOCRACY', *Joint Forces Quarterly* (Spring, 1996), pp. 57-58; Raymond Leach, 'Information Support to UN Forces', *Marine Corps Gazette* (September, 1994), p. 49.

[3] Boyd, 'Joint Intelligence Support of Peace Operations'; Rababy, 'Intelligence Support During a Humanitarian Mission' pp. 41-2; Duncan, 'Operating in Bosnia', pp. 12-15.[3].

[4] *NATO, Peacekeeping, and the UN*, Berlin Information Centre for Transatlantic Security, Germany, 1994, p. 53.

---

[5] Paul Johnston, 'No Cloak and Dagger Required: Intelligence Support to UN Peacekeeping', *Intelligence and National Security*, Vol. 12, No. 4 (October, 1997); Hugh Smith, 'Intelligence and UN Peacekeeping', *Survival* Vol. 36, No. 3 (Autumn, 1994)

[6] International Peace Academy, *Peacekeeper*'s *Handbook* (New York: Pergamon Press, 1984, p. 39.

[7] Canadian Forces Publication 301(3), *Peacekeeping Operations, 1992*, Section 618, Para.1e.

[8] United Nations, *Report of the panel on UN Peace Operations*, A/55/305 - S/2000 801, 21 August 2000. URL:www.un.org/peace/reports/peace_operations.

[9] *Resource Requirements for the Implementation of the Report of the Panel on UN Peace Operations. Report of the secretary-general.* United Nations General Assembly, A/55/507, 27 October 2000, pt. 2, para's. 11 & 12.

[10] *NATO, Peacekeeping, and the UN*, pp. 22.23. NATO involvement in Peace Support missions was approved by its Military Committee, the Alliance's highest military organ, but has not yet been endorsed or even discussed as a policy matter by the legislatures of member states.

[11] John Nomikos, *Intelligence Requirements for Peacekeeping Operations, Research Institute on European and American Studies* Working Paper, Athens, Greece, October 2000.

[12] *NATO, Peacekeeping, and the UN*, pp.22-23.

[13] General Lewis Mackenzie, former UN Commander in Bosnia, speaking in a BBC Radio Interview on 11 February 1994. Cited in Nomikos, *Intelligence Requirements for Peacekeeping Operations*, ff. 12.

Part V is the reference section. It is not indexed—each item is presented as a whole.

The **Brahimi Report** is of extraordinary importance to the future of the UN, and many of the recommendations in that report bear directly on the capacity of the UN to be effective at strategic, operational, and tactical intelligence. The first reference, therefore, is a selection of extracts from the executive summary of the Brahimi Report, together with some explanatory footnotes intended to relate the knowledge contained in this book, to the most urgent and significant Brahimi Report.

Peacekeeping Intelligence Leadership Digest 1.0 is designed to consolidate the lessons, from the 21 contributions in this book, into a 35-page reference (47 pages counting the notes) that can be easily reproduced and circulated apart from the book. This reference is also available as a free digital download from www.oss.net and other web sites associated with peacekeeping such as those in Canada and The Netherlands.

Open Source Intelligence References is deliberately focused on the three most recent and also the most important references relevant to the UN mission: *the NATO Open Source Intelligence Handbook*, the *NATO Open Source Intelligence Reader*, and the NATO guide to *Intelligence Exploitation of the Internet*. Each of these NATO references, in turn, will guide the UN practitioner toward many other relevant references that show how it is possible to do legal, ethical intelligence relying exclusively on open sources of information.

Additional References includes a several off-line references but is almost completely dedicated to many recent (1993-2003) online references that address the urgency and specifics of endowing the UN with intelligence capabilities at the strategic and operational levels. Most of these references are online, and those that are online are immediately available for free download. Included in these references are training materials on the basics of the proven process of intelligence, which is *not* secret and has nothing to do with secrets; and on the larger fields of command and control, communications, computing and intelligence (C4I), and Information Operations (IO).

Abbreviations are listed in alphabetical order with their expansion.

Contributors are listed in alphabetical order, both those who contributed to the conference, and those whose seminal works were selected for inclusion in this book.

The Brahimi Report[1]

EXTRACTS FROM THE EXECUTIVE SUMMARY[2]

The United Nations was founded, in the words of its Charter, in order 'to save succeeding generations from the scourge of war.' Meeting this challenge is the most important function of the Organisation, and to a very significant degree it is the yardstick with which the Organisation is judged by the peoples it exists to serve. Over the last decade, the United Nations has repeatedly failed to meet the challenge, and it can do no better today.

There are many tasks which United Nations peacekeeping forces should not be asked to undertake and many places they should not go. But when the United Nations does send its forces to uphold the peace, they must be prepared to confront the lingering forces of war and violence, with the ability and determination to defeat them.

Each of the recommendations contained in the present report is designed to remedy a serious problem in strategic direction, decision-making, rapid deployment, operational planning and support, and the use of modern information technology. [3]

---

[1] Mr. Lakhdar Brahimi (Algeria) was asked by the secretary-general to lead the Panel on United Nations Peace Operations, with the mission of assessing the shortcomings of the existing system and to make frank, specific and realistic recommendations for change. The recommendations focus not only on politics and strategy but also and perhaps even more so on operational and organisational areas of need. The complete report is at <http://www.un.org/peace/reports/peace_operations>. It was submitted to the secretary-general on 17 August 2000.

[2] All notes in this section are by Robert David Steele, by the Editors' agreement.

[3] Three of these five areas are directly addressable by creating permanent and rapid-response strategic, operational, and tactical intelligence capabilities for the UN. The last, the use of modern information technology, should be guided by what is available

Implications for Preventive Action and Peace-building:
The Need for Strategy and Support

The United Nations and its members face a pressing need to establish more effective strategies for conflict prevention, in both the long and short terms. ... It ... encourages the secretary-general's more frequent use of fact-finding missions[4] to areas of tension in support of short-term crisis-preventive action.

Implications for Peacekeeping:
The Need for Robust Doctrine and Realistic Mandates

The Panel concurs that consent of the local parties, impartiality and the use of force only in self-defence should remain the bedrock principles of peacekeeping. Experience shows, however, that in the context of intra-State/transitional conflicts, consent may be manipulated in many ways.

No failure did more to damage the standing and credibility of United Nations peacekeeping in the 1990s than its reluctance to distinguish victim from aggressor.

This means...that the Secretariat must not apply best-case planning assumptions to situations where the local actors have historically exhibited worst-case behaviour.[5] It means that mandates should specify an operation's authority to use force. It means bigger forces, better-equipped and more costly but able to be a credible deterrent. In particular, United Nations forces for complex operations should be afforded the field intelligence and other capabilities needed to mount an effective defence against violent challengers.

The Secretariat must tell the Security Council what it needs to know, not what it wants to hear, when recommending force and other resource levels for a new mission, and it must set those levels according to realistic scenarios that take

---

from the commercial marketplace, rather than attempting to follow the unilateral and very expensive paths chosen by the various major military forces of the world.
[4] Fact-finding missions are overt, ethical intelligence collection missions.
[5] Strategic threat assessments, including order of battle (OOB), key personalities, plans & intentions, external alliances and covert support, and terrain assessment, must all be professionally prepared and presented to the Security Council if this is to be done.

into account likely challenges to implementation.[6] Security Council mandates, in turn, should reflect the clarity that peacekeeping operations require for unity of effort when they deploy into potentially dangerous situations. [7]

New Headquarters Capacity for Information Management and Strategic Analysis

The Panel recommends that a new information-gathering and analysis entity be created to support the informational and analytical needs of the secretary-general and the members of the Executive Committee on Peace and Security (ECPS). Without such capacity, the Secretariat will remain a reactive institution, unable to get ahead of daily events, and the ECPS will not be able to fulfil the role for which it was created.

The Panel's proposed ECPS Information and Strategic Analysis Secretariat (EISAS) would create and maintain integrated databases on peace and security issues, distribute that knowledge efficiently within the United Nations system, generate policy analyses, formulate long-term strategies for ECPS and bring budding crises to the attention of the ECPS leadership. It could also propose and manage the agenda of ECPS itself, helping to transform it into the decision-making body anticipated in the secretary-general's initial reforms.

The Panel proposes that EISAS be created by consolidating the existing Situation Centre of the Department of Peacekeeping Operations (DPKO) with a number of small, scattered policy planning offices, and adding a small team of military analysts, experts in international criminal networks and information systems specialists. EISAS should serve the needs of all members of ECPS.

---

[6] This suggests a standing strategic intelligence staff with historical and contextual knowledge able to reliably calculate alternative threat scenarios.

[7] Apart from ensuring that the Rules of Engagement (ROE) are appropriate to the threats facing the Force Commander, 'unity of effort' also implies an appropriate mix, from the first day, of military, law enforcement, and relief operating forces *and their requisite intelligence capabilities*. Criminal gangs supported by warlords are a major factor in both arms smuggling and local crime, and must be addressed by integrating law enforcement personnel, and law enforcement intelligence from the beginning.

Improved Mission Guidance and Leadership

The Panel believes it is essential to assemble the leadership of a new mission as early as possible at United Nations Headquarters, to participate in shaping a mission's concept of operations, support plan, budget, staffing and Headquarters mission guidance. To that end, the Panel recommends that the secretary-general compile, in a systematic fashion and with input from Member States, a comprehensive list of potential special representatives of the secretary-general (SRSGs), force commanders, civilian police commissioners, their potential deputies and potential heads of other components of a mission, representing a broad geographic and equitable gender distribution.[8]

Rapid Deployment Standards and 'On-Call' Expertise

The first 6 to 12 weeks following a cease-fire or peace accord are often the most critical ones for establishing both a stable peace and the credibility of a new operation. Opportunities lost during that period are hard to regain.

The Panel recommends that the United Nations standby arrangements system (UNSAS) be developed further...[9]

To support such rapid and effective deployment, the Panel recommends that a revolving 'on-call list' of about 100 experienced, well-qualified military officers, carefully vetted and accepted by DPKO, be created within UNSAS. Teams drawn from this list and available for duty on seven days' notice would

---

[8] It is absolutely essential that there be a senior intelligence officer (SIO) identified from the very beginning, and that this mission leadership have a structured process, from day one, of establishing its Commander's Critical Intelligence Requirements (CCIR), and actually having its CCIR answered, initially by the strategic intelligence element of the UN, but as soon as possible, by the operational intelligence staff formed to support the mission.

[9] Not addressed, but vitally important to this concept of rapid response, is the establishment of an operational intelligence 'cadre', perhaps from Canada and/or the Nordic countries (the latter have perfected quadri-lateral integrated operations and intelligence command centers), that can be quickly mobilized to provide both the immediate operational intelligence support for the mission leadership, and the *in situ* team training of the intelligence personnel assigned to the mission by the various Member States.

translate broad, strategic-level mission concepts developed at Headquarters into concrete operational and tactical plans in advance of the deployment of troop contingents, and would augment a core element from DPKO to serve as part of a mission start-up team.[10]

Parallel on-call lists of civilian police, international judicial experts, penal experts and human rights specialists must be available in sufficient numbers to strengthen rule of law institutions, as needed, and should also be part of UNSAS.[11]

The Panel also recommends that the secretary-general be given authority, with the approval of the Advisory Committee on Administrative and Budgetary Questions (ACABQ) to commit up to $50 million well in advance of the adoption of a Security Council resolution establishing a new operation once it becomes clear that an operation is likely to be established.[12]

Establish Integrated Mission Task Forces
for Mission Planning and support

The Panel recommends that Integrated Mission Task Forces (IMTF's) be created, with staff from throughout the United Nations system seconded to

---

[10] Intelligence specialists from national (civilian), military and law enforcement activities should be included in this 'on call' list.

[11] Established means are available for rapidly identifying internationally recognized Foreign Area and Subject-Matter Experts (SME), for instance, those with deep academic and field knowledge of Rwanda-Burundi. Measures must be taken to identify and hire, for short-term advisory assistance, those world-class experts whose knowledge is not available through any other means, i.e. from Member States' forces.

[12] A mission intelligence budget of no less than $100,000 and no more than $1,000,000, should be allocated at this time and be immediately disposable. This money will be used to buy Russian tactical military maps, commercial imagery, expert evaluations, and preliminary tribal or sub-state actor order of battle investigations (as most countries do not do sub-state orders of battle, this capability is now available in the private sector). If the intelligence function does not get this minimalist budget, then the mandate will be wrong, the force structure will be wrong, the rules of engagement will be wrong, and the mission will be destined for failure before it actually begins.

them, to plan new missions and help them reach full deployment, significantly enhancing the support that Headquarters provides to the field.[13]

Adapting Peace Operations to the Information Age

Modern, well utilised information technology (IT) is a key enabler of many of the above-mentioned objectives, but gaps in strategy, policy and practice impede its effective use. In particular, headquarters lacks a sufficiently strong responsibility centre for user-level IT strategy and policy in peace operations. A senior official with such responsibility in the peace and security arena should be appointed and located within EISAS, with counterparts in the offices of the SRSG in every United Nations peace operation. [14]

Headquarters and the field missions alike also need a substantive, global, Peace Operations Extranet (POE), through which missions would have access to, among other things, EISAS databases and analyses and lessons learned.[15]

Challenges to implementation

…no amount of money or resources can substitute for the significant changes that are urgently needed in the culture of the Organisation.[16]

---

[13] Intelligence, not political analysis or public information, is the proper term for the decision-support function.

[14] There are some who feel that the Department of Public Information (DPI) could, under the right leadership and with the correct mandate, fully integrate its existing responsibilities for outreach, the creation of a global decision-support network, and the establishment of a coherent state of the art information technology architecture that emphasizes open source software standards and open source information access and exploitation.

[15] Perhaps more to the point, past peacekeeping operations have demonstrated the urgent importance of being able to access 'out of area' information sources and propose 'out of area' interdiction of smuggled arms, incoming mercenaries, illegal cash payments, etc. Peacekeeping operations can no longer be planned nor executed in isolation, a Peace Operations Extranet is a form of information peacekeeping that must be exercised globally and constantly.

[16] 'Intelligence', like 'genocide', has a unique meaning and is a word that cannot be replaced by any other word without losing its meaning. The UN must accept this word

The Panel calls on the Secretariat to heed the secretary-general's initiatives to reach out to the institutions of civil society; to constantly keep in mind that the United Nations they serve is *the* universal organisation.[17]

Furthermore, wide disparities in staff quality exist and those in the system are the first to acknowledge it; better performers are given unreasonable workloads to compensate for those who are less capable. …Unless managers at all levels, beginning with the secretary-general and his senior staff, seriously address this problem on a priority basis, reward excellence and remove incompetence, additional resources will be wasted and lasting reform will become impossible.[18]

While building consensus for the recommendations in the present report, we have also come to a shared vision of a *United* Nations, extending a strong helping hand to a community, country or region to avert conflict or to end violence.[19]

---

with its legal, ethical connotations, as representative of the process of finding and using knowledge tailored to the mission and the mandate.

[17] The International Organization for Standardization (ISO), under its new President, is seeking to use standards to promote a global information society. So also can the United Nations unite the 'seven tribes' of intelligence, national, military, law enforcement, business, academic, NGO-media, religious-clan-citizen, into a global information peacekeeping and peace supporting network. In so doing, it will nurture the '*noosphere*' first envisioned by Pierre Tielhard de Chardin, and create the 'world brain' conceptualized by H.G. Wells.

[18] The function of intelligence, new to the United Nations, would be an excellent place at which to begin the establishment and enforcement of the highest standards of professional qualification.

[19] According to Alvin Toffler, information (intelligence) is a substitute for both wealth (poverty) and violence. *PowerShift* (NY: Bantam Books, 1990).

Peacekeeping Intelligence
Leadership Digest 1.0[1]

Executive Summary

The Brahimi Report, in combination with documented field experience from numerous UN peacekeeping missions, and the memoirs and published statements of recent secretaries-general, make it clear that the time has come to establish strategic, operational, and tactical intelligence concepts, doctrine, and tables of organisation & equipment (TO&E) for intelligence support to UN decisions at every level. This Peacekeeping Intelligence (PKI) Leadership Digest 1.0 integrates key expert insights, and represents a first step in the long-overdue establishment of UN competency in the craft of intelligence.

Introduction

Peacekeeping Intelligence (PKI) is substantially different from combat intelligence, which the military is accustomed to, or law enforcement intelligence, which some but not all police forces understand. It requires, above all, *a different mind-set* on the part of the commander and his staff, as well as all personnel, both officer and enlisted. Indeed, it introduces *civilian* personnel, and *non-governmental* personnel, into the actual day-to-day collection, processing, and analysis of raw information from multiple sources. It relies very heavily on *open sources* of information as well as substantially more direct observation and elicitation from varied indigenous sources and largely by non-intelligence personnel, military police and normal infantry patrols, *inter alia*.

Peacekeeping intelligence is different from national intelligence in one other important way. As Hugh Smith has stated so eloquently:

> The concept of 'UN intelligence' promises to turn traditional principles of intelligence on their heads. Intelligence will have to be based on information that is collected primarily by overt means, that is, by methods that do not threaten the target state or group and do not compromise the integrity or impartiality of the UN. It will have to be intelligence that is by definition shared among a number of nations and that in most cases will become widely known in the short and medium term. And it will have to be intelligence that is directed towards the purposes of the international community.[2]

Fortunately, in the 40 years since the first Military Information Branch sought to protect UN peacekeepers at risk in the Congo, there have been dramatic changes in the international information and intelligence environments. The Internet, beginning in the mid-1990's and exploding into global prominence at the beginning of the 21st Century, has made rapid access to vast volumes of information possible from literally anywhere. The implosion of the Soviet Empire, and the emergence of Russia as an interested party in the stabilisation of the Muslim crescent along Russian Southwest border, has had one extraordinary benefit for UN peacekeepers: the release into the public domain of Russian military combat charts, all with cultural features and contour lines, at the 1:50.000 scale, and for ports and capital cities, at the 1:10.000 level. Coincident with the release of the Russian military maps there has been a great leap forward in commercial imagery, with French 10-metre, Indian 5-metre, Russian 2-metre, and American 1-metre satellite imagery now being easily available and even better, easily directed toward any particular target at any particular time.[3]

Partly as a result of the dramatic changes in information technology and the availability of what is now called open source information (OSIF), there has occurred a Revolution in Intelligence Affairs (RIA), and an independent discipline, Open Source Intelligence (OSINT) has emerged, both to meet the needs of organisations that are either nor permitted to, or that voluntary eschew resort to, clandestine and covert means of acquiring information, and to enhance the understanding of nations, the Member States of the UN, that have relied on spies and secrecy for so long that they have in many cases lost touch with the real world.[4] The real world is a world in which tribes rather than armies—criminal gangs rather than political parties—environmental conditions rather than treaties—are the dominant forces that determine whether an areas is stable or unstable, governable or ungovernable. For many national intelligence organisations, the instability of the Third World has been of little concern, and they have no established covert collection assets that can really be brought to bear. Hence, OSINT emerges as a very viable foundation for peacekeeping intelligence.[5]

OSINT is so viable that the North Atlantic Treaty Organisation (NATO), seeking a solution for the challenge of establishing a common appreciation of threats of common concern to NATO and to the Partnership for Peace (PfP) countries, made a commitment to test and develop OSINT as a standard means of meeting NATO requirements. Many do not realise that NATO is actually similar to the UN in that is does not have its own dedicated intelligence capabilities, but has been forced in the past to rely on whatever intelligence the allied powers might wish to share. OSINT represents independence.

Today, as the UN considers how best to implement the recommendations of the Brahimi Report[6], there are three distinct courses of action for any UN leader or Force Commander desiring to substantially improve the possibilities of success for existing and future UN missions addressing complex emergencies:

1) <u>Structure</u>. The Brahimi Report is brilliantly on point when it emphasises the urgency of creating a permanent decision-support structure at the strategic level, while also stressing the importance of being able to mobilise the appropriate mix of experts in advance of mandates being defined, for operational peacekeeping missions. With 75.000 UN peacekeepers deployed around the world, there should be established organic intelligence units for *every* mission at the operational level, and no fewer than 250 intelligence professionals at the strategic level (UN Headquarters).[7]

2) <u>Training</u>. There is an urgent need to establish a complete intelligence training curriculum at all three levels of peacekeeping: strategic, operational, and tactical. Such a curriculum must be able to teach the proven process of intelligence[8], along with a deep understanding of the many open as well as national sources that can be drawn upon to prepare for and guide peacekeeping operations under varying conditions of risk.[9]

3) <u>Open Sources</u>. As NATO has done so well at defining OSINT possibilities for coalition operations[10] we will not emphasise the utility nor the details of OSINT, but rather the cost. The heart of OSINT is that it connects the proven process of intelligence with the *purchase* of legally and ethically available open sources, among which the most important are Russian military combat charts with contour lines at the 1:50.000 level, commercial imagery, tribal orders of battle and anthropological studies, business intelligence on incoming small arms, mercenary hires, and so on. If the UN is to devise a global architecture for proper but legal and ethical intelligence support to strategic decisions about United Nations policies, negotiations and accommodations with Member States, engagements with varied complex emergencies, and subsequent support to missions at the operational and tactical level, then the UN must, quite simply, recognise that there is no element of its budget more important than that which is set aside for the procurement of legal, ethical, open sources of information.

In combination—open sources, training in the proven process of intelligence, and dedicated structure loyal to the UN leadership and responsive to the needs of the UN—these three new capabilities will not only resolve the existing intelligence deficiencies that have been allowed to accumulate, but they will substantially enhance the ability of UN leaders to be effective in their relations with Member States, their crafting of mission mandates, and their oversight of ongoing peacekeeping missions.[11] Once fully implemented, a UN intelligence structure may possibly enable preventive diplomacy, long a cherished objective of this most important universal organisation.[12]

Possibilities for Failure

PKI will often fail at the *strategic* level, either by a failure to perceive deteriorating conditions that will require intervention, such as was the case with the Belgian failure to prepare for the transition in the Congo[13], or, if an intervention is known to be needed, well before the Commander reaches the scene, from a failure of the United Nations and the Member States to arrive at a correct estimate of the situation, in turn resulting in an inadequate or erroneous mandate. A more subtle failure is one of over-extension or irrelevance unrecognised. As one contributor noted, the three main UN missions in the Middle East are routinely ratified each year, with little debate (nor strategic evaluation) of their utility. When such forces disintegrate or deteriorate to the point that they are concerned only with guarding their own security, the UN mission has failed.[14]

PKI may fail next at the *operational* level, where a lack of understanding of the differences between normal military intelligence and PKI will result in poor decisions about what to load and what to 'leave on the pier'. Digital cameras not normally included in Tables of Equipment (ToE), 'mall radios' and cellular telephones in quantity, unclassified computers that can be used to establish a wide-area network (WAN) that includes the varied local authorities and many non-governmental organisations, are but a few examples of what could be and should be introduced into PKI planning by the Commander before departing home base. The other major failure that will occur at the *operational* level is one of historical or contextual misunderstanding of the belligerents, the issues, or the key personalities.

PKI will often fail at the *tactical* level, because neither military nor law enforcement nor national intelligence forces as normally trained, equipped, and organised, are sufficient or appropriate for dealing with what William Shawcross calls 'a world of endless conflict', where humanitarian assistance—meant to stabilise a society—actually creates and perpetuates black markets that empower warlords and criminals.[15] PKI requires an ability to establish orders of battle (OOB) for non-state actors; an ability to cast a much wider human intelligence network with much greater indigenous language capabilities than is the norm; and an ability to share sensitive information with a wide variety of coalition and non-governmental counter-parts who are ineligible for any sort of 'clearance' in the traditional sense of the word.

PKI will frequently fail at the *technical* level, in part because traditional military equipment, including intelligence collection equipment, is not suited for operation in urban areas; for distribution down to the squad level; or for focusing on targets that do not 'emit,' do not wear uniforms or even carry visible arms, and do not ride in conventional military vehicles with clear markings and known characteristics. Conventional militaries are not trained, equipped, nor organised for being effective in 'small wars'.[16]

PKI is, in short, a vastly more challenging endeavour than most military, law enforcement, or national intelligence professional could possibly imagine.

Purpose and Structure of the PKI Leadership Digest 1.0

The purpose of this 'PKI Leadership Digest 1.0' is to provide an orientation for any UN leader, either civilian or military, by distilling the book into 35 pages (47 with notes). The Digest's organisation is shown below.[17]

	Collection	Processing	Analysis	Security
Strategic				
Operational				
Tactical				

Figure 1: Overview of the PKI Leadership Digest 1.0

Strategic Intelligence

At the strategic level, there are three co-equal objectives: first, to discern *early warning* of potentially catastrophic conflicts, both internal and regional, such as would warrant preventive peacekeeping[18]; second, to *inform* the leadership of the UN on a day-to-day basis and during special encounters such as have been common with respect to the efficacy of the sanctions on Iraq; and third, to *prepare* the SRSG and the Force Commander and their staffs for deployment on a peacekeeping mission.[19] The preparation is in turn divided into two parts: the exclusively strategic part requires that the Security Council devise and approve a *mandate* for the mission. The appropriateness of this mandate, the soundness of the strategic appreciation that underlies this mandate, will determine, before a single Blue Beret is deployed, the possibilities of mission success or failure.[20] The second part, what one might call the *strategic-operational transition*, brings together and devises intelligence in support of two groups: the operational command element, which must begin to define its concept of operations and requisite force structure, logistics, and recommended rules of engagement[21]; and the Security Council and supporting Departmental elements (e.g. for peacekeeping or humanitarian affairs), who must ultimately approve the operational plan by confirming the specific forces and rules of engagement proposed by the Force Commander and concurred in by the SRSG.

It is at this time and this level that the SRSG and Force Commander should make a strong personal commitment to championing the inclusion of organic intelligence capabilities within all assigned forces.[22]

At the same time, at this strategic level, the SRSG and the Force Commander should be obtaining the preliminary mandate and operational funded needed to acquire the basic geospatial information needed to both plan the strategic aspects of the deployment, and to support the operational and tactical needs of the mission once in-country. Generally this means the acquisition of at least one full set of the 1:50.000 Russian military combat charts with contour lines for the entire operational area as well as the 1:10.000 Russian charts for ports and capital cities. These are generally also available in digital form for direct integration into aviation and artillery mission support software systems. Ideally the SRSG and Force Commander should also open negotiations with both SPOT Image (FR) and Space Imaging (US) regarding the availability of lower cost archival imagery (generally less than three years old) as well as directed imagery. The US National Imagery and Mapping Agency (NIMA) can be of assistance in this regard.[23] Attention should be given at this stage not only to fulfilling the immediate strategic planning needs, but to ensuring that the Force Commander will have continuing access to commercial imagery and such other geospatial services (e.g. commercial imagery post-processing and target analysis to be done by the provider, with the finished products then digitally transmitted to the operational intelligence staff).[24]

The UN peacekeeping mission is much more likely to succeed if strategic intelligence is available in quality and quantity, *and* if the forces and rules of engagement are proposed *upwards* rather than downwards. It merits emphasis that one reason the UN must have its own strategic intelligence structure is because the larger troop contributing nations generally have not had intelligence assets focused on the 'lower tier' countries where complex emergencies develop, while the smaller troop contributing nations tend not to be able to afford structured intelligence collection, even in areas of immediate interest.[25]

In the course of devising the strategic mandate, both the Security Council and the SRSG/Force Commander must consider the reality that the military peacekeeping endeavour is only the security umbrella for a much more complex mix of civilian actors.[26] Therefore, both parties should ensure that the mandate clearly addresses the desired chain of command and relationships among the various UN parties, and that a strategy is devised that provides for intelligence support to *all* UN elements and for *integrated operational planning across civil-military lines* once the mission is underway.

As the Brahimi Report points out, policy-makers tend to assume best-case conditions when dealing with worst-case behaviour, and this is most dangerous. Both in Ireland and in Bosnia, for example, best-case conditions were assumed, there was no significant intelligence investment authorised, and as a result, the force commanders were severely disadvantaged and opportunities for containing or improving the situation were over-looked, for lack of proper strategic and operational intelligence resources.[27] Speaking of Bosnia, General Sir Roderick Cordy-Simpson has stated quite clearly, '...we did not understand the conflict when we deployed'.[28]

In addition to providing for proper operational conditions, the UN headquarters must plan for a prolonged strategic intelligence endeavour, both in relation to negotiations at the strategic level, including sustained monitoring of embargoes and sanction enforcement by the various Member States, and in relation to strategic-level calculations intended to stabilise 'highly factionalised situations'.[29]

There are several forms such a strategic intelligence activity might take. Among the competing models are those of a 'think tank', a 'joint intelligence centre' that actually processes and analyses information directly, and a 'joint intelligence committee' along the lines of the British model, with the authority to task the various Member States, and to pass judgement on the varied products received in response to its taskings, but without a large specialist staff of its own.[30]

A combination of a modest strategic 'co-ordination' activity at UN headquarters, with standing regional intelligence centres staffed by the Member States in those regions, with a UN liaison presence, offers another alternative for nurturing a non-intrusive but affordable global intelligence network that relies predominantly on open sources of information and shared multi-cultural analysis.[31]

In the long term, the strategic intelligence competency of the UN is going to depend on whether or not the total culture, and especially the culture of the New York bureaucracy, can be modified to fully integrate intelligence *qua* tailored knowledge discovery, discrimination, distillation, and decision-support into the 'art' of UN diplomacy, negotiation, and operations.[32] More than one observer, but General Cammaert especially, has emphasised the urgent need for the establishment of specialised UN intelligence training centres and specific intelligence courses in support of each of the core UN missions and their key personnel.[33] Such training is not only required for operational forces, but for the bureaucrats in the various UN headquarters and agencies. It will take fully twenty years to grow a new culture at the UN, one that is both committed to individual competence, and respectful of intelligence as a legal ethical foundation for information decision-making. A regular training program for entry-level, mid-career, and senior executives is vital if this transition from one culture to another is to succeed.[34]

It merits comment that the lower levels of UN intelligence competency will not be as effective if they are not appreciated at the strategic level. As General Cammaert notes, had the UN in New York understood that the intelligence on the planned genocide in Rwanda was reliable, the outcome may have been considerably more positive.[35]

Finally, at all levels, intelligence may be considered a form of 'remedial education' for policy-makers, commanders, staffs, and belligerents.[36] The proven process of intelligence, drawing primarily on expert open sources both within and external to the mission Area of Responsibility (AOR), can craft 'learning modules' for use within negotiations and between parties. At a higher level, overt intelligence analysis can be channelled through the Department of Public Information and to the public, ensuring that UN concerns and perceptions, based on very sound, objective, and non-partisan intelligence, constitute the foundation for the international dialog about the complex emergency being addressed on behalf of all Member States.

Strategic Collection

As a general rule, all of the raw information needed to make sound strategic decisions can be found through open sources. Open sources have been found by the most sophisticated Member States to provide at much as 80% of the inputs to 'all-source' intelligence on genocide, terrorism, and proliferation, three topics not normally assumed to be 'open'. The key for the UN is to combine a planned and adroitly managed mix of purchased commercial services including academic studies, legal traveller observations, and commercial imagery, with a deliberate collection plan that identifies specific information needs and then mandates appropriate legal and ethical collection efforts to satisfy those needs.

It is important to avoid confusing planned direct collection that is legal, with covert collection that is intrusive. The activities of private military contractors (PMC) are a case in point. Deliberate overt collection efforts can be devised, both in the home country of the PMC and in the country receiving their training, to carefully calibrate the degree and nature of the support being provided. The point is that such information does not get delivered to the UN by Member States who are sponsoring the covert support, nor does it appear in the newspaper. A professional intelligence organisation within the UN must structure and manage the process of collection.

At this level, with an independent collection capability that relies exclusively on open sources of information[37] the UN will find itself liberated from both dependence on such intelligence as the Member States might choose to provide, and from the indecision that attends those who lack sufficient information to make a decision with confidence that they have at least a reasonable appreciation of the complex matter at hand. It is especially important in the early years that UN strategic collection emphasise both commercial imagery and local photography (both air-breather and hand-held). A picture really is

398

worth 10.000 words, and proper pictures will go a long way toward overcoming the inherent attitude in the New York offices of the UN that all intelligence is inherently manipulative and often wrong.[38]

By the same token, little appears to have been done to turn the vast global presence of the UN into a coherent decision-support network. More than one observer has noted the extraordinary reach and inherent expertise of the many UN agencies, most of which seem to feel that they are autonomous entities that do not need to respond to direction or inquires from New York. A common training course on intelligence, and a global electronic database of UN employees and their subject matter as well as their cultural and foreign area knowledge could over time become a very powerful tool for legal direct collection.[39]

'A force commander needs planning information on roads, terrain negotiability, infrastructure, hazards such as minefields and of course tactical positions and strengths of belligerents.'[40] If the strategic element does not put this together before the mandate is devised, the Force Commander will be at a severe disadvantage from day 1.

At the strategic or UN headquarters level, the military information structure should be planned for worst-case scenarios, and include human intelligence and counterintelligence specialists, foreign area specialists, access to satellite imagery and national databases, and all necessary funds and equipment for both obtaining and exploiting (processing and analysing) geospatial information from many sources.[41]

Language skills for the mission area are a special concern. Although some nations such as Norway and Sweden have made a strategic commitment to maintain personnel fluent in key languages (for instance, Swahili, which made a real difference in the Congo operation)[42], most nations do not take foreign languages as seriously as they should. It would be worthwhile, at this point in the process, to have a single staff officer designated as the Language Liaison Officer (LLO), with the specific responsibility of immediately identifying four groups of language-qualified professionals:

1) Intelligence specialists
2) Non-intelligence specialists

3) Private sector parties available for in-country posting
4) Individuals in any capacity who could be contracted to provide either voice or document translation services via remote means (i.e. 'on call').

An on-going aspect of strategic intelligence, one requiring every bit of diplomatic skill and persistence, is that of constantly negotiating and monitoring and nurturing inter-agency information exchanges within individual Member States, and among Member States.[43] In essence, as the sole party with over-arching responsibility for a particular peacekeeping mission, it falls to the UN in New York, and its liaison officers to the capital cities of individual troop contributing and adjacent Member States, to play the role of 'nanny' in gently but persistently ascertaining if there is information to be shared, and then facilitating the sharing both at the strategic level, and downwards to the Force Commander. If the UN chooses to establish a 'world-class' strategic intelligence cadre, these individuals will bring with them a form of global access and global credibility with the various individual national intelligence agencies that may in many instances overcome obstacles to intelligence sharing that emanate from the policy level with its domestic political calculations rather than the needs of the UN, always foremost.

Finally, in the area of strategic collection, the UN can, quite literally, break new ground by pursuing the vision of 'seven standards for seven tribes'. This vision—a logical descendant of the original concept of *noosphere* by Pierre Teilhard de Chardin, and then of the 'world brain' by H. G. Wells—puts forward the notion that in the age of information, globalisation, and increased inter-dependence, there are actually seven intelligence tribes, not only the one national intelligence tribe generally recognised by every government. The other six intelligence tribes are those associated with the military, law enforcement, business, academia, NGO's and media, and religions or clans as well as citizens. By establishing an Internet-based means for harnessing the distributed intelligence of the seven tribes, the UN can become, in effect, the 'hub' for the global brain, and can devise new means of rapidly identifying, contracting for, and leveraging relevant knowledge on a 'just enough, just in time basis'. The seven standards, addressing global open source collection, multi-media processing, analytic toolkits, analytic tradecraft, defensive security and counterintelligence, personnel training and certification, and leadership (with culture development implicit in leadership) are consistent with the new push by

400

the International Organisation for Standardisation (ISO) to use standards as a means of facilitating the global information society.[44]

Strategic Processing

A major advantage of open sources is that they can be shared with every nationality as well as with non-governmental participants in the planning process for addressing complex emergencies. One positive function that a UN intelligence secretariat could offer is that of a 'service of common concern' for digitising, translating, and making available online all available information, including geospatial information, that is relevant to the planned mission.

With the advent of the Internet, standards associated with web-based information entry and access become important. Coding information with Extended Mark-Up Language (XML), and agreeing on standard ways of adding meta-tags for countries, topics, dates, and locations (XML Geo) will considerably facilitate the exploitation of all available information by various parties.

'...the UN has little competency in analysis, scenario building, and prediction. Desk officers do virtually none of this, being overloaded with simple information gathering and a minimal of organising'.[45] If the UN were to consider some innovative processing solutions, perhaps consulting with George Soros, Ted Turner, and, right in New York, David Cohen, the former CIA manager who is now the Deputy Commissioner for Intelligence for the New York Police Department, as well as Goldman Sachs and other major organisations that have taken processing to its highest level, some gains could be achieved in this area, and open sources could be weighted, clustered, sorted, and visualised automatically, freeing up staff to do more human analysis.

Strategic Analysis[46]

It is vital that the analysis prepared on behalf of the Secretary-General be truly independent analysis reflecting the strategic needs of the UN as a whole, rather than the desires of a specific department or a specific Member State whose analyst on secondment has been directed to come to a specific conclusion. As General Frank van Kappen notes, in his experience, the number of reported refugees and the severity of their reported condition often had less to do with reality and more to do with the specific policy being pursued by individual Member States providing the information to the UN.[47]

Although the UN is a universal organisation with global responsibilities, no one appears to expect it to fulfil a strategic intelligence mission of 'Global Coverage'. Instead, the expectation appears to be that the UN will embrace the concept of intelligence at all levels, will establish a structure for strategic intelligence as the Brahimi Report suggests, and then, on a case by case basis, surge up it capabilities, perhaps by temporarily hiring specialists who have exactly the right foreign area and subject-matter knowledge for a specific contingency.[48]

By the same token, UN analysis may be rejected by Member States. General Cammaert has cited the refusal of the USSR to speak to Dag Hammarskjold regarding the Congo; the efforts of the US to discredit U Thant on Vietnam; the problems Boutros-Ghali encountered in Bosnia and Rwanda.[49] While no Member State desires to deal with a UN that assumes supra-national authorities, there is some considerable value in UN analysis, based exclusively on open sources of information, that can be shared with the public and achieve a credibility with the public across the international community. For the UN, insightful analysis that is trusted by the public could become the equivalent of 'the Pope's divisions'.[50]

One means of being effective at the strategic level is to make innovative use of modelling and simulation. Emerging analytic techniques and tools that are 'off the shelf' and therefore not costly, could provide UN intelligence with an advantage in its dealings with national intelligence bureaucracies that have been resistant to change away from the old industrial and Weberian model of information processing along factory lines.[51]

Strategic Security[52]

Although the UN is proscribed from engaging in clandestine and covert actions, it has a need to track any such actions that come to its attention, and in some cases to object and ask a Member State to cease such actions. At the same time, as the UN has long known, but discovered with renewed force in March 2003, it is itself the target of covert operations by a Member State, and has over the course of several months been deceived both tactically and strategically by ostensibly validated secret source material. A security function is needed, not just in terms of protecting the integrity of the UN decision-process, but in terms of critically evaluating all that is put before the UN from the Member States.

At the same time, the UN has a responsibility to protect the confidences of its sources, both those 'in confidence' from the private sector and those that are officially secret from Member States—while also protecting the integrity of its deliberations. This means that the UN must, as an immediate and global priority, establish commonly respected and accepted means for moving sensitive information securely among its various elements.[53] The importance of establishing a reliable trusted means for communicating and protecting sensitive information cannot be under-stated, if the UN is to become a 'smart' organisation possessing increased capabilities for receiving, delivering, and exchanging sensitive intelligence.[54]

Some authorities question the possibility of the UN ever establishing a reliable 'security clearance' process, simply because of the constant change in seconded personnel and the wide variety in nationalities passing through various positions.[55] In the case of UN intelligence, it may be that some combination of permanent military cadre and permanent civilian cadre who are investigated or 'vetted' can be used to manage the *minority* of the information that is sensitive.[56] It is important to stress that while security is important, easily 80% to 90% of the information that the UN must process in order to make sound strategic decisions is *unclassified* and intended to be publicly shared and discussed.

Whilst the UN demonstrates it 'can keep a secret', it needs to work with the Member States to devise new means of communicating vital warning and threat information from sensitive sources down to the Force Commander and the contingent commanders, without excessive security constraints.[57] Stripping a warning of any reference to its national source, or even the discipline that provided it (signals, imagery, human) could in some cases permit a warning to be delivered that would otherwise be blocked by national security regulations. A professional UN intelligence cadre at the strategic level could over time devise new protocols to enhance UN peacekeeping force protection without placing sensitive sources at risk.

According to A. Walter Dorn, over the course of time, the UN will also have to develop some forms of secret intelligence. He says:

> Secret intelligence is even more important in multidimensional PKO's with their embedded responsibilities: election monitoring, where individual votes must be kept secret, arms control verification, including possible surprise inspections at secret locations, law enforcement agency supervision (to 'watch the watchmen'), mediation where confidential bargaining positions that are confidentially shared by one party with the UN should not be revealed to the other, sanctions and border monitoring, where clandestine activities (e.g. arms shipments) must be uncovered or intercepted without allowing smugglers to take evasive action.[58]

In very high risk areas characterised by clandestine arms shipments, secret plans for aggression or genocide, and threats to assassinate indigenous leaders or to assault UN forces, some forms of secret intelligence are inevitably going to be required and the UN must become reliably competent in this area.[59]

At the strategic level, the UN must ensure that any intelligence structure it creates is kept free of Member State espionage. Among the reasons cited for US objections to the earlier creation of a strategic intelligence unit were fears that it would become a surrogate for Soviet espionage. Although managed at the time by an African (James Jonah from Sierra Leone) and drawing its information exclusively from open sources, this was never-the-less how the unit was perceived by some US Senators.[60] It is incumbent on the UN to devise a solution, perhaps involving a Canadian cadre and very strong counterintelligence co-operation with the US, that will protect its strategic intelligence element from both subversion and suspicion.

A subtle aspect of security is that of public perception. Renaud Theunens points out that the international media is actually a competitor of any UN intelligence endeavour, and both are competing to establish a strategic viewpoint on how the peacekeeping operation is actually going.[61] The case could be made that on the one hand, the UN must balance the strictest security and counterintelligence measures to protect sensitive information, but on the other hand it must strive to release to the public the very best open source intelligence analysis that it is

404

capable of generating. Whether the story is positive or negative, it is the UN, at the strategic level, that should be defining the story with its superior intelligence. UN document control and UN declassification both leave much to be desired, and require some sustained professional attention in the very near future.[62]

Notional Strategic Organisation

The figure below depicts a notional 250-person strategic intelligence organisation that is predominantly devoted to the collection, processing, and analysis of open sources of information, including geospatial information. This same structure could be applied to a multi-cultural regional organisation.[63]

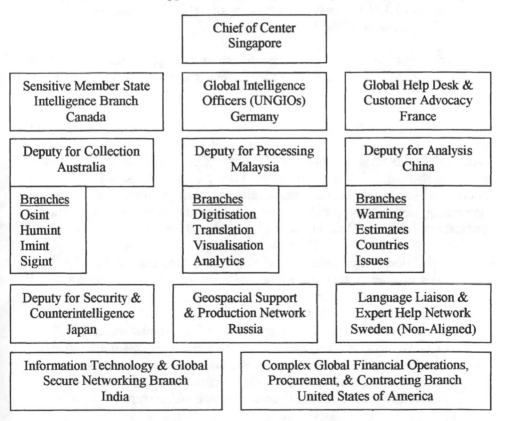

Figure 2: Strategic Intelligence Secretariat, United Nations

Operational Intelligence[64]

Both UN doctrine on 'military information' and UK doctrine on intelligence are outdated and inappropriate.[65] Peacekeeping intelligence is an *emerging doctrine* that is distinct from both of these. Richard Aldrich suggests that low-intensity intelligence doctrine can be generic but does not yet exist. It should stress geographical knowledge and broadly distributed linguistic skills, prior historical knowledge, comprehensive understanding of individual personalities, and extensive liaison to all parties.[66]

> The initial absence of an intelligence structure placed the Force in a dangerously handicapped position which threatened the lives of UN personnel, the success of ONUC operations, and the reputation of the UN itself.[67]

In peacekeeping operations, the normal battalion intelligence staff of 5-6 people simply will not do. In both Ireland and Bosnia, the numbers went up to 30-40 people per battalion.[68] Force Commanders should plan accordingly.[69]

Apart from ensuring that the mission receives the right mandate, the right rules of engagement, and the right force structure, it is possible that there will be no other more important function for the Force Commander than to ensure the establishment of a Force Intelligence Plan that simultaneously creates the operational-level intelligence staff able to manage force-wide collection, processing, and analysis, and also provides for the coherent management of tactical intelligence collection, processing, and analysis.

> Situational awareness' is of paramount importance for the commander, and must include non-military as well as military factors, and must also include the monitoring and understanding of factors external to the immediate mission area. A commander responsible for transitioning an environment toward mission conclusion must maintain an intelligence interest in refugees and displaced persons; politics; economic development; social, cultural, and religious development; and last but not least, crime and corruption.[70]

Peace support operations (PSO) differ considerably from traditional military combat operations. Different mandates, rules of engagement, belligerent 'rules of the game', almost everything is 'different' and this requires that the operational intelligence unit re-orient itself and adjust accordingly. 'The complex operational environment is unpredictable and asymmetric'.[71] One expert suggests that peace support operations not only must pay greater heed to intelligence, but also could in fact be considered 'intelligence-driven operations'.[72]

The selection of specific national contingents and specific national support packages may play a role in the effectiveness of the tactical collection effort. As Dame Neville-Jones observes, in Bosnia 'The zones designated to the different national battalions often became virtually isolated fiefdoms where the forces did their own thing, which, all too often, was not very much'.[73] If not through pre-selection, then through post-deployment liaison and secondments used for cross-fertilisation purposes, the Force Commander must ensure that the various tactical units are melded into an *operational* force and not allowed to conduct either intelligence or operations in isolation.

It is essential, because of the maximum vulnerability faced by the force in its very early days, that the Military Intelligence Preparation of the Battlefield (MIPB) system be in place from day 1. This system must be understood and implemented down to the platoon level and by 'all hands' acting as the eyes and ears of the commander.[74]

'Communications without intelligence is noise, and intelligence without communications is irrelevant'. So said General Alfred M. Gray, Commandant of the Marine Corps, in explaining to Congress why the Marine Corps was the only service that fully integrated the management of communications with the management of intelligence. Modern militaries tend to assume unlimited bandwidth. This is simply not realistic for UN peacekeeping operations in remote areas, and it is incumbent on the Force Commander to ensure that sufficient *tactically-relevant* communications capabilities are introduced into the AOR. In particular, the Force Commander may wish to take lessons from the UNSCOM endeavour and make greater use of concealed networks of video cameras, ground sensors, and remote processing of intercepted signals. In brief, not only must the Force Commander plan for the most robust all-source intelligence network possible, but the Force Commander must also ensure that the redundant and *secure* communications capabilities are there as well.[75]

A Force Commander can make a difference in intelligence by avoiding any assumptions as to competency levels[76], and providing early on for a common base of training and clear understandings as to force-wide intelligence objectives. Asking for a mobile training team fluent in both French and English and able to tour each of the tactical units, stand watch with each unit for a week, and 'set the tone' for the *tactical-operational intelligence interface*, may well be one of the Force Commander's most important contributions to the eventual success of the mission.[77]

The Force Commander can also make a difference by recognising that both the indigenous parties and the various components of the UN humanitarian system, as well as their relief association counterparts, will all have a generally negative view of 'intelligence'.[78] Educating the leadership of all of the parties that the force is in contact with, and stressing constantly the importance of legal, ethical 'situational awareness', is an inherent responsibility of the commander. At the same time, for the next several generations, Force Commanders will be responsible for devising, testing, and documenting emerging doctrine dealing with how aggressive the UN should be in seeking out information under different circumstances; with the degree to which overtly collected information could or should be shared with parties to the conflict; with the degree to which covertly collected information should be used in direct demarches to the offending party, and so on.[79]

Another delicate aspect of the operational intelligence situation is that dealing with lawlessness, crime, and corruption. In most cases, neither the mandate nor the force structure will permit the commander to engage in 'law enforcement' activities, but information and intelligence relevant to these threats to stability will be encountered. The Force Commander must devise, as Lord Ashdown and General Van Diepenbrugge devised, means of exchanging information helpful to one another's distinct mandates.[80] In some instances, the intelligence may be so compelling as to suggest special communications to UN headquarters and a recommendation for a strategic decision to change both the mandate and the force structure, augmenting it with a law enforcement mission and law enforcement specialists.[81]

408

The matter of crime is not one that can be under-stated. In both Ireland and Bosnia, to take two examples, extortion, bank robbing, and petrol smuggling on the one hand; and prostitution and narcotics on the other, were major aspects of the conflict. 'Ireland, and subsequently Yugoslavia, re-affirmed the intense and (generally unappreciated) unseen linkage between the growing importance of 'global issues' such as organised crime, drugs and illegal trafficking in light weapons on the one hand, and local or regional conflicts on the other'.[82]

According to one expert observer, in both Ireland and Bosnia there were three ways in which operational intelligence supported the larger information operations objectives: first, by winning public confidence; second by countering misinformation spread by the paramilitaries; and third, by devising misinformation meant to unbalance the paramilitaries.[83]

Finally, one observer notes that peace operations, unlike normal combat operations, can actually see the international media emerge as policy drivers and therefore an operational factor to be monitored carefully.[84]

Operational Collection

While there will be challenges to the authority of the Force Commander from the national contingents, a basic condition for maintaining good order in the overall collection plan is to require that all tactical collection activities be co-ordinated with the operational headquarters. This is especially intended to apply to French, British, and American special forces.[85] At all costs the Force Commander must guide the tactical units in ensuring that the ground is 'not trampled' and that the modest opportunities for human collection are not corrupted by multiple approaches from different collectors.[86]

In conditions of instability where sub-state actors largely unknown to the Western powers are engaged in deadly conflicts with one another, their locations and capabilities may be known, but their plans and intentions require rigorous attentive collection efforts. For this, there is no substitute for human intelligence.[87]

A primary objective of the operational collection plan is force protection.[88] In this regard, 'The security or insecurity of transport and supplies is also crucial'.[89]

Wireless interception capabilities are fundamental, and include both the monitoring of local language radio broadcasts as well as the interception and, if necessary, decryption of communications by all parties. Such capabilities are discreet and 'invisible'.[90] It merits comment that the Force Commander must specifically address, in advance of deployment, the inclusion of both intercept operators with local language skills at high levels of competency, and of at least one or two trained cryptographic analysts.[91]

Aerial reconnaissance capabilities are valuable *if* they have the photo-interpretation personnel (even one person) and equipment needed to exploit their collection.[92] Fixed-wing aircraft, helicopters carrying cameras with large aperture lenses and high magnification (as well as television cameras), and unmanned drones, are all helpful.[93] The Force Commander should not overlook the simple debriefing of all aviation personnel, this is best done as a mandatory and regular procedure, to which at least one dedicated team of debriefers should be assigned.[94]

The Swedish government's provision of two Saab 29C aircraft equipped for photo-reconnaissance, and a photo-interpretation detachment, was a major contribution to the security of the force in the Congo. Less readily available were radar sets with which to monitor aircraft activity throughout the operational area, something that every Force Commander should ask for.[95]

Critical collection factors at the operational level include population (not just demography but history, culture, religious sites, homes of local leaders); military geography; personalities and detailed background (i.e. military services) of gang leaders; and potential courses of action for each gang, faction, and party, including third parties (private relief agencies, private military contractors).[96]

Targets for operational as well as tactical collection include 'paramilitaries, volunteers, self-declared police forces, freedom fighters, or even criminal networks and the gangs they control'.[97]

Force Commanders should plan for structured intelligence capabilities able to handle as many as 10-20 debriefings a month, in some instances many more. This is a labour-intensive requirement that should not be assigned to intelligence staff as a matter of conflicting routine.[98]

410

The availability of indigenous language skills is a major factor in whether or not the operational collection plan can be carried out. While some have relied on locally hired interpreters, they represent severe disadvantages in that they are vulnerable to blackmail and often cannot move freely into territories controlled by other ethnic groups.[99]

External open sources are relevant at the operational level. Apart from the Internet, there are subscription-based services including regional news services,[100] as well as foreign area expertise, maps, imagery, and directed legal traveller reconnaissance and business intelligence services.

> Recent findings place as a top priority... It is not covert cloak-and-dagger spy work but a carefully planned and executed collection that is sensitive in nature. It requires trained teams working in-theatre for extensive periods of time.[101]

Under conditions of high risk and when facing situations where a mission may change quickly and demand peace enforcement, it is essential that the Force Commander have the mandate and the funding to support confidential-level human information collection (informants).[102] The emphasis on human collection shortfalls, and the urgency of correcting those shortfalls to provide proper intelligence support to the Force Commander, is a constant theme in virtually every professional review of lessons learned from prior peacekeeping operations.[103]

> Effective peacekeeping requires the proactive acquisition and prudent analysis of information about conditions within the mission area. This is especially true if the operation is conducted in a hazardous and unpredictable environment and the lives of peacekeepers are threatened[104]

By the same token, under conditions of high risk and in the face of overwhelming challenges to the adequacy of any UN-controlled operational intelligence endeavour, it appears generally accepted, at least at the highest levels of those engaged in Bosnia, that the American contribution in terms of signals interception from national and field capabilities, are essential. According to General Sir Roderick Cordy-Simpson, '...we would have been in dead trouble in any operation without them…I would emphasise time and time again that the intelligence which the Americans brought with all their capabilities was something that I know that I as a commander on the ground I simply would not have survived without'.[105]

A countervailing point of view is that the Americans are too dependent on technical intelligence sources. The commanding general of Saudi forces during Desert Storm, for example, has stated: 'I was struck by the fact that in their intelligence gathering the Americans depended overwhelmingly on technology, satellite surveillance, radio intercepts and so forth, a very little on human sources'.[106] Because technical sources tend also to be very 'top secret' and over-compartmentalised, one American military expert has commented that the products from these sources are difficult to sanitise and distribute, while also being put forward as a substitute for human assets, whose arrival is consequently delayed.[107]

Unconventional capabilities not normally considered part of the intelligence domain can yield a very good result for the operational commander. General Tony van Diepenbrugge focuses on two in particular: Radio Oksigen, a low-cost high-impact means of reaching youth in the 16 to 25 year-old range; and civil-military co-operation (CIMIC), used to improve relations with local populations, not only through humanitarian assistance, but through direct social contacts such as in the coaching of soccer teams. Both lead to the volunteering of militarily useful information.[108]

Another excellent source that can be tapped informally is that of the UN Military Observers (UNMO). Although not in the same chain of command and operating under a different mandate, they can be helpful.[109]

However, in dealing with non-intelligence observers and collectors of Humint, it is essential to remember that they are not trained intelligence professionals, and their reporting could lead to both information overflow and misinformation. The force commander should endeavour to both provide some training to all of these individuals, and also sponsor a systematic debriefing program that can filter their knowledge within a professional intelligence framework.[110]

The matter of training all personnel through and about intelligence merits emphasis. United Nations Training Assistance Teams (UNTAT) working at the Westdown Camp on Salisbury Plain are said to have made a considerable difference in the effectiveness of forces deployed to Bosnia. Such teams take time to develop.[111] In the Congo, a lack of proper orientation of patrols led to a massacre when a patrol did not understand that the Baluba tribesmen confronting it were dangerous and hostile, the patrol thought they were friendly, and their bows and arrows harmless. Only two survived.[112]

In dealing with national intelligence cells that are not obligated to give the commander anything, two factors can be used to improve access to intelligence: first, the principle of reciprocity, where the commander deliberately sanctions sharing and exchange; and personalities. Personal relations are vital to assuring a positive flow of both sensitive intelligence information among contingents, and commanders must be conscious of the importance of having the right personalities in the role of liaison officers.[113] Renaud Theunens believes the UN should adopt the Military Intelligence Liaison Officer (MILO) concept of the United Kingdom,[114] perhaps asking Member States to identify such individuals, and then providing, as General Cammaert and Van Diepenbrugge have suggested, a common base of training for this multinational capability. Theunens also proposes sharp limitations on independent national intelligence cells, and instead recommends that a Joint All Source Intelligence Cell (JASIC) be formed that is directly responsive to the Force Commander.[115]

National tactical collection capabilities will tend to be sensitive but they must be harnessed. Especially valuable, apart from traditional signals collection capabilities, are Unmanned Aerial Vehicles (UAV), which have 'provided a relatively cost-effective and timely means to deliver imagery on high value targets.'[116] Although the national contingents may initially resist, the establishment of centralised collection management and co-ordination, with a single focal point for each type of collection, is vital.[117] The Baghdad Monitoring and Verification Centre (BMVC) is cited by one authority as an example of a success story.[118]

The U-2 is now being made available to UN forces,[119] and C-130 imagery and signals intelligence platforms can also be requested from the Americans.

The commander should avoid becoming overly dependent on sensors and detectors. The commander will get good intelligence '…only by fully engaging the human factor in all steps of the intelligence cycle, focused on studying and understanding the attitudes and aspirations of *all* of the parties.[120]

Tactical intelligence is vital to the success of the mission 'in detail' and it is the foundation of the mission's credibility. 'If intelligence is not deftly handled, it is easy for the organisation to gain a reputation for being slow to react and for gullibility and political partiality'…counterintelligence may be necessary…[121]

The figure below summarises operational collection options:[122]

Permitted (White)	Questionable (Grey)	Prohibited (Black)
Visual Observation		
- Observation posts	- Observation after forced entry	
- Vehicular observation	- Observers concealed or camouflaged	
- Aerial reconnaissance	- Observers out of mission area	
Sensors		
- Visible (video) - Infrared (IR), radar, X-ray, satellite		
- Ground sensors (acoustic/seismic)		
Human Communications		
- UN personnel: - Clearly, identified	- Unidentified	-Undercover/disguised
- Informants: - Unpaid - Rewarded - Paid (agents)		
- Radio message interception (SIGINT)*		- wiretaps
* clear *and* encoded messages		
Documents (read/copy/distribute)		
- public - private	- confidential	- stolen

◄———————— **Passive** ——————————— **Active** ————————►
Overt   **Covert**

Figure 3. Information-Gathering Spectrum from Permitted to Prohibited

Finally, the commander can make a difference in the totality of the operational collection endeavour by fostering 'complementary footprints', which is to say, spreading the representatives from the various elements out so that no one place has a cluster of duplicative representatives. By dividing locations and developing a system to exchange information in a structured way, with fixed meeting and fixed agenda, the whole does become greater than the sum of the parts.[123]

Operational Processing

Geographic Information Systems (GIS) are worth their weight in gold. Commanders should ensure that they not only have the GIS equipment, but also the $5 cables for connecting the GIS equipment to computers and printers.[124]

The availability of software for link-analysis and other automated data processing is a significant shortfall. In combination with the limited to non-existent ability of analysts within different contingents to leverage multiple databases from one location, the operational processing capability at this time is quite constrained.[125]

Document exploitation is one area where information technology advances can be of considerable assistance to the Force Commander. In addition to equipping patrols with digital cameras whose images can be rapidly transmitted back to the intelligence staff, they should also be equipped with hand-held scanners that can copy and transmit selected sections of captured documents. For larger volumes of captured documents, the Force Commander should consider having a small specialist cell able to screen documents, dividing them into those that are of immediate priority and must be translated in the field; those that are of longer-term importance and should be scanned and transmitted to translators elsewhere in the world; and those that can be set aside.[126]

Until a UN intelligence structure is created, where reliable assessments can be created at each level and are trusted, there will be a tendency for intelligence information to either not flow at all, or flow without control, up and down and sideways. This threatens to swamp the few analysts at each level.[127] It would be helpful for the UN to devise an Internet-based means for entering and accessing all data, using commercially-available security, as a means of at least achieving two goals: one-time data entry with force-wide access; and automated storage and retrieval.[128]

Operational Analysis

'...one or two really sharp officers are of more value to me as a force commander than having an intelligence section of fifteen people who are engaged in a 'process'. That process tells me history, not implications, predictions, and expected belligerent Courses of Action (CAO's) which I need

415

to know.'[129] Rank should not be allowed to inhibit the commander's utilisation of the best available analysts.[130]

'...profile the personalities, monitor the bigger picture, know the history of the conflict, monitor the media and political scene, analyse motives'.[131]

'The intelligence is not only fragmentary, it does not adhere to the rules of regular war. An example: a report about four tanks on a road, if analysed in the traditional way, would be interpreted as a reinforced platoon or a company that would constitute 'only' a reconnaissance patrol. In Bosnia in 1995, the same four tanks would have heralded a major offensive.'[132]

'In traditional peacekeeping operations there is no enemy. Instead you have warring factions toward which you have to remain impartial.'[133] It could be said that unlike normal political or military situations, where there is a given incumbent and an identified 'enemy', in peacekeeping situations there are no constants and no certainties, and the analysis challenge is much greater, every party must be viewed with *equal suspicion* and analysis must be applied to the plans, intentions, and potential course of action of all parties, whether armed, unarmed, hostile or friendly.

One potentially disruptive aspect of operational analysis will be the conflicting views that are generated by senior NATO officers who have access to national sources that may not be shareable with, for example, a Swedish non-aligned officer even if that officer is in charge of the force intelligence campaign.[134] One means of dealing with this is to refuse private briefings, but to sponsor round-table discussions where NATO dissent or input is encouraged on an 'informed opinion' basis, without producing sources or specifics. This at least will ensure that all key force intelligence managers are sharing the same perspective on the battlefield.

The operational intelligence analysis effort must avoid being consumed with day-to-day intelligence requirements. Personnel, time, and resources must be set aside and protected, to focus on longer-term evaluations and assessments.[135] One experienced officer appreciates the distinctions of 'basic-descriptive' (fixed factors), 'current-reportorial' (recent and emerging), and 'speculative-estimative' (future assessments).[136]

416

'To understand a conflict like the one in the Balkans you have to learn the history, religion, cultures, and ways of thinking in the countries concerned. The lesson learned is that what is irrelevant in Stockholm and The Hague may very well be relevant in Pale.[137]

'Due to the nature of the conflict, the local power centres amalgamate military, economical, and political power. The objectives of the local parties are often determined by hard to quantify and qualify political and socio-cultural factors, which may appear irrational in our 'Westernised' judgement.'[138]

Deliberate efforts to create a frame of reference or framework to which analysts can attach and test their ideas to identify patterns, are recommended. So also are role-playing and scenario development, with the caution that these efforts require the participation of many others, not just the staff analysts. Perhaps most importantly, once a scenario has been found to be plausible, it should be delivered to the contingent commanders and their staff in face-to-face mode, and explained properly so they can be alert to indicators that the scenario might be upon them.[139]

It is important, in conducting peacekeeping intelligence analysis, to very clearly understand that traditional military indicators are not the primary signals that must be perceived and integrated. Unconventional combatants do not drive tanks, they drive 'technicals', Toyota pick-up trucks with machine guns crudely mounted in the back. They do not wear uniforms. Over time the analyst will establish a sense of the different things to be looking for, and can promulgate to the tactical units and the varied human collectors a 'playbook' specific to the AOR.[140]

A Force Commander would benefit from instituting a feedback or evaluation loop on all estimative intelligence, seeking to determine over time how well specific analysts and specific predicted course of action came to pass.[141]

Operational Security

The Force Commander has a responsibility to protect the impartiality of the UN mission by ensuring that any information they collect on one belligerent is not inadvertently intercepted by another belligerent. For this reason, establishing reliable secure communications among the units and with higher headquarters is a significant command responsibility.[142]

Among the specific counterintelligence aspects recommended by General Cammaert are a pre-deployment analysis of intelligence collection capabilities by the opposing groups, the assignment of a qualified counterintelligence officer to the headquarters staff; the assignment of a computer network information security specialists to the staff; the early integration of appropriate computer security hardware and software throughout the operational headquarters; and the inclusion of several field investigation/interviewing teams in the planned force structure.[143]

As the UN gets involved in human rights monitoring and the prevention of genocide, it must be prepared to recognise and counter substantial efforts by belligerents who will place UN officials under human and technical surveillance, as happened, for example, in Guatemala in the 1990's.[144]

It is imperative that the Force Commander not under-estimate the ability of non-state belligerents to conduct sophisticated and pervasive human and technical intelligence operations against the UN peacekeepers. Many belligerent groups are able to draw on both direct government support (e.g. as occurred in the Croation-Serbian conflict when the West chose sides secretly) or sympathisers in First World countries who can procure advanced commercial systems; some terrorist groups have a higher ratio of electrical engineering Ph.D.'s than most governments; and some insurgent groups have such a strong will and strong work ethic that they can accomplish amazing feats, such as digging tunnels right up to the G-3 Operations Centre, placing either a human or a microphone directly beneath the chief's desk.[145]

Information security must be a constant aspect of the commander's operational planning and execution.[146] 'At all levels, one of the toughest lessons that UK forces had to learn in both Ireland and Bosnia was that of COMSEC.' This challenge is complicated when forces deploy with poor equipment that will not work in urban areas, when forces substitute commercial cell phones for radios, and when the non-state belligerents are themselves highly sophisticated at technical collection, not just passive airwave monitoring, but active 'bugging' of force headquarters telephones and offices.[147] (NOTE: Force Commanders who feel that cellular telephones are an essential part of their communications

418

flexibility may wish to consult the Finnish military and have them oversee the distribution of Nokia cellular phones with embedded encryption capabilities.)

'Perception security' might be a useful term for focusing attention on situations where the UN could be tainted or threatened by the behaviour of those it is supporting. In the Congo, for example, an individual under escort from the UN made such inflammatory statements that those he was speaking to assumed the UN shared his views, leading to an attack on a 90-man dispersed garrison, of whom 47 were killed.[148] The Force Commander must stress to all hands that they are responsible for constantly monitoring, interpreting, and reporting all that they see, especially when UN armed personal are publicly accompanying belligerent personalities whose actions or words might create an imminent threat to UN forces.

There is another aspect of security that must concern the Force Commander, and that is the necessity, if within the mandate, of training local security forces. Israeli experience suggests that only a local security service is truly capable of dealing with its own terrorists and crime bosses, but Israeli experience in observing American training of the Palestinian Authority also cautions that one must know who is being trained, many of those the Americans trained were, unbeknownst to them, former terrorists. Hence, the Force Commander should be planning for early reconstruction and revitalisation of local security services, but must also plan for intelligence and counterintelligence 'vetting' of everyone to be joined and trained.[149]

The UN is not yet ready for another aspect of intelligence, that of covert negotiations that are secret from the media as well as other parties. As one contributor noted, in the Middle East, many moderate Arab leaders have paid with their lives for being known to be in dialog with Israel, and one benefit of a truly 'secret service' is that it can open doors that will not open in public.[150]

Tactical Intelligence

Tactical intelligence in peacekeeping operations must more properly be considered *tactical-operational* or *operational-tactical*. Because of the political implications of every action, however minor, the contingent commanders must understand, and must direct their intelligence capabilities so as to emphasise, that the SRSG's political objectives, and the Force Commander's operational mission objectives, must be kept in mind at all times.

Tactical Collection

Peacekeeping intelligence collection is a *bottom-up* process, largely requiring that the tactical units collect and evaluate the indigenous order of battle 'from scratch'.[151] At both the tactical and the operational levels, a database of specific *personalities* will be most helpful to the Force Commander and the contingent commanders.[152]

A major distinction between traditional tactical intelligence focused on organised armed and uniformed conventional forces, and peacekeeping tactical intelligence, is that political intelligence gathering becomes of paramount importance, not just the collection of what is said overtly, and the overt observation of behaviours and patterns that may often be at variance with what is said, but also the collection through whatever sanctioned means might be available, of what is said behind closed doors that may help the tactical commander and the Force commander understand plans and intentions.[153]

At the tactical level as well as the operational level, having peacekeepers perform a variety of unconventional civil affairs roles is helpful in collection, and these responsibilities should be entertained by the contingent and force commanders as opportunities rather than distractions.[154]

The 'Mark I eyeball' remains the most valuable tool[155] and every peacekeeper must be trained to observe and debriefed in a timely manner. In addition to the human eye, the value of digital cameras and video recorders cannot be over-stated. With such devices scattered around the force and able to send images back to the operational level (or as appropriate, to New York), 'the commander is already ten steps ahead in the game that he would otherwise be'.[156]

Military police and UN civilian police units should be regarded as human collection assets, and receive commensurate orientation, training, and debriefing.[157] NGO's represent a different kind of opportunity. Here their reluctance to be tainted in any way must be respected, but their value cannot be ignored: their representatives 'have generally been present in the region longer than UN forces, speak the languages of the countries involved, know and have

420

the trust of local officials, and have a deeper perspective on the events surrounding them than UN forces'.[158]

Convoy drivers, patrols, and individuals who have been manning observation posts should all be part of a structured debriefing program.[159]

Indeed, debriefing has been cited by most after-action reports and articles as one of the most important contributors to situational awareness at the tactical and operational levels.[160] However, debriefing is labour intensive, and most force structures do not include sufficient dedicated interrogator-translator teams or funds for sufficient contracted translators (both expatriate and indigenous).

Patrolling is also a vital aspect of intelligence collection as well as public reassurance. One innovation that enhanced the security of patrols was that of covertly emplaced 'overwatch' teams able to observe large areas and warn the patrols of ambushes in preparation.[161]

Translators and ideally translators, who are not from the local area nor restricted by their clan association from free movement through the entire AOR, are extremely helpful. One American success story, a surprisingly unconventional solution borne out of desperation, was the use of contracted Somali interpreters, many of them taxi drivers by trade, who were able to provide reliable unbiased translations, and interpretations of body language (both ways).[162]

As a general rule, overt human intelligence will be extremely important to the tactical commander.[163]

Tactical Processing

Patrol reports and other tactical observers must be debriefed and evaluated as quickly and efficiently as possible. At the tactical level most of the processing is labour-intensive, and staffing should be allocated accordingly. For example, although the battalion intelligence staff can and should conduct debriefings on occasion, it is much more effective to have several professional interrogator-translator teams, each equipped with laptop computers and secure means of sending digital reports.

Tactical Analysis

Irrespective of whether the peacekeeping force is invited or intrusive, tactical units must never take any information offered by any 'host' official or any 'friendly' party at face value. At the same time, whatever covertly obtained intelligence that may be received from 'on high' must be treated with equal suspicion. 'National Intelligence can be wrong, and can certainly be out of date'.[164]

Tactical intelligence collected in isolation from history, culture, and context will be largely irrelevant to the outcome. Among the most important lessons learned (and then promptly forgotten) by the Americans in various peacekeeping operations, are the vital necessity of understanding the culture, who (precisely) makes the decisions, how the infrastructure is designed, and the specific values and taboos.[165] Somalia, for example, will stand for a very long time as an example of the cost of failing to understand sub-state tribal or clan power structures, interests, and intentions.

Tactical Security

Bad things happen in multiples. The American practice of sending CRITIC messages when special events occur (such as a suicide bombing against the Marine barracks in Beirut) could be usefully emulated by the Force Commander. Had there been a similar local area warning network in place, the suicide bombing of the French barracks later on the same day might have been averted.[166]

The issue of warning from higher and adjacent commands is one that merits new doctrine and new methods. At this time most national-level warnings are so imprecise (and sometimes so frequent) that 'warning fatigue' occurs. It may be worthwhile to have one individual assigned exclusively to the task of filtering and considering warnings in the local context, while also pursuing every liaison opportunity to collect on any indications or warning notices that might be made available.

Sometimes, military regulations can place peacekeepers at risk. American regulations in Bosnia, for example, required all personnel, including overt human intelligence collectors, to wear full battle-dress, carry shoulder weapons, and travel in conspicuous four-vehicle convoys.[167] The Force Commander must promulgate reasonable 'rules of engagement' for human collectors that enhance their safety through a reduction of their conspicuousness. Long hair, beards, and local transport can often be superior to bullet-proof vests, and are a required accommodation for selected personnel with collection responsibilities under low-intensity asymmetric warfare conditions.

Concluding Observations

Millions more will die as the great powers compete with one another or vie to fulfil the personal visions of their leaders, some of whom have little regard for the views and concerns of the majority of the global population. In this context, the United Nations stands alone as the universal organisation whose potential for enhancing global security and prosperity is unrivalled. The challenges, however, are great, and the financial and military and civilian personnel resources are small.

Intelligence *qua* knowledge; intelligence *qua* understanding; intelligence *qua* networked minds harnessed for the common good; intelligence converted into *public wisdom* and *shared perceptions*, may prove to be the missing element whose absence has constrained UN effectiveness.

The Brahimi Report is the perfect catalyst for promptly establishing a new UN acceptance of and exploitation of the proven process of intelligence as a legal, ethical, professional means of collecting, processing, analysing, and keeping safe such information as might help the UN leadership establish the correct mandates, establish the correct force structures, and fulfil every peacekeeping mission with precision.

As a group, we are all in agreement. The UN should immediately establish a strategic intelligence secretariat consisting of the very highest calibre of people with direct access to funds for the purchase of open sources of information. The UN should devise an operational intelligence concept of operations that includes increased availability of various standing packages from the Member States and perhaps regular PKI exercises among varied elements. Finally, the UN should immediately commission the creation of a UN intelligence training curriculum, to be offered both as a residency course and as a mobile training course. The way is open for 'UN intelligence'.

Endnotes

---

[1] Digest prepared by Robert David Steele, bear@oss.net, drawing from each of the conference contributions and seminal past publications included in *PEACEKEEPING INTELLIGENCE: Emerging Concepts for the Future* (OSS, 2003). Observations without endnotes are based on Steele's experience. The Netherlands Intelligence Studies Association (NISA) and its board members and editors Ben de Jong and Wies Platje in particular are to be thanked for making this possible by organising the first event dedicated to Peacekeeping Intelligence (PKI), with the kind logistical and financial support of the Netherlands Defence College. It is expected that this Digest will be enhanced as successive annual conferences are held on this vital topic, with an updated version being published on a regular basis. This specific chapter (and future editions) can be downloaded free from www.oss.net (home page, beneath book cover on right) and from the new Peacekeeping Intelligence website hosted by the Center for Defence and Security Studies of Carlton University in Canada, at www.carleton.ca/csds/pki.

[2] Hugh Smith, 'Intelligence and UN Peacekeeping', *Survival* 36/3 (Autumn 1994), p.175. In *PEACEKEEPING INTELLIGENCE*,(hereafter, *PI*), Chapter 14, pp.230.

[3] The best and most responsive provider of Russian military maps for peacekeepers is Eastview Cartographic, founded and led today by Mr. Kent Lee. The maps cost as little as $145 a sheet, and can be delivered digitally as well as in hard-copy.

[4] *Cf.* Robert David Steele, *ON INTELLIGENCE: Spies and Secrecy in an Open World* (AFCEA 2000, OSS 2002), a book severely critical (in the spirit of 'tough love') of the US national intelligence community and its $30 billion a year obsession with covert satellite collection.

[5] As a practical example, a tribal order of battle, down to the village and elder level, can be prepared for between $10,000 and $20,000. Such studies were done by the OSS Nordic team for Afghanistan and Iraq as the US was planning invasions of each of these countries. In the case of Iraq the deliverables included both a complex wall map of relations among tribes and individuals, and a color-coded map of Iraq showing tribal attitudes toward non-Iraqi elements in red (hostile), yellow, and green.

[6] See the extracts with intelligence footnotes, *PI* pp.381-388.

[7] Although some Member States continue to object, the need of the UN for a structured analysis and assessments staff is now beyond dispute. Since Secretary General Boutros-Ghali called for strengthening these arrangements in his book, *An Agenda for Peace* (NY: UN, 1992), to the 1994 findings of the Commission on Inquiry that investigated the attacks on UNSCOM II personnel, to the Brahimi Report, the evidence is clear. The UN cannot be effective without structured intelligence capabilities. *Cf.* Ramsbotham, p.281.

424

[8] Requirements definition, collection management, source discovery and validation, multi-source fusion, compelling presentation. If the wrong question is asked—or accepted for action, time and money will be wasted. If the UN intelligence professional does not know the best sources to access—and at what cost when purchasing imagery or any other legal open source—money will be wasted. Finally, if the UN intelligence professional does not know how to discriminate, distill, and deliver actionable intelligence, the Force Commander or Special Representative of the Secretary General (SRSG) will not receive the full benefit of the intelligence process. On the urgency of establishing a UN intelligence training program, see Cammaert, p.24, and Van Diepenbrugge, p.38. Aid, p.153, also emphasises this need.

[9] Canada would be especially well-qualified to establish both a resident and a mobile training program. Indeed, the author believes that the greatest service Canada might render to UN peacekeeping operations could be in the establishment of a dedicated intelligence brigade from which intelligence battalions and companies can be provided to the various force commanders as a mixed operational-training cadre to whom other nationals can be attached and trained up. This unit would also provide continuity, a requirement emphasised by General Van Diepenbrugge, p.38.

[10] See the page immediately following this Digest, entitled 'Open Source Intelligence References'. Over fifteen international conferences have been held on the topic of OSINT, each producing between one and four volumes of *Proceedings*. Over 6,000 people from over 40 countries have been trained in this newly-appreciated but oldest of the intelligence disciplines, and numerous dedicated OSINT centres now exist in various countries including Australia, The Netherlands, South Africa, and Sweden. Most militaries today have OSINT action officers, and have integrated OSINT into their normal operating procedures.

[11] As Hugh Smith notes in his seminal article, current circumstances confronting the UN around the world 'have made the requirement for good and timely intelligence overwhelming'. Smith, p.230.

[12] Smith, p.231, 246.

[13] Dorn and Bell, p.255.

[14] Shpiro, p.103-105, referring to UNTSO (United Nations Truce Supervision Organisation), UNDOF (United Nations Disengagement Force), and UNIFIL (United Nations Interim Force in Lebanon).

[15] William Shawcross, *DELIVER US FROM EVIL: Peacekeepers, Warlords and a World of Endless Conflict* (New York: Simon & Schuster, 2000).

[16] It takes roughly two years for a conventional force to become competent at low-intensity conflict (LIC) or 'small wars', and they are then *not* competent at 'big war' or conventional tactics. This is a lesson that both the Americans and the British have tended to forget time and time again. Although some have proposed that the Americans limit themselves to providing intelligence and logistics support to peacekeeping

operations, while the smaller and middle powers such as Canada become expert at small wars and at dealing with their own regional uprisings, we must disagree for the simple reason that American intelligence is not now and never will be competent at providing direct support to peacekeeping operations unless it has officers at every level with actual experience in the field.

[17] Although a number of the contributors make reference to the blending or merging of the levels of analysis and operations, in some cases suggesting that it is no longer possible to isolate one from the other, it is still useful, whatever the degree of overlap, to think of and plan for these three levels in discrete terms.

[18] Patrick Cammaert, p.12. General Cammaert makes frequent reference to the Brahimi Report as an essential beginning to the longer-term process of creating strategic and operational intelligence competence in support of UN missions.

[19] The Brahimi Report recommendations represent both an internally-valid process for arriving at conclusions similar to many of those put forward in this book and this PKI Leadership Digest 1.0, and a sensible starting point for over-coming decades of cultural antipathy to the concept of being informed and knowledgeable in a structured way.

[20] 'The Secretariat must not apply best-case planning assumptions to situations where the local actors historically have exhibited worst-case behaviour'. Cammaert, p.15, citing Brahimi Recommendations (see the extracts beginning at page 381), and p.19.

[21] 'Rules of engagement should be sufficiently robust and not force United Nations contingents to cede the initiative to their attackers.' Cammaert, p.15, citing the Brahimi Report. Aldrich, p.87, points out the ludicrous nature of the UNPROFOR rules of engagement, where the running joke was 'if you make a wrong move, I will speak to my colonel who will ask the general to ask our national defence minister to ask the prime minister to ask the rest of the UN to order me to open fire, so be warned'.

[22] Cammaert, p.21 discusses the dismay of a force commander that learns that many of his contingents have no idea what intelligence is, and no organic capabilities. As he has found in his field experience, units with organic intelligence capabilities, especially human intelligence (e.g. interrogator-translator teams), do better at controlling their Area of Responsibility (AOR).

[23] Since the end of the Cold War, Russian military maps have become the primary source of reliable geospatial information for operations in the Third World. There are, however, some concerns about this source being closed at some point—their maps of China for example, have been taken off the market after a demarche from the Chinese. It would be in the best interests of the UN to consult with the most prosperous members of the Security Council, and devise a means of acquiring one complete set of *all* available Russian military maps, at once. Although the Americans have superior Digital Terrain Elevation Data (DTED) from the shuttle mission, and can draw on one-meter sources to create specific maps 'on the fly', the Americans are incapable of

replicating the Russian military maps, which represent hundreds of man-years of effort in both imagery analysis and cartographic production.

[24] Boeing Autometric and SPOT Image both provide excellent post processing services.

[25] Smith, p.232.

[26] Frank van Kappen, p.5.

[27] *Cf.* Aldrich, p.78.

[28] Aldrich, pp.78-79, citing the General's testimony in UK House of Commons, *Select Committee on Defence*, Examinations of Witnesses (Questions 220-242), 2 Feb. 1999.

[29] Aldrich, p.76, discusses the similarities between Ireland and Bosnia, and stresses the greater importance of intelligence in understanding non-military nuances in highly factionalised situations.

[30] *Cf.* Herman, pp.157-170.

[31] Steele, pp.209-212; Smith, p.247.

[32] Johnston provides a lengthy discussion of both the traditional objections to UN intelligence, and the counter-arguments for why the UN must have intelligence. Johnston, pp.319-332.

[33] Cammaert, p.24, 30. In the Steele's view, the Canadian Centre of Intelligence and Security Studies, in close collaboration with the Lester Pearson Peacekeeping Centre and the US Army's Peacekeeping Institute, would be ideally suited to develop both a residency course for mixed civilian-military participants, and a mobile training team able to visit both UN offices in major cities, as well as major field commands. By combining Canadian military intelligence instructors with peacekeeping experience, civilian instructors from varied cultures, and a robust mix of guest speakers recommended by the UN peacekeeping leadership, such a course could quickly establish some basic concepts, doctrines, and acceptances of intelligence as an essential foundation for informed UN decision-making.

[34] The existing culture that is on its way out the door, but still entrenched, is represented by Secretary-General U Thant's message to Lt-Gen Kebbede Guebre, to the effect that 'The limitations [in gathering information] are inherent in the very nature of the United Nations and therefore any operation conducted by it'. Code Cable #6780, 24 September 1962, cited by Dorn and Bell, p.253. The incoming culture that recognises the urgency of adopting the proven process of intelligence in combination with a reliance of open sources of information, is represented by the Brahimi Report and this volume.

[35] Cammaert, p.24.

[36] Dr. Gordon Oehler, then Director of the Non-proliferation Centre at the Central Intelligence Agency (an organisation that recognised that 80% of its raw information could and should come from open sources), articulated the concept of intelligence as remedial education for policymakers when speaking to the third annual Global Information Form (OSS '94) in Washington, D.C.

[37] Open sources include 'gray literature' that can only be obtained locally within the target country, as well as direct observations by legal travellers who are not using false documents or pretexts that could be considered deceptive. Smith provides a useful overview of the existing sources that can be tapped at the strategic level. See Smith, pp.242-246.

[38] 'New York considered General Dallaire's warning another unconfirmed rumour, or even another attempt to manipulate the UN'. Frank van Kappen, p.8.

[39] In the 1970's Samuel Milgram from Harvard conducted a famous experiment in which a stockbroker in Boston was picked as a target and 1000 people across America chosen at random were asked to pass a package to the stockbroker whom they did not know, via someone they did. The most common number of links was in the 4-6 range. If the UN cared to leverage its global presence, there is virtually no one in the world who is more than 2-4 calls away from a strategic intelligence desk officer in New York.

[40] Cammaert, p.20. Under Steele's direction the Marine Corps Intelligence Command (MCIA) prepared 3-7 page reviews of 67 countries and 2 island groups containing specific information about 143 warfighting factors spanning the full range from orders of battle to cultural, language, climate, weather, and terrain as well as port and airfield data. Known now as the *Expeditionary Factors Study*, covering 80 countries, it is based solely on unclassified sources, and can be obtained by the UN from the MCIA through US channels, in CD-ROM.

[41] Cammaert, pp.28-29

[42] Eriksson, p.309.

[43] Aid, p.143, touches on American inter-agency sharing difficulties. OSS experience as well as the experience of selected agencies, such as the Drug Enforcement Agency in Latin America, has shown that often, regardless of the policy that may persist at the most senior levels, when intelligence officers get together 'one on one' there are many accommodations that can be made. Svensson, p.45, makes the same point—he was able to overcome policy restrictions through personal credibility and local exchanges.

[44] Steele, pp.201-226.

[45] Dorn, p.348.

[46] A complete discussion of analysis and assessment in relation to the strategic mission of the UN is provided by Ramsbotham, pp.281-293. He is careful to distinguish between the needs of the SRSG and the Force Commander. Although their needs can be met by the same integrated operational intelligence staff, it is important to observe that each has distinct responsibilities and therefore distinct intelligence requirements in the short, mid-, and long-term.

[47] Frank van Kappen, p.6.

[48] Theunens, p.63.

[49] Cammaert, p.18.

[50] Stalin is reputed to have scorned the power of the Pope, asking where his divisions were, only to learn—as Gorbachev learned after him—that moral authority combined with good intelligence and effective dissemination of that intelligence are indeed the equivalent of several armies. This is an instructive model for the UN, whose leaders need to understand that the Pope *excels* at strategic intelligence.

[51] Wheaton, pp.171-200.

[52] Counterintelligence and Operations Security (OPSEC) are included in this category, at all four levels of action.

[53] Cammaert, pp.17, 19, 29.

[54] Re-activation of the Military Staff Committee might be a means of avoiding the inevitable political obstacles that undermine permanent secure channels as personalities change. This is recommended both by General Cammaert (p.19), and by Helene Boatner, a most senior American manager of analysts, in 'Sharing and Using Intelligence in International Organisations: Some Guidelines' by Helene Boatner, Central Intelligence Agency, in *National Security and the Future* 1/1 Spring 2000

[55] Smith, p.239.

[56] The 1993 proposal by Gareth Evans, then Australian Foreign Minister, for a group of professionals to be recruited from various countries, is consistent with this approach. Gareth Evans, *Co-Operating for Peace: The Global Agenda for the 1990's and Beyond* (Sydney: Allen and Unwin, 1993), p.65, cited by Smith, p.247.

[57] Aid, p.150.

[58] Dorn, p.335.

[59] Dorn, p.336. Dorn provides one of the best available discussions of the UN's aversion to secrecy in contradistinction to the practical needs for secrecy as an aspect of the UN mission. His entire work, pp.333-362, is helpful in that light.

[60] Dorn, pp.347-348.

[61] Theunens, p.64.

[62] Dorn, p.351.

[63] Steele, p.211.

[64] An excellent up-to-date discussion is provided by Par Eriksson, pp.297-315.

[65] Col Jan-Inge Svensson, head of United Nations Peace Forces HQ Intelligence Branch (UNPF G-2—in US circles it would be UNPF U-2), states very clearly that while he arrived to the mission with the intent of following the old 'military information branch' concepts and doctrine, discovered on his first day that the old approaches are wrong, and that a structured military intelligence approach works best. Svensson, p.42. Aldrich, p.85, discusses how the UK had to reinvent intelligence doctrine in Ireland.

[66] Aldrich, pp.94-95.

[67] Dorn and Bell, p.272.

[68] Aldrich, p.92.

[69] A diagram of the organisation of the Military Information Branch of the Operation de Nations Unis au Congo (ONUC) is provided at Dorn and Bell, p.261. Counting the three watch sections as well as all specialist personnel, but not counting national contingent technical collection specialists, the Force Commander should probably plan for 60-75 personnel in the operational intelligence element at the headquarters level.

[70] Van Diepenbrugge, p.33.

[71] Välimäki, pp.48-49.

[72] Theunens, p.61.

[73] Neville-Jones, p.iv.

[74] Cammaert, p.27.

[75] Steele, personal knowledge.

[76] Smith notes that 'The mixture of nationalities involved also makes for difficult communications as well as revealing national differences in operating procedures and significant variations in the level of training and expertise. There are also differences in attitude between the various nationalities [on the acceptability of intelligence as a UN operational function]. Smith, p.232-233.

[77] Cammaert, p.21, emphasises that 'the entire military component should be Humint information gatherers, although ideally every contingent should have a few specialist Humint collection teams which should be planned as part of the force structure.' He also emphasised the value of pre-deployment Humint orientation and training for all personnel in all contingents.

[78] Countless references across the literature document the negative views of many UN officials with respect to the legal ethical function of intelligence (*Cf.* Frank van Kappen, p.3-4), as opposed to the secret covert means that comprise a narrow aspect of the intelligence when practised at the national level. It is vital that over time, in cooperation with the International Organisation for Standardisation (ISO), that all parties eventually understand that intelligence is a proven process for creating tailored useful knowledge, and that it is a process that can and must be shared among the 'seven tribes': national, military, law enforcement, business, academic, NGO-media, and religious-clan-citizen. Smith provides a good discussion of the various reasons why parties external to the UN are reluctant to see the UN become competent at intelligence. Smith, pp.235-236.

[79] Smith, p.237.

[80] Van Diepenbrugge, p.38.

[81] Steele's view is that 'unity of intelligence' and 'continuity of intelligence' demands that law enforcement intelligence and a concern for law enforcement is included in all peacekeeping mandates from day 1. Initially, as military operations are the priority, law enforcement matters will be handled on a contingency or preparatory basis. At the logical point, when the situation has stabilised, it will be imperative for a robust law enforcement endeavour to be launched, and by having law enforcement specialists

engaged from the beginning, the SRSG will be empowered and effective in addressing threats to the society coming from crime and corruption. One prominent authority, Ambassador Robert Oakley, is of the view that the UN must devise a permanent law enforcement cadre. *Cf.* Robert Oakley, Michael Dziedzic, and Eliot Goldberg (eds.), *Policing the New World Disorder: Peace Operations and Public Security* (Washington, D.C.: National Defense University Press, 1998).

[82] Aldrich, pp.80-81. He goes on to point out that troop contributing nations had their favourites in the Bosnian conflict, and [implied but not stated] were therefore legitimate targets for UN intelligence collection [by overt means, naturally] if the SRSG and Force Commander were to be truly effective early on. On page 81 he discusses specific US assistance to the Croatians, including signals intercept equipment, CIA-operated unmanned drones, and encryption equipment for direct intelligence sharing from Washington.

[83] Aldrich, p.88.

[84] Theunens, p.62.

[85] Frank van Kappen, p.8.

[86] In the author's experience, multiple human collection efforts tend to produce increased numbers of fabricators who respond to the market 'demand' by feeding each collector variations on a theme. The tendency of the tactical collectors to 'protect sources and methods' ultimately prevents the Force Commander from exposing these wasteful and misleading activities.

[87] Cammaert, p.13-14.

[88] Cammaert, p.20.

[89] Smith, p.231.

[90] Dorn and Bell, p.262-263. Then Military Advisor to the Secretary General, General Rikhye, concurred in both the urgency of the need for this capability, and its acceptability as a relatively passive or 'invisible' means of enhancing force protection.

[91] The Americans define language competency on a scale of 1 (marginal) to 5 (native). For complex emergencies and the difficult to understand radio environment, nothing less than a 4 level of competency should be accepted by the Force Commander. *The language qualification question must be asked in advance, and high standards specified by the Force Commander.* A useful one-page summary report to keep on hand at all times would identify all personnel in all contingents who are said to speak local language(s), and their level of claimed proficiency.

[92] Cammaert, p.22. However, the UN procurement system is not effective when it comes to reimbursing officers for excess baggage costs—funds should be allocated for such needs as part of the intelligence planning process.

[93] Aldrich, p.93.

[94] Dorn and Bell, p.264.

[95] Dorn and Bell, p.266. General Guebre has described the aerial reconnaissance and photo-interpretation capability as a decisive factor in the success of the UN mission in Katanga in the December 1962-January 1963 period. Dorn and Bell, p.272.

[96] Cammaert, p.26. Or consider, 'Instead of focussing on purely military information, peace support operations require a much broader span of information: political, economical, geographic, ethnic, linguistic, social, sociological, cultural, religious, demographic, biographic, ecological intelligence, etc. Theunens, p.63.

[97] Theunens, p.62.

[98] Three hundred interrogations were conducted in the Congo in the period July 1960 to March 1962. Dorn and Bell, p.267. In today's more complex environment, with many more NGO's and others active in a given AOR, many more debriefings as well as more interrogations should be planned for.

[99] A global foreign language reserve is clearly needed if the UN is to have the full benefit of intelligence at the operational and tactical levels. This could consist of three forms of direct support: Nordic and other European military personnel who are fluent in specific indigenous languages such as Swahili or Tagalog or Urdu, and can be assigned to the Force Commander for the duration; civilian personnel, some academic, some from the business world, who can be hired as contractors and deployed for periods of 30-90 days if not longer; and finally, a 'virtual' reserve of both military and civilian personnel for each of the languages of interest, who can be 'mobilised' without leaving their existing job and location—they simply are on call via satellite telephone and can 'hook in' to serve as a remote translator at any time of day or night during their assigned duty period. In 1999 OSS identified and evaluated 396 terrorist, insurgent, and opposition web sites around the world. On the basis of that experience, we identified the following 29 languages as essential for future low-intensity conflict deployments: Arabic, Catelan, Chinese, Danish, Dari, Dutch, English, Farsi, Finnish, French, German, Indonesian, Irish, Italian, Japanese, Korean, Kurdish, Kurmanji, Norwegian, Pashto, Polish, Portuguese, Russian, Serbian, Spanish, Swedish, Tamil, Turkish, Urdu.

[100] Cammaert, p.28.

[101] Välimäki, p.53.

[102] Cammaert, p.30.

[103] *Cf.* Aid, pp.145-147, also citing Helene Boatner. The decrepitude of US clandestine human intelligence as well as US overt human and open source endeavours has been widely documented in books by various former clandestine case officers. The failure in Somalia, where CIA sent two experienced case officers who did not speak any useful languages nor understand the region, and the hidden failure in Afghanistan in 2001-2002, where Russian intelligence saved the day but CIA claimed the credit, are but two examples. UN operations should focus on informants who are not covert but rather 'in

confidence' and whose contributions reflect their normal direct observations rather than intrusive clandestine penetrations. *Cf.* Dorn and Bell, pp.268-270.

[104] Dorn and Bell, p.253. Their contribution, pp.253-280, is the definitive case study on the fragility as well as the urgency of UN intelligence in support of its missions.

[105] Aldrich, p.84, citing UK House of Commons, _Select Committee on Defence, Examination of Witnesses (Questions 220-242), 3 Feb. 1999. Others have made similar comments about other operations where American support was quite vital.

[106] HRH General Khaled bin Sultan with Patrick Seale, *Desert Warrior* (NY: HarperCollins, 1995), p.203, as cited by Aid, p.144.

[107] Major Harold Bullock, USAF, *Peace by Committee: Command and Control Issues in Multinational Peace Enforcement Operations* (Maxwell AFB: School of Advanced Airpower Studies, June 1994), cited by Aid, p.145.

[108] Van Diepenbrugge, p.37.

[109] Svensson, p.45. He believes UNMO should be directly subordinated to the Force Commander. Eriksson discusses these as well, and is sensitive to their vulnerability to kidnapping and other threats. Eriksson, p.310.

[110] Theunens, p.66.

[111] Aldrich, p.91.

[112] Dorn and Bell, p.270.

[113] Van Diepenbrugge, p.34. He emphasises that liaison officers to both the contingents and to the various non-military parties are frequently underestimated and constitute a vital capability in 'achieving a good and balanced picture'.

[114] Theunens, p.67.

[115] Theunens, p.68.

[116] Eriksson, p.306, 310.

[117] Välimäki, p.53-54. The four Nordic countries are now fully capable of, and routinely operate as, a single integrated intelligence network, to the point of integrating their personnel as well as their assets across the entire intelligence spectrum. At the conference upon which this book is based, there was spirited discussion about the need for Belgium, The Netherlands, and Luxembourg (BENELUX) to begin similar multilateral integrated intelligence operations.

[118] Dorn, p.353.

[119] Eriksson, p.309.

[120] Theunens, p.66.

[121] Smith, p.231-232.

[122] Dorn, p.338.

[123] Van Diepenbrugge, pp.37-38.

[124] Cammaert, p.22. Steele recommends that prior to deployment the Force Commander obtain UN funding for a complete collection of Russian military combat maps for the entire mission AOR, in both hard-copy and digital form; procure the most

recent archived SPOT 10-meter imagery for the AOR in digital form; and purchase Space Imaging 1-meter imagery for those specific base areas or refugee camp areas that must be defended immediately upon arrival. Thereafter, the Force Commander should have *ad hoc* procurement authority for obtaining both 10-meter wide area surveillance imagery and 1-meter urban/targeting imagery delivered by whatever means can be arranged (a JOINT VISION ground station on loan from the US would do nicely).

[125] Van Diepenbrugge, p.36. Theunens emphasises this as well, p.63.

[126] Raids can often produce documentary evidence that is useful not only for force protection, but as evidence of non-compliance that should be transmitted rapidly back to UN headquarters for political evaluation and action. Dorn and Bell, p.274.

[127] Svensson, p.45.

[128] One factor to be considered is that national systems and their databases are not structured for peacekeeping support data. It may be that the UN can become the virtual centre of excellence, and a service of common concern for the storage and exploitation of peacekeeping-specific data, whether collected by national, military, or UN means.

[129] Cammaert, p.21.

[130] Cammaert, p.29.

[131] Cammaert, p.29.

[132] Eriksson, p.311.

[133] Svensson, p.41

[134] Svensson, p.43.

[135] Svensson, p.45.

[136] Välimäki, p.55.

[137] Svensson, p.46.

[138] Theunens, p.62.

[139] Eriksson, pp.311-312.

[140] Eriksson, p.312, discusses this in general terms.

[141] Välimäki, p.51.

[142] Cammaert, p.14.

[143] Cammaert, p.23.

[144] Dorn, p.345. The same has been said of the Bosnia situation.

[145] Steele, personal knowledge. For a remarkable perspective on North Vietnamese accomplishments against Americans (whose OPSEC ranks at the very bottom anyway), see James Bamford, *Body of Secrets* (NY: Doubleday, 2001), and Tom Mangold and John Penycate, *The Tunnels of Cu Chi* (NY: Berkley, 1986).

[146] Cammaert, p.29. Svensson, p.44.

[147] Aldrich, p.93.

[148] Dorn and Bell, p.271.

[149] Shpiro, p.108.

[150] Shpiro, pp.106-107.

434

[151] Dame Pauline Neville-Jones makes reference to this important distinction from conventional operations in her Foreword, p.iii.

[152] Cammaert, p.27.

[153] Aid, p.143.

[154] Aid, p.148, discusses how a US Army intelligence officer assigned the role of 'virtual mayor' for a small town in Kosovo, with all the responsibilities that entailed, ultimately ended up receiving complaints, gossip, and direct information helpful to his primary responsibility.

[155] Cammaert, p.11.

[156] Cammaert, p.28.

[157] Aid, p.149.

[158] Major Harold Bullock, USAF, *Peace by Committee: Command and Control Issues in Multinational Peace Enforcement Operations* (Maxwell AFB: School of Advanced Airpower Studies, June 1994), cited by Aid, p.149. Eriksson makes similar points, p.308.

[159] Eriksson, p.306.

[160] Cammaert, p.26

[161] Aldrich, p.92.

[162] Aid, p.148. Many sources have made mention of this example. To our knowledge, it has not been repeated elsewhere (and was insufficient to overcome all the other intelligence failures in Somalia).

[163] Eriksson, pp.307-308.

[164] Neville-Jones, p.iii.

[165] Aid, p.140, citing American journalist George Wilson.

[166] Aid, p.142.

[167] Aid, p.147. More recently, a very senior Special Operations general officer who should have known better, ordered all Special Forces personnel riding with the Northern Alliance to shave their beards off. The order was quickly rescinded after it was ridiculed in the press and throughout the ranks of the Special Forces, but it accurately reflects the prevailing doctrinal view among many senior military officers— including those assigned to command unconventional and low-intensity conflict forces.

Open Source Intelligence References[1]

NATO Open Source Intelligence Handbook
(SACLANT, November 2001), 49 Pages

NATO Open Source Intelligence Reader
(SACLANT, February 2002), 109 Pages

Intelligence Exploitation of the Internet
(SACLANT, October 2002), 103 Pages

---

[1] Originally conceived by Brig. Gen. James Cox, CA, the Deputy Assistant Chief of Staff, Supreme Headquarters Allied Command Europe (SHAPE), the task of devising an open source intelligence (OSINT) 'solution' for combined operations with the Partnership for Peace and Mediterranean Dialog Nations was delegated to the Supreme Allied Commander, Atlantic (SACLANT). Under the leadership of General William Kernan, USA, and Admiral Sir James Perwone, RN, a NATO OSINT Steering Group was formed at the field grade level, an experimental OSINT unit was formed to provide direct intelligence support to selected operations, and three manuals were written over the course of two years. Capt. David Swain, RN UK and LCdr. Andrew Chester, RN CA, have been the principals staff officers for this endeavour. Taken together, these three references comprise a starting point for any Peacekeeping Intelligence staff interested in optimising their access to and exploitation of OSINT for strategic, operational, and tactical (planning/context) purposes. All three references can be downloaded at no cost from www.oss.net by going to the Archives, then References. They can take between 5 and 8 minutes at the lowest computer connection speeds, but they do download reliably. Contact information for the NATO OSINT specialists is contained in each of the documents. They are not able to provide copies—these are *only* available via download from www.oss.net.

Additional References[1]
On Peacekeeping Intelligence

2003	'If the U.N. Were Being Created Today . . .' Mr. David Malone, former Canadian Ambassador to the United Nations, President of the International Peace Academy, quotes in *The New York Times* 15 March 2003.	**Intelligent Intelligence.** A capacity to collect, analyze and publicize critical information about international conflicts has been lacking at the United Nations since its inception. .... The need for more high-quality analysis of conflict-relevant information was raised by Lakhdar Brahimi (now the United Nations special representative in Afghanistan) regarding peacekeeping reform, but member states shot it down because they did not want inconvenient information on their individual countries highlighted for the Security Council and more broadly. ... A good new initiative, the Conflict Prevention and Peace Forum...aims to make available to the United Nations the very best academic expertise from all over the world on urgent security challenges. But this is not good enough. The United Nations needs to have authoritative analysis generated internally and available to its decision-making bodies and to Mr. Annan's staff. Disagreements among countries would continue (as on the findings of United Nations inspectors in Iraq), but they would be better informed, and we might get better decisions out of the Security Council and other prominent United Nations bodies.

[1] Google search on "peacekeeping intelligence" and then on the two words together but without the quotes, will yield the greatest number of useful references available at search time. Use Google to enter title of documents as fast way to find them online.

2003	Statement by Ambassador Richard S. Williamson, US Representative to the UN for Special Political Affairs, on Peacekeeping, Before the Special Committee on Peacekeeping, 3 March 2003	'The time has come to establish an Information and Strategic analysis Secretariat, within the Executive Committee on Peace and Security (ECPS), to gather and analyse information about conflict situations, and make long-term recommendations to ECPS. This Brahimi recommendation was discussed in two previous Committee sessions, but was defeated because of concerns that the Secretariat would be an intelligence-gathering entity. Nothing is further from the truth.'
2003	Useful Military/Political Sites (Office of the Defence Attaché, U.S. Embassy, Botswana)	Includes Peace Operations
2003	'Intelligence Issues for Congress' (Richard A. Best, Jr., Congressional Research Service, updated 24 January 2003)	Useful insights into Congressional views on where U.S. intelligence is and should be going. Notable for not mentioning support to peacekeeping operations in the aftermath of 9-11.
2003	Command, Control, Communications, Computers, and Intelligence (DefenceLink)	Useful overview of the many considerations and capabilities contained in the US C4I systems environment. The UN cannot afford this environment—but it is a helpful means of considering what the UN should be striving for through lower cost commercial capabilities.
2003	'The Security Gap Between Military and Law Enforcement in Counter-Terrorism' by Mr. J. Wayne Pilgrim, Superintendent, Officer in Charge, National Security Program, Criminal Intelligence Directorate, Royal Canadian Mounted Police	This presentation to the National Defence University highlights some issues and potential solutions for bridging the gap between military and law enforcement intelligence. It concludes that *deep* mind-set changes are required; that collection and analysis can be shared; that joint threat assessments must become more robust, and that interoperable technology is a *sine qua non* if military and law enforcement are to succeed in any joint endeavour.

440

2003	'Intelligence Preparation of the Battlefield for Operations Other Than War', Chapter 6 in US Army FM 30-130	The entire manual is available online. This chapter focuses specifically on peacekeeping and other operations other than war, and constitutes an excellent tutorial for anyone thinking about peacekeeping intelligence from an analytic point of view.
2002	'Operational Intelligence in Peace Enforcement and Stability Operations' by Lawrence E. Cline, *International Journal of Intelligence and Counterintelligence* 15/2 (Summer 2002).	The article provides an excellent summary (and references) from the US military point of view. Of significance is the recognition that even the US with all its investments is severely deficient in both lower tier foreign language capabilities, and integrated tactical-operational-strategic information technology.
2002	'Intelligence Requirements for Peacekeeping Operations' by Dr. John M. Nomikos, Research Institute for European and American Studies (Athens, Greece), 1 July 2002	The author briefly surveys the definition of intelligence, problems with NATO's refusal to share intelligence received from its members, and the consequent emergence of a separate European intelligence network including satellite reconnaissance capabilities. He concludes that 'intelligence sharing is one of the most decisive elements of timely, informed, and well-developed decision-making in the exercise of peacekeeping operations.'
2001	Mr. Graham Day, Senior Fellow at the US Institute of Peace, speaking at the Institute of World Affairs Panel Discussion on UN Peacekeeping, 15 March 2001	'Intelligence gathering and technological leadership are key aspects of this new kind of sovereignty, allowing peacekeepers to access situations and act before they get out of control.'
2001	'The MacKenzie Proposal: Peacekeeping Reform & Grand Strategy', discussion thread around 'A Crucial Job But Not One for a Superpower' by Lewis MacKenzie, *The Washington Post* 14 January 2001, Page B03	General MacKenzie draws on his UN experience as well as his reading of history to propose that the US focus on providing the UN with intelligence and logistics support while retaining its armed forces as 'big war' forces, leaving the 'small wars' to the middle and smaller powers.

441

2000	'Sharing and Using Intelligence in International Organisations: Some Guidelines' by Helene Boatner, Central Intelligence Agency, in *National Security and the Future* 1/1 Spring 2000	Helene Boatner, until her untimely death in the Caribbean on 9 January 2000, was one of the brightest and most innovative of the CIA analytic managers. Her paper is rich with deep understanding of the challenges facing both Member States and the UN in the intelligence arena, and she offers a number of practical solutions.
2000	'Enhancing UN Peacekeeping Capability: A UNA-USA Policy Roundtable', 5 July 2000 (Rapporteur's Report by Martin Skladany, Jr.)	This five-page document from the United Nations Association is a very informed and useful summary of the current deficiencies in UN peacekeeping. It begins by focusing specifically on the lack of intelligence within the UN, to wit, 'in depth information' upon which the Security Council might base its decisions about missions, mandates, and forces.
1999	'Teaching Intelligence: Getting Started' (Dr. John Macartney, 'dean' of the U.S. intelligence trainers, Joint Military Intelligence College)	'Reduced to its simplest terms, intelligence is knowledge and foreknowledge of the world around us...the intelligence process involves the painstaking and generally tedious collection of facts, their analysis, quick and clear evaluations, production of intelligence assessments, and their timely dissemination to consumers. Above all, the analytical process must be rigorous, timely, and relevant...'
1999	'National Intelligence Support Teams' (Mr. James M. Lose, *Studies in Intelligence*, Central Intelligence Agency, Winter 1999)	Although rarely made available to the UN, a NIST is a form of intelligence support that can be asked for. Perhaps more importantly, it can serve as a model for a UN-designed and controlled capability.
1999	*Out of the Closet: Intelligence Support for Post-Modern Peacekeeping* By David Charters Pearson Center, Softcover, 84 pp., 1999 ISBN: 1-896551-26-2.	David Charters' central argument is that post-Cold War conflicts have changed dramatically the character of peacekeeping operations, and that the change will now require peacekeepers to apply the full range of intelligence capabilities in order to bring such conflicts under control. Includes some excellent tables.

1998	'Information Operations: The IFOR Experience' (Mr. Larry K. Wentz, Advanced Communications Systems, Vice President, ACS Services)	This is an excellent overview of all of the various aspects of 'information operations' inclusive of C4I, PSYOPS, InfoWar, and Computer Network Attack. The author is careful to examine the non-military implications.
1997	'Lessons Learned During Peacekeeping Operations in Africa' by Henry Anyidoho, *Conflict Management, Peacekeeping, and Peacebuilding* (Monograph #10), April 1997	The former deputy force commander and chief of staff for the UN mission to Rwanda (UNAMIR) says 'Problems of control have also been exacerbated by a lack of meaningful intelligence. It is common knowledge that for any operation to succeed there is the need for adequate intelligence which will enable cohesive planning. In almost all-African peacekeeping operations, troops have been dispatched to the mission area with very little information about the people, their culture, their beliefs, traditions and customs. Basic geographic information has also been scarce, as few African countries have up-to-date maps, especially those of the military variety which are essential to any meaningful planning'.
1996	'Intelligence and the UN: Lessons from Bosnia—A Canadian Experience' by Capt. Daniel Villeneuve with Sgt Marc-Andr Lefebvre, _Military Intelligence Professional Bulletin) v 4 , 1996.	The authors provide a three-page 'after action report' that emphasises the importance of establishing an end-to-end intelligence process (requirements definition, collection management, source discovery and validation, analytic evaluation and fusion). They note the absence of order of battle information on tribes, the importance of terrain analysis, the value of orienting and debriefing all personnel of all ranks as to the value of their local contacts, and the importance of having good liaison visitation programs to all parties including other contingents.

1995	'Airpower and Peacekeeping' by LtCol. Brooks I. Bash, USAF, in *Airpower Journal* (Spring 1995).	This is an extraordinarily detailed and well-written twelve-page paper on all of the contributions that aviation can make to peacekeeping, with a special emphasis on roles aviation platforms can play in supporting command and control, communications, and intelligence (to include air-breather surveillance of both the manned and unmanned types).
1994	NATO, PEACEKEEPING AND THE UNITED NATIONS (British American Security Information Council, Report 94.1)	'Intelligence gathering and distribution have to be more open and equitable. The desire for contingency planning and for safeguarding secrecy of information must not jeopardise the impartiality of U.N./NATO operations. The UN and the CSCE should either be allowed access to full-scale national and NATO intelligence or be funded to gather their own intelligence.'
1994	*Peacekeeping: Intelligence Requirements*, Richard A. Best, Jr. (Congressional Research Service Report for Congress 94-394F, 6 May 1994)	This excellent paper addresses, from the view of the U.S. Congress and its expert staff, specific intelligence requirements for peacekeeping operations (targets, technologies, infrastructure, human intelligence, and security), as well as constraints and Congressional concerns bearing on US support to UN operations.
1994	*Peacekeeper's Handbook*, International Peace Academy	This frequently-cited manual includes a chapter on information and public relations rather than a chapter on intelligence. It accurately represents the current UN obsession with public relations rather than intelligence as the defining paradigm for UN interactions with the real world.

444

1993	'Intelligence Support to UN Peacekeeping Operations' by Cdr Charles A. Williams, USN, Executive Research Project, The Industrial College of the Armed Forces, 1993.	This 25-page double-spaced paper is a fast light read but worth while as a convenient way of understanding the American military officer's general views about providing classified intelligence support to the UN. The author is favourable toward the UN while reflecting common U.S. military concerns about sharing sensitive information. He concludes, as did Senator David Boren, then Chairman of the Senate Select Committee on Intelligence, that the U.S. can and should share sensitive tactical intelligence with the U.S., and that the best means of doing so is by providing U.S. personnel and U.S. equipment in direct support of the UN Force Commander.

Editors' Note: As the primary purpose of this book has been to aggregate the specific contributions from the conference and the seminal publications, no attempt has been made to create a comprehensive bibliography. We urge all those interested in peacekeeping intelligence to share their recommended references with the Canadian sponsors of the peacekeeping intelligence (PKI) website at www.carleton.ca/csds/pki. That web site will be the permanent home for the virtual library as well as the virtual reference center for PKI.

Abbreviations

AFSOUTH	Allied Forces Southern Europe
ANC	Armee National Congolaise
AOR	Area of Responsibility
APC	Armoured Personnel Carrier
API	Application Program Interface
BHC	Bosnia-Herzegovina Command
BLMF	Banja Luka Metal Factory
BND	Bundesnachrichtendienst (German foreign intelligence service)
BRITFOR	British Forces
BSA	Bosnian-Serb Army
C2	Command and Control
C3I	Command, Control, Communications and Intelligence (also CCCI)
C4	Command, Control, Communications and Computers
C4I	Command, Control, Communications, Computers and Intelligence
C4ISR	C4I plus Surveillance and Reconnaissance
CASIS	Canadian Association for Security and Intelligence Studies
CBE	Commander of the British Empire
CCIR	Commander's Critical Intelligence Requirements
CCIRM	Collection, Co-ordination and Intelligence Requirement Manager
CF	Canadian Forces
CIA	Central Intelligence Agency (US)
CIMIC	Civil Military Co-operation
CINCSOUTH	Commander in Chief Southern Area
CNN	Cable News Network
COA	Course of Action
COMINT	Communication Intelligence
COS	Chief of Staff

447

CP	Check Point
DCI	Director of Central Intelligence
DCSI	Deputy Chief of Staff for Intelligence (U.S. Army)
DFC	Deputy Force Commander
DHA	Department of Humanitarian Affairs (UN)
DIA	Defense Intelligence Agency (US)
DMZ	Demilitarised Zone
DPA	Department of Political Affairs
DPI	Director of Public Information
DPKO	Department of Peacekeeping Operations
ECPS	Executive Committee on Peace and Security
EISAS	Information and Strategic Analysis Secretariat of the Executive Committee on Peace and Security
ELINT	Electronic Intelligence
ESM	Electronic Support Measures
EUPM	European Union Police Mission
EW	Electronic Warfare
FBIS	Foreign Broadcast Information Service
FC	Force Commander
FOA	National Defence Research Establishment (Sweden)
G-2	Intelligence section (US Armed Forces)
GCHQ	Government Communications Headquarters
GIS	Geographic Information Systems
GPS	Global Positioning System
HUMINT	Human Intelligence
ICON	International Communication and Negotiation simulation
ICRC	International Committee of the Red Cross
ICTY	International Criminal Tribunal for the former Yugoslavia
IDL	Netherlands Defence College
IFOR	Implementation Force
IFS	Interactive Function System
IMINT	Imagery Intelligence
INTERPOL	International Police
IO	Information Operations
IPB	Intelligence Preparation of the Battlefield

448

IPE	Intelligence Preparation of the Environment
IPTF	International Police Task Force
IRA	Irish Republican Army
IRMA	Instant Response to Media Attention
ISE	Information Support Element (US)
ISO	International Organisation for Standardisation
ISR	Intelligence Surveillance and Reconnaissance
ISTAR	Intelligence, Surveillance, Target Acquisition and Reconnaisance
JASIC	Joint All Sources Intelligence Cell
JCO	Joint Commissioned Officers (UK)
JIC	Joint Intelligence Committee
JIS	Joint Intelligence Staff
JNA	People's Army of Yugoslavia
KBE	Knight of the British Empire
KFOR	Kosovo Force
LAN	Local Area Network
LINUX	LINus (Torvald's) U(NI)X (A Free Unix-type Operating System for PCs)
MCIA	Marine Corps Intelligence Command
MI	Military Information
MIB	Military Information Branch
MIO	Military Information Officer
MIPB	Military Intelligence Preparation of the Battlefield
MND-SW	Multinational Division South-West
MSU	Military Support Unit
NATO	North Atlantic Treaty Organisation
NBC	Nuclear, Biological and Chemical
NGO	Non-Governmental Organisation
NIC	National Intelligence Cell (Centre)
NIE	National Intelligence Estimates
NISA	Netherlands Intelligence Studies Association
NIST	National Intelligence Support Team (US)
NITAT	Northern Ireland Training Advisory Team
NMIA	National Imagery and Mapping Agency
OHR	Office of the High Representative in Bosnia-Herzegovina

449

ONS	Office for National Statistics
ONUC	Opération des Nations Unies au Congo
OOB	Order of Battle
OODA	Orient Observe Decide Act (Col John Boyd)
OOTW	Operations Other Than War
OP	Observation Post
ORCI	Office of Research and Collection of Information
OSCE	Organisation for Security and co-operation In Europe
OSIF	Open Source Information (raw, not analyzed)
OSINT	Open Source Intelligence (analyzed and tailored)
OSS	Open Source Solutions Inc. (sponsor of OSS.NET)
PfP	Partnership for Peace
PIO	Press Information Officer
PIR	Periodic Intelligence Report
PK	Peacekeeping
PKI	Peacekeeping Intelligence
PLO	Provincial Liaison Officer
PMC	Private Military Contractor
POE	Peace Operations Extranet
PSO	Peace Support Operation
RIA	Revolution in Intelligence Affairs
S-2	Intelligence section (US Armed Forces)
SAS	Special Air Service
SFOR	Stabilisation Force
SHIRBRIG	Stand-by Forces High Readiness Brigade
SIGINT	Signals Intelligence
SIS	Secret Intelligence Service
SRSG	Special Representative of the Secretary General
TAG-I	Technical Advisory Group for Intelligence
TCC	Troop Contributing Countries
TIC	Team Intelligence Cell
TSZ	Temporary Security Zone
U-2	Intelligence Section (United Nations Forces)
UAV	Unmanned Aerial Vehicle
UDA	Ulster Defence Association
UMO	United Nation Military Observer
UN	United Nations

UNAMIR	United Nations Assistance Mission for Rwanda
UNCIVPOL	United Nations Civil Police
UNDOF	United Nations Disengagement Observer Force
UNDP	United Nations Development Programme
UNHCR	United Nations High Commissioner for Refugees
UNHQ	United Nations Headquarters
UNICEF	United Nations Children's and Educational Fund
UNIFIL	United Nations Interim Forces in Lebanon
UNMEE	United Nations Mission to Ethiopia and Eritrea
UNMIO	United Nations Military Information Officer
UNMO	United Nations Military Observer
UNMOP	United Nations Mission of Observers in Prevlaka
UNMOVIC	United Nations Monitoring, Verification and Inspection Commission
UNOC	United Nations Operations in the Congo
UNODIN	United Nations Open Decision Information Network
UNOSOM	United Nations Mission to Somalia
UNPF	United Nations Peace Force
UNPROFOR	United Nations Protection Force
UNSAS	United Nations Stand-by Arrangements System
UNTAC	United Nations Transitional Authority in Cambodia
UNTAT	United Nations Training Advisory Team
UNTAES	United Nations Transitional Administration for Eastern Slavonia, Baranja and Western Sirmium
UNTSO	United Nations Truce Supervision Organisation
UNYOM	United Nations Force in Yemen
WAN	Wide Area Network
WFP	World Food Programme
WMD	Weapons of Mass Destruction
XML	Extended Mark-Up Language

Contributors

Matthew M. Aid is a native of New York City. He holds a Bachelor's degree in International Relations from Beloit College in Beloit, Wisconsin. He has served as a senior manager with several large international financial research and investigative companies for more than 15 years. He is currently a Managing Director in the Washington, D.C. office of Citigate Global Intelligence & Security, where his responsibilities include managing the company's international investigative and security operations. Aid was the co-editor with Dr. Cees Wiebes of *Secrets of Signals Intelligence During the Cold War and Beyond* (Cass, 2001), and is currently completing a history of the National Security Agency and its predecessor organisations. He is also the author of a chapter about the National Security Agency in a book published by the University of Kansas Press in 1998 entitled *A Culture of Secrecy: The Government Versus the People's Right to Know*, as well as a number of articles on signals intelligence in Intelligence and National Security.

Richard J. Aldrich is in the School of Politics at the University of Nottingham and is co-editor of the journal *Intelligence and National Security*. His publications include *Intelligence and the War Against Japan: Britain, America and the Politics of Secret Service* (Cambridge University Press, 2000) and *The Hidden Hand: Britain America and Cold War Secret Intelligence* (Overlook, 2002). His current projects include an examination of intelligence and state formation since 1648.

David J.H. Bell served as a research assistant to Walter Dorn at the University of Toronto in 1994-95. He graduated from Trinity College (University of Toronto) in 1995 with an honours bachelor's degree in Political Science and Ethics. Subsequently, he has held various positions in the public service of Canada.

Patrick C. Cammaert is a major-general of the Marine Corps of the Royal Netherlands Navy. Since early 2003 he is Military Advisor to the Secretary-general of the United Nations. Until October 2002 he was in command of the United Nations Mission to Ethiopia and Eritrea (UNMEE). Before commanding UNMEE, general Cammaert served as Commander of the Multinational United

Nations Stand-by Forces High Readiness Brigade (SHIRBRIG) and as battalion commander with the United Nations Transitional Authority in Cambodia (UNTAC) and as assistant chief of staff of the Multinational Brigade of the Rapid Reaction Force of the United Nations Protection Force (UNPROFOR).

Richard Connaughton is a former officer of the British Army. His last appointment was head of Defence Studies with the rank of colonel, from which he took early retirement. He set up his own consultancy, National & International Consultancy, working for clients in the politico-military field world-wide. He has a post-graduate degree in International Relations from Cambridge and his PhD from Lancaster University is in Politics. He is an honorary research fellow for the Centre for Defence and International Security Studies. He has recently written papers for the *Joint Forces Quarterly, Civil Wars* and *Small Wars and Insurgencies.* Details of his books appear on his website: www.connaughton.org.uk His most recent books are *MacArthur and Defeat in the Philippines* (New York: The Overlook Press 2002) and *Military Intervention and Peacekeeping: the Reality* (Aldershot: Ashgate 2001). His next book, *The Rising Sun and the Tumbling Bear,* on the Russo-Japanese War of 1904-5, is to be published by Orion in 2003.

Tony van Diepenbrugge is a major-general in the Royal Netherlands Army. After his initial Staff course at the Army Staff College in The Hague he was sent on a Peace Support Mission to Lebanon in 1981 where he worked as a member of the UNIFIL staff. In 1996-97, then colonel Van Diepenbrugge served for six months in the former Yugoslavia as director of the Joint Operation Centre of IFOR headquarters in Sarajevo. From September 2001 until September 2002 major-general Van Diepenbrugge was commander of the Multi-National Division South West in Bosnia-Herzegovina. Since October 2002 he is deputy commander in chief of the Royal Netherlands Army.

Walter Dorn is an Associate Professor at the Royal Military College of Canada, a senior member of the external faculty of the Pearson Peacekeeping Centre and an Adjunct Research Professor at Carleton University. A physical scientist by training (Ph.D., Univ. of Toronto), he did graduate work on the detection of chemical weapons and on the technical verification of arms control treaties. After graduation, he was a Research Associate of the International Relations Programme of Trinity College (University of Toronto) and a consultant to Yale University (UN Studies). He served with the UN in East Timor, in Ethiopia, and at UN headquarters as a Training Adviser with the Department of Peacekeeping Operations. He currently teaches courses on peacekeeping and is writing a book titled "Global Watch" on the evolution of UN monitoring. Some of his articles on peacekeeping operations, including those in Rwanda, Namibia, the Congo, Cambodia, Bosnia and East Timor, are available at his web site: http://www.rmc.ca/academic/poli-econ/dorn.

Par Eriksson is an analyst with the National Defense Research Establishment (FOA) in Stockholm, For the past three years he has been involved with projects concerning Sweden 's participation in international peace operations supporting the Swedish Armed Forces HQ, as well as the Swedish government. The views expressed in this article are the author 's own and do not necessarily reflect those of the FOA, the Swedish Armed Forces, or the Swedish government.

Michael Herman served from 1952 to 1987 in Britain's Government Communications Headquarters (GCHQ), with secondments to the Cabinet Office and Ministry of Defence. Since his retirement he has written extensively on intelligence matters, with official clearance. He has been associated with several universities, and is now an Honouree Fellow at Aberystwyth and a Senior Associate Member of St Antony's College in Oxford. His book *Intelligence Power in Peace and War* (Cambridge: Cambridge University Press 1996) has been regularly reprinted, and a collection of his subsequent writings was published as *Intelligence Services in the Information Age: Theory and Practice* (Southgate: Frank Cass Publishers 2001).

Loch K. Johnson is Regents Professor of Political Science at the University of Georgia and author of several books on U.S. national security and American politics. He has won the Certficate of Distinction from the National Intelligence Study Center and the V.O. Key Prize from the Southern Political Science Association. He has served as secretary of the American Political Science Association and president of the International Studies Association, South. He was special assistant to the chair of the Senate Select Committee on Intelligence in 1975-76, staff director of the House Subcommittee on Intelligence Oversight in 1977-79, and special assistant to the chair of the Aspin-Brown Commission on Intelligence in 1995-96. Born in Auckland, New Zealand, Professor Johnson

455

received his Ph.D. in political science from the University of California, Riverside. His latest of many books is *Bombs, Bugs, Drugs, and Thugs* (New York: New York University Press, 2000)

Paul Johnston is a Major in the Intelligence Branch of the Canadian Forces. He graduated with an Honours BA in Military and Strategic Studies from Royal Roads Military College and earned an MA in War Studies from the Royal Military College. He has served in Germany, the Middle East, and various intelligence billets at the tactical, operational and strategic levels, in many cases providing intelligence support to Canadian Forces involved in peace keeping operations. Many of his writings, which have been published in a wide variety of journals including *Parameters* and the *RAF Air Power Review*, are available on his website: http://www.johnston.ca.

Ben de Jong is secretary of the Netherlands Intelligence Studies Association (NISA). He lectures on Russian and East European Politics at the University of Amsterdam, The Netherlands, and recently completed his dissertation on the memoirs of Soviet intelligence officers.

Frank van Kappen is a retired major-general of the Marine Corps of the Royal Netherlands Navy. From 1995 until 1998 he was Military Advisor to the Secretary-General of the United Nations and Director of the Planning Division in the Department of Peacekeeping Operations of the United Nations.

Dame Pauline Neville-Jones is Chairman of QinetiQ Group plc, formerly the Defence Evaluation and Research Agency (DERA) which is in the process of privatisation by the British Government. She is also International Governor of the BBC with special responsibility for BBC World Service (radio) and BBC World (TV). She was previously a Managing Director in NatWest Markets, the then investment-banking arm of the NatWest banking group, and Vice Chairman of Hawkpoint Partners, a corporate Advisory house in the City of London. Prior to that, she was a career member of the British diplomatic service serving, among other places, in Singapore, Washington DC, the European Commission in Brussels and Bonn. She was a foreign affairs adviser to Prime Minister John Major, chairman of the Joint Intelligence Committee in Whitehall and leader of the British delegation to the Dayton peace conference on Bosnia. She was made a Dame Commander of the Order of St. Michael and

456

St. George in 1996 and is an honorary Doctor of London and the Open Universities. She is a Council member of the Royal United Services Institute, a member of the Executive Committee of the International Institute for Strategic Studies and of the Advisory Council of the Centre for European Reform in London.

Wies Platje is a retired lieutenant commander of the Royal Netherlands Navy. For over thirty years he held various functions within the Netherlands Navy Intelligence Service. He is a member of the NISA Board and one the organisers of the NISA/IDL International conference on Peacekeeping and Intelligence in November 2002 in The Hague. He is the author of a book about the Netherlands Navy Intelligence Service, published in 1997 and one of the contributors to *Secrets of Signals Intelligence during the Cold War and Beyond* (London: Frank Cass Publishers 2001).

Sir David Ramsbotham is General (Ret.), British Army, and has served as a consultant to the UN on peacekeeping issues in Cambodia, Cyprus, Israel, Lebanon, Somalia, and Yugoslavia. Apart from his Army experience, rising to Adjutant General (number two on the Army Board, responsible for personnel and training) he has spent three years in the private sector dealing with UN and World Bank post-conflict resolution and de-mining challenges, and was HM Chief Inspector of Prisons from 1995-2000. Today he is a Fellow at Corpus Christi College within Cambridge University and continues to take an interest in peacekeeping intelligence matters.

Martin Rudner is a Professor at The Norman Paterson School of International Affairs, Carleton University, Ottawa, and founding Director of the Canadian Centre of Intelligence and Security Studies at Carleton. Born in Montreal, Quebec, he was educated at McGill University, the University of Oxford, and at the Hebrew University of Jerusalem, where he received his doctorate. Professor Rudner taught at the Hebrew University, and was at the Australian National University in Canberra before coming to Carleton. He is author of over sixty books and scholarly articles dealing with international affairs, including articles in Intelligence and National Security *and International Journal of Intelligence and Counterintelligence*. Professor Rudner is a commentator and analyst on international security affairs for Canadian and international electronic and print media. He is Past President of the Canadian Association for Security and Intelligence Studies.

Hugh Smith is a Senior Lecturer in the Department of Politics, University College (UNSW), Australian Defence Force Academy, New South Wales, and was the Founding Director of the Australian Defence Studies Centre at the Academy.

Shlomo Sphiro is a lecturer at the Department of Political Studies and a Fellow of the BESA Centre for Strategic Studies at Bar-Ilan University in Israel. He specialises in intelligence, security, communications and media. Previously he has conducted research and taught at universities in Britain and Germany, and led a NATO project on improving intelligence co-operation with Mediterranean countries.

Robert David Steele (Vivas) is the founder of OSS.NET, a web site dedicated to international intelligence reform including improved use of open source intelligence (OSINT). He has served in three of the four directorates of the Central Intelligence Agency, as a clandestine case officer, an all-source requirements and collection manager, and as project leader for advanced information technology applications. He was the senior civilian responsible for founding the Marine Corps Intelligence Command. Mr. Steele holds a BA in Political Science with a thesis on multinational corporation operations and home-host country issues; an MA in International Relations from Lehigh University with a thesis on predicting revolutions; and an MBA in Public Administration from the University of Oklahoma with a thesis on strategic and tactical information management for national security. He is a distinguished graduate of the Naval War College, and has earned a certificate in Intelligence Policy from Harvard University. Mr. Steele is the author of *On Intelligence: Spies and Secrecy in an Open World* (AFCEA International Press 2000 and OSS International Press 2002) and *The New Craft of Intelligence: Personal, Public, & Political* (OSS International Press 2002) as well as many monographs, chapters, and articles on information and intelligence strategy and operations. He is the ranking reviewer on Amazon for non-fiction books about national security, information, intelligence, and related ethical issues.

Jan-Inge Svensson is a colonel in the Royal Swedish Army. He is Commanding officer of the Swedish Armed Forces Intelligence and Security Centre. In 1995 he was Head of the G-2 section (intelligence) of the United Nations Protection Force (UNPROFOR) in Zagreb. In 1996 he developed and implemented a Swedish National Intelligence Cell in Sarajevo.

Renaud Theunens has a bachelor degree in social and military Sciences. In 1994-95 he served as G-2 (assessment desk) at the UNPROFOR/UNPF headquarters in Zagreb, Croatia. In 1996-97 he was military information officer (G-2 Analysis) at the UNTAES headquarters in Vukovar, Croatia. In 1998-99 he was chief of the Belgian National Intelligence Cell at the SFOR headquarters in Sarajevo. In 1999 and 2000 he was head of the European desk and senior Balkans analyst with the Belgium Military Intelligence Service. Among his previous publications is 'UNTAES and the Military Challenges in Eastern Slavonia' in M.J. Calic (ed.), *Friedenskonsolidiering im ehemaligen Jugoslawien*, (Ebenhausen, Germany: Stiftung Wissenschaft und Politik) 1996.

Pasi Välimäki is a major in the Finnish Army. As a signals officer he specialised in land forces electronic warfare (EW), later in intelligence. He served two tours in the Balkans. Between May 1995 and May 1996 he was a UN military observer in Sarajevo, Zagreb and in Prevlaka. Between February and September 2000 he was the Chief S2 with the Finnish Battalion in KFOR. Pasi Välimäki has written several papers and articles on strategy and security studies, published in Finland. His main publication is *Intelligence in Peace Support Operations*, published in the Finnish Defence Studies series no. 14. He is presently doing postgraduate studies at Helsinki University on the subject of 'Coercive Diplomacy and Intelligence in Crisis Response'.

Kristan Wheaton is the author of *The Warning Solution: Intelligent Analysis in the Age of Information Overload* (Falls Church, VA: AFCEA International Press, 2001) and is currently busy working on his next book, *Failed States: How to Predict Them, How to Prevent Them*. He is also a Foreign Area Officer for the US Army and is currently serving as an attaché in the Office of the Legal Counselor, US Embassy, The Hague, where he works with the International Criminal Tribunal for the Former Yugoslavia on war crimes issues. He has served as the Chief of the Office of Defense Cooperation at the US Embassy in Zagreb, Croatia, as the Chief of European Analysis in the

459

Intelligence Directorate of the US European Command, as a US Defense Liaison Officer to the Republic of Macedonia and as a Special Assistant for Intelligence to the Commander of Multinational Division North in Bosnia. His recent publications include 'Combat by Tria' in *Proceedings*, (September 2001), and 'Evolution, Ethnicity and Propaganda: Why Negotiating with the Innocent Makes Sense' in *Evolutionary Theory and Ethnic Conflict* (August 2001).

Index

Editors' Note: The Index covers the main chapters (both conference contributors and seminal past publications). It does not include the footnotes nor the references as the latter are self-contained and should be read as a whole. The intent of the Index is to provide direct access to the substantive contributions of the individual authorities on peacekeeping intelligence as they are brought together in this reference volume.

465

470

472

484

486

494

503

509

513

514

Survival has always been a source of knowledge and wisdom in strategic matters.

It still is, but it also has become an

exciting and rich guide to the

complexities, contradictions and contentions

of the post-Cold War international political system.

Professor Stanley Hoffmann, Harvard University

Survival, the IISS's quarterly journal, is a leading forum for analysis and debate of international and strategic affairs.

With a diverse range of authors, eight to ten articles per issue, plus thoughtful reviews and review essays, Survival is scholarly in depth while vivid, well-written and policy-relevant in approach.

Shaped by its editors to be both timely and forward-thinking, the journal encourages writers to challenge conventional wisdom and bring fresh, often controversial, perspectives to bear on the strategic issues of the moment.

It was in Survival that one could read, 18 months before the 11 September attacks on New York and Washington, the warning from Steven Simon and Daniel Benjamin that terrorism's 'new face ... belongs to Osama bin Laden ...who has marshaled a network of operatives in more than 50 countries' determined to 'inflict damage on a grand scale'.

Recent articles include: *After Saddam*, Charles Tripp; *The Taliban Papers*, Tim Judah; and *The New Calculus of Pre-emption*, Robert S. Litwak.

Volume 45, 2003 4 issues, Print ISSN 0039-6338, Online ISSN 1468-2699
Issued March, May, August, November 2003. Print and online subscriptions:
Institutions - $160; Individuals - $77 Journal Subscriptions Dept,
Oxford University Press, Great Clarendon Street, Oxford, England OX2 6DP
tel +44 (0)1865 353907 fax+44 (0)1865 353485 email jnls.cust.serv@oup.co.uk

PEACEKEEPING INTELLIGENCE: Emerging Concepts for the Future
Contributing Journal

International Peacekeeping

Editor: **Michael Pugh**, *University of Plymouth*
Co-editors: **Espen Barth Eide**, *Norwegian Institute of International Affairs, Oslo*, **Adekeye Adebajo** and **Dorina Bekoe**, *International Peace Academy, New York*

International Peacekeeping examines the theory and practice of peacekeeping and reflects the principle that peacekeeping is essentially a political act in which military forces, frequently in a condition of partial demilitarization, are the instruments of policy at an international level. From a broader perspective the journal also reflects debates about sanctions enforcement, monitoring of agreements, preventive deployments, international policing, protection of aid in internal disputes, and the relationship between peacekeepers, state authorities, rival factions, civilians and non-governmental organizations.

International Peacekeeping is an important source of analysis for institutes and universities with an interest in international relations, security and strategic studies, the history of the United Nations, peace research and conflict resolution.

ISSN 1353-3312 Volume 10 2003
Quarterly: Spring, Summer, Autumn, Winter
Individuals £48.00/$65.00   Institutions £200.00/$285.00
New individual introductory rate £38.00/$52.00

Frank Cass Publishers

UK/RoW: Crown House, 47 Chase Side, Southgate, London N14 5BP
Tel: +44 (0)20 8920 2100 Fax: +44 (0)20 8447 8548
North America: 920 NE 58th Avenue, Suite 300,
Portland, OR 97213 3786 Tel: 800 944 6190 Fax: 503 280 883
Website: www.frankcass.com --- Email: jnlinfo@frankcass.com

Intelligence and National Security

Editors: **Christopher Andrew**, *Corpus Christi College, Cambridge;*
Richard J Aldrich, *University of Nottingham* and
Loch K Johnson, *University of Georgia*

'*... the premier journal of intelligence studies.*'
Foreign Affairs

Intelligence and National Security breaks the silence surrounding the secret world of intelligence and special operations. Readers gain insight into the contemporary functions of intelligence and its influence on foreign policy and national security. Articles on the historical background of secret services present the complete picture of their origins and development. Experts on international strategy and the use of intelligence in war, together with cryptanalysts and others who were actively involved in intelligence work for many years, offer new evidence on political incidents in recent history. The journal also contains a major book review section and a bi-annual listing of dissertations on intelligence.

ISSN 0268-4527 Volume 18 2003
Quarterly: Spring, Summer, Autumn, Winter
Individuals £48.00/$65.00
Institutions £235.00/$325.00
New individual introductory rate £38.00/$52.00

Frank Cass Publishers

UK/RoW: Crown House, 47 Chase Side, Southgate, London N14 5BP
Tel: +44 (0)20 8920 2100 Fax: +44 (0)20 8447 8548
North America: 920 NE 58th Avenue, Suite 300,
Portland, OR 97213 3786 Tel: 800 944 6190 Fax: 503 280 883
Website: www.frankcass.com --- Email: jnlinfo@frankcass.com

PEACEKEEPING INTELLIGENCE: *Emerging Concepts for the Future*
Contributing Journal

International Journal of Intelligence and Counterintelligence

Editor-in-Chief: Richard Valcourt, *American Military University*
Editor Emeritus: F. Reese Brown, Founding Editor
Senior Editor: Jefferson Adams, *Sarah Lawrence College*

The *International Journal of Intelligence and Counterintelligence* is a publication dedicated to the advancement of the academic discipline of Intelligence Studies. The Journal serves as a medium for professionals and scholars to exchange opinions on issues and challenges encountered by both governmental and business institutions in making contemporary intelligence-related decisions and policy, and for researchers to access earlier developments and events in this field.

ISSN 0885-0607 Volume 15 Number 4 (Winter 2002-2003)

Taylor & Francis
www.taylorandfrancis.com

530

Peacekeeping Intelligence:
The Conference

- **1st Annual Conference: 2002, The Netherlands**
  - Focus: The Need for UN Strategic & Operational Intelligence
- **2nd Annual Conference, 2003, Canada**
  - Possible Focus: Emerging Definition of UN Intelligence Practice
- **3rd Annual Conference, 2004, To Be Determined**
  - Possible Focus: Institutionalization of UN Intelligence

Host of the 2003 Conference
Carleton University
Norman Paterson School of International Affairs
Centre for Security and Defence Studies
Canadian Centre of Intelligence and Security Studies

Peacekeeping Intelligence:
The Website

http://www.carleton.ca/csds/pki

Available 2002
- **PKI Conference Information & Papers**
- **PKI Leadership Digest 1.0**
- **PKI Directory (Free Self-Registration to Template)**
- **PKI Links (Free Add-a-Link with Comment)**

Planned for 2003-2005
- **PKI Distance Learning**
- **PKI Online Library**
- **PKI Expert Forum**
- **PKI Weekly Open Source Intelligence (OSINT)**
- **Global Intelligence Council (Virtual Network for UN)**

531

OSS.NET
Seven Standards for Seven Tribes

Seven Standards[1]

- Global coverage, 24/7, multi-lingual open source information
- Multi-media, multi-lingual processing including geospatial data
- Analytic toolkits (18 functionalities, plug and play standards)
- Analytic tradecraft (best practices across boundaries)
- Personnel and security certifications
- Defensive security and counterintelligence
- Leadership, training, and culture

Seven Tribes

- National intelligence (only nation-states can practice this level)
- Military intelligence (both state and sub-state)
- Law enforcement intelligence (both state and private sector)
- Business intelligence (includes national economic intelligence)
- Academic intelligence (both social science and technical)
- NGO[2]-Media (including niche industry sources & methods)
- Religious-Ethnic/Clan-Citizen (both organized and informal)

www.oss.net

Daily intelligence commentaries and information of common interest to the seven tribes (Begun July 2002, this is a permanent daily offering).
Annual conference each May in Washington, D.C. (Rosslyn by Georgetown).
Publishing books that help unite the tribes and nurture the new craft of intelligence—a craft that makes possible *information peacekeeping*.

---

[1] OSS has joined the American National Standards Organization (ANSI) and encourages all intelligence practitioner organizations to join their respective national standards organizations, with the objective of establishing Technical Advisory Groups for Intelligence within every nation-state.

[2] Non-Governmental Organizations, including the United Nations (UN), but the latter is a special case in that with Member-State approval and provision, it can have access to sensitive classified intelligence bearing on the safety of peacekeeping contingents.